W9-CKU-983

TOO YOUNG TO DIE

CANADA'S BOY SOLDIERS, SAILORS AND AIRMEN IN THE SECOND WORLD WAR

JOHN BOILEAU AND DAN BLACK

FOREWORD BY
GENERAL JOHN DE CHASTELAIN

JAMES LORIMER & COMPANY LTD., PUBLISHERS
TORONTO

Copyright © 2016 by John Boileau and Dan Black
First published in the United States and UK in 2017.
Maps by Don LaPointe

All rights reserved. No part of this book may be reproduced or transmitted in any form or by any means, electronic or mechanical, including photocopying, or by any information storage or retrieval system, without permission in writing from the publisher.

James Lorimer & Company Ltd., Publishers acknowledges the support of the Ontario Arts Council (OAC), an agency of the Government of Ontario, which in 2015-16 funded 1,676 individual artists and 1,125 organizations in 209 communities across Ontario for a total of $50.5 million. We acknowledge the support of the Canada Council for the Arts, which last year invested $153 million to bring the arts to Canadians throughout the country. This project has been made possible in part by the Government of Canada and with the support of the Ontario Media Development Corporation.

Cover design: Tyler Cleroux

Library and Archives Canada Cataloguing in Publication

Boileau, John, author
    Too young to die : Canada's boy soldiers, sailors and airmen in the Second World War / John Boileau and Dan Black ; foreword by General John de Chastelain.

Includes bibliographical references and index.
Issued in print and electronic formats.
ISBN 978-1-4594-1172-2 (hardback).--ISBN 978-1-4594-1173-9 (epub)

    1. Canada. Canadian Armed Forces--History--World War, 1939-1945. 2. World War, 1939-1945--Personal narratives, Canadian. 3. World War, 1939-1945--Participation, Juvenile. 4. Child soldiers--Canada--Biography. 5. Airmen--Canada--Biography. 6. Sailors--Canada--Biography. 7. World War, 1939-1945--Sources. I. Black, Dan, 1957-, author II. Title.

D810.C4B64 2016   940.53083'510971   C2016-902683-3
                                                    C2016-902684-1

James Lorimer & Company Ltd., Publishers
117 Peter Street, Suite 304
Toronto, ON, Canada
M5V 0M3
www.lorimer.ca

Printed and bound in Canada.

*To the boy soldiers, sailors and airmen who fought — and in
many cases died — for Canada during
the Second World War*

"Older men declare war. But it is youth that must fight and die."

— Herbert Hoover (31st President of the
United States, 1874–1964)

CONTENTS

INTRODUCTION 39

*"I had no knowledge of anything military until one day my father's
oldest brother . . . appeared in uniform . . ."*

YOUTH AND ANOTHER WORLD WAR

PART I 55

FIRST BATTLES: HONG KONG AND DIEPPE

CHAPTER 1 59

*"It had been rather an unusual Christmas day . . . one to remember . . .
one never to forget."*

HONG KONG, THE BATTLE

CHAPTER 2 85

*"I thought we'd be taken prisoner and we're not going to be that long.
I thought maybe six months at the most."*

HONG KONG, THE PRISONERS

CHAPTER 3 111

"I want to be at peace with God."

DEATH AT DIEPPE

PART II 137

ITALY: THE D-DAY DODGERS

CHAPTER 4 139

*"We were — and are — quite proud of the boy's determination and
independence."*

ITALY, THE INVASION

CHAPTER 5 164

*"Well Mother Darling this going to be an awful surprise to you all and
I sure hope and pray that you dont take it to hard."*

ITALY, THE END

PART III 193

NORTH-WEST EUROPE: D-DAY TO V-E DAY

CHAPTER 6 197

"This is it. I'm going to die."

NORMANDY, D-DAY

LIST OF MAPS

ORGANIZATION OF THE CANADIAN ARMED FORCES OVERSEAS

CANADIAN ARMY

After infantry battalions and armoured regiments of the Canadian army were mobilized, they were assigned to brigades, and then further allocated to divisions and corps. (Battalions and regiments are known as units, while brigades, divisions and corps are known as formations.) Once established, the composition of brigades, divisions and corps usually remained fixed. The allocation of artillery units was generally more flexible, depending on the requirements of a particular operation, but they usually had a permanent home formation.

ROYAL CANADIAN NAVY

The ships of Royal Canadian Navy (RCN) were not assigned to higher formations on a permanent basis, reflecting the inherent flexibility of sea power. The organization of naval formations, such as squadrons, flotillas, task forces and fleets was not fixed, but based on many different requirements, from ship type to operational necessity. Ships moved in and out of such formations as circumstances dictated.

ROYAL CANADIAN AIR FORCE

The assignment of Royal Canadian Air Force (RCAF) squadrons to higher formations, such as wings, groups and commands, remained in flux during much of the war, as new squadrons were formed and the Royal Air Force (RAF) — to which all overseas Canadian squadrons were assigned — reorganized on a frequent basis. Squadrons moved between higher formations as circumstances dictated, demonstrating the intrinsic flexibility air power provides.

CANADIAN ARMY OVERSEAS

(Armoured, Artillery and Infantry units only)

First Canadian Army
Elgin Regiment (Armoured Delivery Regiment)
1st Army Group, Royal Canadian Artillery
      11th Army Field Regiment
      1st Medium Regiment
      2nd Medium Regiment
      5th Medium Regiment
2nd Army Group, Royal Canadian Artillery
      19th Army Field Regiment
      3rd Medium Regiment
      4th Medium Regiment
      7th Medium Regiment
      2nd Heavy Ant-Aircraft Regiment (Mobile)
Royal Montreal Regiment (Army Headquarters Defence Battalion)

I Canadian Corps
Royal Canadian Dragoons (Corps Armoured Car Regiment)
7th Anti-Tank Regiment
1st Survey Regiment
1st Light Anti-Aircraft Regiment
Lorne Scots (Peel, Dufferin and Halton Regiment) (Corps Defence Company)

1st Canadian Infantry Division
      4th Princess Louise Dragoon Guards (Division Reconnaissance Regiment)
      1st Field Regiment, RCHA
      2nd Field Regiment

3rd Field Regiment
1st Anti-Tank Regiment
2nd Light Anti-Aircraft Regiment
Saskatoon Light Infantry (MG) (Division Machine
Gun Battalion)
1st Infantry Brigade
    Royal Canadian Regiment
    Hastings and Prince Edward Regiment
    48th Highlanders of Canada
2nd Infantry Brigade
    Princess Patricia's Canadian Light Infantry
    Seaforth Highlanders of Canada
    Loyal Edmonton Regiment
3rd Infantry Brigade
    Royal 22e Régiment
    Carleton and York Regiment
    West Nova Scotia Regiment

5th Canadian Armoured Division
    Governor General's Horse Guards (Division
    Armoured Reconnaissance Regiment)
    17th Field Regiment
    8th Field Regiment (Self-Propelled)
    4th Anti-Tank Regiment
    5th Light Anti-Aircraft Regiment
    5th Armoured Brigade
        Lord Strathcona's Horse (Royal Canadians)
        8th Princess Louise's (New Brunswick)
        Hussars
        British Columbia Dragoons
        Westminster Regiment (Motor) (Brigade
        Motorized Infantry Battalion)

11th Infantry Brigade
> Princess Louise Fusiliers (Brigade Independent Machine Gun Company)
> Perth Regiment
> Cape Breton Highlanders
> Irish Regiment of Canada

12th Infantry Brigade (existed temporarily in Italy by conversion or reassignment of units to meet a requirement for additional infantry in theatre)
> Princess Louise Fusiliers (Brigade Independent Machine Gun Company) (provided by Princess Louise Fusiliers)
> 4th Princess Louise Dragoon Guards (converted from reconnaissance, replaced in 1st Division by Royal Canadian Dragoons)
> Lanark & Renfrew Scottish Regiment (converted from 1st Light Anti-Aircraft Regiment)
> Westminster Regiment (Motor) (reassigned from 5th Armoured Brigade)

II Canadian Corps

12th Manitoba Dragoons (Corps Armoured Car Regiment)
6th Anti-Tank Regiment
2nd Survey Regiment
6th Light Anti-Aircraft Regiment
Prince Edward Island Light Horse (Corps Defence Company)
> 2nd Canadian Infantry Division
> 14th Canadian Hussars (Division Reconnaissance Regiment)

4th Field Regiment
5th Field Regiment
6th Field Regiment
2nd Anti-Tank Regiment
3rd Light Anti-Aircraft Regiment
Toronto Scottish Regiment (MG) (Division Machine Gun Battalion)
4th Infantry Brigade
     Royal Regiment of Canada
     Royal Hamilton Light Infantry
     Essex Scottish Regiment
5th Infantry Brigade
     Black Watch (Royal Highland Regiment) of Canada
     Régiment de Maisonneuve
     Calgary Highlanders
6th Infantry Brigade
     Fusiliers Mont-Royal
     Queen's Own Cameron Highlanders of Canada
     South Saskatchewan Regiment

3rd Canadian Infantry Division
     17th Duke of York's Royal Canadian Hussars (Division Reconnaissance Regiment)
     12th Field Regiment
     13th Field Regiment
     14th Field Regiment
     3rd Anti-Tank Regiment
     4th Light Anti-Aircraft Regiment
     Cameron Highlanders of Ottawa (MG) (Division Machine Gun Battalion)
     7th Infantry Brigade

Royal Winnipeg Rifles
Regina Rifle Regiment
1st Battalion, Canadian Scottish Regiment
8th Infantry Brigade
Queen's Own Rifles of Canada
Régiment de la Chaudière
North Shore (New Brunswick) Regiment
9th Infantry Brigade
Highland Light Infantry of Canada
Stormont, Dundas and Glengarry Highlanders
North Nova Scotia Highlanders

4th Canadian Armoured Division
South Alberta Regiment (Division Armoured Reconnaissance Regiment)
15th Field Regiment
23rd Field Regiment (Self-Propelled)
5th Anti-Tank Regiment
8th Light Anti-Aircraft Regiment
4th Armoured Brigade
Governor General's Foot Guards
Canadian Grenadier Guards
British Columbia Regiment
Lake Superior Regiment (Motor) (Brigade Motorized Infantry Battalion)
10th Infantry Brigade
10th Independent Machine Gun Company (New Brunswick Rangers)
Lincoln and Welland Regiment
Algonquin Regiment
Argyll and Sutherland Highlanders of Canada (Princess Louise's)

1st Canadian Armoured Brigade
    Ontario Regiment
    Three Rivers Regiment
    Calgary Regiment

2nd Canadian Armoured Brigade
    1st Hussars
    Fort Garry Horse
    Sherbrooke Fusiliers Regiment

Canadian units that served with British formations
    Hong Kong Garrison
       Force C
           Royal Rifles of Canada
           Winnipeg Grenadiers
    6th British Airborne Division
       1st Canadian Parachute Battalion
    79th British Armoured Division
       1st Canadian Armoured Personnel Carrier Regiment

Canadian units that served with American formations
    Fifth Army
       1st Canadian Special Service Battalion (part of joint
       American-Canadian First Special Service Force)

PRINCIPAL WARSHIPS OF THE ROYAL CANADIAN NAVY

*destroyed by enemy action (torpedo, mine, aircraft)
**destroyed by other means (explosion, fire, collision, storm, unknown)

Light Cruisers (2)
Ontario   *Uganda*

Armed Merchant Cruisers (3)
Prince David   *Prince Henry*   *Prince Robert*

Escort Carriers (2) (RN, crewed by RCN)
Nabob   *Puncher*

Destroyers (28)

Algonquin	*Haida*	*Restigouche*
Annapolis	*Hamilton*	*Saguenay***
Assiniboine	*Huron*	*Saskatchewan*
*Athabaskan**	*Iroquois*	*St. Clair*
Buxton	*Kootenay*	*St. Croix**
Chaudière	*Margaree***	*St. Francis*
Columbia	*Niagara*	*St. Laurent*
*Fraser***	*Ottawa**	*Sioux*
Gatineau	*Ottawa (2nd)*	*Skeena***
	Qu'appelle	

Frigates (70)

Annan	*La Hulloise*	*Ribble*
Antigonish	*Lanark*	*Royalmount*
Beacon Hill	*Lasalle*	*Runnymede*
Buckingham	*Lauzon*	*Saint John*

Cap de la Madeleine Lévis (2nd)   St. Catharines
Cape Breton   Loch Achanalt   St. Pierre
Capilano   Loch Alvie   St. Stephen
Carlplace   Loch Morloch   Ste. Thérèse
Charlottetown (2nd) Longueuil   Sea Cliff
Chebogue*   Magog*   Springhill
Coaticook   Matane   Stettler
Dunver   Meon   Stone Town
Eastview   Monnow   Stormont
Ettrick   Montreal   Strathadam
Fort Erie   Nene   Sussexvale
Glace Bay   New Glasgow   Swansea
Grou   New Waterford   Teme*
Hallowell   Orkney   Thetford Mines
Inch Arran   Outremont   Toronto
Joliette   Penetang   Valleyfield*
Jonquière   Port Colborne   Victoriaville
Kirkland Lake   Poundmaker   Waskesiu
Kokanee   Prestonian   Wentworth
    Prince Rupert

Corvettes (123)
Agassiz   Galt   Parry Sound
Alberni*   Giffard   Peterborough
Algoma   Guelph   Petrolia
Amherst   Halifax   Pictou
Arnprior   Hawkesbury   Port Arthur
Arrowhead   Hepatica   Prescott
Arvida   Hespeler   Quesnel
Asbestos   Humberstone   Regina*
Atholl   Huntsville   Rimouski
Baddeck   Kamloops   Rivière du Loup
Barrie   Kamsack   Rosthern

Battleford	Kenogami	Sackville
Beauharnois	Kincardine	St. Lambert
Belleville	Kitchener	St. Thomas
Bittersweet	Lachute	Saskatoon
Bowmanville	La Malbaie	Shawinigan*
Brandon	Leaside	Shediac
Brantford	Lethbridge	Sherbrooke
Buctouche	Lévis*	Smiths Falls
Calgary	Lindsay	Snowberry
Camrose	Long Branch	Sorel
Chambly	Louisburg*	Spikenard*
Charlottetown*	Louisburg (2nd)	Stellarton
Chicoutimi	Lunenburg	Strathroy
Chilliwack	Matapedia	Sudbury
Cobalt	Mayflower	Summerside
Cobourg	Merrittonia	The Pas
Collingwood	Midland	Thorlock
Copper Cliff	Mimico	Tillsonburg
Dauphin	Moncton	Timmins
Dawson	Moose Jaw	Trail
Drumheller	Morden	Trentonian*
Dundas	Nanaimo	Trillium
Dunvegan	Napanee	Vancouver
Edmundston	New Westminster	Ville de Québec
Eyebright	Norsyd	West York
Fennel	North Bay	Wetaskiwin
Fergus	Oakville	Weyburn*
Forest Hill	Orangeville	Whitby
Fredericton	Orillia	Windflower**
Frontenac	Owen Sound	Woodstock

Minesweepers (80)

Bayfield	Granby	Noranda

Bellechasse
Blairmore
Border Cities
Brockville
Burlington
Canso
Caraquet
Chedabucto**
Chignecto
Clayoquot**
Comox
Coquitlam
Courtenay
Cowichan
Cranbrook
Daerwood
Digby
Drummondville
Esquimalt*
Fort Frances
Fort William
Fundy
Gananoque
Gaspé
Georgian
Goderich

Grandmère
Guysborough*
Ingonish
Kalamalka
Kapuskasing
Kelowna
Kenora
Kentville
Lachine
Lavalee
Llewellyn
Lloyd George
Lockeport
Mahone
Malpeque
Medicine Hat
Melville
Middlesex
Milltown
Minas
Miramichi
Mulgrave*
Nanoose (ex-Nootka)
New Liskeard
Nipigon

Oshawa
Outarde
Portage
Port Hope
Quatsino
Quinte
Red Deer
Revelstoke
Rockcliffe
Rossland
St. Boniface
St. Joseph
Sarnia
Sault Ste. Marie
Stratford
Swift Current
Thunder
Transcona
Trois-Rivières
Truro
Ungava
Vegreville
Wallaceburg
Wasaga
Westmount
Winnipeg

Armed Yachts (16)

Ambler
Beaver
Caribou
Cougar
Elk

Grizzly
Husky
Lynx
Moose
Otter**
Raccoon*

Reindeer
Renard
Sans Peur
Vison
Wolf

ROYAL CANADIAN AIR FORCE OVERSEAS

Fighter and Army Co-operation Squadrons
RAF Fighter Command
2nd Tactical Air Force RAF
   No. 83 (Composite) Group RAF
        39 (Reconnaissance) Wing RCAF
            400 (City of Toronto) Fighter Reconnaissance
            414 (City of Sarnia/Imperials) Fighter Reconnaissance
            430 (City of Sudbury) Fighter Reconnaissance
        125 (Fighter) Wing RAF
            441 (Silver Fox) Fighter
        126 (Fighter) Wing RCAF
            401 (Ram) Fighter
            411 (Grizzly Bear) Fighter
            412 (Falcon) Fighter
            442 (Caribou) Fighter
        127 (Fighter) Wing RCAF
            403(Wolf) Fighter
            416 (City of Oshawa) Fighter
            421 (Red Indian) Fighter
            443 (Hornet) Fighter
        143 (Fighter Bomber) Wing RCAF
            438 (Wild Cat) Fighter Bomber
            439 (Westmount) Fighter Bomber
            440 (Beaver) Fighter Bomber
   No. 85 (Base) Group RAF
        142 Wing RAF

                   402 (City of Winnipeg) Fighter
         147 Wing RAF
                   409 (Nighthawk) Night Fighter
         149 Wing RAF
                   410 (Cougar) Night Fighter

Air Defence of Great Britain
     No. 10 Group
                   406 (Lynx) Night Fighter/Intruder
     No. 11 Group
                   418 (City of Edmonton) Intruder

Allied Mediterranean Air Command
     No. 211 Group
                   244 (Fighter) Wing
                           417 (City of Windsor) Fighter

Maritime Reconnaissance and Strike Squadrons
RAF Coastal Command
     No. 15 Group RAF
                   422 (Flying Yachtsman) General Reconnaissance
                   423 (Bald Eagle) General Reconnaissance
     No. 16 Group RAF
                   415 (Swordfish) Torpedo Bomber (formerly fighter, later bomber)
     No. 19 Group RAF
                   404 (Buffalo) Coastal Fighter
                   407 (Demon) General Reconnaissance

Air Headquarters Iceland
                   162 (Osprey) Bomber Reconnaissance (temporarily on loan from Eastern Air Command RCAF)

RAF South East Asia Command
   No. 222 Group RAF
         413 (Tusker) General Reconnaissance

Bomber Squadrons
RAF Bomber Command
   No. 6 (RCAF) Group
   No. 62 Operational Base
         408 (Goose) Bomber
         415 (Swordfish) Bomber (formerly fighter and maritime reconnaissance and strike)
         420 (Snowy Owl) Bomber
         425 (Alouette) Bomber
         426 (Thunderbird) Bomber
         432 (Leaside) Bomber
   No. 63 Operational Base
         424 (Tiger) Bomber
         427 (Lion) Bomber
         429 (Bison) Bomber
         433 (Porcupine) Bomber
   No. 64 Operational Base
         419 (Moose) Bomber
         428 (Ghost) Bomber
         431 (Iroquois) Bomber
         434 (Bluenose) Bomber
   No. 8 (Pathfinder Force) Group RAF
         405 (Vancouver) Bomber

Allied Mediterranean Air Command
   No. 205 (Medium Bomber) Group RAF
         331 (Medium Bomber) Wing RCAF (existed temporarily in Mediterranean Theatre)
            420 (Snowy Owl) Bomber

424 (Tiger) Bomber
425 (Alouette) Bomber

Transport Squadrons
RAF Transport Command
    No. 46 (Transport) Group RAF
        437 (Husky) Transport

RAF Southeast Asia Command
    No. 229 (Transport) Group RAF
        435 (Chinthe) Transport
        436 (Elephant) Transport

Air Observation Post Squadrons (attached to First Canadian Army)
RAF Fighter Command
2nd Tactical Air Force RAF
    No. 84 (Composite) Group RAF
                664 Air Observation Post
                665 Air Observation Post
                666 Air Observation Post

THE "BOYS"

Several boy soldiers, sailors and airmen appear in more than one chapter. This list serves as a quick reference for recalling basic details about their service.

Bowen, Gerald — Royal Canadian Navy; schoolboy from Ottawa; enrolled age seventeen.

Cambon, Kenneth — Royal Rifles of Canada; soda jerk from Quebec City; enrolled age sixteen.

Chisholm, Denis — Regina Rifle Regiment; schoolboy from Prince Albert, Saskatchewan; enrolled age sixteen.

Chitty, Bill — 14th Field Regiment, farm boy from Midgic, New Brunswick; enrolled age sixteen.

Durrant, Gordon — Winnipeg Grenadiers; farm boy from Saskatchewan; enrolled age seventeen.

Ewing, Kenneth Alexander — Royal Rifles of Canada; militia soldier from Hampton, New Brunswick; enrolled age fifteen.

Foss, Herbert — Highland Light Infantry; woolen mill worker from Hespeler, Ontario; enrolled age seventeen.

Fowler, Donald — Stormont, Dundas and Glengarry Highlanders (and other units); schoolboy from Kingston; enrolled age fourteen.

Frayne, Ralph — Royal Canadian Navy; schoolboy from St. Catharines, Ontario; enrolled age fourteen in the army, age fifteen in the Merchant Navy and age seventeen in the navy.

Haney, Horace — Regina Rifle Regiment; sawmill worker from Emo, Ontario; enrolled age fifteen.

Hyde, Lloyd — Royal Canadian Air Force (424 Bomber Squadron); delivery boy from Ottawa; enrolled age seventeen.

Lynch, Wilbert — Winnipeg Grenadiers; militia soldier from Portage la Prairie, Manitoba; enrolled age seventeen.

MacDonell, George — Royal Rifles of Canada; militia soldier from Listowel, Ontario; enrolled age seventeen.

MacWhirter, William — Royal Rifles of Canada; farm boy from Hopetown, Quebec; enrolled age seventeen.

Mitchell, Clarence — Royal Canadian Navy; schoolboy from Strathroy, Ontario; enrolled age seventeen.

Muir, Bob — 14th Field Regiment; schoolboy from Como, Quebec; enrolled age sixteen.

Parks, Jim — Royal Winnipeg Rifles; schoolboy from Winnipeg; enrolled age fifteen.

Power, Cliff — Royal Canadian Navy; schoolboy from Mushaboom, Nova Scotia; enrolled age seventeen.

Pringle, Harold — Hastings and Prince Edward Regiment; labourer from Flinton, Ontario; enrolled age eighteen.

Roy, Reginald — Cape Breton Highlanders; schoolboy from Sydney, Nova Scotia; enrolled age sixteen.

Stebbe, Larry — Winnipeg Grenadiers; schoolboy from Beauséjour, Manitoba; enrolled age sixteen.

FOREWORD

*Too Young to Die: Canada's Boy Soldiers, Sailors and Airmen in
the Second World War* is the second of two books by John Boileau
and Dan Black dealing with the stories of underage men who
went to war for Canada, the first one being *Old Enough to Fight:
Canada's Boy Soldiers in the First World War.* The subject of boys
forced to fight has been much in the news in recent years. It was
raised some time ago by Lieutenant-General Roméo Dallaire,
who wrote the Foreword to the first book, and whose experience in Rwanda in 1974 and 1975 — and firmly-held belief since
then — has led him to campaign vigorously for this practice to
end. More recently, the activities of groups like ISIL, Al Shabaab
and Boko Haram, which force children to take part in terror-
ist activities, have brought renewed attention to the subject of
young people at war.

But what the authors write about in their two books is the
antithesis of boys being forced to fight. Indeed, they write about
underage young men who, when Canada went to war in 1914

and again in 1939, defied the rules that, because of their youth, denied their enlistment, and who deployed overseas before being legally entitled to do so. In fact, many who were rejected as too young in one jurisdiction went on to try to enlist in another, and some who succeeded in getting into uniform were subsequently forced to defer when their parents complained to the authorities — only to try again. Many succeeded and did go to war and many came back much changed. Many did not come back at all.

Whereas *Old Enough to Fight* deals largely with young men serving in the army, *Too Young to Die* covers the stories of underage Canadians who joined all three branches of Canada's armed forces. During the 1914–1918 war Canada's Air Force was at an embryonic stage and the role of the recently-formed Royal Canadian Navy was largely to defend Canada's coastal approaches and to shepherd merchant vessels. But by 1939 both the Royal Canadian Navy and the Royal Canadian Air Force had expanded, and by the end of the war they were respectively the fifth and fourth largest naval and air forces in the world. By 1945 Canada's wartime contribution of around a million and a half men and women in uniform, out of a population of only eleven million, was a significant element in the final allied victory. A surprising number of these soldiers, sailors and airmen joined and fought underage.

The first nine chapters of this carefully-researched and highly-readable narrative deal with the tales of those who joined the army and fought in the battles in Hong Kong, Dieppe, Italy, D-Day, the relief of Holland and the breakout into Germany. Three chapters deal with the war at sea, including the experience of young Canadians in the fourth branch of Canada's armed forces, the Merchant Navy. And the final two chapters deal with Canada's war in the air and its huge contribution to the war effort with the Commonwealth Air Training Plan. In each chapter, the emphasis is on the individual experiences of young men who joined underage, the reaction of their families, recruiters and authorities, and their subsequent individual experiences in the war.

The mixture of war, young men and the ever present likelihood of death is a recipe for pathos. The book gives the example of Private Alexander Rose, who enlisted at the age of sixteen in the Black Watch, with three older brothers already overseas: two in the Black Watch and one in the Navy. In November 1943, at the age of seventeen, he was sent first to Britain and then to Italy, where he joined the Carleton and York Regiment. In January 1944 his father wrote to the Chaplain at the reinforcement depot saying that he was a veteran himself, had three other sons overseas, that Alexander was underage, and asking that he not be sent into the line. Given the bureaucratic process that subsequently followed, it was not until after Alexander had been killed in February that measures to remove him from action began. To add further pathos, eleven years after the war ended Alexander's mother wrote to the Canadian Department of Veterans Affairs asking if she could receive a photo of her son's grave in the war cemetery in Italy. The reply she received informed her she could get one by applying through the British Legion in England, at the asking price of $1.65, and 90 cents for each additional copy.

The chapters on Canada's war at sea concentrate on the navy's struggle to counter the U-boat threat off Canada's coastline and across the Atlantic, including the hugely important role of convoying merchant ships carrying vital supplies and arms to Britain and the Soviet Union. It was those convoys that kept Britain and Russia alive and fighting in the early days of the war, in the face of catastrophic losses of ships, cargo and crew sunk by U-boat wolf packs. The book gives much-deserved credit to Canada's Merchant Navy, in which underage men and women found a more ready way to enter wartime service than in the fighting arms, even though the circumstances and conditions under which they then served were unparalleled in their danger and harshness.

The vital role played by the Merchant Navy between 1939 and 1945 was recognized but little rewarded until recently, despite that its casualties were proportionately higher than those of any of the three other arms. It was not until 2001 that Canada approved the establishment of September 3 as a national Merchant Navy Veterans' Day, and it was not until the end of 2012 that Britain finally struck the Arctic Star medal for those who served on convoy runs above the Arctic Circle. In the interests of full disclosure I should add that as one who crossed the Atlantic twice during the Second World War — first in 1940 at the age of three, sailing in a Cunard ship from Southampton to New York, and second in 1943 at the age of six, sailing back in a convoyed freighter from Halifax to Liverpool — I have great respect for those in the Merchant Navy and those who manned the convoy escorts.

The two chapters on the RCAF deal not only with Canadian airmen killed in action but also with many who died in accidents both in Canada and abroad. One such recounts the story of Edward James Wright of Winnipeg, who joined up giving his date of birth as November 7, 1925. The day, month and year were sufficient to allow him to enlist as an eighteen-year-old, but the year he entered on the form should have been 1928, since he was really fifteen. Trained as an air gunner, Wright went to Britain as a flight sergeant and flew first in Wellington bombers, including in several raids over occupied Europe. Eight days after joining 428 Squadron his Lancaster crashed while still in England and he and the rest of the crew were killed. He was sixteen, and perhaps the youngest aircrew member killed on flying duty from any country during the war. Questions were asked how someone so young could have been allowed to join an operational air crew, but as his younger sister Patsy noted: ". . . as I remember him, he would have found another way."

The book reports a number of interesting and little-known facts. As a graduate and former Commandant of Canada's Royal Military College (RMC), I found one to be particularly intriguing. The decision to send two Canadian battalions to Hong Kong shortly before the Japanese invasion of that island stemmed from a conversation between two RMC classmates — Major-General Arthur Grasett, who on graduation joined the British Army and in 1941 was the outgoing commander of the Hong Kong Garrison, and Canada's then Chief of the General Staff (CGS), Major-General Harry Crerar. On his return to Britain via Canada, Grasett called on Crerar and discussed the situation in Hong Kong, giving his opinion that more troops were needed to bolster the defences there. That conversation, followed by a subsequent formal British request to Canada that was approved by the CGS, led to the despatch of the Royal Rifles of Canada and the Winnipeg Grenadiers to Hong Kong, and their subsequent fate at the hands of the Japanese.

Helpfully Boileau and Black have included a complete section detailing the organization of the Canadian Armed Forces serving overseas during the Second World War, and another dealing with the names of the participants who appear in different places in the book. Both sections give the readers the ability to confirm where a particular formation or unit was located in the Order of Battle, as well as allowing them to refer back to find where a recurring individual's name appears and in what capacity.

Readers will find this book both entertaining and informative. Informal in style but with meticulous research and attribution, it provides a record of that aspect of human nature that, regardless of age, motivates the individual to seek to become a part of the whole, where involvement in events of historical importance is the attraction — and the two world wars were arguably the two most important historical events of the first half of the twentieth century. This book is about people, and its personalized stories of the human factor in war is the measure of its success. It joins its predecessor as a welcome and unique addition to the history of Canada at war.

— *General John de Chastelain, CC, CMM, CD, CH (Ret'd)*

PREFACE

In 2009, when we first discussed the idea of a book on Canadian boy soldiers, we thought we would be able to tell the stories of these boys in both world wars in a single book. While that would have been possible, when we settled on a publisher two years later, Jim Lorimer advised us such a lengthy book — more than 200,000 words — would be too expensive for the popular market. We took his advice to tell these stories in two volumes — one for each world war — and that has proved to be the right decision.

Old Enough to Fight: Canada's Boy Soldiers in the First World War was released in the fall of 2013 and was universally well-received. It sold so well Jim released it in a soft-cover edition in the summer of 2015. In that first volume, the stories were over-whelmingly about boy soldiers, as Canada had a miniscule navy and no air force at the time. Despite this, we were able to devote a single chapter to the stories of few underage Canadian sailors and airmen. Additionally, because the First World War is so far removed in time from popular memory, we included — for context — details about various campaigns and battles.

Although the army was overwhelmingly the largest of the three services in the Second World War, Canada also had a large navy and air force. In this volume, we were able to include several stories about Canada's youngest sailors and airmen, and devote a number of chapters to them. Additionally, we felt it was essential to include the stories of boys in the Merchant Navy. Although the Merchant Navy was not a part of the armed forces, during the war senior officials referred to it as the "fourth arm" and it fulfilled an essential role in winning the war. We also believe that, because the Second World War is much more a part of popular memory than the First, we did not have to give as much of the background to campaigns and battles as we did in the first volume.

Surprisingly — or perhaps not surprisingly — the young men who served in the Second World War had many of the same reasons for joining as their predecessors who fought in the First: patriotism, revenge, excitement, adventure, feelings of invincibility, peer pressure, or a burning desire to represent or fight on behalf of their generation. Added to this was the effect the Great Depression had on the economy and jobs, with the armed forces offering much-needed employment for many. Conversely, the creation of a National Registration Certificate during the Second World War, which all Canadians sixteen years of age and older were legally required to carry at all times, made it more difficult for underage youth to join. Yet, thousands of boys were able to "beat the system" by convincing the authorities in one way or another that they were older than their actual years.

The research we undertook to write this book proved to be an amazing experience. In the first place, we were able to interview several of Canada's dwindling number of surviving Second

World War veterans, rewarding encounters that were impossible for our volume about the First World War. Secondly, the immediate families of veterans who had died during or after the Second World War are generally much younger than those from the First World War, making their memories closer in time and therefore more vivid. It also helped our research that more Second World War servicemen wrote first-hand accounts of their experiences — both published and unpublished — than their comrades in arms of the previous generation, which provided an invaluable resource.

Additional research followed many of the same well-known paths that other authors of stories about Canada's soldiers, sailors and airmen use: individual service files held at Library and Archives Canada, burial details of Canada's war dead at the Canadian Agency of the Commonwealth War Graves Commission, Veterans Affairs Canada's Virtual War Memorial and Heroes Remember websites, Historica-Dominion's Memory Project website, as well as numerous organizations ranging from local to national libraries and military museums, and from local volunteers to professional historians, archivists, curators and librarians.

Readers should also be aware that boys who joined before they were legally allowed to enrol or proceed overseas were usually no longer underage by the time the Second World War was over. For example, sixteen- and seventeen-year-old boys who joined in 1939 or 1940 and survived the conflict were twenty-one to twenty-three years old by the time our enemies were defeated in 1945. Similarly, teenage boys captured at Hong Kong in 1941 and who spent the next three and a half years as prisoners of war were no longer teenagers when the war ended. No matter what their age when the global conflict was over, these boys spent a key part of their formative years in the very adult world of the armed forces during war.

This volume and its companion one about the First World War tell for the first time the stories of boy servicemen in a Canadian context. They are stories of which all Canadians — both young and old — should be aware.

JBB
"Lindisfarne"
Glen Margaret,
Nova Scotia

DRB
Merrickville,
Ontario

June 6, 2016 — 72nd anniversary of the D-Day landings in Normandy, involving Canadian soldiers, sailors and airmen.

INTRODUCTION

"I HAD NO KNOWLEDGE OF ANYTHING MILITARY UNTIL ONE DAY MY FATHER'S OLDEST BROTHER . . . APPEARED IN UNIFORM . . ."
Youth and Another World War

Ralph Frayne was fourteen years old when he thumbed a ride into Hamilton, Ontario, to join the Canadian army. He was discharged when his mother found out, but that did not stop him. A short time later, he hitchhiked to Halifax, joined the merchant marine, then the Royal Canadian Navy (RCN) — all before his eighteenth birthday.[1]

There were Canadian boys younger than Frayne serving in the Second World War, the vast majority in their mid-teens — sixteen- and seventeen-year-olds who marked or came close to marking their eighteenth birthdays overseas. How many were under the age of eighteen when they joined is difficult to say, but research points to significant participation in the army, the navy, the air force and the "fourth arm of the fighting services" — the merchant marine.[2] The exact number is unknown because the majority of them got in by fudging their birthdate by as much as two to three years. Some went beyond that and passed themselves off as an older brother.

When it came to age, the qualifications stated volunteers had to be between eighteen and forty-five,[3] although boys under eighteen were legitimately welcomed in with the rank of "boy soldier," "boy sailor," "boy bugler" or "boy drummer." While applying to the Royal Canadian Navy (RCN) at age sixteen, Kenneth Watson of Revelstoke, British Columbia, was asked to produce a signed consent form from a parent as well as character references. He got in as a Boy (Seaman Class) in 1941 (Chapter 10).

The Royal Canadian Air Force (RCAF) also took in sixteen- and seventeen-year-olds, although it may have been more reticent due to the dangers of wartime flying and the cost of replacing aircraft. That did not stop Edward Wright or John Dowding from becoming air gunners. Both enrolled at sixteen. Another teenager, Lloyd Hyde of Ottawa, completed several tours as a tail gunner and got home before the war ended while moving on to adulthood (Chapters 13 and 14).

The minimum age for overseas service was nineteen,[4] but recruits also had to have a minimum height of five-foot-four, be in good health and be British subjects "of good character."[5] While many were welcomed as "boys," adolescents under the age of eighteen, or perceived to be underage, ran the risk of being rejected on the spot at the recruiting centres. Many were, but countless others got in with few questions asked and served alongside older men overseas. Birth and baptismal certificates were not required at the recruiting centres, where those in line were simply asked to state their age. As in the First World War, the sergeants or corporals manning the recruiting centres were looking to fill quotas and so they often looked the other way or advised the young lad standing in front of them to add a year or two to his age — if the youngster had not already done so.

Adolescents who joined the Non-Permanent Active Militia (NPAM) before the war were generally viewed more favourably

A lone sentry walks guard duty outside a recruiting centre in this 1941 watercolour titled Recruits Wanted, *by Orville Fisher.*

than those who had not joined Canada's part-time military. Denis Chisholm of Prince Albert, Saskatchewan, enrolled in the Regina Rifles in June 1940 at sixteen, after a year in the militia. At first he said he was promptly told "to go home and grow up. So I went home and a few days later the phone rang and they said, 'You're a bugler, aren't you?' I said yes. Then they asked me how old I was. I told them I was nineteen, and they said, 'Well, come on down.'"[6]

That same year, the NPAM was redesignated the Reserve Army and a new policy required "that future enlistments would be restricted to men not eligible for the Active Force — i.e., those between 17 and 19 years of age or over 35." During the war, the Reserve produced a proportion of recruits for the Active Force by training young men of pre-enrolment age.[7]

This may help explain the large number of boys under the age of nineteen serving in Canada.

In 1943, the Canadian Technical Training Corps was formed, which established the Canadian Army Trades School at locations across Canada. Boys enrolled at age sixteen as apprentices and trained as auto mechanics, clerks, draftsmen, electricians, machinists and surveyors. The idea was that by age nineteen, they would be ready to join the army as trained tradesmen.

Meanwhile, at the recruiting centres, boys who were told to come back in a year or two often waited only a few days or weeks before trying again. Intervention from an irate mother, father or older sibling ended or delayed the adventure for some who had managed to slip in undetected, as in the case of seventeen-year-old Clifford Power of Mushaboom, Nova Scotia, who was discharged six months after his mother caught up to him. Three months later, well before his eighteenth birthday, Power snuck away from home, signed up again and in September 1942, nearly died when HMCS Ottawa was torpedoed, with significant loss of life, in the North Atlantic.[8] Sadly, for others the protests from home arrived too late.

Attestation papers, completed at the time of enrolment, contain much useful information, but cannot always be trusted when it comes to verifying date of birth. Neither can the official provincial death certificates, which often relied on the Canadian military to provide the dates of birth and death, taken from the soldier's service records. There is one form, however, in the files of deceased soldiers, sailors and airmen that can be viewed with more confidence when it comes to determining age. This four-page, legal-size document was mailed to next of kin by the Department of National Defence's Estates Branch and was usually filled out by the serviceman's mother or father — weeks after the soldier's death. Its purpose was to gather information should there be any service estate available for distribution. The instructions to next of kin noted the "particulars required are to be carefully filled in" and the declaration "should be signed in the presence of a Clergyman, Priest, Local Magistrate, Commissioner for Oaths, Notary Public or a Commissioned Officer of any of His Majesty's Forces who should be asked to complete and sign the Certificate." It included space for next of kin to state the date of birth of the deceased. In the majority of the files we reviewed, the date of birth given by the next of kin was a year to three years younger than the date of birth given by the serviceman when he joined.

* * *

More than a million Canadian men and women served in the Second World War between 1939 and 1945. The total number of males who enrolled in the army, air force and navy was approximately 940,000. There are no official estimates, but if only one per cent of the total male enrolments were underage when they joined, the figure is significant. However, we believe the percentage was higher, somewhere around three per cent or upwards of thirty thousand.

In addition, boys too young to join the army, navy or air force were among the twelve thousand who served in Canada's Merchant Navy. Boys as young as twelve or thirteen — and perhaps younger — worked on board Canadian- or foreign-flagged merchant ships that hauled everything from molasses to high-octane aviation fuel during crucial convoy runs. These lads toiled in the galley, on and below decks, in the mess or in dark and dusty bunkers, where they shovelled coal into the chutes feeding the boiler rooms (Chapter 12). Some of them went down with their ships or experienced harrowing situations adrift at sea. Most gained valuable experience, including Frayne, who could not wait to join the regular navy after watching the bodies of merchant mariners drift past his ship in the North Atlantic.

Roy Spry in Toronto, 1943. He was sixteen when he joined the Merchant Navy in December 1944.

In the First World War, it is estimated at least twenty thousand Canadians enrolled underage, most of them in the Canadian Expeditionary Force. This equates to roughly three per cent of the males who served, a percentage in line with our estimate for the Second World War.

It is also interesting to note the average age of Canadian soldiers in the Great War was twenty-six, although it was younger in front-line battalions. In the Second World War, the average age of a rifleman was twenty-three,[9] suggesting the average age of those serving at the sharp end was younger compared to Canada's First World War experience. Overall, fewer Canadians died in the Second World War than in the First, partly because of the amount of time Canadians spent in Britain prior to being engaged in major campaigns, but largely due to the changed nature of warfare. This is also true for the number of underage soldiers. Records supplied to us in 2010 from the Canadian Agency of the Commonwealth War Graves Commission (CWGC) show eighty-six Canadians were fourteen, fifteen, sixteen or seventeen when they died during the war. The matching number for the First World War is 474. The youngest soldier identified by the CWGC in the Second World War is fourteen-year-old Claude Brooks, a reservist who was killed, along with two others, when the armoured vehicle he was in fell off a bridge on Prince Edward Island in September 1944.[10] For the purpose of this book, we have included boys like him, as well as those who enrolled underage but continued to serve as they grew older during the war.

* * *

So why did young adolescents join? Why were they so eager to leave home and family to put their lives at risk? And more importantly, what was it about the late 1930s and early 1940s that compelled boys too young to shave or graduate from high school to want to fight a foreign enemy? The reasons given then and later were similar to what was heard during and after the Great War: there was a ruthless enemy to defeat; their friends were signing up; they could earn regular pay, drop out of school or swap a dead-end job with an opportunity for adventure — a chance to "be somebody" and see the world. There were also angrier responses: to escape an orphanage or an abusive situation at home, or to avenge the death of a father, brother or close friend killed overseas.

Underlying most of it, though, was a feeling that went beyond patriotism. Young people wanted to contribute and to be seen supporting the war effort in a meaningful way — at home or abroad — even if it meant leapfrogging past their adolescent years into the world of adulthood. That was true for Gerald Bowen of Ottawa, who suddenly went from a boy delivering newspapers to a sailor on the high seas.[11] Those growing up in the late 1930s and early 1940s took the war very seriously and their responses were heavily influenced by the Great Depression; like Jim Parks of Winnipeg, for instance, who hopped freight trains in search of work in Saskatchewan and Alberta before enrolling at age fifteen.[12] In the West, amid the dust of the drought, there were "hobo jungles," relief camps and grasshoppers that chewed through clothes. People were paid with eggs and chickens, or a day's work for a day's work.[13]

The war introduced a new set of dangers for anyone who survived the Depression. Now, instead of losing the family home, the farm or a low-paying job, young men and women faced losing their lives or becoming horribly maimed in a war just twenty-one years after the last one. But it also brought prosperity as industries ramped up to produce wartime equipment and armaments. Young people, who had scraped by with their families during the Depression, were among the thousands who benefited. "The war," Canadian historian Cynthia Comacchio

Many posters, like this one by Hubert Rogers, encouraged civilians to do their part for the war effort.

noted, "also bestowed their first opportunity to be productively engaged, adequately clothed and fed, and earning wages."[14] For some, shift work was not the answer. After quitting school in Brockville, Ontario, Jack Shepherd worked at a milk plant before joining the army at age fifteen. "I got teed off because some of the guys working in the plant were drunk and you couldn't get them to work. I was doing so much that one morning I just went in and said goodbye to the guy in charge — told him I was finished — that I had had enough."[15]

For Shepherd and other adolescents, the most obvious way to contribute was to get into uniform and get overseas. Those who were underage and got in were admired by peers who could not enrol, and all around them, the pressure to support the effort

Youthful and resourceful Jim Parks of Winnipeg, prior to heading overseas in 1941.

grew, even though — compared to 1914 — there was less public enthusiasm for going to war. However, schools, churches, community groups, businesses and government departments all promoted the effort and publicly encouraged youths to participate. In and out of the press, boys and girls were recognized for planting Victory gardens, making bandages, shipping seeds to Britain, knitting socks, canvassing neighbourhoods for salvageable materials, building model airplanes for aircraft recognition and studying first aid. Mandatory military drills were introduced at high schools, where teachers shaped classroom courses around events overseas. The Boy Scouts and Girl Guides were heavily involved, so were high school cadet corps. This activity was in contrast to the low to moderate amount of interest the war-weary public had for the military during the interwar years. But for many young Canadians, the pull towards military service was noticeable and it grew as the 1930s ended.

Donald Fowler's interest began to peak after a visit from his uncle in Peterborough, Ontario. "I had no knowledge of anything military until one day my father's oldest brother — he was a regimental sergeant major — appeared in uniform at our home. It shocked me because he was wearing a Sam Browne belt and he looked so officious he frightened me. That was the start of all things military for me."

After moving to Kings-
ton, the Fowlers settled
into a modest home near
the armouries. "I could
throw a snowball from
the front yard of our
house on Montreal Street
and hit the front of the
armouries . . . I used to
marvel at the guy who
came out of the building
— the quarters where the
men slept. He'd walk out
to the centre, to a metal
plate in the rugged field
and he'd stand there and
he would play the trum-

Jack Shepherd enrolled after leaving a job at a milk factory in Brockville, Ontario.

pet. I was fascinated by his Reveille and Last Post. The horses also
held my interest and they had a little pony there and they would
let me ride it in Artillery Park. I would have been about ten."
Fowler became a boy bandsman at eleven and enrolled with the
Stormont, Dundas and Glengarry Highlanders at fourteen. His
father, Gunner H.J. Fowler, joined the Royal Canadian Horse
Artillery in 1939 and went overseas that year, but was sent home
on the hospital ship the *Lady Nelson* in 1943 after he was seriously injured when his motorcycle collided with a truck during
the compulsory period of darkness known as blackout. Fowler's
younger brother, Karl, born in 1928, joined as a boy soldier at
age twelve. He did not get as far as Donald, who headed overseas
in 1941, saw service in Britain and North-West Europe, and was
only nineteen when the war ended.[16]

At home, the sights and sounds from overseas were everywhere. Families who could afford a radio gathered to listen with

bated breath to the news, and adults were quick to admonish the young if they interrupted the broadcasts. In downtown movie houses, graphic newsreels showed the devastating effects of the Blitz and the smoking carnage from battlefields. In black and white, the images illuminated the silver screens where teenagers spent Saturday afternoons or evenings. They took the news seriously, as they did the war. Many were frightened, confused and alarmed by a world that seemed to be crumbling, yet rushing forward at an alarming rate. Looking for reassurance, they discussed matters with peers or talked to parents, clergy and teachers. On the whole, they were deeply moved by what they saw and what the future might hold for them.

All of this and more caused young Canadians to commit themselves to the war effort in the most obvious way possible — in uniform. Thousands got in and helped carry the burden of war, which since the beginning of humanity has been created by older men, but placed on the backs of the young.

* * *

Wracked by the Depression, Canadians did not welcome war in 1939. But it was unavoidable. On September 1, Germany, in an unprovoked act of aggression, invaded Poland. Intent on protecting Polish sovereignty, Britain and France demanded the Germans withdraw. When that warning went unanswered, Britain and France declared war on Germany. The date was September 3. Seven days later, Canada joined in, with the idea of waging a war of "limited liability," hoping to avoid a repetition of the terrible loss of life in the First World War.

Initially, Canada agreed to provide economic assistance and raw materials and to ramp up wartime industrial production. The country would host and train pilots and aircrew under the mammoth British Commonwealth Air Training Plan, while overseas,

Life as a boy bandsman was not enough for eleven-year-old Donald Fowler, who joined the army in Kingston, Ontario, at age fourteen.

Britain and France would fight the battles. But by December, the first ships carrying 7,500 troops of the 1st Canadian Infantry Division were arriving in Scotland.[17] As Canada raced to rebuild its badly depleted fighting forces, the policy shifted, especially after Germany invaded Denmark and Norway in April 1940 and followed with the Blitzkrieg that swallowed North-West Europe. After the evacuation of British forces from Dunkirk in late May and early June, and the subsequent fall of France, Britain was alone, facing an enemy on the opposite side of the English Channel.

The Canadians arriving in Britain trained while trying to adjust to the damp weather, new traffic rules, blackouts and the British way of life. Any Briton old enough to remember the Canadians during the First World War was somewhat surprised by the "colonials" who arrived this time and stayed longer. While nearly half of the First World War's Canadian Expeditionary Force were British-born, the vast majority of Canadians serving in the Second World War were Canadian-born.[18]

By early 1942, many Canadians were bored and anxious for action, having read about the December disaster at Hong Kong and the terrible U-boat attacks on passenger ships in the North

Atlantic. The horror show in Hong Kong marked the first of many bloody land, sea and air battles that killed approximately 44,000 Canadians. Thousands of others were wounded and spent the rest of their lives with missing limbs, horrific disfigurements and deep psychological scars. For parents, the sharp, silent pain of losing a young son never ended, regardless of how old he was when he died.

Sadly, many young Canadian soldiers, sailors and airmen did not die on a battlefield at all. They were claimed by disease, road accidents, drownings and other causes. Seventeen-year-old Trooper John Huggins of Fort San, Saskatchewan, was very athletic, but did not stand a chance when he was struck by a hit-and-run motorist in downtown Toronto in 1943. He had been in the army a month. Private Evan Desjardins was only sixteen when he enrolled at Ottawa in late November 1941, and was five months past his seventeenth birthday when he died December 27, 1942. He was a passenger on a local train that was struck from behind by a troop train at Almonte, Ontario.[19] That horrific crash, one of the worst in Canadian history, claimed the lives of nearly forty people, including nine servicemen — all of them on the local train. More than two hundred others were injured.[20]

Private Lucien Paiement of Montreal enrolled at sixteen and was marking his seventeenth birthday when he arrived in Iceland with Les Fusiliers Mont-Royal. His unit was assigned to garrison duty as part of Z Force, which freed up British infantry units for deployment elsewhere. Less than three months later — on October 1 — he died of acute appendicitis at No. 50 General Hospital, Reykjavik, leaving behind his grieving mother, sick father and a younger sister.

Overseas, Brookwood Military Cemetery became known as the Dispatch Riders Holding Unit, owing to the number of motorcycle fatalities.[21] Gunner John Callahan of Galt, Ontario,

This 1944 watercolour titled Dispatch Rider *by Donald Anderson, shows RCAF LAC W. Dalton at Station Croft in Yorkshire.*

enrolled at seventeen; Signalman Ian Ferguson of Montreal and Driver Thomas Steed, born at Brantford, Ontario, both joined at sixteen. All three died in motorcycle mishaps and are buried at Brookwood. Private Hubert Blanchard of Regina is there, too. He was sixteen when he enrolled in June 1940 and two weeks shy of his eighteenth birthday when he was accidently shot in the chest by a sentry on February 16, 1942.[22]

Many other young Canadians survived their time in Britain and not all were bored by or hated the experience. In fact, many admired the country and its people. "I was in the UK for three years before I went over to France and during that time I never heard one Brit say we might lose the war — never heard that once," noted Denis Chisholm, recalling his young impressions of British stoicism and courage. "They were upbeat and they were getting the hell bombed out of them. They were on rations like you wouldn't believe, but they were the most cheerful, stiff-upper-lip types you ever met in your life — just amazing."[23]

The main goal, however, was to stop Hitler and Mussolini. Following the disastrous raid on Dieppe in August 1942, Canadians were sent to Sicily in 1943 and then to the Italian mainland. Less than a year later, they were part of the greatest seaborne invasion of all time — the D-Day landings in Normandy and eventually the liberation of Europe. The Canadian contribution on land, on sea and in the air was outstanding, and a good part of it was paid for in blood by the youngest of the young.

PART I

FIRST BATTLES: HONG KONG AND DIEPPE

"We can see today that the decision to reinforce Hong Kong was a mistake . . . [and] the raid on Dieppe . . . tactically . . . was an almost complete failure."

Colonel C.P. Stacey, *Six Years of War: The Army in Canada, Britain and the Pacific, The Official History of the Canadian Army in the Second World War, Volume I*

MAP I

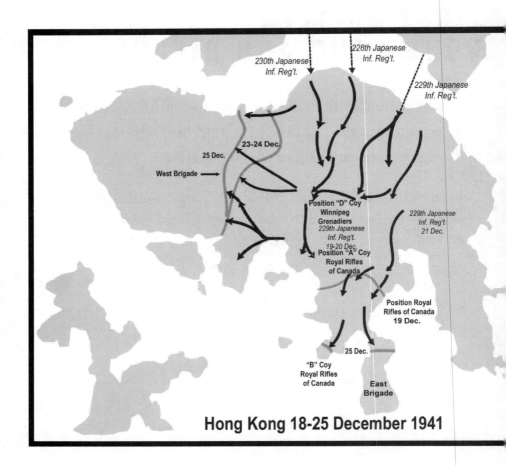

230th Japanese
Inf. Reg't.

228th Japanese
Inf. Reg't.

229th Japanese
Inf. Reg't.

23-24 Dec.

25 Dec.

West Brigade

Position "D" Coy
Winnipeg
Grenadiers
229th Japanese
Inf. Reg't.
19-20 Dec.
Position "A" Coy
Royal Rifles
of Canada

229th Japanese
Inf. Reg't.
21 Dec.

Position Royal
Rifles of Canada
19 Dec.

25 Dec.

"B" Coy
Royal Rifles
of Canada

East
Brigade

Hong Kong 18-25 December 1941

MAP II

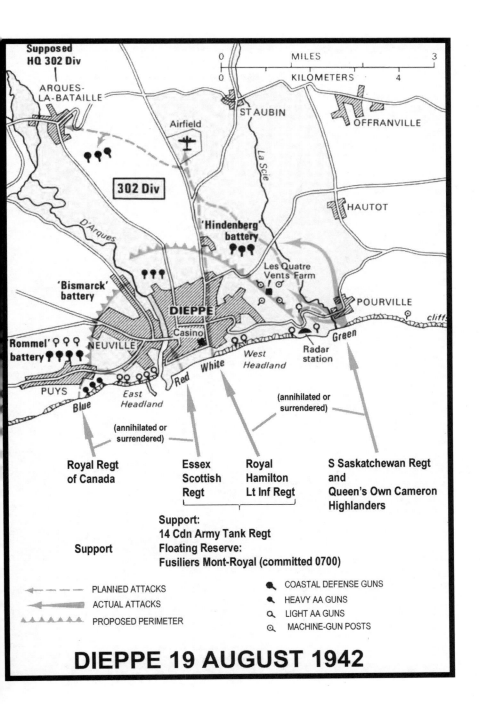

DIEPPE 19 AUGUST 1942

"IT HAD BEEN RATHER AN UNUSUAL CHRISTMAS DAY . . . ONE TO REMEMBER . . . ONE NEVER TO FORGET."

Hong Kong, The Battle
(Map I)

Grenadier Gordon Durrant had never been so afraid in his young life. After surrendering to victorious Japanese troops on Christmas Day 1941, his sergeant told Durrant and his fellow soldiers that everyone had to go to battalion headquarters by a certain time that afternoon; anyone in uniform or with a weapon after that would be shot on sight by the Japanese. Durrant, who enrolled at age seventeen, wondered what his fate would be, knowing the enemy had killed any Chinese they captured. His sergeant did not calm the soldier's fears when he added, "Now we don't know what they're going to do, whether they're going to line you up and shoot you or whether they are just going to put you in the prison camp and keep you."[1]

At battalion headquarters, their Japanese captors lined the Canadians up and tied them together with wire that looped around their wrists, hands behind their backs. Then they marched them off to the nearby village of Aberdeen. Durrant recalled one Canadian who was trying to help his wounded brother, who kept falling down. "The Jap sentry come and just stuck a bayonet in him and broke the wire and put the wire from him around another one and then pushed his body over the [edge of the road], and his brother is yelling his head off and they were hitting him with the rifle . . . and we yelled at him to keep quiet, to not make any noise or they will put the bayonet in you."[2]

What other horrors lay ahead for the Canadian prisoners of war?

* * *

In July 1941, the outgoing commander of the British Garrison in Hong Kong, Major-General Arthur Grasett, returned to Britain via Canada. Grasett, a Canadian serving in the British army, stopped in Ottawa to see an old friend from their student days together at the Royal Military College of Canada and the Imperial Defence College, Major-General "Harry" Crerar, who was Chief of the General Staff at the time. Their discussion turned to Japan, which had been fighting China intermittently since 1931 before it launched major offensive operations in 1937. Japan's aim was to establish what became known in 1940 as the Greater East Asia Co-Prosperity Sphere; in effect, a Japanese empire. The Japanese rationale was straightforward: Western nations had established their colonial empires and now it was the turn of Japan — a latecomer on the scene — to become an imperial power.

Grasett had a low opinion of the Japanese fighting abilities, a not-uncommon attitude towards non-whites at the time. He told Crerar the addition of two or more battalions to the two British and two Indian infantry units already in Hong Kong would make it strong enough to withstand a Japanese attack during an extensive siege. When Grasett returned to Britain, he recommended increasing the garrison and suggested Canada might provide troops. The British had already decided not

A 1941 recruiting poster by M. Gagnon for the Royal Rifles of Canada, one of two infantry battalions sent to Hong Kong.

to commit more of their own forces to the colony, based on various studies that showed it would be extremely difficult to defend. Despite this conclusion — which apparently was never communicated to Canadian authorities — a formal request for additional soldiers was sent to the Canadian government in mid-September, which Crerar supported. On October 11, the British asked for the addition of a brigade headquarters and various specialist elements to the Canadian commitment. The government agreed and the headquarters, plus signals, medical, dental and postal detachments were included. The contingent was designated C Force, under the command of newly-promoted Brigadier John Lawson, a regular force officer. As well, because the two battalions would be far from replacement depots, a reinforcement company was authorized for each of them.

The fate of 1,973 Canadians, including lads who had enrolled under the age of eighteen, was sealed.[3]

* * *

The war to date had not been a good one for either the Winnipeg Grenadiers or the Royal Rifles of Canada. And it was about to get much worse — far beyond what any of the soldiers in the two battalions could have imagined. The Grenadiers were initially mobilized for active service as a machine-gun battalion in September 1939 (later converted to a conventional infantry battalion), while the Rifles were called up later, in May 1940. Rather than being selected for service in Europe, both infantry units were sent to garrison some of Britain's North American island colonies: the Grenadiers to the warmth of Jamaica the same month the Rifles were mobilized, and the Rifles to the chilly, fog-shrouded shores of Newfoundland a few months later, in November. While garrison duty may have been safe, it was boring — endless hours of mind-numbing sentry duty and patrols — especially for the younger members of the battalions, who were eager to get into action. In October 1941, when the Rifles concentrated at Valcartier, an army camp hewn out of the bush north of Quebec City for the First World War a generation earlier, and were told they were going overseas, Sergeant George MacDonell noted, "the camp was in an uproar as hectic preparations were made for a long journey to some unknown foreign destination. The excitement was high."[4] Although the new location was initially unknown, the mere fact the government had chosen them for service abroad was generally greeted with enthusiasm by all ranks.

Before the war, the Edmonton-born MacDonell had been living with an aunt and uncle in Listowel, Ontario, since the

A young sergeant George MacDonell poses in front of his tent in Gander, Newfoundland, on his birthday, August 5, 1941.

separation of his parents when he was twelve years old. In the winter of 1938, he joined the 100th Battery, a local militia artillery unit. The sixteen-year-old became a signaller, transmitting fire orders from an observation post back to the battery's 18-pounder field guns. When Britain declared war on Germany on September 3, 1939, MacDonell's battery was mobilized. Less than a week later, with Canada's declaration of war — and based on his Grade 10 commercial qualification — he was put to work full-time typing enlistment papers of those who volunteered to serve in the active force. MacDonell found it an exciting time. "No more high school for me," he remembered. "I was employed on more serious business, that of saving my country from the Nazis."[5]

He had just celebrated his seventeenth birthday three weeks earlier.

When MacDonell's uncle phoned his nephew's commanding officer to point out the lad was only seventeen and ineligible to join, MacDonell ran away, hitchhiked to London and enrolled in the Royal Canadian Army Service Corps as a private, claiming to be eighteen. A few days later, he phoned his uncle to tell him what he had done, adding if he interfered again, he would "go out

west and enlist again, and sever our relationship forever."[6] His
uncle backed off. Due to a shortage of vehicles, MacDonell's unit
trained as infantry on the plain behind London's Wolseley Barracks. The facilities were primitive: tents without floors, palliasses
on bare ground, no indoor toilets or showers, cold water only and
no mess tents. When it rained, the camp was turned into a muddy
morass, but spirits remained high among the new soldiers.

On December 7, 1939 — two years to the day before Japan
attacked outposts of the Western powers in the Far East and
Pacific in an event that changed the lives of George MacDonell
and hundreds of other Canadian soldiers forever — Mac-
Donell's commanding officer announced the unit would be
going to Britain with the 1st Division when it sailed in the
next few weeks. The young man's initial excitement was soon
diminished when he learned the next day only those who were
over nineteen could go; those under that age would be sent to
the nearby training depot of the Royal Canadian Regiment. The
disappointment MacDonell and his comrades felt was "painful
indeed"[7] as they watched their older mates prepare for their
journey overseas.

At the Royal Canadian Regiment training depot, quickly nicknamed "Boys' Town," the young soldiers were put in the charge
of the regiment's overage officers and senior non-commissioned
officers, veterans of many years' service and a fine group of
instructors. The difference between these old regular force soldiers and the part-time militiamen who had been their trainers
up to now was remarkable. Under the veterans' guidance, the
youthful recruits learned valuable skills and over the next few
months were turned into the goal of all army training — a team.
MacDonell lapped up the rigorous regimen and felt at home in
the rigid, hierarchical structure of the army. Towards the end
of his recruit training, he was called into the office of the regimental sergeant-major, a man who was regarded by the boys as

The Royal Rifles of Canada entrain for Vancouver at Camp Valcartier, October 1941.

only slightly below God in rank, and informed the next day his appointment to lance corporal would be published in unit orders. At a rugged six-foot-four and two hundred pounds, MacDonell was following an informal army tradition that especially tall soldiers, who were usually used as "right markers" when parades were forming up, would find themselves as lance corporals near the end of recruit training.

Two months later he became a corporal, earning $1.75 a day. He was not yet eighteen.

Near the end of September 1940, MacDonell and two of his friends were informed they were being promoted to sergeants and posted to the Royal Rifles of Canada, a Quebec City unit, then training at Camp Sussex, New Brunswick. The former Grade 10 commercial student was now the youngest sergeant in the Canadian army. Garrison duty followed in Newfoundland

before coastal defence duties in New Brunswick and concentration again at Camp Valcartier, where preparations for overseas
commenced. The issue of tropical kit caused great speculation
regarding the unit's destination, with service in the North Afri-
can desert as part of the British 8th Army the top choice. That
changed on October 23, when the regiment boarded a train
heading west to Vancouver, instead of east to Halifax. During a
stop in Ottawa, elements of the brigade headquarters joined the
Rifles on the train.[8]

Other boy soldiers were on the train with MacDonell as it
travelled through the night across the great expanse of Northern
Ontario's Precambrian Shield. Rifleman Bill MacWhirter was
attached as an immediate reinforcement soldier to D Company,
the same company in which MacDonell was No. 18 Platoon sergeant. MacWhirter had been born in Niagara Falls, New York, on
January 10, 1924, when his family was living there. A few years
later, due to hard times caused by the Depression, the family
returned to Hopetown, a hamlet on the south shore of Quebec's
Gaspé Peninsula, where MacWhirter completed Grade 8. When
the war broke out, his father, a veteran of the First World War,
joined the Veterans' Guard, and two older brothers also joined
up. At the tender age of fifteen, MacWhirter suddenly found
himself head of the family farm.

In 1941, he followed his father and brothers in uniform and
enrolled at nearby New Carlisle when he was seventeen.

Rifleman Ken Ewing was in A Company. The Hampton,
New Brunswick, native was born on August 7, 1925, the fourth
oldest of twelve children and the son of a civil engineer who
had been a lieutenant during the First World War. Ewing quit
school in Grade 10 to join up, but was unsuccessful in his
attempt to get into the Merchant Navy. As he and a couple of
friends showed up at the docks in nearby Saint John, the ship
they intended to serve on was sailing out of the harbour. "And

thank God for that," Ewing recalled later, "because it was an Estonian ship and it probably didn't survive too long."[9] He promptly enrolled in a local militia unit, the 8th Princess Louise's New Brunswick Hussars — one of the country's oldest units — in the spring of 1940, when he was only fifteen. When the Hussars mobilized in July, Ewing was sent home along with one of his brothers and a few friends because they were too young for overseas service. Undeterred, Ewing joined another militia unit, the New Brunswick Rangers, still hoping to get into an active unit. When he learned the Royal Rifles of Canada were only thirty kilometres away training in Camp Sussex, he and a friend made the short journey.

On November 4, Ewing enrolled, claiming to be nineteen although he was only fifteen at the time. He thought the unit authorities knew he was underage — perhaps seventeen or eighteen — but did not realize how young he actually was.

Rifleman Ken Cambon came from a family with military connections. His father was a musician in the band of the Royal 22e Régiment, Quebec's famous "Van Doos," while his maternal grandfather had been the garrison commander in Barbados before immigrating to Canada with his family in the early years of the twentieth century. Cambon was born on July 29, 1923, and lived with his parents, two sisters and a brother near the historic Plains of Abraham Battlefields Park, where Wolfe defeated Montcalm in 1759 and transformed Canada forever. After completing Grade 11 in 1940, the reluctant scholar got a job as a soda jerk making ten dollars a week plus the odd tip. Then, a minor event one day changed his life when he accidentally broke a coffee pot and immediately had his wages cut in half. Somewhat dejected by this turn of events, Cambon was walking home from work when he passed a Royal Rifles of Canada recruiting sign advertising $1.30 a day. He went in and signed up, lying about his age.

The Winnipeg Grenadiers entrain for Vancouver at Winnipeg, October 1941.

It was July 1940 and Cambon was a few days from his seventeenth birthday.[10]

About the time the Rifles passed through Winnipeg on their way westward, a train carrying the Winnipeg Grenadiers began its journey. One of those aboard the second train was Grenadier Larry Stebbe, who had been born in Beauséjour, Manitoba, on February 25, 1923, and enrolled when he was sixteen years old on September 18, 1939, a few days after Canada declared war. Trained as a signaller, Stebbe went to Jamaica with his battalion in June 1940, where the unit guarded prisoners of war. Little did the young soldier realize how soon the tables would be turned and roles reversed. His main job was to man the telephone switchboard in the town of Newcastle. Stebbe later recalled, "[My] memories of Jamaica are of a tropical paradise," an impression "made all the more vivid because it contrasted so vividly with what followed."[11]

Portage la Prairie, Manitoba, native Wilbert Lynch was born on April 6, 1923, and raised on a farm with two brothers and three sisters. In the middle of the Depression, when he was thirteen, he left home and worked on a few local farms for room and board plus five dollars a month. On April 9, 1940, just three days after his seventeenth birthday, the six-foot, 196-pound Lynch enrolled. Initially he served in the 12th Manitoba Dragoons, headquartered in Virden in southwestern Manitoba and was sent to nearby Camp Shilo for machine-gun training on the Bren gun before transferring to the Winnipeg Grenadiers.

Grenadier Gordon Durrant grew up on a farm in Saskatchewan, where he and his four brothers and seven sisters put in long hours helping their father, who suffered with a disabling injury from the First World War. Born on December 20, 1921, Durrant left school after Grade 8 to work full time on the farm before joining the army at seventeen. His motive was purely economic: "There was no money around . . . you were rich if you had a quarter . . . money was very scarce . . . it was $1.30 a day for to go into the army . . . a lot of money! . . . so pretty near all the young people joined pretty well right away."[12] Durrant was sent to Jamaica in April 1940 with the Grenadiers for garrison duty. He sailed from Halifax on the *Lady Drake*, one of the famous "Lady Boats" pressed into wartime service instead of the normal Canada–West Indies passenger and cargo runs of peacetime. During the voyage, Durrant and his buddies heard on the radio that the Germans claimed one of their U-boats sank a ship carrying Canadian soldiers to Jamaica with the loss of all on board.

"I was quite scared at the time,"[13] Durrant admitted. When he got to Jamaica, he cried for a week.

The two trains carrying C Force arrived in Vancouver on October 27, and the majority of the troops immediately boarded the HMT *Awatea*, only recently converted to a troopship. Due to insufficient space on the ship, C Company of the Rifles had

Military equipment is loaded aboard HMT Awatea *at Vancouver, October 27, 1941.*

to embark on the RCN armed merchant cruiser HMCS *Prince Robert*, assigned to escort *Awatea* to Hong Kong. In the best of naval traditions, Ken Cambon and his fellow soldiers slung hammocks in *Awatea* over mess tables "deep in the bowels of the ship," where "they bitched about the monotonous diet of mutton and griped about the luxurious quarters of the officers in privileged possession of the exclusive and finely appointed saloons."[14] Gordon Durrant's comment on the lack of food choice was more succinct: "Nuttin' but mutton!"[15] It was a sentiment echoed by many others aboard *Awatea* as the troopship chugged westward across the Pacific Ocean.

Awatea and *Prince Robert* sailed that night. Sealed orders were opened at sea disclosing C Force's destination: Hong Kong. It came as a complete surprise to most; many had never heard of the British colonial outpost on the southeast coast of China. As George MacDonell admitted: "Well, we knew nothing about Hong

HMT Awatea *alongside at Manila in the Philippines in mid-November 1941, en route to Hong Kong.*

Kong and we were just amazed at this modern, beautiful Chinese city — Kowloon on the mainland and Victoria on the island."[16] Despite two days of seasickness after leaving Vancouver, Rifleman Ken Ewing was pleased with their destination. "This is great," he thought. "New country, new, new experience, I was quite happy about it."[17] Due to a combination of bad luck and inefficiency, none of the battalions' 212 vehicles, including fifty-seven Universal carriers, forty-five motorcycles and an assortment of trucks of various sizes, arrived before the ships sailed. Although there was space for only a small portion of these vehicles aboard *Awatea,* a lack of effort by the Quartermaster General's Branch ensured none of them arrived in time. They followed on an American freighter, which sailed a week later. Routed via Honolulu and Manila by United States naval authorities, the ship reached the latter port after the Japanese attack began and were diverted —

Soldiers of the Royal Rifles of Canada disembark at Kowloon, November 16, 1941.

with Canadian approval — for the use of American forces defending the Philippines.

The Rifles and Grenadiers would have to protect Hong Kong without their vehicles.[18]

After a twenty-one-day voyage, the Canadians landed at Hong Kong on November 16, disembarked at Kowloon and marched through the streets to Shamshuipo Barracks, just over three kilometres away. Rifleman Ken Cambon remembered it as "a grand day . . . Our two battalions marched down Nathan Road steel-helmeted and obviously invincible. The main street . . . was lined by cheering crowds waving small Union Jacks." The only drawback was that his platoon was positioned halfway between the two regimental bands, which were not synchronized to the same beat. The result was the march to the barracks was "a continuous ballet of changing step."[19]

At the barracks, according to Rifleman Bill MacWhirter, "We were living like kings. The Chinese: they made our beds, they cleaned our rifles . . . in the morning they would wake us up and they would shave the boys. They went to shave me and I had no whiskers. So I said, 'Don't put that razor on my face.'"[20] Cambon was astonished by the luxury of the camp, where even "the lowly rifleman had a single bed with sheets and a mosquito net. East Indian orderlies came in each morning with a cup of tea and an offer to shave you in bed and shine your shoes . . . all for a pittance. It was a shock to be addressed as Sahib, sir. Others were ready to press your uniform and even make the bed."[21] MacDonell described Shamshuipo as "a beautiful barracks, with gleaming, one-storey, white concrete buildings surrounded by manicured green spaces and connected by wide boulevards flanked by flower beds," while Victoria was "a beautiful, modern city."[22] Other soldiers did not share MacDonell's opinion of Hong Kong. MacWhirter felt that "it was a dirty city . . . The hundreds of Chinese women, children, laying out on the street, sores on their heads."[23]

The colony consisted of two parts: first, the island of Hong Kong and a peninsula on the mainland, which contained the major city of Kowloon; and second, to its north, the largely uninhabited, rough terrain of the New Territories. A narrow channel, in some places only half a kilometre wide, separated the two parts. The commander of the British Garrison was Grasett's replacement, Major-General Christopher Maltby, who had only taken over in July. Maltby decided to defend forward and organized the fourteen thousand troops at his disposal into a Mainland Brigade under British Brigadier Cedric Wallis and an Island Brigade under John Lawson. The only Canadian unit in the Mainland Brigade was the signals section. Wallis placed his three battalions along the colourfully named Gin Drinkers Line, made up of fortified positions that stretched for fifteen kilometres across rugged hill country. The line got its name "not so much from the habits of the soldiers . . . as by virtue of the fact that it began in Gin Drinkers Bay, the scene of happily alcoholic expatriate picnic parties in good weather."[24] On the

Kowloon on the mainland part of the Crown Colony, as seen from the island of Hong Kong.

island, Lawson concentrated his one British and two Canadian battalions on its south side to defend against a possible attack from the sea.[25] Five obsolete non-fighter aircraft and a naval squadron consisting of three obsolescent destroyers, four river gunboats, eight older motor torpedo boats and a number of small auxiliary vessels rounded out Maltby's force.[26]

The Canadians had little time to enjoy life in the semi-tropical outpost — or as Cambon put it, "vegetate in lotus land"[27] — before they moved into the steep hills of Hong Kong Island to train and familiarize themselves with the terrain. At 11 a.m. on December 7, Maltby ordered battle positions occupied and the Royal Navy recalled two of their three old destroyers to their nearest base at Singapore, two thousand kilometres away (the third was in drydock). At 8 a.m., Monday, December 8 (December 7 at Pearl Harbour because of the International Date Line), a mere three weeks after the Canadians' arrival, airplanes appeared in the sky over Kowloon. While the rest of the battalion was occupying their positions on the island, Bill MacWhirter and forty to fifty other recruits had remained in Shamshuipo Barracks to undergo drill. Before the training commenced, he and some friends were enjoying a bite to eat in the local Navy, Army, and Air Force Institutes (NAAFI) canteen. According to Mac-Whirter, suddenly, "some Chinaman jumped out and he said, 'There's some planes.' So we run out and we said, 'Look at our planes from Singapore.' And all at once they come into a dive. It was the Japanese . . . they machine gunned our barracks and the burst of bullets just about cut a Chinese guy . . . in two. That's the first death I saw."[28]

Japanese aircraft bombed and strafed the airfield and destroyed or damaged all British airplanes within minutes. Meanwhile, combat-experienced Japanese soldiers of three 38th Division regiments (each equivalent to an Allied brigade) moved against the Gin Drinkers Line. On the night of December 9–10, they captured a key position and the highest point along the defence line. D Company of the Grenadiers was dispatched to the mainland in darkness to reinforce this sector.

When the company saw action on the next day, it became the first element of the Canadian army to fight in the Second World War.

Japanese forces broke through the Gin Drinkers Line on December 11 and continued their advance towards Kowloon, forcing Allied units back under a heavy artillery and aerial bombardment. When Kowloon fell on December 13, the surviving British forces retreated to Hong Kong Island under cover of D Company. Maltby now reorganized his units into an East Brigade (containing the Royal Rifles) and a West Brigade (containing the Grenadiers), the latter under Lawson's command. On the island, Grenadier Larry Stebbe worked in his battalion headquarters, manning the telephones. He was moved so quickly his rifle and personal belongings never did catch up with him, leaving him "with only the clothes [he] was wearing."[29] Grenadier Wilbert Lynch ended up manning his Bren gun in a mountainside pillbox at the Wan Chai Gap, overlooking one of the vital water reservoirs. He stayed there for the rest of the battle; when the fighting ended more than two weeks later, his position was virtually on the line the Japanese had reached.[30]

The Japanese paused to offer the British two opportunities to surrender, both of which were firmly rejected by the colony's governor. Rebuffed, the enemy moved to the next phase: a nighttime amphibious assault against the island. While preparing for the invasion, the Japanese had continued to bombard the island's north shore. Three new Japanese regiments crossed the harbour in small boats on the evening of December 18 (as narrow as five hundred metres at Lye Mun Passage), landed at four locations on the northeast side of the island and quickly overwhelmed Allied defensive positions. As the Japanese fanned out, they forced the defending troops to fall back into the mountains to the south. Confusion, chaos and casualties followed. Later on December 19, the invaders overwhelmed the West Brigade headquarters and shot Brigadier Lawson after he reported by telephone he was "going outside to fight it out."[31]

The Japanese swarmed across the island, cutting the brigades in two and forcing the defenders back towards the island's western and southern shores through rugged, steep hill country. On December 19, Rifleman Ken Ewing's platoon was tasked to reinforce Mount Parker, a key position on the northeast corner of the island. The soldiers set off, intending to defend the mountain "at all costs." But when they got there, "the Japanese . . . were already in possession . . . [They] lost two corporals . . . in that skirmish, withdrawing from Mount Parker." From there everything got "sort of hazy."[32]

George MacDonell recalled the Rifles attempting "again and again . . . in broad daylight, without any supporting mortar or artillery fire, to counterattack the Japanese positions on top of prominent peaks" they had occupied. MacDonell continues, "This entailed scaling the heights with their thick cover of entangling scrub in the face of grenades, enemy machine guns and mortar fire from above. In each case, by the time we finally reached the top of these peaks and drove the Japanese off, we were out of water, had no food and little ammunition, and were nearly dead from the exhaustion of the day's climb and battle in the heat."[33] Colonel C.P. Stacey, author of *Six Years of War: The Army in Canada, Britain and the Pacific*, agrees with MacDonell's assessment and notes "the extraordinarily rugged terrain of Hong Kong was one of the hardest battlefields on which Canadians fought in any theatre."[34] As far as the enemy's capabilities, Larry Stebbe thought the Japanese were "wonderfully equipped and trained for hill fighting."[35]

Ken Cambon's experiences in C Company were similar. He recalls spending "most of the time struggling up and down hills, seldom knowing where we were fighting, always either being shot at or bombed." While resting at a beautiful house called Palm Villa, his platoon was ordered to counterattack the Japanese on a hilltop the Canadians had already abandoned. Cambon and his comrades crawled on their bellies to another summit overlooking the enemy position, "already exhausted, tired and hungry, but, considering the situation, still in remarkably good spirits." The fatigued Rifles finally made it to a position overlooking about seventy enemy soldiers some fifty metres away. When the Rifles opened fire, their "first burst took them completely by surprise and they scattered for shelter."[36]

Elated by their success, a Canadian lance-sergeant "blew caution to the winds and let out a whoop." The general euphoria was soon dampened when a corporal arrived with the disappointing news that instead of receiving the expected rations, ammunition and reinforcements, they were to go back down the hill to participate in a different counterattack tomorrow. Cambon said, "[I] felt a deep sinking sensation in my stomach, my mouth was dry and I found myself cursing the world about me." Then, to add to his dismay, it started to rain as darkness fell. They groped their way back in the inky blackness, "slipping and slithering into crevices, not at all sure if [they] were heading for Palm Villa or into a Japanese ambush." The icing on the cake occurred as the Canadians approached Palm Villa, "only to be welcomed by the sentry at the gate shooting at [them]."[37]

Because of his familiarity with the area from an earlier reconnaissance, on December 20 young George MacDonell volunteered to lead his platoon in an attack against the Japanese and silence an enemy artillery battery along the way. MacDonell believed that by using the concealment offered by now-dry water catchment canals, he could penetrate the Japanese lines to get close to the battery. The platoon made it undetected to about two hundred metres from the Japanese guns, in a location slightly above the enemy position. As MacDonell was about to give the order to fire, a Japanese staff car drove up and stopped, according to MacDonell, "right under the muzzles of our guns . . . Just as the Japanese officer and his aides stepped out of the car, our weapons opened fire. The chaos was indescribable."[38]

On the plus side, the short, sharp and largely one-sided battle was over in minutes and the battery silenced. But on the negative side, the Rifles had expended most of their ammunition and alerted other nearby Japanese troops. It was time to leave — and quickly. MacDonell ordered his men to run down the water catchment as fast as they could, while he brought up the rear with his Bren gun, intending to slow down any pursuers. Meanwhile, enemy soldiers ran along the ridge lines above the Canadians, hoping to cut them off. When MacDonell caught up to his men, they were huddled in the bottom of the water catchment canal, pinned down by a Japanese machine gun at the very point where he had hoped to exit the canal for the cover of a wooded area. As he pondered his limited choices, a second Japanese machine gun began to enfilade the catchment.

"For sheer, heart-stopping terror, it had no parallel," he recalled. "We were trapped!"[39]

MacDonell had already decided he would not surrender and hit upon a plan. He ordered two Bren guns loaded with tracer rounds and positioned one where he could fire at the first Japanese machine gun. Firing tracer bullets, he was able to bring accurate fire on the gun and quickly put it out of action. He next turned his attention to the second gun, and in the middle of firing his fourth or fifth magazine at it, ordered his men to run to the trees. When they were not fired on by either Japanese gun, he scrambled to join them as they escaped into the cover of the trees and made it back to their company's location. MacDonell marvelled at the success of their audacity: "Not one of my platoon was killed that day, and only six were wounded."[40]

After Ken Ewing and the soldiers of A Company withdrew to Repulse Bay on the island's south shore, on December 21 they were ordered forward to try to link up with the Grenadiers at the Wong Nai Chung Gap. They made it as far as The Ridge, a British ordnance depot manned by soldiers, "none of whom had seen a rifle for dozens of years," when they were stopped by a strong Japanese defence. That night, two platoons were ordered into the hills to prevent the Japanese from using a water catchment as a supply route. During this move, the Japanese ambushed young Ewing and his comrades soon after midnight, causing several casualties.[41]

After Ken Cambon and a comrade spent the night in the luxury of a well-appointed upstairs bedroom after their return to Palm Villa where, in his words, "For a few short hours we were the most contented and pampered members of the Eastern Brigade,"[42] they awoke the next morning to find the rest of the platoon had departed. The two soldiers set off southwards for Stanley Village, hoping to find their comrades. After a fleeting encounter with a small Japanese armoured vehicle and rescue by some British machine gunners, the two late risers managed to link up with the rest of their group. The platoon commander took one look at Cambon, the youngest man in the platoon, and sent him to battalion headquarters, ostensibly to help out. Cambon, who usually fought against any special treatment because of his age, did not object this time. At the headquarters, he was told to man the telephones. Since there was only one line to brigade headquarters and a second one that worked sporadically to Maltby's headquarters, he felt it was "a rather useless endeavour," although it was interesting to witness "the antagonisms between the Canadian Commanders and the British Staff."[43]

The success of MacDonell's limited operation and those of his fellow Canadian, British, Indian and Hong Kong soldiers could not delay the inevitable. Steadily pushed back across the island, low on ammunition, rations and water, and with their numbers decimated by death and injuries, their situation quickly changed from desperate to disastrous. By the morning of Christmas Day, the Rifles were clinging to Stanley Fort at the end of the most southerly point of the island, Stanley Peninsula. At 8 a.m., MacDonell was told in a few hours his company would counterattack Stanley Village, which had been occupied by the Japanese the previous day. The village was about fifteen hundred metres away, at the base of the hill where Stanley Fort was situated. As MacDonell reflected on the "sheer stupidity of the order . . . without artillery, mortar or machine-gun support into a village full of Japanese, in broad daylight," he was convinced it would be his last day on earth. When he informed his men of their mission, so fatigued they could hardly stand, they stared at him through "exhausted and unbelieving eyes," yet not one asked to be excused.[44]

The mission of MacDonell's platoon was to attack the left flank of the village and secure a row of houses, which would give excellent fields of fire across the rest of the hamlet. After MacDonell issued orders and reorganized his platoon due to recent deaths and injuries, the men replenished their ammunition and grenades, cleaned their weapons and grabbed a few hours restless sleep. At 1 p.m., MacDonell led his platoon into the village by crouching low in a ditch beside the road. Although the enemy responded immediately with rifles, machine guns, mortars and artillery, the platoon got to within a hundred metres of the settlement without any casualties. In front of them and slightly higher across open ground was a graveyard, occupied by Japanese soldiers.

MacDonell realized that unless his men advanced to the cemetery quickly, they would suffer heavily, so he ordered his men to spread out, fix bayonets and charge. The swift action worked and took the enemy by surprise. A "confused and bloody melee of hand-to-hand fighting with bayonets" followed, from which the Canadians emerged victorious. The Japanese survivors fled into the village and took a stand in the first row of houses, which resulted in another hand-to-hand battle as MacDonell and his men cleared the houses with Tommy guns and bayonets. As they moved deeper into the hamlet, they came upon an unsuspecting Japanese platoon rushing forward, likely sent to reinforce the position. "A roar of machine-gun fire" wiped them out.[45]

MacDonell led his men deeper into the village and passed the line of houses that was their objective. Stiffening enemy resistance began to cause casualties among the Canadians, so MacDonell ordered them back to their objective, where they took up positions and poured a heavy fire onto the counter-attacking Japanese. When the commander of No. 17 Platoon to their left was killed, MacDonell took command of it as well. When the Japanese paused to regroup and register their

The site of the counterattack by A Company, Royal Rifles of Canada, at Lye Mun
Battery, December 19, 1941.

artillery on the Canadians' position, MacDonell considered
his situation. He had several casualties, ammunition was running low, they were out of water, and the enemy was about
to remount his attack and outflank the Canadians. It would
only be a few minutes before the small force was encircled and
cut off. Then a runner appeared with the order to pull back.
MacDonell sent his men back in small groups, covering their
withdrawal along with the platoon sergeant from No. 17 Platoon. To MacDonell's great regret, he had to leave behind at
the mercy of the enemy the wounded who were unable to walk.
That night, as they prepared to meet what would undoubtedly
be the last Japanese attack, they were informed the governor of
Hong Kong had surrendered.[46]

Of the 148 men in D Company that day, 104 became casualties, an astonishing 70 per cent casualty rate. Historian Carl
Vincent believes D Company's counterattack, "for idiotic futility,

ranks with the Charge of the Light Brigade" and is "reminiscent of nothing so much as one of the more mindless attacks on the Western Front during the First World War."[47] When MacDonell recalled the actions of his men years afterwards, he, in his own words, felt, "both proud that I was a member of that courageous band and full of sorrow," as well as "haunted by the tragic and unnecessary loss of those young lives." He continued to "marvel at their courage and their willingness to die rather than fail to do their duty."[48]

When Cambon rejoined his platoon after his stint at battalion headquarters, the unit had been reduced to about three hundred soldiers. On December 25, he witnessed the futile counterattack of MacDonell's D Company against Stanley Village. The remainder of the day was "a nightmare of confusion"[49] as Japanese mortars, artillery and dive bombers pounded the area incessantly. The forces on Stanley Peninsula continued to resist until a staff car carrying a large white flag appeared with two British officers and informed them the rest of the island had surrendered earlier in the day. As firing ceased, Cambon recalled thinking, "It had been rather an unusual Christmas day . . . one to remember . . . one never to forget."[50] Larry Stebbe echoed Cambon's thoughts. Up to then it was "one of bleakest Christmases I had ever spent, but by no means as bleak as some which were to come."

After the Canadians surrendered, Stebbe recalls his "first vivid memory of the Japanese was their diminutive size. They looked almost like dwarfs at first. It was humiliating to think that such small men had defeated us."[51]

When the Allies laid down their arms, 290 Canadians had been killed in action and a further 493 wounded. Among the dead were several who had been among the wounded. They were bayoneted or machine-gunned after they surrendered, in a killing orgy by victorious Japanese soldiers.

Another 1,683 were marched off to endure for another forty-four months the subhuman conditions of Japanese prisoner of war camps.

Many did not survive.[52]

And boys who had joined the army as teenagers would come of age as prisoners of cruel captors.

CHAPTER 2

"I THOUGHT WE'D BE TAKEN PRISONER AND WE'RE NOT GOING TO BE THAT LONG. I THOUGHT MAYBE SIX MONTHS AT THE MOST."

Hong Kong, The Prisoners

(Map I)

Finally — in his sick and weakened condition — Rifleman Geoffrey Marston somehow found the strength to get up and go to the toilet in the prisoner of war camp, where, he recalled, "I reeled back from the awful stench of . . . five peanut-oil cans that were in constant use, and those who couldn't control their body functions had to use the floor. Cakes of excrement and pools of urine lay everywhere. The filth proved a mecca for rats who were scampering about in large numbers. We were deathly afraid that they would attack our buttocks, thereby devouring chunks of flesh." The rats became a greater threat when those "swimming around the floating muck tried to clamber into our beds. Some succeeded and began attacking the flesh of the patients. But they didn't feel it. The flesh was dead"[1]

* * *

For the nearly seventeen hundred Canadian survivors captured at Hong Kong, their ordeal as prisoners of war had just begun.

North Point prisoner of war camp photographed from an American aircraft after Japan surrendered.

They were kept in camps in Hong Kong until 1943, when almost twelve hundred of them were sent to Japan. There, Canadian soldiers were forced to work as slave labour in dockyards and coal mines. In both locations, they endured subhuman treatment. The prisoners of war (POWs) became weak and malnourished from a starvation diet, lived in primitive, vermin-invested huts, endured abuse and mistreatment from their guards and contracted many diseases, usually without any medicines to cure them.

Initially a few of the Japanese treated some of the Canadians with kindness. Sixteen-year-old Rifleman Ken Ewing remembered enemy soldiers giving their thirsty prisoners "a mouthful of beer." But even then, he was aware he was probably "in for a rough ride," as he soon saw first-hand the treatment the Japanese handed out to prisoners of war and civilians indicated "they didn't care very much for human life." Ewing accepted

his possible fate with remarkable maturity and recalled thinking, "there was a pretty good chance that I wouldn't [come
back]." Although he did not personally witness any of the
immediate killings after the surrender, he knew two or three
wounded soldiers in his unit were murdered by the Japanese.
The men had been left with an orderly in some houses as Ewing
and the others made their way to Repulse Bay.[2]

But the atrocities had begun even before the shooting stopped.

On the evening of December 18, after they had successfully
crossed to Hong Kong Island, the Japanese overran a Hong Kong
Volunteers anti-aircraft battery, captured twenty of the Chinese
manning it and bayoneted them. Two survived by playing pos-
sum beside the rapidly decomposing bodies of their comrades for
two days before sneaking away.

It was the first known massacre of soldiers during the invasion.
It was not to be the last.[3]

Early on December 19, the Japanese overran an advanced
dressing station in the charge of a Canadian army doctor at the
Salesian Mission. The victorious soldiers herded eighteen Canadian and British soldiers and three civilians to the edge of a cliff,
lined them up and bayoneted the unsuspecting men in the back
so their bodies tumbled over the precipice. Only three survived.[4]

A Japanese battalion had taken over Eucliffe House, the resi-
dence of a wealthy Chinese businessman near the Repulse Bay
Hotel, as their headquarters. On December 22, a number of
Canadian and British prisoners were roped together in threes
and shot.

Later, fifty-three bodies were found in the area — "shot, bayoneted, or beheaded."[5]

On December 24, at the Repulse Bay Hotel, the Japanese painfully bound several British soldiers and their officers with rope,
many of whom were in agony from earlier bayonet wounds. All
were still being tortured. A Dutch civilian noted the captives were

"glassy-eyed, their tongues lolled and their chins dripped blood." On the orders of a Japanese senior officer, the guards "brought their rifles to their shoulders and shot all those bound British fighting men before our eyes. Then they walked among them and bayoneted a few in their death struggles."[6]

But the "most sadistic massacre" took place at the St. Stephen's College Hospital on Christmas Day.[7] In the predawn hours that day, when the civilian superintendent of the hospital rushed out to tell the approaching Japanese that the building was protected because of its status, he was shot in the chest and bayoneted to death. Some twenty wounded soldiers were next, bayoneted in cold blood as they lay on their cots.[8] Another fifty — including a number of Canadians — would be murdered before word was received of the garrison's capitulation later that afternoon.[9]

At the hospital, surviving British, Canadian and Chinese patients, doctors, nurses and orderlies were herded into a dark storeroom. Later that morning, they were ordered out of the room. As they exited, the Chinese nurses were taken to another room, where the Japanese had dragged the bodies of the soldiers they had executed earlier and covered them with the torn, bloodied mattresses on which they had been killed. The Chinese nurses were raped repeatedly on the mattresses by enemy soldiers, and then murdered. The seven British nurses were gang raped next. Three were killed and their bodies mutilated, while two others were returned to a room holding other female prisoners only to be taken out later and violated again.[10]

Such atrocities are partly explained by the fact the Japanese government never ratified the 1929 Geneva Convention that revised the rules of conduct for prisoners of war. According to long-time Canadian Department of National Defence historian Ben Greenhous, this was ostensibly because the Japanese army would not embrace a concept that could possibly induce its soldiers to surrender. But when the Allies announced they intended to abide by the provisions of the Convention, Japan declared its intention to follow suit.

The problem was the Japanese did not share the same view as the Allies as to who constituted a prisoner of war.

The Japanese army did not formally recognize any enemy soldier captured alive as a prisoner until he was turned over to a POW camp or hospital. Soldiers who surrendered unwounded were regarded as active opponents who could escape and continue the fight. In this view, killing was often the "preferred alternative."[11] John Masters, an experienced pre-war British Gurkha officer who fought the Japanese in Burma for three years, put the differing national philosophies about prisoners into stark perspective: "By 1944 the number of Japanese captured unwounded, in all theatres of war, probably did not total one hundred. On the Burma front it was about six."[12] For some unknown reason, large bodies of troops that surrendered to the Japanese at Hong Kong were generally not seriously mistreated, except for those at hospitals and dressing stations. On the other hand, soldiers who surrendered singly or in small groups were likely to be slaughtered outright.[13]

But when it came to treatment in POW camps, it was an entirely different story, where starvation, brutality, mistreatment, degradation and torture were daily facts of life.

* * *

After surrender, the surviving members of the Royal Rifles of Canada and other East Brigade units were held near Stanley Fort until December 31, when they were marched across the island to North Point Camp, originally built to house three hundred Chinese refugees.[14] During the march, seventeen-year-old Rifleman Bill MacWhirter first experienced the brutality of his captors: "This is where they started to get rough . . . Some of our boys were wounded quite bad, and as they fell out, they bayoneted them. We could not do nothing about it. They just would bayonet them on the side of the road and that was it and you just had to keep going or you would die too." One incident in particular stood out in MacWhirter's memory. As they struggled across the island, a Japanese soldier drove his bayonet through the wrist of a wounded Canadian and left him.

MacWhirter marvelled that somehow the soldier survived the march and the prison camps as he saw him later with "the wrist twisted because of no treatment. When he came back from the war he had a twisted arm, like the wrist."[15]

On the march, MacWhirter's fellow rifleman, Ken Cambon, now eighteen, said he felt that "it was humiliating to see so few guards assigned to guard the straggling column. I suspect this was done purposely to impress the Chinese, in case they needed any further convincing of the superiority of the Imperial Nipponese Army." At the camp, he noticed "the guards were relieving everyone of their watches, as they filed through the gate." Cambon quickly slipped his into his heavy sock, "one of the few smart things I ever did, as it later became a valuable bargaining item."

Conditions in the camp were appalling. It had been heavily damaged during the battle. Several of the huts were burned to the ground and those still standing had been looted of anything still serviceable. To make matters worse, the Japanese had used the camp to quarter their horses and mules, leaving "a stinking mess!" A dump at one end of the compound had been shelled, uncovering the old garbage and drawing hordes of flies, while the other end "was littered with the dead bodies of Chinese civilians and Japanese pack animals who had been killed by the defenders."[16]

After the Rifles arrived at North Point, George MacDonell, nineteen, noted that the exhausted survivors "simply lay on the ground or on the cement floor of the shattered, windowless huts."

They were "filthy and battle-stained," and within a short time, many began to succumb to a virulent form of amoebic dysentery, hastened by a lack of any medical supplies, a hospital or provisions for the sick and wounded. Those who were badly wounded or suffered from dysentery simply lay on their stretchers, "covered with their own blood and filth and crawling with flies. This was our introduction to a Japanese camp and to how the Japanese treated their prisoners."[17]

Number 37 wooden identification card had to be carried by Bill Mac-Whirter at all times while he was a prisoner of war.

Initially, the survivors from the Winnipeg Grenadiers were kept overnight in Mount Austen Barracks. The next few nights were spent in various locations before they were moved across the harbour to Kowloon on December 30 and incarcerated in their former home at Shamshuipo Camp, along with other soldiers of West Brigade.[18] Despite being taken prisoner, Grenadier Wilbert Lynch, also nineteen, recalled he was not too worried at the time. "I thought we'd be taken prisoner and we're not going to be that long. I thought maybe six months at the most . . . I was confident that . . . the war was going to end . . . I didn't think that the Japanese had that much force, you see."[19] Ken Cambon and others felt the same: "Most people thought it would be only a matter of a few months before the Americans and British came to our rescue."[20]

How very wrong they were.

At no time during the last days of December did the Japanese issue any rations to their prisoners. Grenadier signalman Larry Stebbe, still only eighteen, well remembered the lack of food:

Larry Stebbe (centre, standing) and other liberated prisoners of war on their way back to Canada.

"From the first day we were captured, hunger was never absent from our camp . . . Two meals a day was our ration and each meal was a spoonful of rice and a bun and hot water in between for our lunch. Our own cooks had to bake the buns and they used the old sourdough technique, keeping a piece of fermented dough to make the next batch." When the Grenadiers returned to Shamshuipo, Stebbe said, "We found a disaster. It was stripped of doors, windows, lighting and cooking equipment. Many of us were without clothing, blankets and eating utensils. It was demoralizing sitting in the sun for warmth and huddling on the cement floor at night."[21]

Sixteen-year-old Rifleman Ken Ewing echoed Stebbe's comments about food and accommodation. "We got, twice a day, about the equivalent of a tea cup full of rice gruel and nothing else," he remembered. In the camp, "the toilets . . . the water lines, everything had been torn out by the Chinese, the windows

Ken Cambon was photographed by his Japanese captors in the fall of 1943.

. . . the window sills, window frames had all been taken." This left "a platform out over the sea wall" as toilet facilities. Sleeping arrangements consisted of a bunk bed with bare boards and no blankets or pillows. Insect infestations followed. "We had everything from . . . body lice, to fleas, to crabs, to . . . bed bugs."[22]

When food was first issued at North Point the day after the Canadians' arrival, George MacDonell remembered it "consisted of mouldy rice full of rat droppings and worms." Like Ken Ewing's, his initial daily ration was two bowls of rice and a sourdough bun. During the first few months of captivity, daily rations were at their lowest point, perhaps nine hundred calories per man: an average-sized male requires thirty-five hundred calories to maintain health and weight. The food was also of poor quality and worsened by an almost complete absence of essential vitamins, especially the B complex — leading to the condition known as avitaminosis. Those wounded or exhausted from the battle were the most badly affected by the substandard rations and usually died.[23]

Ken Cambon also remembered squatting on the sea wall, holding on to a wire fence to keep from falling into the water. Unfortunately, he was one of the first of many to be stricken with dysentery, and "spent some of the worst hours of [his] life hanging on to that fence. Truly this was the lowest ebb." Perched precariously on the seawall and hanging on to the fence while "very weak with fever, nauseated and racked with the cramps that only bacillary dysentery can create" was not the only horror there. When he glanced down into the water, he saw "a bloated face drift by." Cambon "shivered and shook, as the cold damp dawn heightened the chills and fever of the dysentery, and deepened the despair of the breaking day." Fortunately, an Indian army medical officer gave him some precious sulfa tablets that saved his life.[24]

"They took all our clothing away from us," recalled Wilbert Lynch, "and give us just a Japanese khaki . . . thin Japanese khaki clothes . . . We didn't have any underclothes or anything. They give us them G-strings they called them." The G-string was a new experience for the Canadians. It was "just a long piece of [narrow] cloth . . . it had a string on one end of it and then you tied the string and you pulled the other [end] up between it and it flapped over the belt, over the string and it would hang down."[25]

A fellow sergeant in George MacDonell's D Company kept a secret diary, an act that could have gotten him killed if his captors discovered it. A sample of his entries from the first few months at North Point records a downward spiral of despair and death:

> *Stench is terrible . . . We put some ground over some of the bodies . . .*
> *We are almost frozen and our roof leaks . . . Dysentery is widespread . . .*
> *I believe they are going to starve us to death. We are terribly hungry. Just talk about food.*
> *We are getting lousy as coots.*
> *Heat getting bad . . . Mosquitoes eating us alive . . . Bedbugs getting worse.*

*Food is awful . . . Heavy rain all night. Sleep out-
doors on concrete so many bugs.*
*Man died. Many going blind — gradually getting
weaker.*
*Conditions getting unbearable, we will all die in
this terrible place.*
*Two men died last night . . . first man of my sec-
tion died with dysentery . . .*
More men falling sick every day.
*Another died today . . . another death in my pla-
toon . . .*
*Very hot. Men dying at the rate of three a day,
malaria, dysentery, fever.*
More sick. Some going blind. Three died today.[26]

Recalling his experiences, MacDonell wondered how "any of us survived." He and his fellow Canadians knew they were slowly starving to death, but they also realized "a bout of amoebic dysentery would speed up the process and almost certainly guarantee a very unpleasant death."[27]

Geoffrey Marston, another member of the Rifles, recalled his experience with dysentery in particularly graphic terms: "I was experiencing persistent bowel movements followed by extreme stomach cramps, nausea and weakness." At first, he thought it was a bad case of diarrhea caused by the terrible diet, but "not long afterwards I noticed my stool streaked with blood and mucous" and realized he had dysentery. The soldier went to the camp's "ramshackle hospital, which reeked with undescribable stench." He lay huddled on a cot, wet with rain that seeped through the rotten roof. To him, "the atmosphere was frightening." Those unable to find the strength to leave their beds to totter "at a snail's pace . . . to reach a closed-in quarter at the end of the ward that was used as a toilet . . . lay

George MacDonell was photographed by his Japanese captors on July 7, 1943.

in their own muck. Dirty, blood-stained pieces of toilet paper littered the floor."

Miraculously, Marston beat the odds, recovered and survived the war; but when he was liberated, his weight had fallen to ninety-two pounds. Canadian officers who confronted the Japanese and firmly requested they fix the roof and provide better toilet facilities were refused. The Japanese added if the officers bothered them any more, all prisoners would suffer a cut to their food rations.[28] Ken Ewing remembered the casual brutality of the Japanese guards: "You had to salute every guard . . . and you better do it or . . . you were going to get beaten up."[29]

On January 23, 1942, the Winnipeg Grenadiers moved from Shamshuipo to North Point to join the Royal Rifles of Canada, in effect reconstituting C Force. When the remaining non-Canadian prisoners were removed in April, North Point became an all-Canadian camp and the Japanese allowed the Canadians to administer their own affairs — to a degree.

During August 1942, medical officers diagnosed additional diseases at North Point: beriberi and pellagra, both caused by nutritional deficiencies.

Rifleman Bill MacWhirter recorded a side effect of the malnutrition, something called "electric feet": "I've seen men, big tough men, with their toes in their mouth, crying with pain," he recalled. "Some of them, they'd go out and walk on the cement because the cold seemed to stop the pain."[30] Electric feet (peripheral neuritis or dry beriberi) was caused by a lack of thiamine (vitamin B1). It started with numbness in the toes and continued with twitching feet, called "happy feet" by some soldiers. This was followed by sharp, shooting pains like "multiple needles being plunged into . . . [the] flesh"[31] from the arch of the foot to the tip of the toes, sometimes radiating as high as the knees. For unknown reasons, the pains were worse at night, when hospital patients who had the condition screamed in the ward housing them. Many soldiers tried to ease the pain by exposing their feet to cold, including soaking them in ice-cold water all night and even all day. The camp doctors forbade this latter form of temporary relief due to the resulting maceration and secondary infection of the skin.[32]

MacWhirter also remembered another affliction, "what they called dhobi's itch. It was in the private parts, oh my God, some of them suffered." Ken Ewing echoed MacWhirter's comments: "We used a very descriptive term for . . . this, they called it strawberry balls. And . . . that particular piece of your anatomy was just like a piece of raw meat, very, very itchy and very sore." MacWhirter believed he had avoided both painful experiences because of "school and the needles," although at the end of his captivity, he "only weighed ninety-five pounds." Bizarrely, the malnutrition did not affect his gain of height and the teenager continued to grow taller, perhaps adding another six-and-a-half to seven inches to his stature.[33]

Bill MacWhirter (right) and some friends pictured in the Philippines on their way home after liberation from the Omine prisoner of war camp.

Despite the subhuman conditions and poor quality of the meagre rations, the majority of Canadians resolved to live. Initially Ewing "couldn't eat or . . . didn't feel like eating . . . as the rice tasted like sawdust and felt about the same consistency." He was giving it to a British sailor when he suddenly realized he'd "better start eating or . . . end up like some of the others." It was then that the determined young Canadian soldier made his decision: "I would survive if, if even I was the last one."

Without that resolve, "people just curled up and died, that's all."[34]

George MacDonell noticed the same phenomenon. "Those who could not stand the psychological and emotional shock of these conditions and starvation tactics and studied brutality of our captors soon died to escape what, for them, was intolerable." Fortunately, "they were a small minority. For the rest, we maintained strict discipline," consisting of daily orders, conduct sheets, formal military structure and ranks. "Each individual was constantly reminded that he was a Canadian soldier who was only temporarily under the control of the Japanese." MacDonell believed that "this discipline and philosophy saved countless lives and provided concrete support for the survival of many who would otherwise have died. The will to live is very strong. The desire not to disgrace your uniform or to let your officers and comrades down through personal weakness is just as strong."

Like Ken Ewing, MacDonell had decided he would live. "The worse the conditions got, the more determined I was that I would not crack . . . Above all I was determined that we would live to see the inevitable Allied victory, no matter what."[35]

At Shamshuipo in mid-June 1942, the Canadians started work on extending the runway at Kai Tak Airport. To accomplish this, a large hill had to be removed, "with pick axes, shovels and baskets with poles — one pole and two small baskets or one large basket for two men" according to Larry Stebbe. Just before midnight on August 19, four of Stebbe's fellow Grenadiers escaped from North Point Camp. When the enraged Japanese discovered this, they ordered all prisoners to parade in a downpour, no matter what their condition. Stebbe had just been "discharged from the agony ward, very weak and emaciated." He said, Sores developed on my mouth, eyes and nose with blisters in my mouth making it hard to swallow." He had to be helped out to the square and stand there in the heavy rain. When he walked over to be identified, he passed out, and for many days after could "only remember bits of what was going on."[36]

The four escapees were picked up a few hours later by the Japanese navy after the leaky sampan they stole sank halfway to the mainland. The navy turned them over to the Kempeitai, the much-feared military police — which functioned more like secret police — who beat them with baseball bats, tied them up with barbed wire and then executed them. Fearing loss of face, Japanese authorities informed Tokyo the Canadians had been shot while trying to escape.

Their unmarked graves — which they were probably forced to dig for themselves — have never been found.[37]

Today a marker stands on the site where four Winnipeg Grenadiers were summarily executed by the Japanese for attempting to escape in August 1942.

To George MacDonell, "Japanese cruelty could not be exaggerated." He "personally witnessed their actual behavior and they were savage in the extreme. Once aroused, they behaved with no restraint — like madmen." Yet, he found "in the private soldiers themselves, especially if they were combat troops, out of sight of their officers, little of this ferocity and cruelty . . . and they sometimes turned a blind eye to prisoners' infractions of the rules, which, if discovered, would have enraged their superiors."[38]

September also saw the move of the Canadians back to Shamshuipo Camp in Kowloon on the mainland, probably due to the first movement of slave labour to Japan — about eighteen hundred British troops from Shamshuipo.[39] The same month, a diphtheria epidemic broke out in the camp that lasted six months. MacDonell estimated that "at its height, men died every day, and by the end of this period another 54 men in our regiment had needlessly died of a combination of malnutrition and diphtheria." Unfortunately, "the Japanese refused to supply serum to fight the disease and showed a callous indifference to [the] doctors' repeated pleas for some, or any, form of medication for those afflicted." The senior Japanese medical officer even "accused . . . doctors and orderlies of neglecting their patients, for which they were beaten." Fearing to be criticized by their superiors, the Japanese medical authorities ordered that diphtheria "should not appear as the cause of deaths" on official reports.[40]

At Kai Tak Airport, Ken Cambon found the work parties enjoyable, "despite the odd beating for 'sabotage,'" as "it felt great to get outside the fences of the camp." When mixing sand and cement to make concrete for the runaway, the Canadians put as little cement in with the sand "as could escape the attention of the foreman." Later, he heard that "the first planes to use the new runway crashed as they sank into the tarmac." It was probably "apocryphal but we hoped the story was true."[41]

In January 1943, the first Canadians were sent to Japan as slave labour, packed into the hold of a freighter like cattle. Three further shipments followed in August and October of that year, with a final shipment in April 1944. In all, 1,184 Canadian POWs were sent to Japan to work in mines and at the docks. Those left behind at Shamshuipo were in the worst physical shape, but the condition of several began to improve due to less crowding and the arrival of the first shipments of bulk Red Cross supplies in October 1942 and of coveted individual Red Cross parcels the next month. In contravention of the Geneva Conventions, the Japanese had held up these shipments and then shamelessly pilfered some of their contents.[42]

Brothers Armand and Hector Bourbonniere from Eriksdale, Manitoba, served in the Grenadiers together. Armand was the youngest of ten children and left school at fourteen to help his father in his dairy products transportation business by picking up cream and eggs at local farms. When he turned sixteen, he moved to Winnipeg and worked at a clothes cleaning company until he joined the army in September 1939, when he was seventeen.

The brothers were interned together, but when Canadian prisoners were being sent to Japan as slave labour, Hector had beriberi and was too sick to make the voyage. The siblings were separated, with Armand in one enclosure with others going to Japan and Hector in another with the beriberi patients. Somehow, Armand managed to get out of his compound to visit his older brother.

The sight shocked him.

"They were all guys with beriberi . . . all puffed up and they had them against the board so they could breathe . . . when I saw him I couldn't believe it. When he saw me he started crying . . ."

Armand told Hector he had no choice in leaving, but would see what he could do for him before he left. At the risk of death, he jumped the fence and traded an army shirt for some soy bean milk from a Chinese civilian. When he returned he "mixed [it] with water in a little can" and forced Hector to drink it over his protestations. "I lifted his neck, and he don't want to swallow, he don't want to open his mouth even. Anyway I got it open and started pouring it in, slowly. He got a part of it in," and the first night, Hector lost "fourteen pounds of water. That's what brought him back to Canada . . . all the guys told me after . . . They told me it saved his life."[43]

George MacDonell went to Ohashi Camp in Japan with the first group in January 1943: "[we were] battened down in a cargo hold below the waterline . . . for our run through the American-submarine-infested waters of the China Sea." The concern was real. The previous draft of British prisoners had been torpedoed with the loss of fifteen hundred POWs. When the Japanese abandoned ship, they left the British below deck under battened-down hatches. Most of the small number who somehow escaped drowning were machine-gunned in the water by Japanese navy escort ships.

Few survived.[44]

Grenadier Larry Stebbe was part of the same 650-man draft as MacDonell and ended up working in a Tokyo shipyard. He said that, to his surprise, "This was about the best treatment we received during our whole captivity, though it was still not much." He started out in a blacksmith shop, but when he suffered a few injuries, he was employed on lighter tasks until he improved and was then put to work breaking up bars of pig iron with heavy hammers to be resmelted. This labour, especially on a meagre diet, "was very strenuous." Stebbe even became "partially blind from malnutrition," although he eventually regained his sight.[45]

In the hold of his ship, a "small, dirty collier" taking him to Japan in August 1943, Rifleman Ken Cambon and 375 fellow Canadians "could not all lie down at the same time as there was insufficient room to stretch out." The conditions were appalling. "There were no toilets, only buckets passed up to the deck when full . . . Food and fresh water were lowered in big tubs." Perversely, as "many were seasick, and unable to eat, the rest of us were better fed than we had been for a long time."[46]

In Japan, the Canadians were spread through several camps to work in coal or nickel mines, factories or dockyards. Cambon and about three hundred others were sent to open up Camp 5-B in Niigata, which was to become, according to Cambon, "the worst camp in Japan, by any standard," where "the morbidity and death rate were to be staggering, much higher than any other camp in Japan." The captors divided the prisoners into three groups: one to work in a coal dock, one in an iron factory and the third in a general cargo dock. Cambon ended up in the

Ohashi prisoner of war camp — where George MacDonell was held — photographed from an American aircraft after Japan surrendered.

coal dock, which was unfortunate as it was "by far the toughest place to work." The first day began at five o'clock with a breakfast of a potato and some greens, followed by a three-kilometre walk to the coal dock, where the Canadians met the manager of the operation and the foremen, or honchos, who were to supervise them.

"Whiskers," as the prisoners named the manager after his long, black beard, proved "to be a hard taskmaster in the months ahead, and was indirectly responsible for many deaths." The job of the Canadians was to push small railcars, each carrying about a half-ton of coal, along a raised trestle and dump it into various storage areas or occasionally into a full-sized railway car. "Any error or slowdown was rewarded with a sharp whack of the honcho's stick." Few of the foremen were decent individuals; "others were just ornery and mean while still others were plain psychotic."

"Without doubt," Cambon continued, a foreman named Sato was "the worst of the honchos . . . a sadist who was only happy if he was beating or shouting at some unfortunate." Cambon later realized that "he almost certainly was a paranoid schizophrenic" who had been "discharged from the army as mentally unfit. On the slightest suspicion he would unmercifully beat some poor soul into semi-consciousness."[47]

* * *

Rifleman Bliss Cole was ready to die.

Perhaps he should have listened to his parents, who had not wanted the teenager to join the army. Cole's father, Elmer, a native of Turtle Creek, New Brunswick, was a veteran of the First World War. He had enrolled in the 145th (New Brunswick) Battalion, based in nearby Moncton, and sailed overseas in September 1916. When he returned, he brought back a war bride with him: Dorothy Taylor was from Shoreham-by-the-Sea, Sussex. One night Elmer received a call from a recruiter.

"Do you have a son named Bliss?" the caller inquired. "What's he trying to do, join up?" Elmer responded.

The senior Cole let his wife have the final say. She would let her son join, but on two conditions: he had to promise not to drink, and to come home. The younger Cole readily accepted his mother's caveats and promptly enrolled in the Royal Rifles of Canada on August 16, 1940 — along with his father. Bliss ended up in A Company, while Elmer was made a staff sergeant and appointed company quartermaster sergeant. Out of four sons and seven daughters, three of the brothers were now serving in uniform: two in the army and one in the air force. Father and son, one forty-two and the other seventeen, sailed off to war together. They were captured at Hong Kong and held at North Point Camp before being sent to another POW camp near

Yokohama, Japan, in January 1943. Then, in early March 1944, Elmer was admitted to the camp hospital with pneumonia and dysentery. He died a few days later, on March 16, with his son at his side.

Bliss was despondent.

After staying together and helping each other to survive the horrible conditions of slave labour, father and son were now separated forever. Bliss was prepared to curl up and die himself. An officer took the young man aside and reminded him, "your mother has just lost her husband, she doesn't need to lose a son." Bliss took the advice to heart and survived, although his normal five-foot-ten, 150-pound frame was reduced to a skeletal eighty-five pounds when he was released from captivity at the end of the war. He returned to New Brunswick, got married, settled in Saint John and raised five children with his wife. He died in 2011 at eighty-seven.[48]

Through clandestine radios — the discovery of which could have resulted in death — and other means, the Canadian POWs followed the progress of the war as it turned against the Japanese during their years of captivity. Sometimes, the effects of the Allied war effort were experienced first-hand, when American aircraft bombed targets near some of the camps. As the end of the war approached, a general improvement in food and working conditions signalled the Japanese were prepared to accept defeat and wanted to be shown in a more favourable light. At the same time, disturbing rumours circulated that the Japanese intended to butcher all prisoners if the Allies invaded, a chilling prospect the Canadians could easily believe. Then, in early August 1945, word came of a massive new type of bomb, which obliterated the cities of Hiroshima and Nagasaki.

Japan surrendered.

Shortly afterwards, American airplanes appeared over the camps, dropping food, medicine and other supplies to the prisoners. It was a heady time. Suddenly, the prisoners were in charge. Virtually unlimited food supplies caused many POWs to gorge on items they had not experienced in more than three years. Inevitably, those who did so quickly regurgitated foods too rich for bodies unaccustomed to them or too plentiful for shrunken stomachs. Doctors marvelled at the almost instant results of a new drug — penicillin — that had been dropped, along with instructions on how to use it.

One Canadian's POW experience resulted in his marriage. John "Jesse" James was from Lac du Bonnet, Manitoba, and, like Bliss Cole, the son of a First World War veteran and a British war bride. When the family farm was flooded because of a new hydroelectric dam, which caused his parents to move to a farm on the British Columbia coast, seventeen-year-old Jesse stayed behind and joined the Winnipeg Grenadiers.

During the fighting for Hong Kong, James was wounded by shrapnel and had to have his left leg amputated below the knee. Because of infection during captivity, it had to be amputated two more times. (After the war, James required another amputation — still below the knee — "because the bone was sticking out.") James believed his injury made him "one of the lucky ones," because he got to work as a records clerk for the senior medical officer at Shamshuipo Camp, where he survived on a steady diet of rice and "whatever insects [he] could catch for protein."

After Japan surrendered, one of the prisoners that James was helping was in a hammock on an intravenous drip. When he brought his patient some chocolate dropped by American airplanes and "helped him to a taste," the grateful prisoner said the chocolate "never tasted sweeter." The next morning his "friend was dead but he knew the taste of freedom."

A British hospital ship took the Canadians to Manila, where American medical personnel looked after them. Because of his

HMCS Prince Robert *arrives at Esquimalt, British Columbia, with liberated Canadian prisoners of war from Japan.*

amputation, James had to undergo physiotherapy. His physio-therapist was Lieutenant Marcine Hefner, from Ohio. Hefner had joined the Women's Army Auxiliary Corps in May 1943 and, after basic training in Georgia, was sent to Aberdeen Proving Ground in Maryland as a truck driver hauling supplies from one part of the base to another.

When a recruiter arrived looking for students to attend an army physical therapy school, Hefner applied and was accepted. On completion of six months schooling and a further three months on-job training at a hospital, she was promoted second lieutenant. On April 13, 1945, she arrived in Manila and ended up at the 248th General Hospital. In early September, a group of thirty-two Canadian POWs arrived from Hong Kong. Jesse James was one of six amputees among them.

Hefner "massaged their legs and arms that were left and exercised the muscles that had not been used for nearly four years," but the Canadians complained the physiotherapists "were pretty rough on them." One of them, a curly haired young man," told

Canadian prisoners of war are greeted by sailors from HMCS Prince Robert *after their liberation at Shamshuipo Camp.*

her the "only way to get even with you is to marry you." Hefner replied she could not do that, as she "was an officer and he was just a gentleman, as an enlisted person."

But the difference in rank could not withstand love.

James and Hefner were married in February 1946 and lived in Winnipeg for five years before settling permanently in Emo in Northern Ontario, along the way raising a family. Jesse James died in 2005.[49]

* * *

When the gaunt and emaciated Canadian POWs were liberated at the end of the war, they were 264 fewer, largely the result of harsh treatment at the hands of the Japanese. In Hong Kong, 128 had died of disease and malnutrition, while a further 136 had died of disease, malnutrition or accidents in Japan. Additionally, almost every soldier who returned to Canada after the war was plagued by physical and psychological problems, the results of their cruel imprisonment. These problems continued to plague the survivors and many suffered for the rest of their lives.[50] Their life expectancy was, on average, ten years less than other Canadian veterans of the Second World War.

Sergeant George MacDonell of the Rifles reflected on the effects of his long captivity: "No one who survived to return after the ordeal escaped the emotional and physical trauma of the Battle of Hong Kong and the starvation, malnutrition, slave labour, anxiety and humiliation suffered in Japanese prison camps."[51]

After the war, Rifleman Ken Cambon thought he had been "so lucky," but that feeling was not shared with so many of his comrades. He felt the reasons for this were complex and "not always entirely related to physical disabilities. Perhaps," he reasoned, "some never really escaped from those dreadful years" of captivity.

"Freedom," he believed, "is more than a lack of a barbed wire fence."[52]

CHAPTER 3

"I WANT TO BE AT PEACE WITH GOD."
Death at Dieppe
(Map II)

Private Robert Boulanger of Les Fusiliers Mont-Royal hunkered down in the flimsy wooden boat as it sped towards the beach at Dieppe. He tried to make himself as small a target as possible against the lethal rifle, machine-gun, mortar and artillery fire coming his way — all of which seemed to be directed at him personally.

It was August 19, 1942, and the early morning raid was the amphibious equivalent of the Charge of the Light Brigade.

Aboard twenty-six R-boats ranged in four long lines offshore, 584 Fusiliers surged forward on orders from their commanding officer, Lieutenant-Colonel "Joe" Ménard. Although the battalion was supposed to land at Red Beach and then move west towards White Beach, enemy fire from the heights just east of the French port forced the unit to angle westward towards the latter beach while still off shore. During the run-in, several boats were blown out of the water by ten minutes of enemy artillery fire. As the boats approached the beach, very heavy machine-gun fire opened up

Assault craft carry Canadian troops toward the Dieppe beaches.

from positions onshore and the western cliff. This was quickly followed by mortar fire and grenades pouring down from positions on top of the cliff, ripping into the boats and the men on board. Despite the carnage, the Fusiliers were not discouraged. Incredibly, many boats survived the onslaught and ran — at speed — up onto the slippery shingle, which was being swept by enemy fire. The soldiers who managed to get out of the boats charged into utter chaos.[1]

A falling tide had forced some of the surviving boats to drop their troops in knee-deep water, already filled with the bodies of dead Canadians from the first assault waves. Firing from the hip as they waded ashore, many Fusiliers were killed or wounded before they reached the beach. Those who made it in were instantly trapped by mortar, machine-gun and sniper fire. Anyone who tried to move forward was cut down or wounded. Few made it off the beach and into the town.[2] One hour and forty minutes earlier, the main attack had gone in by the Royal Hamilton Light Infantry and southwestern Ontario's Essex Scottish, supported by the Calgary Tanks. The results were disastrous. The proverbial "fog of war" was perhaps nowhere thicker than at Dieppe that day. Due to a lack of accurate information and the mistaken impression troops were doing well across all beaches, Les Fusiliers Mont-Royal, the assault force's floating reserve, had been ordered to attack in what was the most tragic of the many tragic errors made that day.[3]

Quickly jumping out of his boat as it grounded on the bottom, Boulanger dashed forward, and then fell, a bullet between

The Dieppe Raid *by Charles Comfort vividly depicts the action of tanks and infantry on White Beach in front of the casino.*

his eyes. He had enrolled a month after he turned fifteen and was the youngest Canadian to die at Dieppe, having celebrated his seventeenth birthday less than two weeks earlier.[4]

* * *

Before the main assault in front of Dieppe, the first attack of the day had gone in two kilometres to the east on the narrow beach at Puys at 5:07 a.m., where another boy soldier — Private Jimmie Burnett of Toronto's Royal Regiment of Canada — had already met the same fate as Robert Boulanger would.

As Burnett's unit approached the beach, the fear that had gnawed at him during his last leave in Scotland came back with a vengeance. Back then, he'd even considered deserting, but with the help of his grandmother, he faced up to his fears and dutifully returned to his regiment — albeit a few days late.

Now, in the final few minutes of the run-in to the tiny pebble beach, he consciously willed himself to stare down his fears again and overcome them. Whatever happened, Burnett was prepared to meet his fate.

But as transpires so often in wartime, fate had already intervened and the unit was seventeen minutes late. The slim — very slim — advantage the cover of darkness would have given was gone.

But it might not have made any difference.

The slaughter began as soon as the hulls of the landing craft scraped bottom several metres offshore and their bow doors opened at Blue Beach, the code name for the narrow beach at Puys. From concealed positions and pillboxes on the beach and dominating cliffs, intense German rifle and machine-gun fire poured into the first wave of the Royal Regiment as they attempted to storm ashore.

The valiant soldiers of the Royals rushed into a hail of bullets; many were cut down before they could reach the shingle beach. Soon, dead and wounded alike piled up in the doorways of the assault craft or sank, dead or struggling, in the shallow water that quickly turned red. It was only thirty-five or so metres to the heavily wired, 2.5- to 3.5-metre-high seawall, but not more than fifteen men of the first wave — consisting of A and B Companies and battalion headquarters — reached it.

Hunkered down at the seawall, this depleted force fought back as best it could; even the wounded continued to fire their weapons. But it was to no avail. Failure was reinforced twenty minutes later when C and D Companies touched down in the second wave, having been under fire during their entire run-in to the beach. More of the second wave made it to the seawall, only to become as hopelessly trapped as their comrades. In addition to small arms and machine-gun fire, German mortar bombs and grenades rained down on the few survivors. A third wave, consisting of an attached company of the Black Watch (less company headquarters), landed ten minutes later about

Bodies of Canadian soldiers lay on Dieppe's shingle beach beside destroyed tanks and landing craft.

ninety metres west of the seawall, but was captured except for one soldier.[5]

The Royal Regiment of Canada had been given an impossible mission. Within three hours, the unit was reduced from a battalion of 554 soldiers to a few men huddling defensively behind whatever protection they could find. Half of the battalion had been killed, the heaviest loss of any unit involved in the entire Dieppe operation. Only sixty-five Royals returned to England.[6]

Among the dead sprawled grotesquely on the shingle at Blue Beach was Private Jimmie Burnett, who had enrolled a year earlier when he was only sixteen.[7]

* * *

Combined Operations Headquarters under the dapper Lord Louis Mountbatten had developed Operation Rutter, a commando raid on the heavily fortified French resort town of Dieppe to test

Mock casualties are evacuated from a British
beach during an exercise prior to the Dieppe Raid.

the German defences, intending to occupy it for a few hours before withdrawing. When the Canadian army was offered the leading role, senior commanders jumped at the chance. They selected Major-General "Ham" Roberts's 2nd Division for the task. Canadian officers accepted the plans developed for the raid by the British staff, pronouncing themselves satisfied with them. In preparation for their mission, the Canadians practised amphibious operations and focused on physical and tactical training.[8]

As a result, Boulanger, Burnett and their comrades from the other units selected for the raid began to move to the Isle of Wight for training in combined operations on May 18. The next few weeks were taken up with navigating obstacle courses, bayonet fighting, unarmed combat, climbing cliffs, firing weapons from the hip, embarking and disembarking from landing craft, demolition training and river crossings.

Then the tempo of training intensified and training with landing craft commenced. On June 1, for example, the soldiers of the Royal Regiment boarded landing craft, moved out to sea, landed in two waves on a narrow, sandy, gently shelving beach once crowded with peacetime holiday-makers, and then withdrew under cover of a smokescreen.[9] On June 11 and 12, Exercise Yukon, a large-scale combined operation, was held for all units on a stretch of Dorset coast that resembled the Dieppe area. Although Yukon was in fact a dress rehearsal for the raid, it did not go well. Mountbatten decided further rehearsal was necessary and Yukon II followed on June 22–23 at the same location. Although results were generally more favourable, shortcomings still remained. Written assurances that these weaknesses had been corrected led senior Canadian commanders to give their final endorsement to the raid.[10]

A little over a week later, on the morning of July 2, Boulanger, Burnett and other soldiers embarked on three landing ships, ostensibly for Exercise Klondike I. Once they were all aboard, their commanding officers announced the training exercise was in fact an actual operation against the enemy. But the weather conspired to thwart the plans and the operation was delayed, only to be cancelled when the weather cleared but the tides were wrong. Units were sent back to their various camps, with troops warned not to discuss the operation under any circumstances.[11]

Despite the Canadians' acceptance of the assault plan, it had serious flaws. Perhaps the most significant shortcoming was the decision to carry out the raid under the new name of Operation Jubilee after it had been postponed several times and then cancelled — critically compromising security.

Late on the evening of August 18, 1942, 237 ships and landing craft left five ports along the English south coast, bound for a sixteen-kilometre stretch of French shoreline. They carried 4,963 Canadians in six infantry battalions, a machine-gun battalion and a tank regiment from 1st Canadian Tank Brigade. Their task was to assault the main beaches at Dieppe, as well as the flanking villages of Puys to the east and Pourville to the west. In addition, 1,075 British commandos and fifty American rangers were to attack two coastal artillery batteries on the outer flanks about half an hour before the main assault.[12]

Dawn of the single worst day in Canadian military operations during the Second World War was only a few hours away.

On Green Beach at Pourville, the Canadians had their greatest success of the day, limited as it was. At 4:52 a.m. on August 19, the South Saskatchewan Regiment began to land. Unfortunately,

through errors in navigation, they landed to the west of the Scie
River, instead of on both sides of it, and were held up trying to
cross a bridge to get to their objective. A short time later, Winnipeg's Queen's Own Cameron Highlanders of Canada also landed
at Green Beach. They managed to penetrate the farthest inland
of any unit that day, but were soon forced back to the beaches.

* * *

Robert Boulanger was born in Grand-Mère, Quebec, on August
6, 1925, into a family consisting of two older brothers and two
sisters.[13] Another brother and four more sisters followed Robert's
birth. He enrolled in nearby Shawinigan Falls on September 10,
1940, having worked for a time as a driver and farmer. On his
attestation paper, he claimed a birthdate of August 6, 1921, which
made him four years older than his actual age. Boulanger had only
turned fifteen thirty-five days earlier.

On enrolment, the brown-eyed, brown-haired lad was only
five feet, four-and-a-half inches tall, although he weighed a solid
132 pounds. In November, Boulanger transferred to Les Fusiliers Mont-Royal at his request and commenced training at A13
Canadian Infantry Training Centre, Valcartier, a short distance
north of Quebec City. In June of the next year, he was sent to 2nd
Canadian Infantry Holding Unit in Britain for additional training.
Two months after his arrival there, Boulanger wrote a letter home,
describing his Atlantic crossing and some of his experiences in
Britain. It also included a caution for a relative or family friend:

August 28, 1941
My dear parents,

It is my pleasure to write a few words to you and
tell you I am in perfect health. Duty has called me

Private Robert Boulanger of Les Fusiliers Mont-Royal was killed during the Dieppe Raid.

to defend our beautiful Canada. There is one thing I must advise you about. Robert, who has just been married, should not come overseas. You have done enough in sending your Robert.

I frequently go to London, the largest city in the world. I have travelled five thousand miles from Canada and to Germany it is another five hundred miles. It is close.

In the next letter I will send you a picture of the boat in which I crossed the ocean. We saw some whales and we also saw some German aeroplanes which flew over the larger boats. However, they were unable to sink us.

You must tell all my friends in Grand-Mère that I send them my fond wishes. I must finish my letter my dearest parents, who have been so good to me for almost 18 years. I do not know if I will return. Here I am, along with all my friends, sleeping in tents. It is with tears of sadness that I must

Les Fusiliers Mont-Royal on a training exercise in Britain in preparation for the raid on Dieppe.

send you a fond goodnight, dearest Mom, Dad and all the family.
From your son Robert, who has not forgotten and loves you all.[14]

Boulanger was finally posted to Les Fusiliers in mid-January 1942. A month later, he went absent without leave. His absence cost him about a day's pay for each hour he was absent: five day's pay for five and a half hours absent.

In many ways, the history of Les Fusiliers Mont-Royal during the Second World War is similar to that of many other infantry battalions: mobilization for active service; a period of recruitment, equipping and training in Canada; deployment to Britain for further training; and participation in large-scale general manoeuvre exercises. In the case of the Fusiliers, there were two additional events they, the Royal Regiment of Canada, and only a few other units experienced: garrison duty in Iceland as part of

Z Force — which freed up British infantry units for deployment elsewhere — followed by specific exercises for Operation Jubilee.

Boulanger's last letter home was written over a three-day period as he waited on land and sea with his fellow Fusiliers to sail across the English Channel to Dieppe:

17–18–19 August 1942

Dear Dad and Mum,

A few minutes ago, we were gathered together to learn that we'll finally be embarking to go and fight the enemy in the next 24 hours. Even though I shouted "Hurray" like all the others in the platoon, I don't feel very brave, but rest assured that I'll never dishonor the family name.

We've been training hard for this day. I have a lot of confidence that we'll be victorious in our first engagement and that you'll be proud that I was one of the participants. Since we arrived in England, we've heard talk from other comrades from all parts of the Empire, as well as the English, who are fighting on so many fronts. Now, we Canadians, it's our turn to join them in the battle.

Where we are right now, our Colonel, Dollard Ménard, just confirmed the news and, in secret, told us the place where we'll be attacking the enemy. I'm sorry, but I can't reveal either the name, or the location. We know exactly the situation we'll be fighting in, and we'll attack with confidence.

Our chaplain, Padre Sabourin, gathered together everyone who wanted to receive general absolution, as well as Holy Communion. Almost

*everyone answered the call. I want to be at peace
with God in case something happens to me. My
good friend, Jacques Nadeau, went too.*

*After the detailed instructions, which we were
given by our officers and non-commissioned officers, we were invited to participate in a sumptuous
meal. We were served by members of the Women's
Royal Navy Service. The tables were covered with
white table cloths and each one had a complete
place setting. It's been a long time since we've been
treated like this by the military.*

*. . . I am continuing my letter on board our
assault craft, which is taking us to our target.
We're lucky, because the sea is very calm, the
temperature and the weather are good. They told
us that our engagement with the enemy will take
place around 5:30.*

*In the meantime, I'm using the time to check
my rifle once more and my equipment, for a third
time, all the while listening to my comrades talking
about different things. Some are telling jokes, but
listening to them I can feel their tension, which I
feel myself too.*

*Lieutenant Masson gave us his last advice, just
as we were dropping the mooring lines. Sergeant
Lapointe asked lots of questions because it's the
first time that he'll be leading a platoon of men.
Jacques is busy making adjustments to his bike and
seems bothered by something, as he is muttering
like he usually does in such a case.*

*The moon is bright enough so I can continue.
We've been sailing for two and a half hours, and I
have to be quick before it gets too dark. I'm taking*

*advantage of the time to ask for forgiveness for all
my faults and the pain that I've caused you, especially during my enlistment.*

*Roger told me how much trouble I've caused
you; I hope that if I come home alive from this
adventure, and if I return home at the end of the
war, I'll do everything that I can to dry your tears,
Mum; I'll do everything in my power to help you
forget all the anxieties I've caused.*

*I hope that you received my letter from last
week. I know that I celebrated my eighteenth
birthday on the 13th [his actual birthday was on
August 6], and that I have no reason to go into
combat. But when you learn how bravely I fought,
you'll forgive me for all the pain I have caused you.*

*Dawn is just starting on the horizon, but dur-
ing the night I've recited all the prayers that you
taught me, and with more fervour than usual. A
few minutes ago, I thought that we were already
in action with the Germans. Over there, on our
left, the roar of cannons and the lit-up sky made
us think so. Our embarkation group is moving
slowly and Lieutenant Masson told us that the first
assault wave is moving towards its objective.*

*It's much brighter now, and I can see much
better to write, I hope that you can read my writing. They've told us that we're very near the French
coast. I think so, as we can hear the gunfire as well
as the noise of explosions, even the whistling of
shells passing overhead.*

*I've finally realized that we're no longer on an
exercise. A landing craft right beside us just got hit,
and it disintegrated along with all on board. We*

*didn't have time to see much, because in the space
of a minute or two, there was nothing left.*

*O my God! Protect us from a similar fate. So
many comrades and friends who were there a couple of minutes ago gone forever. It's horrible. Other
boats in our group and other groups have been hit,
and have suffered the same fate.*

*If I should be among the victims, Jacques will
tell you what happened to me, because we promised to do this for each other, in case one of the two
of us doesn't come back.*

*I love you a lot, and tell my brothers and sisters
that I love them with all my heart.*

Robert Boulanger[15]

Robert Boulanger was not the only Fusilier killed at Dieppe; the battalion suffered heavy losses there. Only 125 Fusiliers returned to Britain, fifty of whom were wounded. Seven officers and ninety-eight soldiers were killed.[16]

The "Jacques" referred to in Boulanger's last letter home was Jacques Nadeau, his best friend. Nadeau saw Boulanger fall with a bullet between his eyes. Nadeau was seriously wounded that day and left for dead when the hastily arranged evacuation took place later that morning. He was found by German troops and sent to Stalag VIII-B, a notorious prisoner of war camp near Lamsdorf, Germany (now Lambinowice, Poland), along with many others captured at Dieppe. The Russian Army liberated the camp on March 17, 1945.

After the war, Nadeau was finally able to tell Boulanger's family what had happened to his friend. In August 2012, on the seventieth anniversary of the Dieppe Raid, Nadeau was one of the veterans who attended the official ceremonies and stood at Boulanger's grave to salute the young soldier.[17]

German artist Franz Martin Lunstroth's oil painting Mopping Up After the Battle *depicts the carnage at Dieppe.*

Not far from the cemetery is a recent tribute to Boulanger. On January 21, 2014, the city of Dieppe inaugurated seven streets in a new development, each named after an individual connected in some way to the raid. One of them is "Rue du Soldat Robert-Boulanger." Immediately below the name of the street, the signpost notes "1924–1942" and below that is the inscription "Le plus jeune combattant Canadien tombé sur la plage de Dieppe lors du Raid du 19 août 1942."[18]

* * *

Jimmie Burnett's home life was not without its trials and tribulations. He was born in Cullen, a small village on the North Sea coast of Moray, Scotland, on June 30, 1924, to a loving mother and a troubled father. In April 1927, Burnett emigrated to Canada with his family. They landed at Saint John, New Brunswick, before travelling to Ontario. At the time, George Sr. and Margaretta (who was nine years younger than her husband) had two children in addition to Jimmie: older brother George (nicknamed "Mac") and younger sister Reenie. In their new country, the Burnetts settled into a house on Aylesworth Avenue in the Toronto suburb of Scarborough, where three new family members followed in due course: Lily, Margie and Isobel.[19]

George Sr. was a veteran of the First World War, having spent four years as a private with the Royal Scots Fusiliers in France, and had been wounded in his left leg, which left him unable to bend it at the knee when seated. He continued to be "tormented by demons" from his wartime experience and developed a reputation as both a womanizer and a drunk. On many occasions, Mac and Jimmie had to protect their mother and sisters from his "drunken rages," staying in the house in the face of their father's repeated threats to toss them out on the street. One evening, the two young boys turned the tables on their father and actually forced him out of the house to sleep in the porch all night.[20] To support their mother and sisters, the boys left high school and went to work, the younger Burnett as an apprentice machinist.

In high school at Scarborough Collegiate, Burnett had been an army cadet and later joined the 2nd or reserve battalion of the Royal Regiment of Canada in February 1941. His reasons are unknown — patriotism, love of military life, escape from his home situation — any or all could apply. Whatever his motives, a few months later, on April 29, he transferred to the Royal Regiment's 1st or active battalion at Toronto's No. 2 District Depot. Burnett claimed a birthdate of June 29, 1922, a date supported by a handwritten, signed note from his father, which read: "I, George Burnett, Father of James Burnett, cer-

Jimmie Burnett's family (from left): Reenie, George Sr., Mac, Margaretta and Jimmie.

tify that James is 18 years and 10 months old and I do not wish to have him taken out of the army." George also enlisted the support of his landlord, a sergeant with the Toronto police, who helped forge Jimmie's paperwork, as well as those of other eager young boys from Scarborough Collegiate who wanted to join up.[21]

In fact, the "devilishly charming" Burnett was only sixteen years and ten months old. His true age was reflected in his size. The fair-haired, blue-eyed youth was less than five feet, seven inches tall and weighed only 119 pounds.

The next month, his older brother, now married and with a pregnant wife, joined the Royal Canadian Army Service Corps. His mother and his eldest sister, Reenie, also helped the war effort, working as so-called "bomb girls" in a new munitions factory recently created in Pickering Township on Lake

Ontario, just east of Scarborough. In those peaceful, rolling farmlands, an instant community sprang up: Ajax, named after a Royal Navy cruiser.[22]

On May 21, Burnett commenced his military training at No. 22 Canadian Army (Basic) Training Centre in North Bay, Ontario, where he got into a spot of trouble shortly after his arrival. Like many other soldiers — especially young ones — he was absent without leave. He was charged and found guilty of being absent for thirteen hours and forty-five minutes, for which he forfeited a day's pay of one dollar and thirty cents and was confined to barracks for seven days. Nine days later, he was absent again, this time for four hours, and received a punishment of five days' confinement to barracks.

On completion of his training, Burnett was posted to A11 Canadian Infantry Advanced Training Centre at Camp Borden north of Toronto from late July until mid-September, where he learned to be an infantryman. He was then temporarily attached to No. 12 Canadian Army (Basic) Training Centre in Chatham, Ontario. Lance Corporal Charles Kipp was an instructor at the Chatham training centre before he was sent overseas, where he endured eight months of hard fighting in North-West Europe with the Lincoln and Welland Regiment. He ended up as a platoon sergeant and was wounded in action nine times. Many years later, Kipp recorded his wartime experiences, which included his duties as a recruit instructor at Chatham:

> *Every day, the recruits had to be on parade at*
> *8:00 a.m. They were taught platoon drill: how*
> *to march, how to make left, right or about turns,*
> *either standing still or on the march; and how,*
> *when and who to salute. Then they were issued*
> *rifles and taught rifle drill, musketry and small*
> *arms. They learned how to clean and take care of*

their weapons, how to use them and how to fix a
bayonet. Then we taught how to kill a man with
a bayonet. We had fencing instructors, teach-
ing them how to fight with a bayonet — how to
parry, point and draw a bayonet from a body.
Real gruesome work . . . Basic training lasted two
months. Then, men had to pass tests in everything
we had taught them. If they were reserve soldiers,
they then went home. If they were active service-
men, then they went to advanced training for
whatever branch of the service they were going
to. This meant that every two months, we got
new men to train, and the process started all over
again. It also meant that we got very raw throats
out on the parade square.[23]

Although what Burnett did at Chatham is unrecorded, he was likely employed on the euphemistically termed "general duties" — a catch-all army phrase for a "go-fer." But his attachment was short-lived and he spent only two weeks at Chatham before he was back in Camp Borden in early October to wait for a posting overseas. While there, his sisters Reenie and Margie travelled north from Toronto to visit him, the last time any of the girls would see their brother.

Burnett did not have to wait long. He sailed for Britain and arrived on October 19. He was then sent to No.1 Canadian Infantry Holding Unit at Witley Camp, near Godalming in Surrey. Witley and other temporary camps in the area — Bramshott, Liphook, Bordon — had a long association with the Canadian army and were used during the First and Second World Wars, becoming virtually complete Canadian towns.

In Britain, Burnett was given landing leave, and then briefly attached to a Royal Canadian Ordnance Corps detachment —

probably for general duties again — before he was sent to 2nd Canadian Division Infantry Reinforcement Unit in early December. At Witley, Burnett was housed in Laurentide Camp, which, with Algonquin and Jasper, made up the overall larger Witley Camp. The young soldier's penchant for getting into trouble manifested itself in two incidents at Laurentide.

In the first, Burnett was charged with the old army standby of conduct to the prejudice of good order and discipline on January 5, 1942, when he "failed to carry out his duties as a guard in a proper manner." Five days' confinement to barracks — along with the opportunity to properly learn the duties of guards during three extra shifts — were his punishment. During this period, Burnett and his brother, Mac — who was also stationed in Britain — travelled to their birthplace in Scotland, where they visited a favourite aunt, Jessie Patterson, who lived at what became known to the boys simply as "18," a reference to their aunt's civic address. In Cullen, they were "welcomed into the open arms of their aunts and grandmother" and were to visit the village while on leave on more than one occasion.[24] In February, Burnett failed to return from a week's leave to Cullen on time and was thirteen hours late. He lost four days' pay as a result.

On March 27, Burnett was finally posted to the unit he had originally joined: the Royal Regiment of Canada. To date, the war had been a relatively easy one for the regiment — but in less than five months, that would change in a very tragic way, a way no one at the time could have imagined.

When Jimmie Burnett joined the Royal Regiment five months after his arrival in Britain, it had been there for almost a year and a half. He moved from Laurentide Camp to the unit's temporary billets at Eastbourne, a south coast town, and arrived in the midst of a very busy training regime. On April 19, Burnett and his comrades moved into tents near the picturesque village of

Hellingly in East Sussex, about sixteen kilometres from the south coast. After one exercise was greatly hampered by rain and mud, the soldiers returned to their tents to discover the campsite had been bombed by German aircraft and, consequently, they had to move again.

Following a series of exercises to prepare his unit for the raid on Dieppe, a period of leave was granted, with up to thirty per cent of the unit allowed to be away at any one time. Burnett was one of those who benefited from this and received seven days leave to visit his Scottish relatives. It was to be the last time. In Cullen, he confided in his grandmother about his feelings as a soldier. He said he was "terrified" and had "a bad feeling" about the battle he had so narrowly avoided. For the first time, it seemed he was frightened and, as a result, did not want to return to his unit. His grandmother reminded him of his obligations to his family and his country and insisted he return.

Soon after this visit, Mac also intervened and attempted to get Burnett transferred to the Royal Canadian Army Service Corps, a somewhat safer place than an infantry battalion. This was likely based on his younger brother's age, but the request was denied.[25] Burnett did rejoin his unit, but six days, fourteen hours, and thirty minutes after his leave expired. Lieutenant-Colonel Doug Catto, the new commanding officer who had taken over the battalion on July 19, was obviously concerned about Burnett's illegal absence and sentenced him to a stiff penalty on August 7: fourteen days' confinement to barracks and the forfeiture of twenty-one days' pay.

Five days later, all leave was suddenly cancelled, and at 10 a.m. on August 18, the Royal Regiment received a curt telephone message from 4th Brigade Headquarters: "The show is on." Against all precepts of military security — and on the recommendation of Mountbatten — the raid on Dieppe had been resurrected under the code name Operation Jubilee.

The last entries on Burnett's statement of service note his final movements in terse military terminology:

Embarked UK for France Jubilee Oper[ation] 18 Aug 42
S[truck] O[ff] S[trength)] to X List Missing 19 Aug 42

On August 25, Burnett's mother received an official telegram notifying her that her son was missing in action. Such telegrams were received by many who had relatives on the raid, as death could not be confirmed until information was received from the Germans through the International Red Cross. Margaretta gave up her job at the munitions factory to be sure she would be at home when the news arrived.

On October 29, Margaretta wrote to military authorities in Ottawa in an attempt to learn more. After noting she had "heard nothing" since the August cable, she added somewhat bitterly, "His assigned pay [twenty dollars per month] did not come out on the 30th Sept. I phoned headquarters in Toronto but the lady there was anything but civil. I understood it was only deserters of the British Army that had pay stopped not a Hero of Dieppe 18 years of age." After her signature, she added: "A volunteered Comando [sic] of The Royal Regiment of Canada."

Margaretta received two responses to her query. The first was from the records section advising her no further information was known about her missing son's circumstances, while the second was from the paymaster general. It explained the rules regarding discontinuance of pay and allotments of soldiers reported missing, until they were either found or presumed dead. It also noted the Dependents' Allowance Board would investigate her particular case, to ascertain if she were "dependent on the missing soldier," in which case, "the assigned pay may again be put

A Toronto newspaper clipping announced Private Jimmie Burnett's death.

into force until the soldier is presumed dead or a pension is granted."

Whatever hope this reply may have given Margaretta was dashed a week later when a letter from the Dependents' Allowance Board arrived: "As your husband is living with you and providing for your support, it is regretted that you are unable to be considered for an interim allowance." But it did helpfully add that "if the soldier turns out to be a prisoner of war, the account will be reinstated."

The family's worst fears were confirmed in a telegram on December 5, which stated Burnett was "now reported by Berlin through International Red Cross Geneva killed in action nineteenth August 1942." Two days later, a *Toronto Daily Star* article titled "Waiting to send Yule gifts learn Dieppe sons killed" contained the results of interviews with parents who had lost sons during the raid. This article, noted that Margaretta "'had not given up hope until now her son was a prisoner, but the family's greatest fears had now come true."

Burnett's death caused tensions to rise within his family. Margaretta blamed her husband for encouraging their son to enrol, called him a "bastard" and feared for Mac's life. Burnett family lore maintains it was guilt that led George Sr. at age fifty-two to join the Veterans' Guard of Canada a month after learning of his son's death. He served at Camp 30, a prisoner of war camp at Bow-

manville, Ontario.[26] Burnett's
death also hit his sister Reenie
— to whom he was particularly
close — extremely hard. Although
Reenie had a boyfriend, he was
also killed during the war and she
never married.[27] It took until June
14, 1943, before the Burnetts were
informed their son's remains had
been interred in Des Vertus cemetery on the outskirts of Dieppe,
based on advice received from the
Vichy French government.

But events then took a bizarre
turn.

On July 18, Margaretta wrote
a letter to the Canadian director
of records, in which she acknowl-
edged the information about her
son's burial place, but went on to state:

BUCKINGHAM PALACE

The Queen and I offer you
our heartfelt sympathy in your
great sorrow.

We pray that your country's
gratitude for a life so nobly
given in its service may bring
you some measure of consolation.

The sympathy letter from King George VI to the Burnett family following Jimmie's death.

*It has come to my knowledge by a soldier that has
been writing home saying he visited my sons [sic]
grave in Success [the recipient has written "ssex"
above "ccess"] England. If that is the case surely
there must have been an awful blunder. You will
have to let me know wright [sic] away what is
the truth. This suspense has been terrible I really
can't stand much more of it. My only other son is
a soldier in England also my husband served all
through the Great War is now the Veteran Guards.
Please write and let me know where my boy is
really buried at.*

The authorities immediately asked Margaretta the name of the soldier who provided the information. They then asked Canadian military records personnel in England to investigate. As it turned out, a soldier in 4th Canadian Armoured Division Transport Company, Royal Canadian Army Service Corps (the same corps in which Burnett's brother served), had heard Burnett was a casualty from Dieppe and he had been informed such casualties were buried at Brookwood Military Cemetery in Sussex. "To have something to write," he sent a letter to Margaretta, telling her this. He was later directed to write an apology.

At about the same time, Margaretta was informed by the administrator of estates that her son's personal effects had arrived in Canada and would shortly be sent to her. The same letter advised that since Burnett had been paid in full for the month of August 1942, there were "no funds available to this Branch for distribution." Margaretta subsequently applied for a war service gratuity, which was denied because she was "not dependent upon [her] son, either in whole or in part, immediately prior to his death." It also noted any gratuity to which Burnett was entitled would form part of his service estate and be distributed in accordance with his will. This gratuity was eventually calculated as $211.28, based on total days of service plus a supplement for time spent overseas. In accordance with Burnett's will, the full amount went to Margaretta, but it took until September 1945 before it was paid to her.

Burnett's older brother, Mac, returned home safely at the end of the war but, after having survived the conflict, passed away in 1954 from Hodgkin's disease. Margaretta, who was still alive at the time, had lost both her sons before their time.[28] After the war, the Commonwealth War Graves Commission created the Dieppe Canadian War Cemetery out of the cemetery at Des Vertus. It is unique among Commonwealth cemeteries as it was originally constructed by the Germans to bury Allied soldiers killed in the raid. As such, it was laid out in the traditional German way, with headstones placed back to back in long double rows. After the Canadian army captured Dieppe in 1944, it was decided not to disturb the graves, so this unusual layout remains today. In 1949, it became the first new cemetery of the Second World War to be completed. Burnett's headstone bears the epitaph "In Life, Loved and Honoured. In Death, Remembered."

* * *

On the ground, the Dieppe Raid resulted in 907 Canadians killed[29] and an additional 1,946 taken prisoner. From a force of 4,963 men engaged for only nine hours, the Canadian army lost more prisoners than in the whole eleven months of the later campaign in North-West Europe from D-Day to V-E Day.[30] The Dieppe Raid remains a major controversy to this day, and continues to generate endless debate and discussion about its usefulness, especially with regard to application of the hard lessons learned there to the D-Day invasion almost two years later.

Today, in a small park beneath Dieppe's cliffs, a memorial erected by the grateful French attests to the Canadians' sacrifice. It reads, in French: "On the 19th of August 1942 on the beach at Dieppe our Canadian cousins traced with their blood the road of our final liberation portending in this way their victorious return on the 1st of September 1944."

And in the Dieppe Canadian War Cemetery, Jimmie Burnett and Robert Boulanger lie only two rows apart for all eternity, closer in death than they ever were in life.

PART II

ITALY: THE D-DAY DODGERS

"The men who wore on their shoulders the name of Canada were identified with the costliest struggles of the entire campaign."

Lieutenant-Colonel G.W.L. Nicholson, *The Canadians in Italy, 1943–1945: The Official History of the Canadian Army in the Second World War, Volume II*

MAP III

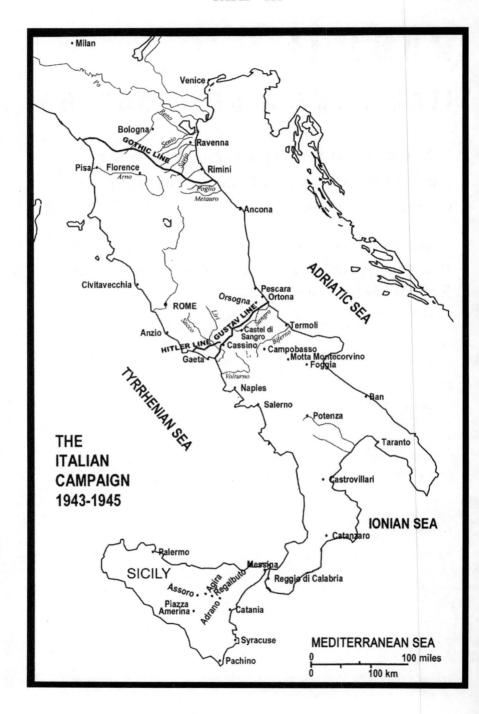

THE
ITALIAN
CAMPAIGN
1943-1945

Milan

Venice

Po

Reno

Bologna
GOTHIC LINE
Senio
Ravenna
Savio

Pisa
Florence
Arno
Rimini

Poglio
Metauro

Ancona

ADRIATIC SEA

Civitavecchia

Pescara
Orsogna
Ortona
ROME
Liri
Sangro
Anzio
Sacco
GUSTAV LINE
Termoli
HITLER LINE
Castel di
Sangro
Cassino
Biferno
Gaeta
Campobasso
Motta Montecorvino
Foggia

Volturno
Naples
Bari
Salerno
Potenza

TYRRHENIAN SEA

Taranto

Castrovillari

IONIAN SEA

Catanzaro

Palermo

SICILY
Messina
Assoro
Agira
Regalbuto
Reggio di Calabria
Piazza
Amerina
Adrano
Catania

Syracuse

Pachino

MEDITERRANEAN SEA

0   100 miles
0   100 km

"WE WERE — AND ARE — QUITE PROUD OF THE BOY'S DETERMINATION AND INDEPENDENCE."

Italy, The Invasion
(Map III)

Victor Innanen was a tough kid in a tough outfit doing a tough job. His unit, the 3rd Regiment of the First Special Service Force, was tramping through the frozen foothills and gullies of Italy's Monte Majo hill mass in early January 1944, struggling to survive the high winds and subzero temperatures as they rooted out the last of the area's determined German defenders. On January 8, there were one hundred casualties, nearly half due to frostbite and exposure and the rest from battle. The next day, 122 soldiers were casualties, again almost half due to non-battle injuries. On January 10, seventy-three names were listed on the casualty report, forty of them with frostbitten feet.[1] The seventeen-year-old Innanen — already a three-year veteran — had managed to keep up so far, but was beginning to wonder how long he could continue this daily slugging match across the freezing, snow-covered slopes, harassed by enemy artillery fire and never knowing when the next deadly skirmish would occur.

Would this punishing ordeal ever end?

Reginald Roy's identification discs, showing his initial rank of "Boy."

* * *

Reginald (Reg) Roy, the son of a First World War pilot and his English war bride, joined the Cape Breton Highlanders before the war. Born in New Glasgow, Nova Scotia, on December 11, 1922, he was only sixteen when he enrolled in the spring of 1939 in Sydney on Cape Breton Island. He quickly became known in the unit as "Boy" Roy and was one of three boy soldiers in the battalion whose rank was actually "Boy." Roy and his young companions were paid seventy cents a day and eagerly awaited the time when they would turn eighteen and be promoted to private — along with an increase of forty cents a day.

When the Cape Breton Highlanders received the telegram to mobilize in the early evening hours of September 1, 1939, the order to report to company locations was relayed over the local radio station, CJCB, a few minutes before midnight. Roy was one of those who heard the radio message and reported to the armouries at Victoria Park in north-end Sydney the next day.[2] At the armouries, Roy noted, "There was a parade for everything — pay parade, bath parade, medical parade and what not . . . I remember when we were informed there was to be a short-arm inspection.

The three boy soldiers of the Cape Breton Highlanders in 1939; Reg Roy is on the right.

In my innocence, I brought along the shortest weapon I had, my bayonet! That was not quite what they were interested in. But we were learning, we were learning."

Meanwhile, training continued, but at a very basic level as the Highlanders lacked uniforms, weaponry, ammunition and vehicles. Towards the end of September, the government announced Canada would send a contingent overseas, but the Cape Breton Highlanders were not part of it. Volunteers were requested to make up manpower shortfalls in 1st Canadian Division units, and several Highlanders responded, with most of them going to the West Nova Scotia Regiment. The unit also handed over a fair amount of its much-needed equipment, which it could ill afford to do. The next time the Highlanders saw their mates was in films of Canadian soldiers arriving in Britain.[3]

* * *

Harold Joseph Pringle came from the tiny rural community of Flinton, north of Napanee in eastern Ontario. He had attended school only until Grade 6 (a common practice at the time) when he was fourteen, and then tried his hand at various

Harold Pringle at his home in Flinton, Ontario, before he joined the army in 1940.

jobs — lumberjack, highway road crew, farmer, hydroelectric worker. He gave most of his earnings to his parents; usually everything but twenty-five cents, which he kept for himself. Pringle's father, Billy, was a forty-two-year-old veteran of the First World War and had served as a sniper in the 4th (Central Ontario) Battalion Canadian Mounted Rifles. Despite its name, the unit was a standard infantry battalion, having turned in its horses early in the war. Young Pringle was extremely proud of his father's wartime service.

Although the Pringles farmed a few acres of land, father Billy also trapped, fished and hunted to supplement the family diet, and worked on road crews in the summer to earn money. With the outbreak of war in Europe, Harold Pringle was keen to join the army, as his father had done. But Billy was concerned about his son, so on February 5, 1940, both father and son took the train from Flinton to Picton and together joined the Hastings and Prince Edward Regiment (colourfully nicknamed the "Hasty Ps"). Although it was a few days after his eighteenth birthday, young Pringle claimed a birthdate of January 16, 1920, instead of his actual one of 1922. The elder Pringle had enrolled to be with his young son in order to protect him.

Pringle and his father trained at Picton before moving to Camp Borden for further training. In August 1940 — with the son still too young to be sent overseas — they sailed to Britain in a draft intended for the Hastings and Prince Edward Regiment, but once they got there, they were disappointed to be sent to No. 1 Canadian Infantry Holding Unit, rather than the regiment. Despite the soul-destroying routine of a holding unit, Harold's father managed to keep an eye on his son and keep him out of trouble. Then, in April 1942, the elder Pringle was returned to Canada on release for medical reasons, leaving his twenty-year-old son on his own. Without his father to guide him, it did not take long for the younger Pringle to get into trouble, partly as a reaction to his father's curt dismissal.

During the next two years, Pringle was frequently absent without authority. He also struck up a "friendship" with a British woman — Pringle, a good-looking young man, never had any difficulty in attracting women — who lived in Portsmouth and whose husband was serving overseas in the British army. By now, his periods of absenteeism had become intolerable and he was court-martialled. Pringle was sentenced to six months in the "Glass House," the Canadian army's infamous prison at Headley Down. After less than a month of enduring the sadistic daily routine of the warders, he escaped and went into hiding. A month later, he surrendered to the London police. This time, Pringle was sentenced to nine months' detention.

In January 1944, Pringle, now almost twenty-two, was released from prison early because he volunteered for active service, providing it was with the Hastings and Prince Edward Regiment. The army agreed, as the regiment had been fighting in Sicily and Italy with 1st Canadian Infantry Division since early July and was

The Cape Breton Highlanders' signals platoon, of which Reg Roy was a member.

in need of reinforcements.[4] In early March 1944, Pringle arrived in Italy, two months after the meat-grinder of Ortona.[5]

* * *

In January 1941, while the Pringles were training in Britain, the Cape Breton Highlanders were ordered to Saint John, New Brunswick, to replace the New Brunswick Rangers in garrison coastal duties. On arrival in Saint John, the soldiers marched two and a half kilometres from the rail station to their new quarters at the armouries at Barrack Green, "slipping and sliding on the icy streets." Reginald Roy, who had just turned eighteen, was not impressed. An exhibition building next door was used for messing and "it was cold and drafty. In the short time it took to move with a meal from the serving line to a table, the food would be cold and the tea tepid." Additionally, the food was "below standard and heat was virtually non-existent."[6]

What Barrack Green lacked in creature comforts was frequently made up by the people of Saint John. Roy said he found them "remarkably funny and nice to the soldiers. They always want to make us happy." One thing Roy found especially kind was every Sunday evening when about forty or fifty Highlanders were invited to supper in local homes. Cars were sent to pick up the soldiers, and on arrival, Ray noted, "[We] greeted by the good lady, lavish luxuries are spread at our feet and in time we sit down to an excellent home cooked meal." Roy and fellow boy soldier Ray MacDonald went to two such dinners.[7] Roy wrote in a letter to his girlfriend: "Of course we are the little gentlemen — and at last I have convinced Ray not to eat the bread before it is sliced."[8]

At the end of March, Roy and the Cape Breton Highlanders were thrilled to learn they would become an infantry battalion in the new 1st (later 5th) Canadian Armoured Division. More moves followed in rapid succession: to Camp Sussex, New Brunswick, in April; to the Connaught Ranges outside of Ottawa in May; and to Camp Borden, north of Toronto — one of the army's six main training locations — in June.[9]

In another letter to his future wife, Roy gave his initial impressions of the camp:

> Cars, trucks, Bren carriers, tanks and heaven
> knows what else are continually buzzing hither and
> yon. The roads leading into and out of camp are
> strewn with marching troops all day long. Planes,
> both bomber and fighter are continually roaring
> overhead swooping, stunning and swanning about
> trying to scare the life out of everybody and usually
> succeeding in doing so. Camp Borden is hot, sandy
> and dusty. I have never been honestly clean since I
> have arrived here and never expect to be until we
> leave . . . Our whole unit is under canvas, the tents
> are all pitched in a grove of pine trees . . . It is very
> similar to a desert oasis . . .

*Blending in with the roar of vehicles is a steady
hammering chatter of heavy machine guns heard
in the distance firing on the range.*

*In the morning, at reveille, it seems as if a
thousand buglers are trying to outdo each other
with their shrill calls, rousing some thirty thousand
men who, in turn, tell the buglers individually and
collectively in slightly drowsy voices their opinion
of the person who dares arouse them from such a
lovely sleep.*

*Later in the day . . . the various bands start
marching up and down the road, playing away
like men possessed. There is more music in Camp
Borden during that hour than there is in an entire
season of the Metropolitan Opera.*[10]

Roy was promoted sergeant at eighteen and sailed to Britain
with his battalion in November 1941. While the Highlanders
spent the next three years training in Britain, Roy was selected for
officer training in Canada. After interviews and IQ tests in London, Roy and his fellow potential officers were sent to a prisoner
of war camp for a week to learn how to handle German prisoners,
as, in his words, "we were to be employed as their guards on the
trip to Halifax." It would be well over a year before he returned.

In Canada, after successfully passing his training at the
Brockville Officer Training School, Roy was promoted second
lieutenant and sent to Camp Aldershot, Nova Scotia, where
he received his second "pip" as a lieutenant. Roy and his fellow officers were keen to return overseas, but in the summer of
1943, there was a surplus of officers, so they were sent to Home
Defence regiments. Ironically, Roy ended up in the barracks at
Victoria Park in Sydney, where his army career had begun. As far
as he was concerned, it was back to "square one."[11]

***

From all indications, Freeman Hector Grant did not have an easy life. Born on Remembrance Day, 1926, in Yarmouth, at the southwestern tip of Nova Scotia, he started work as a helper in a mill at an early age. When he joined the army on December 15, 1942, he had turned sixteen only a little over a month earlier, but claimed a birthdate in 1923. At the time of his enrolment, he had been employed as a labourer for three months. Although Grant's father, Hector, was alive when he was growing up and was employed as a mechanic, it appears he had little to do with raising his son, especially after the boy was ten. As well, his mother, Rowena, seems to have been out of the picture. Grant did not name her on his attestation paper and listed his father as his next of kin, while most soldiers claimed their mothers as next of kin when they enrolled. Instead, a local woman stated she had looked after the youngster for several years before he joined the army.[12]

Although Grant's physical development was noted as "good" on enrolment, he had been quite ill in 1932, when he suffered from both pleurisy and pneumonia. This led to empyema, a condition in which pus and fluid from infected tissue collects in a body cavity — most often in the space around the lungs — and is usually a complication of pneumonia. He still bore the scar of a thoracostomy on his right side, which had drained the infected fluid from his chest. Apart from this — and a few missing teeth — the fair-complexioned Grant was normal size for his age, at 137 pounds and five feet, seven inches tall, and possessed 20-20 vision.

Early in 1943, Grant was sent to No. 14 Advanced Infantry Training Centre at Camp Aldershot in the province's picturesque Annapolis Valley. He completed basic infantry training there and also qualified as a 6-pounder anti-tank gunner before the end of May. Twenty days later, he was on his way to Britain. He was sent to 2nd Canadian Division Infantry Reinforcement Unit on arrival in June.

The infantry reinforcement unit had the task of collecting and training personnel earmarked as reinforcements for the division, a job made all the more urgent after the losses at Dieppe the previous August. Despite being assigned to 2nd Division's reinforcement unit, Grant was sent to Italy on September 12 to 1st Division, where he joined — appropriately enough — the West Nova Scotia Regiment in the division's 3rd Brigade.

The infantrymen of the West Novas — mainly from the Annapolis Valley and South Shore of Nova Scotia — had landed in Sicily on July 10, fought through the dry, rugged hills and mountains of the island until August 7, and then were the first Allied troops to land permanently on continental Europe when they led the way at Reggio at the toe of the Italian boot in the early morning hours of September 3. When Grant joined the unit, it was on the coast south of Catanzaro, enjoying a four-day "rest" period, marked by daily practice marches without water bottles and with strictly enforced march discipline.

Rest time was short-lived, and Grant and his new mates from the West Novas soon found themselves advancing steadily northwards against skilled and determined German troops, who delayed the Allied advance with every means at their disposal on narrow, twisting mountain roads and steep gorges. By early December, 1st Division had relieved 78th British Division in front of the medieval town of Ortona, perched on steep cliffs overlooking the Adriatic Sea.[13] Canadian soldiers were about to begin one of their toughest battles of the war, but young Grant never got to take part in it.

The attack towards Ortona commenced with an assault on the rain-swollen Moro River on December 6 and ended three hard-fought days later when a few infantry battalions succeeded in getting across, supported by tanks.[14] With a number of crossings

Canadian soldiers search German prisoners of war near the Moro River, Italy, December 1943.

on the north side of the Moro in Canadian hands, the advance towards Ortona continued. But they encountered a natural obstacle, simply known as "The Gully." Heavily defended, it presented a formidable barrier to all forward movement.

The battle for The Gully began on December 11, with the three battalions of 2nd Brigade attacking. By noon — with tank support — they had closed up to the enemy's defences but could not break through. Battalions of 1st Brigade then moved forward on both flanks of 2nd Brigade, but they too could not advance.

At noon, division commander Major-General Chris Vokes called on 3rd Brigade to break the log-jam. Grant and his mates in the West Novas — less B Company — set off at 6 p.m. to push through the forward units, cross The Gully and capture a lateral road near Casa Berardi, a prominent stone farmhouse that was key to the whole position. The fourth company and a tank squadron were held in reserve, ready to move when required. A few metres short of The Gully, the West Novas were silhouetted against the moonlit landscape and stopped short by heavy German fire from the long depression across their front. The soldiers, including Grant, dug in for the night, ready to resume their attack the next morning, when artillery support would be available.

But they never got the chance: the Germans pre-empted them with four fierce counterattacks. While the Nova Scotians grimly held their ground, Vokes decided to continue the assault elsewhere.[15] Two patrols from B Company had penetrated as far as a major lateral road running westward from Ortona on the afternoon and evening of December 12 and found a spot passable for tanks. B Company's commander decided to exploit this information and ordered a platoon forward, carried on three tanks. Their attack went in at 7 a.m. on December 13, covered by the noise of one of the German counterattacks against the main position occupied by the West Novas.

The platoon's attack was a complete surprise and succeeded in killing or capturing more than one hundred Germans. At the same time, the rest of the battalion was undergoing another "long and bloody day," now reduced to a little more than one hundred all ranks. That afternoon at about 4:30 p.m., this handful of survivors made another attack on The Gully opposite Casa Berardi. They met with limited success but were forced to withdraw under the cover of darkness. By then, the battalion had been so reduced it was doubtful if it could have held out against a determined German counterattack. B Company — less a platoon left at the site of the successful attack that morning — was recalled from its independent mission. Once it rejoined the regiment, the remaining

Canadian soldiers carry a comrade killed by shellfire on the Ortona Front,
December 1943.

soldiers of the unit, including Grant, were reformed temporarily
into two under-strength companies.

  For the next four days — from December 14 to 17 — the
West Novas continued to hold their positions in front of The
Gully.[16] Somehow, Grant had managed to survive to this
point, but his luck was about to end. Sometime on December
14, the seventeen-year-old was killed in action, having served
only one year less a day. The exact circumstances of his death
remain unknown.

* * *

Victor Innanen was — if nothing else — persistent. In July
1941, he travelled from the small, rural village of Harriston (now

After being released for being underage, Victor Innanen managed to re-enrol while still fifteen and served in the First Special Service Force under the surname of Coja.

known as Minto), about eighty kilometres north-west of Kitchener-Waterloo, enrolled in the army in London, Ontario, and was assigned to 15th Field Ambulance. The five-foot-seven, 122-pound, blue-eyed, fair-haired youth claimed to be nineteen, when in fact he had only turned fifteen three months earlier.[17]

The teenager was also independent. His parents, Alexander and Ida (then deceased), had been born in Finland and emigrated to Canada, where they raised a family of six boys and four girls, of which Victor was the second youngest. Although he was born in nearby Arthur Township, Innanen left home at twelve to work in Harriston as a farmhand.

Two weeks after Innanen enrolled, he was sent to Camp Valcartier, Quebec, for training, before moving on to Camp Sussex, New Brunswick, where he joined his unit. He was able to keep his secret for nearly seven months. He was serving with 15th Field Ambulance when his true age was discovered and discharge proceedings followed. On January 31, 1942, Innanen was released for being underage. In accordance with regulations, he was given a thirty-five dollar clothing allowance to buy civilian clothes.

Less than two weeks later, Innanen, still fifteen, was back in London, where he re-enrolled in the army, this time under the assumed name of Victor Coja, his mother's maiden name. As before, he claimed his birth year as 1922, although he changed the date and month. A week later, Innanen was posted to the Canadian Fusiliers (City of London Regiment), stationed in nearby Listowel. He must have found life in a Home Defence infantry battalion an unexciting prospect because he volunteered for a unit that was unique in the military annals of Canada and the United States — and of any other country for that matter.

In July 1942, the Canadian government had approved the assignment of seven hundred officers and men to a new unit called 1st Canadian Parachute Battalion. But no such unit existed. The name was an administrative cover designation for Canadian military personnel that were recruited and sent to train with a unit just being formed: the joint American-Canadian First Special Service Force. During the Italian Campaign, the unit was dubbed *die schwarzen Teufeln* (The Black Devils) by their German adversaries.

When the Canadian army did raise an actual parachute unit shortly afterwards, it became known as 1st Canadian Parachute Battalion, while the cover unit for Canadians in the Special Service Force was changed to 2nd Canadian Parachute Battalion. Innanen and other soldiers destined for the First Special Service Force were sent to Fort William Henry Harrison near Helena, Montana. There, they underwent a rigorous training program in parachuting, hand-to-hand combat, use of demolitions, skiing, rock climbing, physical fitness and other specialties. Innanen qualified as a parachutist on August 24, even as many of his comrades were returned to their home units due to injuries sustained during jumps — or because they failed to jump. In March 1943, Innanen was appointed acting sergeant, although he was still only sixteen years old. Considering the fitness, robustness and physique of most of his comrades, it was an amazing accomplishment.

The 2,200-man First Special Service Force consisted of three six-hundred-man regiments, each of two battalions. Each battalion had three one-hundred-man companies of three platoons, further broken down into two sections. Canadians made up almost half of the combat element. A service battalion, manned only by Americans, looked after the administrative needs of the unit.[18] Innanen was assigned to 1st Company, 1st Battalion, 3rd Regiment.

Following its initial training in Montana, the Force moved to Norfolk, Virginia, in April to undertake amphibious training at the request of General Eisenhower, in preparation for possible deployment to the Mediterranean. After very successful completion of this training, it moved to Fort Ethan Allen in Vermont, where it was held in readiness pending orders to proceed to Europe. Then, on June 9, the First Special Service Force received orders for a completely different mission.

Accordingly, in early July, the unit arrived in San Francisco, its port of embarkation for its first operational mission: to assist in the recapture of Alaska's Aleutian Islands from the Japanese. In an unexpected move in June 1942, about eighty-five hundred Japanese military personnel had occupied the islands of Attu and Kiska at the western end of the Aleutian chain. The Japanese wanted to distract the Allies from other more important areas in the central Pacific and push out their defensive perimeter.

On May 11, 1943, the U.S. Army's 7th Division, supported by three battleships, had attacked Attu. Japanese defenders fought to the death and inflicted almost four thousand casualties on the larger American force, which took twenty days to defeat the Japanese. Meanwhile, Canadian and American government officials and military staff had been discussing the possibility of a Canadian army contribution to the recapture of the second Japanese-occupied island, Kiska, garrisoned by six thousand of the enemy. In the end, Canada decided to provide a brigade group based on the headquarters of 13th Infantry Brigade.

The 13th Infantry Brigade was a Home Defence formation.

It had gone through many changes of units, but for the Kiska operation, one of its infantry battalions was — ironically — the Canadian Fusiliers (City of London Regiment), which Innanen had transferred from to join the First Special Service Force. Innanen disembarked at Amchitka Island on July 24, his unit's staging area for the assault.

In the pre-dawn hours of August 15 — after bombardment by ships and aircraft — soldiers of the 1st Regiment landed from rubber boats along Kiska's north shore and moved inland. The landings were unopposed and no Japanese soldiers were encountered as the units moved inland. The next night, the 3rd Regiment landed at the north end of the island, where Innanen was one of the first two dozen men to go ashore. The results were the same — no enemy found. In fact, the Japanese occupiers had slipped away by submarine three weeks earlier.[19]

The next mission assigned to First Special Service Force was a tougher one: assist the Allies in the conquest of Italy. For this operation, it was to operate as light infantry, but against objectives considered too tough for ordinary soldiers. Innanen and his buddies departed Newport News, Virginia, by ship in late October and landed in North Africa in early November. On November 18, they disembarked at Naples, Italy, ready to face the German foe.

Lieutenant-General Mark Clark, commanding Fifth U.S. Army, was eager to be the liberator of Rome, but first he had to break through several lines of formidable German defences. The first of these was situated in the peaks and ridges before Monte Cassino, in an area known as the Camino hill mass. While two divisions from X British Corps operated on the left against Monte Camino, the First Special Service Force would assault on the right against two high peaks: Monte la Difensa in front, with Monte la Remetanea behind. Both were more than nine hundred metres high.

The Force's 2nd Regiment was tasked with taking the mountain, with Innanen's 1st Battalion, 3rd Regiment in reserve. It was a two-day operation. The first night saw a gruelling seven-hour climb up the sheer face of Monte la Difensa, with all supplies — including water — carried by the soldiers, followed by a layup during daylight. On the second night, the assault force scaled the remaining 350 metres to the top and attacked before dawn on December 3, taking the Germans by surprise in a final rush. By 7 a.m., soldiers of the 2nd Regiment's 1st Battalion were firmly in control of the peak. Behind them, the remainder of the regiment was climbing upwards to reinforce the attack, while Innanen and his mates concentrated on bringing ammunition forward and evacuating casualties to the rear.

For the next two days, the 2nd Regiment held on to Monte la Difensa and repelled a German counterattack on the morning of December 4. Throughout this time, pack trains from Innanen's regiment toiled beyond the point of exhaustion to carry water, ammunition, rations and blankets to the top. Meanwhile, 1st Regiment's 1st Battalion was ordered up the mountain to reinforce 2nd Regiment. Seen by German forward observers, the battalion was caught in artillery barrage in the open and suffered heavy casualties. The bombardment targeted the 3rd Regiment's pack trains as well, which also suffered several casualties as they laboured under trying conditions to carry cans of water, small arms ammunition, mortar shells and other commodities up the mountain.

On the afternoon of December 5, two of the Force's battalions attacked forward along the narrow ridge that led to Monte la Remetanea, about nine hundred metres to the north. The battalion came under enemy machine-gun and mortar fire from Monte Camino, and it was not until the next day that one of the battalions was able to move on and take the objective.

The next day, Monte Camino fell to a British division, and by December 8, the entire Camino hill mass was in Allied hands. In its first action, the First Special Service Force had fought with

A mule pack team carrying supplies travels along a snow-covered mountain road in Italy during the winter of 1944-45.

distinction and achieved its objectives — but at a cost of more than five hundred casualties — many of them due to exhaustion or frostbite. Canadian losses amounted to a third of the total; fortunately, Innanen was not among them.

On December 9, the Force withdrew from the line to the village of Santa Maria for a well-deserved period of rest and recovery. Roughly a quarter of its combat strength had become casualties, although many would be able to return after medical treatment or rest. These losses were particularly difficult for the Canadians to absorb as — bizarrely — neither the Canadian army nor the Canadian government had made any arrangements for casualty replacements. In fact, the official policy was losses would not be replaced, a situation that — if unchanged — would eventually lead to the Canadians becoming non-effective and would require their removal from the Force.

Soldiers of the First Special Service Force prepare a meal.

On December 21, the Force began moving forward to its next objective: the Mignano Gap, part of the German lengthy defensive position known as the Winter Line. The task of Innanen's 3rd Regiment in this next operation was to secure the dominating hill mass of Monte Majo. The regiment ascended snow-covered hills overlooked by the mountain's heights, securing several nameless peaks in the process. At the same time, it struggled to keep open lines of communication with the rear for mule trains and pack boards; the only ways to deliver ammunition and other requirements to the front.

Casualties grew as high winds and low temperatures daily reduced the Force's strength due to trench foot, exhaustion and hypothermia, exacerbated by harassing artillery fire from the Germans. To make up for losses, the American corps commander augmented the First Special Service Force with two infantry battalions, an engineer company and a division's artillery in direct support. Suitably reinforced, 3rd Regiment set out on the night of January 6 to attack the crest of Monte Majo. Innanen's 1st Battalion led the way.

At 10 p.m., as the battalion moved steadily towards the summit, German machine guns opened up from several locations, including some to the rear. Company commanders reacted immediately and led their troops in flanking attacks against the enemy's main positions on the summit. By midnight, the crest had been taken. Reacting in typical fashion, the enemy launched a series of counterattacks, as well as heavy artillery and mortar fire, over the next two days. Using large numbers of captured German machine guns and quantities of ammunition, Innanen and his 3rd Regiment comrades were able to stop each attack against them.

For a week after Monte Majo was captured, the soldiers of the entire Force were committed to endless patrolling throughout the hill mass as they tried to root out the remaining enemy troops. Skirmishes were a daily occurrence, as arduous terrain, vicious cold and dogged German resistance reduced the Force's strength further. Survivors remember this period as one of "utter weariness . . . of firing not at people, but grid squares on the map, wisps of smoke, muzzle blasts in the darkness." Then, on January 11, during one of these forays, Sergeant Victor Innanen, only seventeen, was killed in action and joined so many of his mates. Four days later, the Force was withdrawn from the front lines to begin reorganizing for the next phase of the Allied offensive. During this period, the total strength of the Force had been reduced from 100 officers and 1,498 men to 63 officers and 770 men — a 50 per cent loss.[20]

A week later, Colonel Robert Frederick, the founder and commander of the First Special Service Force, sent a letter of condolence to Mr. A. Coja in Toronto, erroneously believing Coja was the family name. In it, he noted:

Wounded Canadian soldiers of the First Special Service Force await medical evacuation.

Your son was a member of this command and went with his unit into combat against the enemy. He and his comrades behaved bravely and well in the face of danger and acquitted themselves proudly. The unit successfully accomplished its battle missions but, as must happen when brave men engage in combat, some of our comrades fell, killed or wounded . . .

The death of your son is deeply felt in this command. While I fully realize the magnitude of your loss and the degree of your sorrow, I assure you that our feelings of loss and bereavement can be second only to that of your lost comrade's loved ones.

Canada and the Army can well take pride in the gallant service of your son. He shall live in our memory and his sacrifice for the nation he served in the cause of liberty and justice shall inspire us in

the fight against a ruthless and dangerous enemy.
Please accept my sincere and heartfelt sym-
pathy for the irreparable loss you have suffered.
"Greater love hath no man that this, that a man
lay down his life for his friends."

On January 23, Innanen's brother-in-law, Clayton Bender, who was a gunner in the artillery, sent a letter to F.G. Sanderson, a federal Member of Parliament. In it, he sought advice on how to proceed to correct Innanen's records to reflect his real name, rather than Coja, as "his mother is dead and the father's whereabouts are rather uncertain and his interest more uncertain." Bender was married to Innanen's sister, Esther, and had been contacted by another sister, Elsie, whom Innanen had named as his next of kin. Together, the two sisters had decided the record should be corrected.

Bender asked if Sanderson could possibly help them in this matter, as "we were — and are — quite proud of the boy's determination and independence. He has a good record as far as I know and the fact that he attained the rank of Top Sergeant when he was really just sixteen says enough." Bender closed his appeal by noting, "He has made the supreme sacrifice and it can now do the military effort no harm to tell this and have the records corrected."

While Bender was writing his letter, Innanen's brother, Walter, then serving overseas with the engineers, had his unit chaplain send a letter to the records officer at Canadian Military Headquarters, essentially requesting the same action as Bender had. These appeals had the desired results, and on March 31, 1944, all of Innanen's documents were corrected to reflect his proper name, which is engraved on his headstone in Italy's Cassino Military Cemetery.

* * *

Freeman Grant's father, Hector, was first informed of his seventeen-year-old son's death by telegram on December 26, followed by a letter from the adjutant-general on January 7, 1944. Young Grant possessed little in life and even less in death. His personal belongings consisted of three locks with keys, a flashlight, a Sam Browne belt, a kit bag handle, miscellaneous photographs and postcards, a notebook, a handkerchief, a leather wallet, a haversack and a silver signet ring. He signed a will at the end of August, just before he left Britain for Italy, in which he left everything to his father. Blake Grant, a Yarmouth blacksmith, was named as executor. Hector Grant was unaware of this, as after his son's death, he noted on one form, "Would like to know if Freeman made a will."

Shortly after Grant's death, events took a bizarre twist in an unseemly manner over his estate. A Miss Bernice Sweeny wrote to authorities on January 5, before Grant's father had received the letter about his son's death. In it, she claimed ". . . I maintianed [sic] clothed and schooled him for six years before he inlisted his father did not help in anyway . . . if theres anything either money or belongings. It should come to me."

Sweeny followed this with another letter on February 21 in response to information that Grant's estate had not been settled:

> When it is settled would you kindly notify me. As I
> wish to take it up with the father . . . [who] never
> once gave the son a meal or the price of one. I cared
> for him wholly at my expense . . . He contributed
> to my support what he could . . . I have a letter he
> wrote me from North Africa telling me he bought
> a bond in my name? I tried to make the father pay
> me board. But he never did anything but promise.
> Its easy to prove him a (no-good) my lawyer knows
> the proceedings . . . If you would inform me when
> it is settled, if its in the father's favour.

At this stage, Sweeny procured the services of Yarmouth lawyer Peter Judge, who wrote to the authorities on April 12, enclosing "Miss Sweeney's [sic] statement of account for board of the late Freeman Grant from April 29th, 1937, to September 8th, 1942, amounting to $667.50."

More than a year after Grant's death, the executor of his will, Blake Grant, entered the fray with his own letter to the authorities on January 23, 1945. He asked if Grant had bought a fifty-dollar bond, as he had been told that Miss Sweeny "as his gardine [guardian] received money every month if it is not too much trouble kindly check up on it."

On August 11, 1947, Miss Sweeny (now Mrs. Murray Forbes) wrote again to the authorities and asked to be informed by letter if the will had been probated or not. The final letter on file, dated September 22, informed Forbes that as the total distribution of the service estate had been made to Blake Grant, she should contact him direct.

Since the matter was out of official hands and now a private matter, any further action Forbes may have taken to obtain the few dollars in Grant's estate remains unknown.

CHAPTER 5

"WELL MOTHER DARLING THIS GOING TO BE AN AWFUL SURPRISE TO YOU ALL AND I SURE HOPE AND PRAY THAT YOU DONT TAKE IT TO HARD."

Italy, The End

(Map III)

Harold Pringle of Ontario's Hastings and Prince Edward Regiment stood alone in a long, barren strip of ground along a dusty road in an area known by the locals as *le Breccielle*, or "broken ground." He was silhouetted in the bright, early morning sunshine against a three-and-a-half-metre concrete wall that stood at one end.

Suddenly, ten shots rang out in unison. The force of the bullets hitting Pringle's chest slapped his body back. His feet buckled and he slumped forward, dead in a heartbeat.

Incongruously, it was July 5, 1945, nearly two months after the war in Europe ended.

And the soldiers who killed Pringle were not Germans; they were Canadians.

Pringle, who had been sent overseas at eighteen — under the legal age — was the only Canadian soldier executed during the Second World War by his own side. Although several other Canadians had been condemned to death for various crimes —

including eight for murder (some for murdering their superior officers) — all of those sentences had been commuted.[1]

* * *

John Anderson's military career started in July 1941 when he joined the 2nd/10th Dragoons and attended the unit's annual training at Camp Niagara that summer. Before the war, the Dragoons had been a unit of the Non-Permanent Active Militia (NPAM or simply "the militia"). They were not mobilized for active service until June 1, 1942. At that time, the unit was converted to an infantry battalion, although it retained its former cavalry name.[2] Anderson claimed a birthdate of June 19, 1923, when he enrolled, but when the Dragoons were called up to active service, the hazel-eyed seventeen-year-old was only five feet, four inches and 140 pounds.[3]

Anderson had left school at fourteen, having completed Grade 8. He entered the workforce and was employed at McKinnon Industries in St. Catharines, Ontario, where he assembled automobile parts. He lived at home with his father, James — a security guard — and his mother, Jennie. Anderson had three brothers, two of whom were serving overseas in the army, and two sisters, one of whom was in the RCAF, stationed at Sydney, Nova Scotia.

The 2nd/10th Dragoons were assigned to 7th Canadian Infantry Division, a Home Defence formation serving in Atlantic Command. In the fall of 1942, the division's 15th and 20th Brigades were stationed at Camp Debert, Nova Scotia, while its 17th Brigade was at Camp Sussex, New Brunswick.[4] Anderson must have gotten a little homesick because on October 5, he was missing from morning parade. Seventeen days later, he was apprehended in St. Catharines and returned to Debert under escort.

Anderson appeared before his commanding officer on October 30 and was found guilty of being absent and sentenced to twenty-eight days detention. He also had to pay the cost of his and his escorts' transportation and meals — a total of $70.91. Coupled with the automatic punishment of stoppage of pay that accompanied detention, Anderson forfeited fifty-three days' pay and allowances. The only bright spot was that his commanding officer released him from detention three days early.

Ironically, on release from detention, Anderson was granted two periods of leave, one for a week and another for two weeks, a week after the first one ended. When the second leave period ended December 22, the wheels were in motion to send him overseas. He arrived in Britain on January 7, 1943, and was sent to 3rd Division Infantry Holding Unit. By February 1, Anderson was posted to the Royal Canadian Regiment, and by April he was in B Company of the Perth Regiment.

The Perth Regiment had been mobilized on the outbreak of war in Stratford, Ontario, as a corps machine-gun battalion and spent two years training in Canada. In March 1941, a year and a half into training as Vickers machine-gunners, the Perths became a motor battalion in the newly formed 5th Canadian Armoured Division. They sailed to Britain in October 1941, where they continued their motorized training regimen. The unit spent two years in Britain, moving through a number of locations in rural southern England.

In January 1943, the regiment's role changed again; it would become a standard infantry battalion in 5th Armoured Division's 11th Infantry Brigade. One of the Perths' fellow infantry battalions in the brigade was Reg Roy's Cape Breton Highlanders. Although Anderson and the Highlanders sailed to Italy in late October 1943, Roy, who had joined as a boy soldier at sixteen, was not with them. He was in Canada, desperately waiting to return overseas.

Canada, meanwhile, had been pressing Britain for another division to be sent to Italy to gain combat experience. With some reluctance, the British gave in, with the caveat that only the soldiers would be sent; vehicles would be taken over from departing British units because of a shortage of shipping. Anderson sailed from Liverpool aboard the *John Ericcson* with his regiment on October 27 and docked at Naples on November 8, where the unit bivouacked in a depressing slum area on the outskirts of the city. The stay was short-lived, and on November 19, the Perths moved across the Italian peninsula to a camp near Altamura, not far from the Adriatic — where living and training conditions were much better — about 210 kilometres behind the front lines. Before it left Naples, the regiment picked up its vehicles from a British infantry battalion: a collection of old, worn out, two-wheel-drive vehicles, instead of the four-wheel-drive vehicles they had in Britain. Many of the vehicles broke down before they reached the Canadians' destination. Some had to be towed the rest of the way.

Anderson and his mates knew their first action could not be far off. They were right; on January 4, 1944, 11th Brigade was ordered forward to relieve 1st Canadian Infantry Division's 3rd Brigade "to get its first experience of contact with the enemy." The area it was moving to was on the coastal sector of the front, north of Ortona.

The Perths arrived in their sector on January 12. Initially, it had been the intention of senior officers to give the Perths and their two sister battalions a "holding and patrolling" mission, allowing them to become accustomed to front-line duties. This changed the day the Perths arrived at the front to a mission to "putt pressure" on the enemy, to prevent him from moving troops to the west coast, where the Allied landings at Anzio were planned for January 22.

Following a fifteen-minute artillery barrage at 5:30 a.m., Janu-

Canadian soldiers advance along a rain-soaked road.

While on radio watch, two Canadians grab a bite to eat.

ary 17, the Perths advanced towards the Riccio River to seize the high ground on the far side. When this was accomplished, the Cape Breton Highlanders were to attack on the right. A and C Companies led, with Anderson's B Company to follow once the two leading companies were across the river. As soon as the artillery fire lifted, the defending German paratroopers emerged from the safety of their dugouts. Mortar and machine-gun fire pinned A Company in the valley bottom, along with most of C Company. B Company was then ordered forward to reinforce A Company, but not enough of its soldiers made it through the enemy mortar and machine-gun fire to make an appreciable difference.

Further moves by D Company and the Cape Breton Highlanders met with the same results, and both battalions were ordered to withdraw as darkness fell. Their first day in action cost the Perths 137 casualties, forty-seven fatal. Anderson was not among them. As the Perths' regimental history proudly notes, it was "the first, last and only time in the Second World War that the Perths failed to capture an objective."

In the weeks following their abortive attack across the Riccio, the Perths "endured one of the most miserable periods of their war experience" as they rotated through a typical static front routine of two weeks in forward positions, a week in the counterattack role, and then back in the front lines. The weather was a bone-numbing mixture of rain, sleet and wet snow, while temperatures were a few degrees above or below zero. Front-line duty meant crouching in slit trenches and weapon pits — military terminology for what quickly became little more than water-filled holes in clay and mud.

The regiment had occupied a portion of the front line near the town of Orsogna, about thirty kilometres inland from the Adriatic. In the area held by each company, the three platoons rotated daily so every platoon got the opportunity every third day to get a couple of hundred metres behind the front lines, where some relaxation was possible, although it still involved sitting in the mud. On February 5, Anderson and a number of his mates were at the B Company kitchen, located in a cave in the side of a ravine. The route to the cave was along a narrow ledge, from which there was a steep nine-metre drop. Soldiers returning from the forward trenches for lunch queued up along the ledge, waiting to enter the cave. All hell broke loose when a German mortar round landed. The explosion blew most of the men into the ravine, killing fourteen and injuring twenty-three, five of whom later died from their wounds. It was the worst day in the regiment's eight-week stay in the Orsogna area. One of eight soldiers from the reserve company position who volunteered to go forward to assist in the recovery recalled the carnage as "soul-shattering." Dismembered and twisted bodies were scattered all over the muddy floor of the ravine. The regimental chaplain, who prepared the bodies of the dead that night for

Canadian soldiers dig out a comrade who was buried alive in the rubble of a building.

burial, believed a small difference either way — much less than a metre — in the flight of the mortar round would have missed the soldiers. A bit shorter and it would have hit the crest above the ledge; a bit longer and it would have fallen to the bottom of the ravine.[5]

Among the dead was John Anderson, who had joined the army at seventeen and was nineteen when he was killed in action.

* * *

Alexander Rose left school in Montreal's Rosemount district when he was fifteen, having completed six years of schooling. When he enrolled on October 2, 1942, he had been working for two years as a stamper at Fairchild Aircraft Ltd. in Longueuil, across the St.

Lawrence River from Montreal. Rose came from a large Scottish family of six boys and two girls. (His parents had been married in Glasgow in 1913.) Three of his older brothers were overseas in the armed forces: twins in the Black Watch and another brother in the navy. Rose claimed a birthdate of August 3, 1924, exactly two years earlier than his real birthdate. When he joined, the blue-eyed youth stood five feet, eight a half inches and weighed 131 pounds. His claimed date of birth made him eighteen, when in fact he was only sixteen, three years below the minimum age for overseas service.[6]

Rose was allocated to the infantry, and his military training began at Number 41 Canadian Army (Basic) Training Centre at Huntingdon, Quebec, a mere fifteen kilometres north of the American border. On completion of his training in late January 1943 — and because he was thought to be eighteen — Rose was posted to the 2nd Battalion, Black Watch (Royal Highland Regiment) of Canada. The Black Watch's 2nd Battalion was a unit of the Reserve Army, in which many boys who joined the army legally between the ages of seventeen and nineteen were held and trained until they were old enough to proceed overseas.

Like John Anderson in the 2nd/10th Dragoons, Rose and the Black Watch were assigned to 7th Canadian Infantry Division. Within Atlantic Command, the Black Watch was subsequently detached from 7th Division to be part of the garrison of the Halifax Fortress, along with a coastal artillery regiment, an anti-aircraft regiment and another infantry battalion. Seven months later, Rose was sent overseas, arriving in Britain on September 1, 1943 — a month after he turned seventeen — where he was taken on strength of 5th Canadian Infantry Replacement Unit. In November, he disembarked in the Mediterranean theatre and was sent to B Company, 1st Battalion, No. 1 Canadian Base Reinforcement Depot. First Battalion held reinforcements destined for the infantry, organized on a territorial basis. Rose was destined to become a member of New Brunswick's Carleton and York Regiment in 1st Canadian Infantry Division's 3rd Infantry Brigade.

The Carleton and Yorks had been fighting in the Italian Campaign since they landed in Sicily on the first day of the invasion of the island in July 1943, were part of the initial assault troops to land on mainland Italy in September, and had subsequently fought their way up the Italian boot, including the slugfests of the Sangro River Valley and The Gully in November and December 1943. On January 4, 1944, the battalion was relieved in the front lines by the West Nova Scotia Regiment and went into reserve for ten days. Then, all of 3rd Brigade was relieved by 11th Brigade of the newly arrived 5th Canadian Armoured Division and moved to the rear for three weeks of training in the San Vito area.

The next four months saw the Carleton and Yorks divide their time between training and forward positions. The Italian winter weather and ground conditions resulted in static operations. In Ortona, the battalion received reinforcements: five officers and fifty-one soldiers. Rose was among the latter.

The late winter and early spring of 1944 saw 1st Canadian Division engaged in a "dispiriting kind of warfare" which, although it may not have been obvious to the ordinary soldier huddled in the bottom of a cold, damp slit trench, did have a purpose. The aim was to "keep the Germans on their toes and to do everything short of a major offensive to stop them withdrawing troops," so they could not redeploy troops to reinforce their defences against renewed Allied offensives on the west coast of Italy. During much of this period, all three brigades of 1st Division were in the line.

Operations consisted mostly of patrolling under hazardous weather and the ever-present threat of enemy action in the killing fields on the approaches to the Arielli River, an area of gentle uplands riddled with steep-sided gullies. The seventeen-year-old Rose was killed on February 17, one of nine fatalities the battalion

A Canadian soldier, killed by shellfire, is buried in a temporary battlefield grave.

suffered that month out of forty-one battle casualties.[7] Eight days later, Rose's mother received the telegram all families dreaded, stating her son had been killed in action. In mid-March, the telegram was followed by letters from the director of records and the adjutant-general confirming the news.

Ironically, on January 9, 1944, about the time Rose was preparing to join the Carleton and York Regiment, his father had sent a registered letter to Honorary Captain Claude Laboissière, the Roman Catholic chaplain for No. 1 Canadian Base Reinforcement Depot:

> *Sorry to give you the trouble But I have A Son he*
> *is under Age he was 17 Years of Age last August*
> *he was Born the 3rd of August 1926, Sir I May tell*
> *you that he likes the Army But I don't want him to*
> *go in the Fighting Line because he is under-Age his*

*Mother is very worried over him he has other three
Brothers some where over there. I am a Vet myself
and was Discharged from this war, Sir Don't put
him out of the army As he really likes it And I
think he would break his heart if he was put out.
Sir Don't tell him I write to you.*

By this time, Rose had been moved to the Reinforcement
Depot's 4th Battalion, which held a proportional mixture of
soldiers of all trades before they were posted to units. Laboissière sent a letter to 4th Battalion's commanding officer, in
which he enclosed the letter from Rose's father. The commanding officer requested verification of Rose's details from the
records section, and on February 10, the records officer sent a
letter to the commanding officer of the Carleton and Yorks —
where Rose was now serving — for this information. But Rose
had already been killed, before he could be removed from Italy
for being underage.

Subsequently, Canadian Military Headquarters in London
looked into this situation, specifically asking if Rose's case had
been investigated as expeditiously as possible. Chaplain Laboissière (now a major) was asked why he had dealt with this matter
personally rather than through the proper channels at the Canadian Section General Headquarters Second Echelon. Laboissière
believed he had taken the correct action, as Mr. Rose's letter had
been addressed to him personally. He was under the impression
the action he had taken would achieve the desired results, and
he was not aware he should have passed the correspondence
through the appropriate headquarters.

In addition, Laboissière very much regretted his actions had
caused a delay. As a result of this incident, the headquarters issued
instructions to all chaplains at base reinforcement units that in
the future, such matters must be passed to it. The headquarters

also took those involved to task for not handling Rose's case "as expeditiously as possible." Instead of a series of letters, a signal message should have been sent, which could have resulted "in the withdrawal of Pte. Rose."

Eleven years after the war ended, Rose's mother wrote to the Department of Veterans Affairs in June 1956, asking if she was entitled to a photograph of the grave of her late son. She noted she had received a picture with a wooden cross on the grave, but thought she would receive another one when "the Permanent stone was placed on it or do I have to buy one?" She also mentioned her son had been killed in Italy when he was seventeen and a half years old.

The reply from the director of war service records advised her to:

> kindly note that Canadian Government has made no arrangements to provide next-of-kin with photographs of overseas graves showing the permanent headstones which have been erected. You can, however, obtain the desired photo through the British Legion in England, and order forms in connection are available in this country from the Dominion Command, Canadian Legion . . . The price is $1.65 for the original photograph of the grave and 90 cents for each additional copy. Pictures of the cemetery itself are also available at 25 cents each.

Rose's personnel file held at Library and Archives Canada contains his Canadian Army Soldier's Service and Pay Book, a small booklet each soldier usually carried in a breast pocket of his battledress. It has a hole in it, most likely caused by shrapnel. The hole cuts below the word "Soldier's" on the front cover and goes through the entire book. There is another hole along the book's

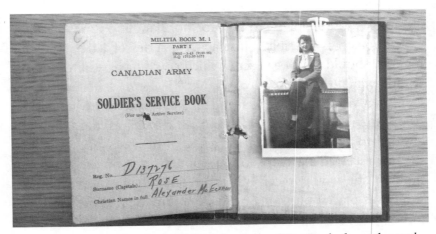

The inside of Alexander Rose's Soldier's Service and Pay Book shows shrapnel damage.

spine, about half way down, while pages 12, 13 and 14 appear to have blood stains on them. Clipped to the back inside cover of the booklet is a black-and-white photograph of what appears to be Rose's mother sitting on a fence. There is a hole through the picture as well.

* * *

Reg Roy finally got his wish and sailed to Britain in the fall of 1944. On arrival, he was given the choice of joining the North Nova Scotia Highlanders, who were then fighting across North-West Europe, or returning to the Cape Breton Highlanders, in which he had initially enrolled when he was sixteen. Now a young man of twenty-one, he immediately opted for the Cape Breton Highlanders and found himself aboard a troopship bound for the Mediterranean and a landing at Naples.[8]

As he waited at a Reinforcement Depot before rejoining his unit, Roy took the opportunity to tour Naples. He was not impressed. "The people, especially the poor, are in rags," he wrote in a letter to Canada on October 11, "and beg and borrow or steal anything you have." For hygienic purposes, the army had taken over several Italian cafes. "Personally," he added, "I wouldn't think of eating at one of these dirty, smelly, fly-infested cafes run by the local inhabitants." In the smaller towns, "whole families, plus chickens and donkey, all eat, sleep and live together in the same one or two rooms."[9]

From Naples, Roy travelled by train and truck to the east coast, where he rejoined his unit on October 17. With him he had brought a draft of thirty-two soldiers.[10] Ten days later, he was writing home about his first night in the line. Although he did not shoot any Germans, he did get a prisoner. "A nice young fellow," he wrote, "about 25 years old, good-looking, blond, etc. who had fought in France and Russia. He gave himself up to me just yesterday after I had been in [the battalion] just four days too." Roy searched his prisoner and "got some nice souvenirs . . . They will be useful to me but no good to him . . ." In return, he gave the German "half a package of cigarettes and my rum ration so we were 'even' I thought. I wish they were all that easy to capture."[11]

The next day, Roy was put in command of the battalion's pioneer platoon, a position he had held before. His predecessor as platoon commander had had his hand blown off the previous day. On October 29, the Highlanders were relieved by a British battalion and transported by trucks one hundred kilometres to the rear, to the medieval hill town of Urbino, birthplace of the famous Renaissance painter Raphael. Roy was pleased with his new accommodation in a civilian house, where he shared a room with another lieutenant.

The contrast with living in a hole in the front line was staggering. "We have two nice spring beds, mattresses, dresser and all the trimmings," he noted. "Also we have good silverware, cups and plates, a tablecloth and whatnot." The two Canadians got along very well with their hosts, a family of four. Roy was also impressed with the fact "Raphael was born three doors away. What do you know?"[12]

After a month of inactivity in the rear, 5th Canadian Armoured Division launched a major operation in early December. Its mission: cross the Montone and Lamone Rivers and advance to the Senio. The Cape Breton Highlanders' role was to force a crossing of the Lamone, with the Perth Regiment assaulting to their left. The attack was cancelled due to high water levels, but reinstated on December 10.[13]

Roy and his pioneers had just occupied new positions along the Lamone when a runner from battalion headquarters showed up with a message from the commanding officer. About two hundred metres away, a large barn near a crossroads was filled with mines and booby traps. Roy was ordered to examine the barn and defuse the mines. He brought three of his men to the barn, where they discovered "several hundred mines of all sorts — R-mines, Schu-mines, Topf-mines and a variety of other anti-tank mines. If a shell had hit the barn, there would have been the darndest explosion you could imagine."

Roy was familiar with the mines and knew how to defuse them. After explaining to the others what to do, all four toiled diligently at their hazardous task for about fifteen minutes. Roy worked at the riskiest job and suddenly realized if he made a mistake, he would not only blow himself up but "the whole damned place." As a result, he decided to move to a nearby farmhouse and continue his task by himself, with one of the soldiers carrying the slabs of solid explosives removed from the mines by the other two soldiers, so he could remove the detonators and render the explosive safe.

They worked like that for ten or fifteen minutes, but as a soldier carrying two or three slabs of explosive in his arms came in the kitchen door, Roy "heard the damnedest explosion. At about the same time, the kitchen window blew in over [his] head, hitting the opposite side of the kitchen wall." He "knew immediately what had happened" and raced for the barn. The big double doors of the barn had been blown off and smoke billowed through the opening. The corporal was extremely badly burnt and unconscious and died within an hour or so, while the private had been killed instantly. Roy marvelled at the fact that by some quirk of fate, all the explosives did not go off. "If they had, the farmhouse that I was in would have been completely flattened as well. It was a bit of a shattering experience."[14]

As the Cape Breton Highlanders spent their first Christmas in the front line, Roy recalled what had been a "rather nasty" experience at times:

> I had to go on what is called a Reconnaissance
> patrol with soft hats, blackened faces, etc. That
> lasted from 9 p.m. to 12 p.m. Christmas Eve. At
> times I was within 5 to 10 yards of Jerry and other
> times didn't quite know where he was. However, he
> didn't see us . . . The patrol ended just as Christ-
> mas day was starting. A cold, starlit night and on
> our way back we would drop into platoon and
> company headquarters reporting our safe return.
> Everyone greeted us with Merry Christmas and a
> cup of hot tea and a tot of rum . . . and very often
> generous slices of fruit cake . . . it wasn't Canada, it
> hadn't snowed, the country was foreign and always
> dark . . . but those Merry Christmases . . . carried
> a warmth of feeling and such memories of better
> Christmases in Canada that I hadn't forgotten
> them for a long, long time.[15]

In early January 1945, Roy was ordered to conduct a recon-naissance near a town on the southern side of the Valli di

Lieutenant Reg Roy (right) and other members of the Cape Breton Highlanders pose with a captured Nazi flag in Holland at the end of the war.

Comacchio, a large area of brackish lagoons and wetlands northwest of Ravenna. As he approached his objective, he was unnerved by the sight of a leg in a field, severed from a soldier's body. When he reached a partly destroyed bridge, Roy came under machine-gun fire, bullets pinging off girders overhead. He moved up a road and, when shells began to land nearby, sought cover near a rectangular metal box. It was only when the firing stopped that Roy realized he had thrown himself down beside a German anti-tank R-mine, which held four kilograms of TNT and was known for being easily detonated.[16]

As the Canadian presence in Italy was winding down in preparation for the move to North-West Europe, one of Roy's last letters from the peninsula was to his parents, in which he described the ancient soldierly art of "liberation." He noted "the peasants, who we 'liberate' in more ways than one, are usually quite generous with their eggs and potatoes and such. If they aren't, we merely liberate the said articles from the peasants." Roy went on, "There's no such word as stealing. Heaven forbid. It's all liberation. There's an old saying that Jerry steals everything he sees, whereas the Canuck steals everything they hide."[17]

* * *

On arrival at Naples in March 1944, Harold Pringle, who had turned twenty-two in January, was sent to the Canadian Reinforcement Depot at Avellino, nestled in the Apennine Mountains some fifty-five kilometres east of the port city. From there, he was dispatched to the Hastings and Prince Edward Regiment, which he joined on March 23 on the Arielli River and was assigned to D Company. Pringle and his fellow reinforcements were sorely needed by the regiment. The battles leading up to Ortona and in Ortona had taken a heavy toll on the unit. Even after Ortona, during a supposedly "quiet" period while both sides held their positions in the line and restricted offensive activities to patrolling, casualties occurred daily.

Despite a long record of being absent without authority and lengthy periods of detention, Pringle was remembered as a "good" soldier. His platoon sergeant at the time, Tony Basciano, recalled him as "the nicest guy, a good-looking young fellow . . . His dress was just perfect . . . He was a likeable guy. Always trying to get along. Just A-1." Basciano noted there was also a dark side to Pringle: "He had a hell of a temper. God, he had an awful temper. He would have made sergeant easy, if he wanted to, if he didn't have that temper. He took orders but he didn't like it."[18]

On April 11, the regiment was dug in near the town of San Tommaso a few kilometres west of Ortona. Three of the companies sent patrols out that night. D Company's, led by

The oil painting Reinforcements Moving up in the Ortona Salient *by Lawren P. Harris depicts the devastation caused by fighting in the area.*

Captain Beauclerk and including Pringle, was a fighting patrol to "Daisy," a fortified house in the German lines. The men slipped away after dark, moving silently, slowly and cautiously towards their objective. As he always did whenever he had the chance, Pringle had extra grenades tucked into his battledress tunic.

As the Canadian patrol approached Daisy, its defenders opened fire with machine guns and grenades. The Canadians returned fire, but were outnumbered and outgunned. When Beauclerk and two privates were hit, Pringle and the others gathered them up and began to withdraw. Pringle and another private provided covering fire as the patrol extricated itself and made it back to Canadian lines, with the extra grenades Pringle

Campobasso, *painted by Charles Comfort. The hill town was a major Canadian leave centre.*

had brought along proving their worth. Beauclerk was badly wounded and evacuated to a hospital, while the two privates were dead.[19]

Patrols continued unabated, a seemingly unending struggle in the steep gullies and ravines that marked no man's land. Then, on April 20, the regiment and the rest of I Canadian Corps were deployed to the other side of the Italian peninsula for the next major Allied offensive. The unit did not arrive until May 8, as it rested en route and spent a few days near the Canadian leave centre at Campobasso.

The Allies' objective was the Liri Valley, a ten-kilometre-wide stretch of open fields pockmarked with orchards, vineyards and

Charles Comfort's oil painting, The Hitler Line, *depicts tough and experienced infantrymen of 1st Canadian Division advancing across a devastated battlefield.*

dense woods between two mountain ranges. Route 6 ran up the valley, which offered the only motorized approach to Rome. After 8th Indian Division had burst through the imposing defences of the Gustav Line at the start of the valley, it was the Canadians' turn. Their mission was to pass through the Indians, take the lead and breach the major defences of the Hitler Line further up the valley. Pringle and the Hasty Ps entered the battle on May 17, a confusing melee of company actions fought through thick woods. When D Company rejoined the regiment, it had suffered seven killed and thirty wounded.[20]

By May 23, the Canadians were facing the formidable main defences of the Hitler Line. Pringle and the units of 1st Brigade were in the second assault wave, following 2nd Brigade. As they waited, units came under artillery and mortar fire, which had a

devastating effect on one of the Hasty Ps sister battalions, the
48th Highlanders. D Company was ordered forward to support
the Highlanders. By 3 p.m., after several nasty firefights, D Company, the rest of the regiment and several other Canadian units
had breached the Hitler Line. The road to Rome — which both
sides had declared an open city — lay open. Although losses were
heavy, Pringle survived.[21]

Despite the Canadian soldiers' victory, they were deprived
of the right to enter Rome as the Eternal City's liberators. That
honour was stolen from them by the egotism of American Lieutenant-General Mark Clark, the commander of Fifth U.S. Army.
Canadian troops were incensed at this snub to their triumph,
a feeling that was multiplied many times over when military
authorities banned them from all Italian towns, ostensibly as
a way of preventing the spread of venereal disease. Following
on the heels of missing the opportunity to occupy Rome, this
decision led many to vote with their feet. Absenteeism and
desertion among Canadian soldiers increased dramatically.
Two days after the liberation of Rome, Pringle joined the exo-
dus. Three weeks later, he was caught in the newly freed city and
placed under arrest. With so many other incidents of absenteeism and desertion on his record, Pringle probably realized he
faced some years of hard time in a military prison. He escaped
from custody at a field punishment camp and headed off to
Rome again.[22]

Under the American occupation, Rome indulged in endless
merrymaking. Parties and dances continued all night, while
women and wine were in abundant supply, in marked contrast
to the situation during the brutal German occupation. Once in
Rome, Pringle started to live with a woman, whom he may have
met on his previous foray into the city. Whatever the case, he
stayed with her and began to learn a little of her language before
venturing out. Then, in August, he met an American deserter,

Staff Sergeant Bobbie Williams of the 4th Ranger Battalion, a veteran of the debacle at Anzio the previous January. He convinced Pringle there was no point in returning to his unit; Rome had too much to offer.[23]

Many deserters were active in the flourishing black market that had grown up in Rome, with much of the goods on offer being supplied by trucks and drivers of the Allied armies. A survey conducted by the provost marshal's office discovered an astonishing 50 per cent of black marketeers were servicemen. In August, Pringle and Williams bumped into Petty Officer Bill Croft, a deserter from the Royal Navy, in a restaurant. Croft convinced his new acquaintances the situation was ripe for deserters to organize themselves into a gang to participate in the lucrative black market. In fact, there was already one such group in operation, known as the Lane Gang, which allegedly contained deserters from every army in Italy — including Germans. The Lane Gang hijacked military and civilian vehicles alike, trafficked in drugs and ran prostitutes. Its members became rich and lived luxuriously.

Croft's idea was to operate on a much smaller scale than the Lane Gang to attract less attention from authorities. His plan won over Pringle and Williams, and in September, the three deserters scouted out Rome and its environs, looking for likely targets. On one such trip, the trio encountered John "Lucky" McGillivary, a fellow Canadian Pringle had met in prison in Britain. McGillivary was a deserter from the Cape Breton Highlanders and his disciplinary record was even worse than Pringle's.[24]

Other deserters joined the group, including Lucky McGillivary. By then the Sailor Gang, named after Croft's naval background, had six members: two Americans, two Britons and two Canadians. In October, the gang recruited its final member, another deserter from the British army. Regular army personnel assisted the gang, providing goods for the black market and even blank three-day pass forms, crucial to the unrestricted movement and continued freedom of the gang's members. At night, Pringle went out in an American army uniform and was known as "Joe," but during the day, he preferred civilian clothes.[25]

Life in the Sailor Gang was rough-and-tumble. There was plenty of drinking, day and night, and some of them became belligerent and started fighting, perhaps none more so than McGillivary. One night in late October, after a particularly long alcohol-fuelled session, a fight between McGillivary and another gang member, Charlie Honess, resulted in the murder of McGillivary. His body was later found by an Italian farmer, dumped in an irrigation ditch with three gunshot wounds.[26]

By then, military police and special investigators were closing in on the Lane and Sailor Gangs. One by one, the men were arrested. Pringle's turn came on December 12. After he was captured, he and three other gang members — Croft, Honess and Holton — were charged with McGillivary's murder. Pringle's court-martial began on February 14, 1945. Seven days earlier, Pringle's experienced defence lawyer, Lieutenant Michael Cloney, who had never lost a case, was replaced by Captain Norman Bergman, without explanation. This would be Bergman's first trial.[27]

Despite his inexperience at trials, Bergman conducted a masterly defence. He shredded the conflicting statements of gang member Holton, who had been given immunity by the British in exchange for his testimony. Holton testified Honess shot McGillivary in his room, and then all four of them jumped in a jeep to seek medical attention for the wounded man. But instead of going to the nearest military hospital, they headed for one outside the city. Somewhere along the way, they turned into a field where they placed McGillivary on the ground and then decided to disfigure McGillivary's face to prevent identification. Although he aimed at McGillivary's face, Pringle flinched as he fired and the bullet went into McGillivary's left lung. Croft was next and fired into McGillivary's head, using Pringle's pistol.

Bergman also countered the testimony of the British army pathologist who conducted the autopsy on McGillivary and stated the man was alive when the final two shots were fired. Bergman called on his only witness, a Canadian army pathologist, who provided expert evidence that the abdominal wound caused by Honess resulted in McGillivary's death during the jeep ride. When Pringle and Croft fired their shots, he was already dead. Regardless of these facts, the officers of the court martial found Pringle guilty of murder and sentenced him to death.[28]

Separate British court-martials followed Honess and Croft. Both were found guilty of murder and sentenced to death. Honess was executed by firing squad in April, while Croft followed in May, after the war in Europe had ended.[29]

Captain Bergman filed a petition against Pringle's guilty verdict on March 26, shortly after Croft's court-martial ended. It was based on testimony from Croft's trial that claimed McGillivray was already dead when Pringle fired a bullet into his chest. But in-depth reviews of Bergman's petition at Canadian Military Headquarters in London did not change the conviction of authorities that Pringle was guilty. Ottawa was requested to confirm the finding and sentence.

There was only one small problem: a federal election in June. The executing of a Canadian soldier before the election would not look good, especially to the thousands of servicemen who already detested Prime Minister Mackenzie King. Ottawa hesitated. Meanwhile, Canadian authorities in London were growing impatient. The longer Pringle's execution was delayed, the longer a number of Canadian soldiers had to remain in Italy to guard Pringle, administer themselves and form a firing squad.

On June 20, after the election, which returned King's Liberals to power, the prime minister met with senior staff to consider Pringle's case. Although eight Canadian servicemen convicted of murder during the war had their death sentences commuted, Pringle presented a unique problem. The British had already executed their two servicemen involved in the incident, and to spare the Canadian soldier might anger them, as well as make Canada appear weak when the country had aspirations of greatness based on the part she played in the war.

The wily King understood the national and international ramifications of executing or sparing Pringle. The sentence would stand, but the government would not issue a press release about it, it would not be mentioned in official reports of court-martials, Pringle's records would be sealed for forty years, the soldiers involved in his execution would be told never to discuss it and Pringle's family would not mention it or they would lose his military pension.[30]

Pringle was awoken in his cell at 6 a.m. on July 5 and informed of the confirmation of his execution. His last request was for tea, cigarettes and strawberry jam, but he turned down the option of a shot of morphine traditionally offered to servicemen about to be shot. He then wrote his last letter home:

My Darling Mother + Dad + Brothers + Sisters

Well Mother Darling this going to be an awful surprise to you all and I sure hope and pray that you dont take it to hard. But the papers have just come back from Canada and the army has found me guilty so they say and I guess the good Lord wishes for me and I sure will pray and do everything in the world for you all. Well Mother darling I received a very nice letter from Marion

*yesterday. But I don't think I will have the time
to answer it. I am sending this short note by
Father Tom.
So again Dear Mother + Dad + Brothers + Sisters, May the Good lord keep you all in the very
best of health.*

*To My Darling Mother + Dad + Brothers + Sisters
From your Lonesome Son Harold.*

Good by My darling

With lots of Love to all.

PS xxxxxxxxxxxxxxxx

*If you would Mother please let my darling Doreen
Woods know wont you. Also give her my love.*

Pringle was taken from his cell at 7:45, his arms secured behind his back with leather straps. Although he shook off a cap the officer in charge of the firing squad tried to put over his face, he allowed him to pin a piece of red cloth over his heart. Pringle was then driven to the place of execution at *le Breccielle*, where the firing party had assembled. On arrival, he was tied to a post at his feet and torso.

His execution followed immediately.[31]

After his death, Pringle's mother, Mary, as his sole benefi- ciary, received $161.91, being the outstanding balance in his pay account.

Her application for a war service gratuity, which was calcu- lated as $505.77, was denied due to the circumstances of her son's death.

An early pocket-book edition of Colin McDougall's novel, Execution, *which was based on Harold Pringle's story.*

Maria Fedele, the Italian girlfriend and later wife of Bill Croft, leader of the Sailor Gang, was paid fifteen thousand lire by Canadian authorities to cover her expenses while testifying at Pringle's court-martial.[32]

* * *

Between 1952 and 1957, Colin McDougall wrote a novel, *Execution*, based on Pringle's story. McDougall was a former officer of the Princess Patricia's Canadian Light Infantry who had served in Italy. The book was universally praised on its publication and won the Governor General's Award for Fiction in 1958. McDougall never wrote another novel.

PART III
NORTH-WEST EUROPE: D-DAY TO V-E DAY

"During this period the First Canadian Army advanced some 450 miles in a direct line, and fought and won a series of battles as terrible as any in the history of the ancient and famous lands where the campaign took place."

Colonel C.P. Stacey, *The Victory Campaign, 1944-45: The Official History of the Canadian Army in the Second World War, Volume III*

MAP IV

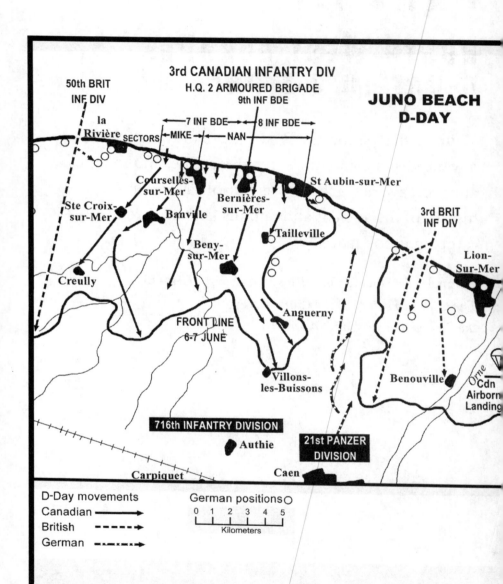

3rd CANADIAN INFANTRY DIV
H.Q. 2 ARMOURED BRIGADE
9th INF BDE

JUNO BEACH
D-DAY

50th BRIT
INF DIV

la
Rivière

SECTORS

7 INF BDE

8 INF BDE

MIKE

NAN

Courselles-
sur-Mer

St Aubin-sur-Mer

3rd BRIT
INF DIV

Ste Croix-
sur-Mer

Banville

Bernières-
sur-Mer

Tailleville

Lion-
Sur-Mer

Creully

Beny-
sur-Mer

Anguerny

Benouville

Orme

Cdn
Airborn
Landing

FRONT LINE
6-7 JUNE

Villons-
les-Buissons

716th INFANTRY DIVISION

Authie

21st PANZER
DIVISION

Carpiquet

Caen

D-Day movements   German positions ○
Canadian ——————➤   0 1 2 3 4 5
British - - - - - ➤   Kilometers
German -·-·-·-·-➤

MAP V

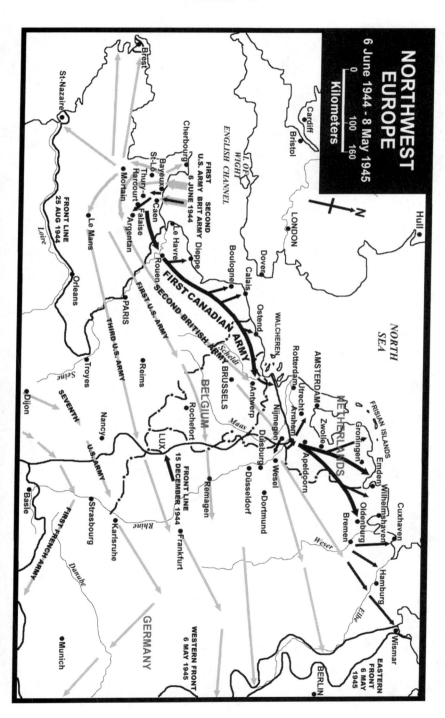

NORTHWEST EUROPE
6 June 1944 - 8 May 1945

Kilometers
0   100   160

CHAPTER 6

"THIS IS IT. I'M GOING TO DIE."
Normandy, D-Day
(Map IV)

Private Jim Parks was a breath away from drowning.

He could not find anything to grab onto in the grey swells off Normandy, France. Sliding up and over waves more than two metres high, Parks saw dust and black smoke rising against a heavy overcast sky. The young soldier from the Royal Winnipeg Rifles was trying to orient himself when he was nearly sideswiped by a Landing Craft Assault (LCA) that had survived the shelling and underwater mines. The vessel's wake crashed over his head and propelled him downward. "This is it," he thought. "I'm going to die," without ever having set foot on Juno Beach.

Determined to give himself a fighting chance, Parks, who had enrolled at age fifteen, was a strong swimmer. He kicked towards the surface, hoping to fill his lungs with air, but all he took in was another mouthful of salt water, accompanied by the cold realization he was still sinking, pulled down by the weight of his battledress and boots.[1]

* * *

It was June 6, 1944, and the day was not going exactly as planned. While the armada heading across the English Channel towards Normandy was the largest in history, the Allied operation was a gamble. The odds against success had continued to stack up even as the final decision was debated on whether or not to launch Operation Overlord, and the naval and assault phase, Operation Neptune. The invasion's land force commander, British General Bernard Montgomery, had shared dire predictions of high casualties, but the "Victor of El Alamein" and his staff instilled confidence among the troops through meticulous planning and an arduous training scheme. American General Dwight D. Eisenhower, the Supreme Allied Commander, also wore the cloak of confidence, but was braced for disaster. On the eve of the assault, he drafted a letter taking full responsibility for the operation's failure — and kept it handy, just in case.[2]

Eisenhower's private fears were warranted. British army predictions for the Canadian and British landings on D-Day were 9,250 killed, wounded or missing out of seventy thousand soldiers. Of these, three thousand could drown. The ominous prediction for Canadian casualties was nearly two thousand out of an invasion force of fifteen thousand, including members of the 1st Canadian Parachute Battalion.[3]

Frightful as those predictions were, there was no turning back for the three airborne divisions that had left hours earlier to secure the flanks, or for the seaborne invaders as they approached their designated objectives. The entire Overlord front extended for more than eighty kilometres and its geography ranged from towering cliffs to sandy beaches, with the higher ground in front of the Americans at Utah and Omaha. The British faced Gold and Sword while the 3rd Canadian Infantry Division, directed by I

Landing craft from HMCS Prince Henry *prepare to go ashore during a training exercise prior to D-Day.*

British Corps, had the relatively flat and sandy coastline between the British beaches, code named Juno. On the waterfront in front of the Canadians were the villages of Courseulles-sur-Mer, Bernières-sur-Mer and Saint-Aubin-sur-Mer.

Besides the sheer size and complexity of Overlord, the weather was bad. Originally set for June 5, the invasion had been postponed by a day because of a vicious storm. This further reduced the window of opportunity Allied planners had to work with after meteorologists identified June 7 as the last day of favourable tides for a month. With high tides and the concurring light of dawn, the assault vessels heading to Juno had a better chance of avoiding the rocky offshore ledges. For the troops, it also meant less distance to travel once they disembarked from the landing craft. However, high tides still brought the risk of being sunk or blown to bits by deadly beach obstacles hidden beneath the water.

Getting the infantry ashore and supporting them with fire-power was another massive undertaking. The D-Day naval fleet, commanded by British Admiral Sir Bertram Ramsay, was comprised of 7,016 vessels, including six battleships, two moni-tors, twenty-two cruisers, ninety-three destroyers, seventy-one corvettes and thousands of landing craft. The RCN contributed more than 110 ships, including destroyers, corvettes, motor torpedo boats, armed merchant cruisers converted into land-ing ships and sixteen minesweepers. In all, nearly ten thousand Canadian sailors supported the assault.[4]

Overhead, 171 squadrons of Allied fighters and fighter-bomb-ers were busy attacking the Luftwaffe or ground positions. The preparations included a pre-invasion aerial bombing campaign that targeted Germany as well as roads, bridges, railways and radar installations in France. Hoping to convince the Germans they were right, that the assault would fall some 230 kilome-tres to the east, on the Pas de Calais or even further east in the Scheldt estuary, Allied planners used deception by employing a fictional army group in southeast England. Other tricks were also used to support the ruse and the air force did its part by dropping almost an equal number of bombs on the Pas de Calais as it did on Normandy.

All this, however, did not guarantee success on D-Day, a goal that had occupied the minds of leaders and strategists since Dunkirk in 1940. Under General Field Marshal Erwin Rom-mel, the Germans had fortified their coastal defences, but more worrisome for Montgomery in 1944 were the panzer and pan-zer grenadier divisions and the possibility they could be used to counterattack the beach landings, resulting in widespread slaughter. Well before D-Day, Allied planners identified the

Jim Parks (right) and his brother Jack prior to heading overseas.

ground the enemy was most likely to use to achieve that, and it
fell directly in front of the Canadian plan of attack.[5]

* * *

Jim Parks knew it was going to be a tough day.

He had enrolled underage without difficulty, with his sixteen-
year-old brother Jack, and was to arrive on the beach immediately
west of Courseulles-sur-Mer with his five-man mortar detachment. Jack, who was also part of the assault wave, was to arrive
a little later. After leaving the south coast of England, Parks and
the other men on the Landing Craft Tank (LCT) had endured a
cold, wet and nauseating voyage while crossing the stormy English Channel in the creaking, flat-bottomed vessel.

The last couple of weeks in England had been a mixture of
boredom and excitement. Many Canadians had spent five years in
England, and they were anxious for combat. They had witnessed

the horrific aftermath of the Dieppe Raid in 1942 and the departure of fellow Canadians headed to Sicily in 1943. Finally, something was on — something in which they would participate.

In May, tens of thousands of Allied troops began moving into designated areas along the south coast. By May 26, these high-security locations resembled concentration camps. All leaves were cancelled and no one was allowed in or out without a pass. Charles ("Bill") Chitty, who enrolled in New Brunswick at age sixteen, was with the 14th Field Regiment, Royal Canadian Artillery, when his unit was ordered — on May 29 — to prepare to move out of a sealed encampment at Farnham.

His thirty days at Farnham had been uncomfortable. Chitty and his fellow Canadians were closely supervised by British soldiers who were considered non-combatants. He and others at the camp had grown tired of these men, "their attitude and their cooking." The latter consisted of porridge and weak tea for breakfast, sandwiches and more weak tea for lunch and "ghastly chunks of mutton for dinner." Tension ran high and tempers flared amid rumours about where the next big "show" would be. "We knew what was about to happen but we didn't know when or where."[6]

Parks remembered that men were parcelled out in order of their role in the operation. "They referred to it as a sausage machine . . . you'd go in, come out, and be assigned."

The massive transfer of men, weaponry and other war *maté-riel* went fairly well, and by June 1, the first Canadian units began boarding ships or landing craft.[7] It was cold, with light rain when Parks boarded his LCT at Southampton. The wind picked up and the sea became quite rough. Ships had already begun to move into the Channel on June 4 when the invasion was postponed. Chitty, who had been dining on hard rations, joined a throng of men who marched off the ship into a huge shed converted into a shower, where he washed a week's worth of grime off his body.[8]

Bill Chitty (right) poses with a pal. The young farm boy from New Brunswick landed on D-Day and served throughout the fighting in North-West Europe.

Less than twenty-four hours after it was postponed, Operation Overlord was on again. Eisenhower gave the final "go" after receiving a favourable weather report and consulting his top commanders. "One of the ship's crew came around and said, 'This is it, we're going in!'" recalled Chitty.[9]

Bill Tindall, who had enrolled in 1940 at age seventeen, was not among the men heading to the docks just then, but he witnessed part of the 6th British Airborne Division's task. "We were stationed in Denham, northwest of London — right by a RAF airfield. We could hear just a steady drone so we looked out . . . and these planes were taking off, towing gliders with paratroopers on board . . ."

Ahead of the gliders were transport planes carrying the paratroopers, including 543 members of the 1st Canadian Parachute Battalion. Tindall had joined the Governor General's Foot Guards, but was transferred to the Royal Canadian Engineers.

Fully loaded and camouflaged, a vast assortment of vessels is prepared to embark from Southampton.

Once in England, he was assigned to the Canadian Chief Engineer Works, 21st Army Group Headquarters. "At the time we didn't really know what was happening, but we knew something was . . . because all our leaves were cancelled, you couldn't get any more than 24 hours if you could get a pass."[10]

Jim Parks remembered, "We finally left during the night of June 5–6. It was still windy and rough, but we were on the high seas heading towards the beach. It was pretty exciting."

Measuring forty-six metres in length, the LCT Parks was on carried two sections of the Winnipeg Rifles' mortar platoon, consisting of two carriers and a trailer stocked with ammunition and enough food for twenty-one days. Also on board were two large armoured bulldozers and a detachment of engineers.

The LCT was roughly 230 metres from shore when all hell broke loose. On the rising tide, it ploughed into a mine lying just below the surface. The explosion blew a hole in the steel-plated bow ramp, seriously wounding the sailor assigned to lower it. Minutes later, a German 75 mm shell flew through the open bow and slammed into the front of one of the giant armoured bulldozers. Luckily, the armour-piercing shell struck the machine's blade at such an angle that it only left a large gash in the steel plating.

Parks, who was crouched on deck between the carriers, felt the craft shudder, then heard "little pops" as machine-gun bullets ricocheted off the sides of the vessel and the steel plating on the earthmovers. The bulldozers, which could operate in up to two and a half metres of water, would be first off the LCT. Equipped with ropes tied to grappling hooks, the machines would chug towards shore while sappers bravely attached the hooks to the wooden, steel and concrete obstacles that formed a formidable part of the enemy's beach defences. The idea was to clear a path for the carriers and the smaller craft loaded with infantry. In addition to the crashing surf and exposure to enemy fire, the sappers had to contend with the beach obstacles themselves, which were built with jagged edges and festooned with explosives.

"Our job was to land with our section of two mortar carriers — right on the beach — and then set up our mortars to provide cover for the combat engineers and the infantry coming ashore," Parks recalled. "Our time was to be two minutes before the landing craft with the infantry came in. At least that was the plan. Of course everything — the enemy defences — was to have been blown away by then and we were to wade ashore and do our job. Everything was to have been neutralized, but it wasn't neutralized at all."

The men attacking the beach had no way of knowing how thick

the enemy's massive, steel-reinforced concrete gun positions were. The Courseulles strongpoints were no exception. Located at the western edge of the seaside village — on both sides of the entrance to the harbour — the bunkers were too thick to be destroyed by naval gunfire.[11]

The Winnipeg Rifles — with an extra company of Canadian Scottish from Victoria, British Columbia, attached — and the Regina Rifles Regiment were 7th Canadian Infantry Brigade's lead assault battalions on D-Day. They were supported by tanks of the 1st Hussars from London, Ontario, part of 2nd Canadian Armoured Brigade, and 12th and 13th Field Regiments of the Royal Canadian Artillery. While the Winnipegs headed towards the west side of the Seulles River, the Reginas aimed for the beach directly in front of Courseulles on the east side of the river. C Company of the Canadian Scottish was given the task of eliminating the pillbox on the beach further to the west. From there, they would attack Château Vaux, where the enemy had established a field gun battery protected by wire and machine guns.

Leading the 8th Canadian Infantry Brigade's assault on the eastern sector of Juno Beach were the Queen's Own Rifles of Canada — supported by Le Régiment de la Chaudière, the brigade's reserve battalion — and the North Shore (New Brunswick) Regiment. In support were tanks from 2nd Canadian Armoured Brigade's Fort Garry Horse and 14th and 19th Field Regiments. In front of the Queen's Own was Bernières-sur-Mer, while the North Shores had the western outskirts of Saint-Aubin-sur-Mer to the east.

"For our part, we knew exactly where we were going and as we moved closer to the beach we could see the church spires," recalled Parks. "It was getting daylight and we saw tanks with flotation devices on them."

The tanks Parks saw were the new Shermans equipped with a temporary, inflatable canvas screen around the hull to displace water and a special gearing device — known as Duplex Drive (DD) — which enabled the thirty-ton armoured vehicles to operate with tracks on land or propellers in the water. Designed to swim in calm seas at a maximum speed of six knots, the DDs were scheduled to arrive on shore before the infantry, but it soon became apparent the heavy seas and enemy shelling would interfere with that plan.

Parks had a front row seat as two of the "swimming" tanks of the 1st Hussars entered the water. "Right away they were swamped and began sinking. None of the men got out of the first and only two got out of the second. It was hard to watch. And there were five guys to a tank."

Meanwhile, waves were crashing over the bow ramps of the smaller LCAs, each loaded with roughly thirty-five men, including a four-man boat crew. Soaked to the skin and with bits of vomit and cold ocean spray dripping off their faces, some of the men on board swore they would rather die on the beach than endure another nauseating second on board. Life for some ended well before that when various landing craft were destroyed by mines or artillery shells, or were raked by machine-gun fire. One young soldier to die in an LCA was Rifleman Russell (Junior) McCallum of the Queen's Own Rifles. Just twenty years of age, he had joined the Toronto Scottish at age sixteen. Discharged on account of his age, he had quickly re-enlisted and was overseas by July 1941.[12]

Young Bill Heron of the Canadian Scottish was fortunate enough to be on a larger LCT, but still remembers the crowded vessel and the relentless pounding the various landing craft endured. "We had seventy-five miles of water to cross to reach France. It was terrible storms that day as well and most of us were terribly seasick and really didn't care whether we lived or died. We were still very scared naturally . . . being human."

The young man could have waited another year before skip-

Orville Fisher's iconic oil painting D-Day — The Assault *depicts the moment of truth for the Canadians who fought their way onto Juno Beach.*

ping school to enrol in the army in 1940 at age seventeen. Born on May 29, 1923, and raised in the rural town of Brooklin, Ontario, north of Oshawa, he had worked for his father, who owned a small farm as well as a hay and straw business. Waiting until his eighteenth birthday would have undoubtedly unrolled a different set of life experiences for Heron, but more than likely, they would not have interfered with his participation on D-Day. While based in England, Heron met the girl who became his beloved war bride. Her name was Olive, but she insisted everybody call her Bobbi. The young couple had a son named Billy, born on February 5, 1944. Heron saw the baby once before embarking for Normandy.[13]

Bill Chitty and Bob Muir were also underage when they joined. They were considered to be the youngest in 14th Field Regiment and both were on board the same LCT on D-Day.[14] Approaching Bernières-sur-Mer, Chitty was sitting in a Priest, a self-propelled, armoured artillery vehicle equipped with a 105 mm howitzer and a .50 calibre machine gun. Every available space in the Priest and on deck was jammed with shells and spare ammunition for the infantry. The latter included PIAT (Projector, Infantry, Anti-Tank) guns, mortar bombs and machine-gun rounds. There was also an "extra supply of ammunition stacked beside each Priest," which was to be used in the barrage to be fired from the LCT.

Chitty, who was born in Brighton, England, on May 28, 1924, enrolled when he was only sixteen, on March 8, 1941, after serving a year with the 2nd Battalion, New Brunswick Rangers. He joined by giving a false date of birth, May 22, 1922. Just a toddler when his family moved from Brighton into a London row house owned by his grandparents, Chitty used to watch his father, a First World War veteran, head off to work at the London, Midland and Scottish Railway. His mother, Dorothy, was a concert pianist, and while there were youngsters to care for, Chitty recalled children in those days were to be "'seen, not heard.' That was the rule, and family life was quite rigid and we had to stay out of the way most of the time."[15]

Feeding stale bread crusts to ducks in Regent's Park, trips to the zoo with his father to see the "man-eating tiger" and recitals in the upstairs drawing room where his mother entertained guests while playing her grand piano were happier moments. Darker days included the time he almost died of pneumonia, the illness that killed his baby sister, Barbara. Then there was the day — while walking home from school — when Chitty decided to tempt fate with a speeding ambulance. He had gotten used to the emergency vehicles roaring past his house, with their clanging bells. "I thought the people in them were very kind and wouldn't hurt anybody." Chitty decided to test the driver's kindness by stepping onto the street, assuming it would stop and let him cross. "Luckily the driver was able to swerve in time . . . I never tried that again."[16]

A few years later, his father quit the railways, intent on trying his luck abroad — in Canada — where the weather was hot and dry and where "everyone turned brown" — at least that was the story Chitty and his older sister, Pamela, were told when their mother broke the news. With their luggage and high hopes, the Chittys boarded a steamship and crossed the Atlantic. By June 1930, they were facing a hard-scrabble existence on a rundown farm at Midgic, New Brunswick, approximately ten kilometres northeast of Sackville.

While crossing the English Channel on D-Day, Chitty thought about what he had left behind. He could see his mother and father on the farm and remember how he sometimes joked with his sisters while milking the cows. He could also remember the hard work of sawing logs, tilling the fields with a horse-drawn disc harrow and going without electricity or running water. The two-hole toilet, which had to be cleaned once a year, was in the grain barn. Chitty's main chore was gathering firewood and making sure there was enough water. He remembers waking up on winter mornings and moving pails of frozen water from a bench in the scullery to above the stove. Sometimes — if it was a long winter — there would not be enough wood. Chitty took the job seriously, but if he slipped up, his father would pounce. "My name was Git Wood and I didn't know any different until I was fourteen years of age."[17]

For most farm boys, attending school was secondary to farm work. "There were no funds to pay for hired help. When seasonal work had to be done, such as planting, cutting wood, haying or tending crops, school time was sacrificed . . ." Chitty remembers

Manual farm labour toughened Bill Chitty, seen here carrying a large log.

being ridiculed at school for falling behind and the frustration felt by teachers who were constantly trying to bring farm kids up to speed.

The Chittys were poor, but resourceful — willing to trade a day's work for a day's work. One source of food was the nearby Tantramar Marshes, influenced by a tide that inundated the land, but brought in saltwater fish. "We would go out at night with a large scoop net and bring home a supply of gaspereau, which would be put in our smokehouse. On occasion we would scoop a large Atlantic salmon."[18]

Some of the family's modest income came from the sale of eggs and butter — even rabbits that Chitty trapped and sold to farmers who raised silver foxes. The produce was loaded onto a horse-drawn cart and delivered to regular customers, including students and staff at Mount Allison University in Sackville. In winter, the cart was loaded onto a sled. "We would start the twelve-mile journey across the marshes and through a covered bridge . . . On bitterly cold days we would get across the open marshes and stop and turn into the first house . . . I would go to the door and tell them we were cold and they would invite us in and give us something hot to eat . . . The trip took four hours each way" and often Chitty and his sisters would take turns jumping off the sled and running alongside to keep warm.

Chitty's formal schooling ended after Grade 7. There was no money to put towards higher education, but there was plenty of farm work. A radio, purchased in the late 1930s, brought news of war overseas. Chitty saw an opportunity for adventure and wasted no time enlisting. "When I told my parents what I had done, they were upset. But I told them I would not be going overseas due to my age and this seemed to put them at ease. At least my mother seemed more at ease, but my dad didn't say anything!"

At Camp Petawawa, the teenager had just returned from his first leave when orders came to proceed overseas. He was granted five days embarkation leave, plus travel time, but on his way back to New Brunswick, he had a problem to solve. How was he going to explain to his parents he was heading overseas? "I was required to take my kit home, including my rifle. So in order to avoid letting my folks know what was happening, I got to Sackville by train and a CNR policeman, who I knew at the Sackville station, agreed to keep my kit there so I wouldn't have to take it home."

Before he stepped foot in the door, Chitty was greeted by his sister Peggy, who figured something was up. "What are you home again for?" she asked. "Is this all you do is go back and forth from home to your army base?"

It was his sister Pamela who returned him to Midgic Station, where he confided in her. He pleaded with her to keep the secret. At Sackville, Chitty recovered his kit from the co-operative CNR policeman and took the next available train to Petawawa. A few days later, he was off to Halifax and the "old country" his family left behind.[19]

The world Chitty entered after enlistment was far removed from rural New Brunswick. And now he was hunkered down in his Priest self-propelled gun with Juno Beach in front of him. He was frightened — most men were — but he was ready to fight.

The winters were always cold, but the work never stopped on the Chitty farm. A horse and sleigh were used to deliver produce to neighbouring farms.

There was no turning back and he was proud of the invasion force spread out around and above him. Instead of snaring rabbits, he was firing live rounds at other human beings. "Here we were joining this massive barrage prior to landing, supported by the air force and long-range guns from the battleships."[20]

With their flat bottoms, the LCTs were not ideal platforms for firing artillery rounds accurately while trying to remain stationary in the water. The problem was discovered before D-Day, and so was the solution. Instead of slowing down and holding a position to fire, the vessels would maintain speed, allowing the guns to fire more accurately as the LCTs reached various distances from shore. However, rough seas and enemy fire still made the job difficult.

Chitty recalled that "something went wrong with the landing plans and we were ordered to cease fire." Then the LCT struck a mine, crippling the mechanism used to lower and raise the bow ramp. "There we were, like sitting ducks out in the water with no cover." He remembered an order came down to stop firing, and the men were ordered to throw hundreds of rounds of ammunition overboard. "The loose ammunition on deck had to be removed" before the Priests could be driven off.

In the same LCT, Bob Muir, meanwhile, was anxious to "score some hits." In his mind, his own safety was secondary to killing the enemy. Focused on his task, he had endured the crossing without throwing up, and years later politely — and curtly — recalled the vomit-filled morning. "It was very rough and stormy. It was not very nice at all."

Soaked by ocean spray, he had spent part of his time thinking about the Canadians killed at Dieppe in 1942. "We were looking for this battle to pay . . ." Beneath the naval and air force bombardment, "we fired all the way in then turned around and went out to allow the infantry to land."[21]

Muir was only sixteen when he enrolled in the spring of 1941, and just seventeen when he got overseas three months later. He and his older sister Babs were born in Detroit, where his father — a Canadian First World War veteran from Montreal — worked as a graphic artist for the Ford Motor Company. The young family moved across the river to Windsor, Ontario, and during the summer, journeyed to Hudson, Quebec, where his grandfather — his mother's father — owned a summer house. When war broke out, the Muirs moved into a cottage at nearby Como.

Thin, but rather tall for his age, Muir was a likeable boy who attracted people "like moths to a light." He was willing to try anything and was a natural athlete. He loved hockey and played on the provincial golf team. "Bob left school at age fifteen and went into Montreal to enrol in the air force. His father, who had already joined the air force, agreed to sign something stating he would be kept in Canada for a year," recalled his widow, Grayce.

Babs recalled how her brother had been "told to go home and wait for another birthday."

With his father's help, Bob Muir was prepared to serve in the air force until he was told to go home. He then discovered a faster way to get overseas.

Somehow Muir became convinced the quickest way overseas was with the Royal Canadian Artillery. "I remember him finally coming home to Como . . . in the dark, early one morning to tell us he had enlisted and was being posted to Debert [Nova Scotia]. Poor Mom was in tears," recalled Muir's younger brother David.[22]

When Muir headed home during his embarkation leave from Debert, he surprised his mother by arriving with four other soldiers. "He said, 'But Mom, they can't get home.'" Babs was working as a lifeguard at the Hudson Yacht Club when she saw the train coming around the bend. "It was going to take my brother off to war."

"He weighed only 117 pounds," added Grayce. "When I look at the photos that were taken of him then, he still looks like a little boy."

Ironically, one of his first jobs was riding on a truck equipped with loud speakers through which his young voice would beckon others to enrol.

Muir was also a keen observer. "I watched what the other guys did and did the same and that amounted to my basic training," he recalled. During his short stint at Debert, Muir was asked if he could drive a truck. "They put me in this gun tractor with a limber and gun on behind and we went for a drive and coming down this long, long hill you are supposed to start shifting down and I didn't know how to shift down." By then, the truck and the trailer were doing about eighty kilometres an hour and there was a sharp right turn at the bottom of the hill, which took the road across a narrow bridge. All along the road, people were shouting and waving at him to slow down, but he could not because he did not know how to shift gears. "So I go whipping through this little bridge at sixty miles an hour and around the corner and the old gun slides across, and there I am barely able to look over the steering wheel."[23]

He could still laugh about it, but Debert was now a distant memory. After striking the mine, the LCT had to be abandoned. "We were still in about six feet of water but the tank was water-proof to about eight feet." The artillery made it to shore, but the men had to find cover while engineers set charges against the sea-wall in front of Bernières-sur-Mer. "We just sat on the beach and were subjected to all kinds of nonsense." Muir remembered how vulnerable he and his buddies were because each self-propelled gun carried a huge quantity of high explosives, including a string of land mines that the engineers put to good use. All of this was exposed to enemy fire.[24]

To the east, facing the west side of Saint-Aubin-sur-Mer, Private Gerry Macdonald and several other men from the North Shore (New Brunswick) Regiment were crouched in their land-ing craft, nervously waiting for the bow ramp to be lowered. Running towards the opening, the men were mere seconds away from leaving the craft when the vessel was struck by a mortar shell. "It drove the ramp right back up in our face, everybody got knocked down . . . Then they almost finished us off. And it happened a second time, but we got off OK, but of course these Germans were shooting at us. But you never had time and I was seasick so it never made any difference to me . . . And being young it is different altogether," recalled Macdonald, who, like Muir, enrolled at age sixteen and was only a year older when he arrived overseas.

Once on the beach, the young medic was busy. "[It's] not a pretty thing to talk about, but it should be talked about," he remembered while being interviewed in 2012 at Camp Hill Veterans Memorial Building in Halifax. "We took care of the guys on the beach, everybody who got shot up no matter who they was, German, [or] what." Before the end of the war, he would lose his twenty-three-year-old brother, Ron, killed in Italy while serving with the Cape Breton Highlanders. Both boys were born into the military. In fact, Gerry's mother gave birth to him while living on base at Halifax.[25]

To the west, Parks and the rest of his mortar section had been in no rush to leave their LCT. He was incredulous when the order came to offload the bulldozers and carriers while the vessel was still more than a hundred metres from shore. The water looked too deep, especially for the carriers, which, unlike the bulldozers, were designed to operate in up to a metre and a half of water. "One of the sergeants said, 'We can't go in the water yet,' but they ordered us off . . . The bulldozers were about twelve feet high. When they went in, the force of them going forward pushed the LCT backwards. Once in the water, waves lapped at the top of their cockpits. The first mortar carrier that went in ahead of us floated a bit and then sank, while tracers from enemy fire flew over our heads. The guys on the first carrier jumped off, grabbed onto some compo boxes and began swimming."

Anticipating he was going to end up in the water, Parks decided to leave his Lee-Enfield rifle on the rack in the mortar carrier, which he figured would soon be on the bottom of the English Channel. At the last minute, he also elected to leave behind the metal base plate, which weighed approximately nineteen kilograms, and the aiming post for the mortar he was assigned to carry. "All I had on was some of my web equipment and the sight for the mortar. I thought the less equipment, the better. As soon as our carrier left the LCT, it began to sink. I got my foot on the top as it was going under, and gave myself a shove."

The waves took Parks to the left until the wash from the smaller LCA forced him under in roughly two and a half metres of water. "I had swallowed a lot by then, but my foot touched bottom and I pushed myself up. The goal was to get ashore."

Reaching the surface, Parks saw bodies in the surf. He grabbed onto a tetrahedron, a beach obstacle with iron bars intersecting at right angles. "It had a wine bottle [explosive] attached to it. I waited a bit and then latched onto two bodies. I was wearing a lifebelt, but it wasn't keeping me afloat. The surface was very rough. I caught my breath and then made my way to shore. Along the way I bumped into a couple of guys who were face down. They had been shot. I grabbed them by the collar and dragged them in and then ran forward to this other guy from B Company. He said, 'Drag them in, Jimmy.' Together we dragged more guys in. At one point I got down beside this corporal who was lying face down on the beach. I thought he was alive so I took cover the same as he was. Then I realized he'd been hit. We were not too far out of the water — maybe ten feet. There was a lot of noise."

Nearby, men were dying or bleeding out on the sand or in the water. Some were caught dead in their tracks while others, who had not made it out of the blood-stained water, sank or drifted away or took their last breath tangled in barbed wire, where their lifeless forms remained in men's memories for years. "I could hear machine-gun fire and mortars coming down," Parks recalled. "I figured the corporal next to me was already dead. It showed later that he had died of wounds, but as far as I could tell he was dead. I took his Sten gun and some other stuff. I got behind this pillbox. The enemy machine-gun fire had let up, just mortars landing here and there."

Parks, who was with a group of other soldiers taking cover behind the pillbox, soon spotted his brother Jack coming in with his own mortar section and the mortar platoon headquarters. "Somebody had brought in this guy — Lance-Corporal Bill Martin. He had been seriously wounded. My brother was holding him and then he asked me if I would hold him for a while. I did and Bill looked up at me and said he was cold. He had been hit in the stomach, lungs and legs and was all frothy at the mouth. He died in my arms."

Still concerned about the men he saw in the surf, Parks helped pull more of them in. "We were worried about the tanks running over their bodies, and some of the men could have been alive . . . and some could have drowned."

Parks could relate to the fear of drowning, and not simply because of his own experience that morning.

He had grown up in one of Winnipeg's working-class neighbourhoods, and remembered the day Jack nearly disappeared beneath the ice-covered waters of the Red River. The river was only eight blocks from their two-bedroom house on Lizzie Street. Jim was five years old, Jack was six. Jack's friend fell through and Jack went in to save him. Both boys were close to being swept beneath the ice when a couple of fishermen, who had heard Jim's screams, hurried over and pulled the boys out by the hair. "It was close," recalled Parks. "It would have been a terrible blow to my mom if Jack had died. She had already lost two children to whooping cough. The cops took our friend home and then us. I remember coming into the house ahead of the policeman who had Jack in his arms. I said, 'Mom, Jack fell in the river!' My mother stood up and then fell back against the door — in shock. Then she looked past me and saw Jack and the policeman. She thought she'd lost another one."

Harry Mayerovitch's poster stresses the importance of 1944 to the war effort, as the Allies close in on Nazi Germany from all directions.

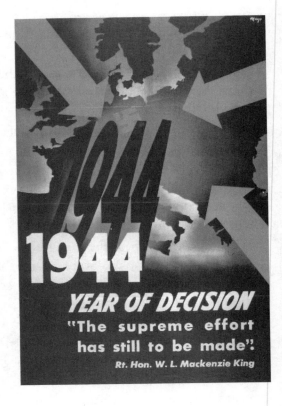

The Parks boys were close, having spent their younger years contributing what they could to the family's meagre income — even if it meant hopping freight trains to find work. "When we were eleven or twelve, we used to tell our parents that we were going haying — to work on a friend's farm for a few days. We told them we would sleep in the barn and they would think we were just outside of town when we were actually out near Saskatoon, Regina, Lethbridge, Calgary or some other place. It was the Depression and there were all kinds of people riding the rods. Some of the farmers were pretty damn miserable, but some were OK. If you were fifteen you could get about twenty-five cents a day — younger boys could earn ten cents. More importantly than that, you could get fed on the farms. Big lunches, sometimes with cake or pie and ice cream . . ."

Sometimes, the boys would visit hobo jungles, makeshift camps where scrounged food — usually stale bread or burnt cookies obtained from bakeries — could be shared, helped along with a tin of sardines. Times were tough, but not without adventure, and the brothers always returned home with cash.

Both were in the army cadets when war broke out and had recently returned from summer camp on Lake Winnipeg, just north of Grand Beach. Parks recalled, "There would be about thirty of us cadets up there. We lived in tents and there was a reservation nearby. We learned how to use a compass and we got a lot of exercise because we would hike at least three times a week. The natives taught us how to trap and skin squirrel and muskrat. We looked forward to it every year."

Although both were underage, it was not difficult for Jim or Jack to enrol in the regular army. Jim began by joining the Queen's Own Cameron Highlanders of Canada — another Winnipeg regiment — after war was declared. "My brother joined first — the Princess Patricia's Canadian Light Infantry — and later switched to the Camerons. The pals he signed up with were only sixteen or seventeen. So I figured I would not have any trouble. I had gone through a growth spurt and was five-foot-nine and nearly 140 pounds. So I was big enough."

Parks remembered being handed a type of registration card while with the Winnipeg Rifles Reserve. "You had to be eighteen years old to get one of those, but they handed them out carte blanche. I got one even though I was underage. So when I was going through the process of getting into the regular force with the Camerons, they asked what proof of age I had and I just showed them the card. They said that was good enough. Otherwise I would have had to run home and forge one or something."

In spring 1941, the Parks brothers were among twenty Camerons who volunteered to be transferred to the Royal Winnipeg Rifles. A short time later, they were settled into a coach on a CNR train bound for Nova Scotia.

Both boys knew how lucky they had been on D-Day. They had never experienced combat, and while catching their breath on that beach, they could appreciate the unpredictable nature of war. One soldier in the surf would haunt Parks for years. "He was with B Company, lying face up and all I could see were his intestines coming out around where his belt was. The poor guy had got it right in the guts."

East of the Winnipeg Rifles, the 1st Hussars had managed to get enough DD tanks ashore to support the Regina Rifles. Attacking with the Reginas that morning was seventeen-year-old Rifleman Horace Haney, who enrolled on June 11, 1942, at age fifteen.

Born and raised in the rural northwestern Ontario town of Emo, located along the Rainy River, approximately 190 kilometres southeast of Winnipeg, Haney finished a year of high school, then took a job at a sawmill as a tail sawyer. It was sweaty, dangerous work, but he stuck it out, earning fifteen dollars a week while occasionally hearing news about some of the men who were overseas or on their way.

Anxious to join them, Haney quit his job and headed west to Port Arthur, Ontario (part of present day Thunder Bay), where he enrolled on June 11, 1942. Bouts of bronchitis and asthma when he was eleven, coupled with kidney and bladder trouble when he was ten, were noted by the doctor conducting the medical exam, but these "previous medical conditions" did not stand in the way of the teenager's wish to enrol.

At five-foot-eight, 131 pounds, with a 37-inch chest, Haney was big and strong enough, and the scar on the back of his left hand suggested he was not afraid of hard work. But even with those physical attributes, the brown-eyed youth figured it was safer to fudge his age, which was recorded as January 16, 1923. It was his mother, Sarah, who finally set the record straight after his death when she told authorities he was born on January 27, 1927.

Although Haney would not live to see his eighteenth birthday, he made it to the beach and continued to see action into early July.[26] There is no record of what his experience was after the Reginas landed, but like other members of his unit in the first wave, he was grateful for the support they received from the 1st Hussars. The German defences at Courseulles had been barely touched by the naval bombardment. One massive strongpoint — ten metres across with concrete walls more than a metre thick — was particularly troublesome. In addition to its three protected machine-gun positions and an anti-tank gun mounted on a swivel behind the structure, it featured a concrete-walled trench that led to the water's edge. The massive bunker also contained underground chambers that protected the gun crews. The tanks dealt with one 75 mm gun by putting a round right through its gun shield. Direct hits from another DD tank silenced another position.

The Reginas fought on by working their way from the beach into the village — tough going every step of the way. The battalion's reserve companies had different experiences. While C Company had little trouble landing and clearing the beaches, D Company lost men and several assault landing craft to underwater mines. Fewer than fifty survivors reached shore.[27]

* * *

Canadian casualties on D-Day were 340 killed and 574 wounded. In less than a month, twenty-six of the wounded men would be dead.[28] Canadian, American and British blood was in the water and on the beach, but D-Day was a major Allied success. More than 155,000 troops had been landed by sea and air and the number of casualties was nowhere near the predictions. Still, there were many families back home that mourned the loss of a son, a father or a brother. Many would also have to care for a loved one injured on a day mostly full of positive news. For the men on the ground, there was no rest. The toehold they had established along the coast had to be defended and extended against an enemy bent on throwing them back into the sea.

CHAPTER 7

"I WOULD HAVE GOT IT RIGHT ACROSS THE MIDDLE OF MY CHEST."
Normandy, The Road to Carpiquet
(Map IV)

It was June 8, 1944, and Bombardier Frederick Barker of Oakville, Ontario, was moments away from dying. Sitting "brazen as brass" on his Norton motorcycle, the young dispatch rider with the Cameron Highlanders of Ottawa had just pulled up to a T junction on the northwest side of Putot-en-Bessin, Normandy, when he heard a voice bellowing, apparently at him, "Get down! Get down!"

Barker, who enrolled at age seventeen after a year in the militia, hopped off his Norton and dove behind a mound of earth. Seconds later, machine-gun fire scalped the top of the berm, spraying him with dirt. The voice belonged to Company Sergeant-Major (CSM) Charlie Belton of the Royal Winnipeg Rifles, who had wisely taken cover behind a Bren gun carrier. "Had Charlie not told me to get flat, and had I not done so at that moment, I would have got it right across the middle of my chest."[1]

It was going to be another long and costly day in Normandy.

Personnel of the Cameron Highlanders of Ottawa on their motorcycles near Caen, France, July 1944.

* * *

While much of the world was celebrating the triumph of D-Day, Allied planners knew the ultimate fate of the invasion force depended on the crucial hours and days immediately after the landings. In the Canadian sector north of Caen — in villages such as Putot-en-Bessin, Norrey-en-Bessin, les Buissons, Buron and Authie — the Germans struck with successive counterattacks against 3rd Canadian Infantry Division and 2nd Canadian Armoured Brigade. The enemy's goal on either side of the northward-flowing Mue River was to pry the Canadians off their D-Day toehold and throw them like "little fish" back into the sea.

For their part, the Canadians would have none of it. But the price for their bravery and dogged determination was paid for with vast quantities of young blood spilled on farmers' fields, along dusty country roads and amid clusters of houses that barely passed for villages. Most of the Canadians killed during the first six days of the invasion fell in battle, but many others were murdered in cold blood by maniacal German youth serving in the 12th SS (Hitlerjugend) Panzer Division. A lot of these boys were only seventeen — some younger — but had been raised to believe in the German master race and were quite prepared to die for the Führer while led by experienced and — in some cases — bloodthirsty officers.

The idea of pressing German youth into military service was first put forward in the winter of 1943. Germany's armed forces had suffered huge losses during the Russian campaign, resulting in a serious manpower shortage. Historian Howard Margolian believes the idea of recruiting youth most likely originated with Reich Youth Leader Artur Axmann, whose pleasure-time pursuits included hosting "lavish sex-and-booze parties for the Nazi brass." Axmann's idea was presented to Hitler by Reich Leader of the SS and Police Heinrich Himmler, and recruitment began almost immediately. The focus then was on youth born in 1926, and the physical requirements included a minimum height of five feet, eight inches. While some youths were coerced into joining, the practice was stopped by Hitler's personal secretary, Martin Bormann, after complaints were received from parents and others who were opposed to the idea of young boys being forced to join. The youths who volunteered attended a six-week military instruction camp, which included physical training, followed by four weeks in the Reich Labour Service. Next was sixteen weeks of intense SS military drill.[2]

By June 1943, the effort was paying off. More than ten thousand recruits were training at Beverloo, Belgium, and as they moved through the training schemes with their young and impressionable minds, most had a romantic view of war and service to the Führer. "For the vast majority of the young troops, the idea of fighting and dying for the Fatherland was held in almost mystical reverence," Margolian noted in his book *Conduct Unbecoming: The Story of the Murder of Canadian Prisoners of War in Normandy.*

Their indoctrination was deep. Under the Nazis, German youth were taught to hate Jews, Communists and the Western allies that defeated Germany during the First World War, a shameful and disastrous outcome that was still fresh in the minds of all Germans.

Many of the 12th SS Division's officers had transferred from Waffen-SS divisions, and within that group, dozens had served in the ruthless Adolf Hitler Bodyguard Division (Leibstandarte SS Adolf Hitler). In Normandy, the Hitler Youth were under the leadership of men who "viewed enemy prisoners as objects of hate and who considered their murder to be a powerful and legitimate weapon of war."[3] By June, the conditions were ripe for cold-blooded murder and other mayhem perpetrated by fanatical teenagers and ruthless officers.

Estimates vary on the strength of 12th SS on June 6, but it probably had seventeen thousand all ranks out of an authorized strength of twenty-two thousand.[4] Of those, roughly two-thirds were eighteen years old or younger.[5] These teenagers were well-armed, cocky and fuelled by a volatile mixture of duty and idealism. The Hitler Youth was a powerful force, moving forward when serious command and control issues were plaguing the enemy's larger war efforts in Normandy.

* * *

Although they fell short of their final D-Day objective, the inland advance of 7th Canadian Infantry Brigade's Royal Winnipeg

Youthful-looking members of the German 12th SS Division await transfer after being captured in Normandy.

Rifles and Regina Rifles was impressive. The men were glad to be back on land, but every step held the weight of what they had endured on the water and the beach. During the rough crossing, many had not eaten or had thrown up what they had. Most had gone forty-eight hours without sleep.

Meanwhile, young Jim Parks of Winnipeg, who nearly drowned on D-Day, was assigned as a runner to brigade tactical headquarters. He had not gotten very far into his first assignment when he was overcome by exhaustion and the effects of salt water. "Some of it caught up with me and so I went over to this tree and barfed up." Taking pity on him, his sergeant-major suggested he stay put and catch up with the boys later. "I was really tired and so I fell asleep for about an hour or so." Earlier, when other mortar crews arrived on the beach, Parks became a voice of experience when he warned an overly confident soldier to slow down and watch for snipers. "He said, 'You're crazy' and he stuck his arm above the embankment to prove it. Bang! A shot went through the arm and he had a Blighty."[6]

Sheldon Nattrass, who enrolled at age seventeen and landed on D-Day with the 44th Battery, 13th Field Regiment, Royal Canadian Artillery, was, like Parks, exhausted and banged up after landing at Courseulles-sur-Mer. "I don't remember too much of it except that there were a couple of guys with me that just looked like I felt — like an old rag doll."[7] Four of the regiment's officers who landed with the Reginas were now dead, blown up by enemy shelling or a land mine. The officer commanding the regiment's 22nd Battery and his signaller were also dead, killed when a shell hit their landing craft.[8] "It was terrible and well, I was stunned through the rest of it . . . But later in the day, I recovered a bit," recalled Nattrass, who grew up in the southeastern Saskatchewan town of Gainsborough, but enrolled at Winnipeg.[9]

By nightfall, the Winnipeg Rifles were dug in south of the village of Creully, eight kilometres southwest of the beach, while the Reginas had covered roughly the same distance to Le Fresne-Camilly. In between was the Canadian Scottish Regiment around Pierrepont. With very little sleep, the Winnipegs and Reginas got an early start the next day, and by noon, both of these depleted regiments arrived at Objective Line Oak, the name given to the third D-Day objective, along the Caen-Bayeux highway.

Further back and to the east, the 8th Canadian Infantry Brigade's North Shore (New Brunswick) Regiment was enduring a bloody introduction to Normandy. Instead of rubbing shoulders with the British 3rd Division, which had landed on Sword, east of Juno, the Canadians were advancing with an exposed left flank. This left them vulnerable to elements of the 21st Panzer Division,

Canadian wounded on Juno Beach, prior to being transferred to a Casualty Clearing Station.

which had access to the coast. The flank was exposed because the British 3rd Division's advance had been stymied by a narrow beach, a solid secondary line of German defence and "the only serious panzer attack of the day,"[10] which had pushed the British to the east.

The New Brunswickers continued to run into fierce resistance while advancing from Tailleville, captured after an eight-hour battle on June 6. Facing them on June 7 was a wooded area and the Douvres radar station. The latter was a massive complex on several acres that extended five storeys underground. The Luftwaffe garrison of 230 had recently been strengthened by members of the 192nd Panzer Grenadier Regiment. Protected by two strongpoints surrounded by minefields and barbed wire, it included half a dozen 50-millimetre guns, sixteen machine guns and three heavy mortars. Supporting the

North Shores was a squadron of Fort Garry tanks and guns of 19th Army Field Regiment.[11]

With the North Shores was Private Warren Lanning, who enrolled at the tender age of fifteen on October 8, 1941, at Botwood, Newfoundland. He had come a long way since the day he fudged his age by saying he was eighteen. "I was only fifteen. I think he knew, because he gave me a small wink." Lanning figured he was lucky because Newfoundland did not belong to Canada, and he was sure if he had tried to enrol in Nova Scotia, the authorities would have asked for a birth certificate.

After training at Debert, Lanning embarked for England, where he transferred to the North Shores in time to land on D-Day. "I was a private . . . a straight infantry, old foot slogger," he recalled. "We often were behind tanks when advancing and that helped. In tough situations like that you had close relations with everybody."[12]

While attempting to clear the woods south of Tailleville, the North Shores endured the wrath of Germans who had snuck back into trenches and shelters among the trees. Adding to the confusion, enemy snipers suddenly appeared in Tailleville and fired on the Canadians while they were preparing their attack. At one point, enemy fire wreaked more havoc when it struck an ammunition dump. The ground beneath Tailleville was a warren of bunkers and interconnecting tunnels that extended into the woods. It was thought they had been cleared, but the enemy got back into them.

The North Shores cleared a section of the woods, but came under intense small-arms and mortar fire from another location and the radar station. By late afternoon, the woods were cleared, but a communications breakdown between divisional commanders resulted in more confusion and risk for the Canadians when a British battalion, which had arrived on Sword that day, attacked the radar station. Unaware that friendly forces were in the woods, the British unit, supported by tanks, fired away until a Canadian major put a stop to it. The Germans, meanwhile, did not let up, and it was decided to pull the North Shores out to Anguerny.[13]

Lanning was among those who survived the first two days in Normandy.[14]

The 9th Canadian Infantry Brigade, 3rd Division's reserve brigade, which also arrived on D-Day, had moved into the beachhead secured by 8th Brigade. By late afternoon, it was moving towards Bény-sur-Mer, roughly five kilometres from the coast. The North Nova Scotia Highlanders and Sherbrooke Fusiliers had orders to advance south and cut across the Caen-Bayeux highway towards Carpiquet and its airfield, west of Caen. By then a significant portion of 21st Panzer Division was west of Caen and half the infantry of 12th SS and one third of its artillery were facing the left flank of 9th Brigade's leading forces. Twelfth SS, which included 25th SS Panzer Grenadier Regiment led by Colonel Kurt Meyer, had orders to counterattack along the east side of the Mue and push the Canadians back into the Channel.

Following intense house-to-house fighting, the Canadians forced the Germans out of the village of Buron while the bulk of the Canadian force advanced to Authie. By early afternoon, 9th Brigade's vanguard was dug in at Authie, only two kilometres from Carpiquet. The Canadians hung on, fighting exceptionally well even though they were vastly outnumbered and without artillery support and wireless communication. The latter would have allowed them to call in naval fire support. What the Canadians faced at Authie and Buron was the first major German counterattack against the Allied bridgehead, led by elements of 12th SS. And while the Canadian force was "driven back by a force more than three times its size," 12th SS did not come close to pushing the Canadians into the sea. For both sides, the casualties were high, but by day's end, 9th Brigade was secure at les Buissons, less than two kilometres north of Buron.[15] The dead included Canadians who were murdered in cold blood after they were captured by the SS, the first of 156 Canadians to die at the hands of the Hitler Youth. These prisoners were either shot at close range in the head, machine-gunned or bludgeoned to death. Some were deliberately struck by vehicles while being marched away. Another horrific and well-documented incident occurred when the bodies of two murdered prisoners were ground to pulp beneath a tank after they were deliberately pulled out into the street.

Lieutenant-Colonel Charles Petch, who earned the Order of the British Empire for his actions in Normandy, was shocked when he first encountered the Hitler Youth. The officer commanding the North Novas was amazed by the "cockiness and fanatical arrogance" of the teenagers. He described them as sixteen to eighteen years old, but some looked about twelve. "I remember my sergeant saying 'How can I fire at them when I have kids of my own their age?'"

Petch remembered one boy who was manning a machine-gun post. He "refused to give up until he used up all his ammunition. Then the squirt calmly strode out of his mudhole combing his hair."[16]

Herbert Foss of the Highland Light Infantry of Canada, who enrolled in London, Ontario, when he was seventeen, was not part of the attack towards Carpiquet, but was helping to hold 9th Brigade's left flank south of Villons-les-Buissons on June 7. He remembered how his battalion from southwestern Ontario, which had not suffered any casualties or "fired a shot" since landing on D-Day, was part of the costly effort to recapture Buron a month later. "They [the Germans] had dug all the nice trenches and that for us, which was nice of them. And that night, we knew why. Boy, did they ever blanket us with shells and mortars and whatever. I lost both my friends that night."

Foss never forgot the loss of his buddies. However, their deaths served to strengthen his resolve to fight on with other boys who, like him, had been keen to enrol, even though they were much too young. "Five of us were standing on a street corner in . . . Hespeler, Ontario, and people were getting into the military all around us — all except us fifteen-year-olds. We thought, well, everybody is getting in, why not us?"

After being rejected in Hespeler, Foss and his chums were annoyed, but not discouraged. They waited and eventually learned that "it was easier to enrol in London." One of his friends had a grandfather with a Ford sedan. "The five of us pooled all our money and headed out on the highway . . . and we finally made it after many stops. We went in and they hired us on — enrolled us." The next day, the boys were in Stratford, Ontario, where they joined the Highland Light Infantry. It took a year or two, and it definitely was a roundabout way to get in, but it worked.

Foss, who was seventeen when he boarded a troopship bound for Britain, loved sports, especially lacrosse, hockey and baseball. He was bright and energetic, and had worked at the local woolen mill, where his older brother, Tom, was a foreman. Tom and two other brothers, John and Bill, also served during the war as did their sister, Sue.

Like a lot of boys, enrolling in the army presented Foss with an opportunity for adventure and to serve King and country, but it also saved him from a difficult and at times dysfunctional family situation. Born at Rose Blanche, a tiny, barren, windswept fishing village on the southwest coast of Newfoundland, Foss moved with his family to southwestern Ontario. His mother had died and he was not particularly close to his father, and he did not get along well with his stepmother. Foss and his siblings were raised by their older sister, Anne, who was only eight when their mother died. Once in the army, Foss had a heightened sense of purpose and earned respect. He made friends easily and could handle the training. It was as though he had found a new kind of family. The losses at Buron in July were certainly hard to take, but the memories of those boys remained with him.[17]

*　*　*

In 7th Brigade's sector, on June 8, while crouched behind the berm near the T junction at Putot, Frederick Barker of the Cameron Highlanders of Ottawa had good reason to be fearful. The young dispatch rider had Charlie Belton of the Winnipeg Rifles to thank for making it this far, but what would happen next was anybody's guess.

As part of their failing effort to push the Allies back into the sea, the Germans also launched a series of attacks west of the Mue, against Canadian positions along and just south of the Caen-Bayeux highway. Opposite them were the Regina Rifles at Norrey-en-Bessin and Bretteville-l'Orgueilleuse and the Winnipegs at Putot and Brouay. The enemy plan included exploiting the terrain between the Canadian right flank and the 50th British Division to the west. Thrown against the Canadians was the 26th Panzer Grenadier Regiment of 12th SS, commanded by a sociopath, Colonel Wilhelm Mohnke, who had become addicted to morphine after losing part of his right foot in 1941.[18]

Like Meyer's 25th Panzer Grenadier Regiment, Mohnke's regiment was more powerful than any standard Anglo-Canadian infantry brigade, and its companies were well reinforced. Compared to the Reginas and the Winnipegs, which suffered serious losses on D-Day, the Hitler Youth were fresh and at full strength.

The enemy's early-morning attack on Norrey and Bretteville on June 8 was repelled, in large part due to the Reginas' intense small-arms fire and supporting artillery fire from 13th Field Regiment. The Hitler Youth who tried to storm the village

A Canadian dispatch rider takes cover from snipers near Buron, France, July 1944.

from the east were met with anti-tank guns and then infantry from the Reginas' B Company, who engaged the enemy in close combat. The fighting was brutal — lasting about seven hours — but the Reginas prevailed through skill and courage. That same day, tanks from 12th SS Panzer Regiment threatened 7th Brigade's left flank at Cairon, a village that straddled the Mue northeast of Norrey. Disaster was avoided when the Sherbrooke Fusiliers arrived. The tankers just happened to be passing through on their way to Camilly.

In setting up his defences at Putot, Lieutenant-Colonel John Meldram gave A Company the responsibility of covering the bridge over the railway tracks just west of the village and the tracks in front of Brouay, further to the west. It was hoped those soldiers would link up or establish contact with elements of 50th British Division. Meldram positioned C Company along the south side of Putot, where the railway tracks dropped into a cutting, and D Company was located east of Putot along the railway line. Belton and the rest of B Company — and battalion headquarters — were situated near the northwest side of the village.

The SS assault on Putot began at 10 a.m. and was supported by an artillery barrage and armoured vehicles. Anxious to prove themselves, and prepared to die for the Fatherland, the Hitler

Youth advanced. To the west, they got in behind the Canadian positions and some broke into the vulnerable corridor on the Canadian right flank. After swarming into the village, the enemy cut off the Winnipeg Rifles, who were still fighting it out along the railway line to the south.[19] Barker's savior, Charlie Belton, saw the enemy attack "across the fields in droves" and pin men down inside the orchard on the north side of the village. "It was just hell flying all over the place."[20] By afternoon, three of the Winnipeg companies had been cut off and surrounded.

The exact timing of Barker's encounter with CSM Belton at the T junction is unknown, but it occurred shortly after Belton had spotted the young man resting next to a crucifix on the northeast side of the village. "I was so tired," recalled Barker. "I hadn't had any sleep at all and I lay down beside the Crucifixion and picked up a brief snooze." Barker's slumber was interrupted by the sound of Bren gun carriers rumbling up the road. He jumped to his feet and saw they belonged to the Royal Winnipeg Rifles. Suddenly, someone was waving and yelling at him to get moving because the Germans were advancing. That someone was Belton. Barker jumped on his motorcycle and took off after the carriers, which, by the time he caught up to them, had stopped near the T junction.[21]

Barker was only sixteen when he joined the Lorne Scots (Peel, Dufferin and Halton Regiment) of Oakville, Ontario. He repre-sented himself as an eighteen-year-old then — and again in April 1941 when he signed on for overseas service with Canadian army at age seventeen. He got overseas that same year, and in 1943, transferred to the Cameron Highlanders of Ottawa. Assigned to No. 13 Platoon, a 4.2-inch mortar platoon, Barker served as part of an observation post (OP) crew and a dispatch rider. His platoon and No. 14 Platoon had landed without too much dif-ficulty on D-Day and proceeded to the town of Banville, where No. 13 took up positions in support of the Winnipeg Rifles. "The

7th Brigade's front — though noisy and rather fluid was not as uncertain as 8th Brigade's front, and consequently our mortars were not asked to fire."

Barker recalled advancing to Secqueville and on to Putot, June 7, where he got his first "minor scare" while returning from Putot to the mortar platoon's position north of the Caen-Bayeux highway. "One of our Colonels — I forget which one — was coming up. He stopped me and asked me for my password. Stupid me, I couldn't remember it." Barker was allowed to proceed, but was stiffly warned to learn the password.

Prior to the German attack on Putot, Barker was helping to establish an OP near the bridge on the west side of the village. He watched in horror as an American bomber, crippled by enemy fire, crashed on the other side of the railway tracks. Soldiers from the Winnipeg Rifles bravely dashed across the tracks to rescue the airmen, and one of them brought two airmen out. "The other two [airmen] had parachuted out, but one hit the ground just as the chute opened, and the other I believe the Germans shot while he was still in the air."

The events leading to Barker's near-death experience at the T junction began when he was at the mortar platoon's main position, in a wooded area north of the Caen-Bayeux highway. He had agreed to help the captain of his OP search for a piece of paper that had some firing coordinates on it. It was thought that the information had been left at a chateau they had visited. Hopping on Barker's motorcycle, the officer and the bombardier sped to their destination east of the village where they conducted a search, but came up empty. "I rode him back down again to the Platoon. Then he sent me back up on my own to recheck as the papers were very important." Barker's second search produced nothing, so he headed back. The running around had tired him out; the quiet field next to the crucifix looked like a good place for a nap.

A Canadian sapper emerges from a dugout in Normandy, July 1944.

While still hiding behind the berm near the T junction, the young man heard Belton tell him the Germans had crossed the railway tracks and had taken the rest of the village. Barker told the CSM he had to get back to his platoon. Belton thought that was a bad idea, but he helped the young man get his motorcycle upright and alongside the carrier. Barker slid onto the seat, started the engine and then sped off, knowing he could easily be struck down. He made it back to his platoon, but seconds later, an enemy scout car and a number of armoured vehicles appeared, heading along the highway towards Caen. "Our No. 5 Machine Gun Platoon and some anti-tank guns opened up on them . . . [but] our mortars were useless at such a close range." Barker was running across an open field when the captain of his OP was hit in the lower leg by a bullet or piece of shrapnel. Both men made it to Secqueville, where the captain was later evacuated.[22]

Parks, who was near battalion headquarters, was also busy. He recalled how the enemy used the wheat fields for cover during their main attack on the village. "The wheat fields were three to four feet high. We couldn't see much and Jerry was able to come in almost on top of our people — as close as twelve feet away, they would show up. All of a sudden the guys were surrounded on three sides. That was Putot — once we got overrun."

Parks's brother Jack, who also enrolled underage, was inside the village, hugging a wall, when he peered around a corner and came face to face with a Hitler Youth soldier who had been doing the same thing. "Jack was trying to figure out where they were. So he takes a quick look and suddenly sees this guy right there in front of him. He runs back. So does the other guy. It scared the hell out of both of them." That heart-pounding moment came just after Jack had a German potato masher [grenade] land on his lap while he was sitting in a Bren gun carrier. "Another soldier reached over and threw it overboard." The Winnipeg Rifles gave as good as they got in and around Putot, but it was not enough to repel the Hitler Youth. Many men were dead, wounded or captured, and ammunition was running out. Jack and the rest of his mortar section were in the midst of delivering ammunition to a group of C Company men who were surrounded and under fire inside the village. It was decided to load up the carriers and get everybody they could out. "On the way out the men in the carriers fired their weapons and threw grenades everywhere," recalled Parks.

At one point, Jim Parks and a corporal from C Company were busy trying to kill a sniper who was targeting battalion headquarters. Armed with Sten guns, the two soldiers set off with five magazines of ammunition each. "We went along this hedge and the corporal fired a few and then I would jump ahead of him and fire a few. We got quite a ways down and we ran out of ammo. I had nothing left and he had one or two rounds left and he said he would go back and get more ammo. After standing there awhile I sort of felt rather lonely and decided, well, I'm not going to stick around . . ."

In June, it does not get really dark in Normandy until around 11 p.m. Slipping into the cover of darkness was, therefore, not an option in the early evening hours. Parks decided to stick close to the hedgerows and shadows as he cautiously worked his way north from Putot towards Secqueville. His heart seemed to skip a beat when he "heard some voices." Convinced they were Canadian, he was just about to say something when he suddenly realized he was listening to German. "I looked through the hedgerow in front of me and only about ten feet away I could see there were about five of them."

Without ammo, Parks turned and ran as quietly and as fast as he could to the end of the hedgerow. "There was a road and there was this field and across that was La Bergerie Farm where the Canadian Scottish were." The field between Parks and the farm was being hit by shellfire. "I was scared as hell of this bloody SS . . . I had to make a decision right away. Do I stay put or do I run across the field to the farm, which was about 300 yards away? I thought if I ran and dropped down, ran and dropped down, then I might make it across the field. That's what I did and got to the farm, which was surrounded by a stone wall."

Parks had always been quick on his feet. Growing up in Winnipeg, he played baseball and hockey, and got lots of exercise delivering *Liberty* magazine, hocking newspapers on street corners and selling peanuts, popcorn, cigars and cigarettes in the bleachers at the baseball park. His physical activity usually involved running, and not just around the bases in the schoolyard. More than once, he and his chums had to run from police after they were spotted taking ice from railcars parked next to a fruit storage depot. "We called it fruit row and the sooner you got there the better because you could load up and then take your wagon and run around the neighbourhood selling ice for ten or fifteen cents a block. One time we could see the police cars coming and we jumped off and ran like mad. They definitely knew who we were."

With shells exploding behind him, Parks reached the stone wall and frantically began looking for a way to get in. "It [the wall] was about twelve feet high. Someone — a Canadian Scottish soldier — looked out through a small hole, and then a rope ladder came over. I climbed up and dropped down the other side. That's when I learned that the Canadian Scottish were about to launch an attack against the Germans in Putot. One of them asked me if he could swap his Lee-Enfield for my Sten. I told him I had no ammo and he said he had plenty. I sat there for a while and noticed the corporal who had been out with me earlier. He was sitting on the other side of the farm."

The Canadian assault to retake Putot began when the Canadian Scottish Regiment advanced on the village, supported by five field regiments. Artillery, which included a smoke barrage and the Cameron's 4.2-inch mortars, kept the Germans pinned down and isolated. Advancing behind a creeping barrage through an open wheat field, the Canadian Scottish faced an enemy hidden behind buildings and stone walls and in small orchards. With their own barrage raining down in front of them and enemy mortars and shells crashing down as well, the men were advancing inside an inferno. Providing additional fire support were tanks from the 1st Hussars and 62nd Anti-Tank Regiment, Royal Artillery. The fighting was bloody and costly, but it ended roughly an hour after it began.[23]

Three days later, elements of Le Régiment de la Chaudière and the Fort Garry Horse participated in an effort to expel SS Panzers from the vicinity of Rots. The attack succeeded, but it

was a brutal fight. That same day, at 2:30 p.m., tanks of the 1st
Hussars rumbled across open fields from Norrey to Le Mesnil-
Patry, south of Putot. With them was infantry from the Queen's
Own Rifles. Although some infantry and tanks got into the vil-
lage, the attack fell apart when enemy armour and anti-tank guns
opened up.

Canadians fought with tremendous courage during their first
six days in Normandy. Weakened by D-Day bloodshed, battalions were often overwhelmed by much larger forces. But on both
sides of the Mue River, they robbed the enemy of momentum and
stopped the counterattacks aimed at destroying their crucial toehold. The continuous fighting cost 3rd Canadian Infantry Division
and 2nd Canadian Armoured Brigade 1,017 dead and nearly 2,000
wounded. Battle exhaustion also took a very heavy toll.[24]

The Canadians got some much-needed rest and reinforcements, although many of the greenhorns that arrived in late June
were not well trained.

William Berrow, who had enrolled at age seventeen — following several unsuccessful attempts to join — was delivering
ammunition with waterproof lorries to artillery positions near
Caen. His unit was the 69th Tank Transporter Company, Royal
Canadian Army Service Corps. Berrow's first night in mid-July
was an eye-opener. "We were given orders, don't move, bed
down." He and a pal named Alf found an old slit trench and put a
camouflage net down. They recovered the wing from a destroyed
German fighter and placed it over the hole for protection. "We
were down there . . . real comfortable. We were smoking and
talking and all of sudden these guns opened fire and these planes
went over . . . Well, I was so scared. I said to Alf, 'You know
what? I wish I was home with my mother.' I was supposed to be
a soldier. I'm a brave soldier, but I cowered down pretty quick
that night." His fear was justified when a red-hot shell fragment
melted through the wing, landed between him and his friend,

A rifleman keeps watch from behind a partially destroyed wall. Many of the ruins throughout Normandy provided cover for both sides.

and set the netting on fire.

Berrow was fifteen when he tried to enrol the first time. His older brother told him he was too young, but Berrow had a plan: he would tell the recruiters he was eighteen. During the medical, the doctor observed that Berrow weighed only 109 pounds; recruits, he explained, had to be at least 120 pounds. "He said 'I'm going to let you go and you go home and tell your mother to put some lead in your pockets, and come in and see us.'" Berrow tried the air force, then the navy. He got into the army on his seventh try.[25]

Well before then, Supreme Headquarters of the Allied Expeditionary Force was frustrated by what was seen as a lack of progress in front of Caen. Following a British attack on June 26, the 8th Brigade's North Shores, the Chaudières, the Queen's Own Rifles and 7th Brigade's Winnipeg Rifles advanced on Carpiquet and its airport. Supporting them were twenty-one regiments of artillery as well as armour from the Fort Garry Horse and 79th British Armoured Division. The attack was also supported by the 16-inch guns of HMS *Rodney* and two squadrons of Typhoon fighters. But as the infantry moved through chest-high wheat, soldiers began noticing their rolling artillery barrage had stopped. The Germans had successfully shelled the start line and were saturating the wheat fields with accurate artillery fire.[26]

Parks remembered jumping for cover after his mortar platoon came under fire. "We got shelled like hell. I was sitting at the end of a trench and I had my greatcoat spread out. My buddy and I were eating our meal when these Moaning Minnies [mortars] came in. They made a lousy noise and we didn't know where they were going to land. I threw my meal aside and then dove down, but my greatcoat got hung up in the roots of this tree, which had been hacked up by shelling. I was hung up about a foot and a half below the level of the trench. When I finally got out and looked at my greatcoat, it was in shreds. A little while later we got shelled again. I don't remember a thing — just a big flash."

Buried in his slit trench, Parks felt someone tugging on his helmet, causing the strap to pull tight against his chin. It was his trench buddy, who had also been buried, but managed to free himself. "He grabbed each side of my helmet and just gave me a yank. When I looked at the landscape afterwards I was left wondering how they missed us. There were shell holes everywhere. It was a good thing we had dug our slit trench a little deeper."

On the fields in front of Parks, the Winnipeg infantry were falling quickly in a futile attempt to attack the hangars on the south side of the airfield. The attack stalled under ferocious enemy fire and was called off. A second attempt was made but

Machine-gunners of the Cameron Highlanders of Ottawa (MG) in action near Carpiquet, France, July 1944.

the men were finally withdrawn that night. North of the airport, the North Shores and the Chaudières got into Carpiquet village and dug in, joined later by the Queen's Own. That night, they were hit repeatedly by mortar and artillery fire. By morning, the final German counterattack was repelled. The fighting resulted in more than 371 Canadian casualties, including more than a hundred dead.[27] "We lost a lot of men there," recalled Parks. "So did the other battalions. I lost good friends, including Izzy Freeman who arrived in June, part of a reinforcement draft. I hadn't seen him since I joined the army in 1940 because he was still in school back in Winnipeg."

Parks and Freeman had attended the same school and played in the same baseball league. "He was a Jewish kid from Poland and we would play against each other. They weren't very well off. His uncle was a ragman. He'd come up the street with a little wagon on wobbly wheels and a nag pulling it . . . selling wine

Battle for Carpiquet Airfield *by Orville Fisher shows some of the destruction caused during the tough fighting to capture the airfield.*

bottles, three for a cent. Izzy was a really good guy. When he was killed it made me think back a bit."

Parks knew the battles were not getting easier. He accepted that fear was part of his day. "The fighting was nasty. Every time something happened you were losing people. It seemed we were always short of men . . . I had this will to live — I think everybody had that, but you always had that fright. Sometimes it would leave you, but most times you had it, but you just kept going."

Ahead were several more weeks of bloodletting in the wheat fields ripening under the hot sun. More men would breathe their last, including the youngest Canadian killed in Normandy.

"WHENEVER WE WERE MOVING WE WERE LOOKING FOR DEPRESSIONS IN THE GROUND — SOMEPLACE TO DIVE INTO."

Normandy, Caen to Falaise

(Map V)

Denis Chisholm turned his head and looked across the narrow space between his cot and the boy's. His name was Kurt and he was lying on his side, breathing heavily as the smell of infection rose inside the British hospital tent. Chisholm stared, becoming more aware of how life is eradicated by war. Kurt was sixteen years old, but he looked like an old man beneath the blanket; gone was any sign he had fought in the Hitler Youth.

Chisholm was sixteen when he left high school in Prince Albert, Saskatchewan, to join the Regina Rifles. He was still young in August 1944, but was no longer untested in battle. The deep shrapnel wound on the base of his right thumb was not life-threatening, but was serious enough to pull him out of the fighting north of Falaise, France.

The hospital tent, he recalled, was shaped like the letter H, with two wards parallel to each other and a smaller tent in the middle for ablutions. Like other hospitals in the Bayeux area, No. 106 British General was busy. Every stretcher case was different and some wounds defied description. Gangrene was a particularly grotesque and painful infection. Flies, grime and the ubiquitous brown dust of Normandy penetrated wounds before buddies or medics could apply temporary dressings on the battlefield. The wounded were carried by stretcher bearers to a Regimental Aid Post (RAP). Those unable to return to battle usually passed through a series of medical field units before arriving at one of the hospitals near the coast. Chisholm remembered the ambulances, jeeps, trucks and other types of vehicles arriving with the wounded. "I couldn't believe how many came into that place. The operating theatres were just tents and they were going twenty-four hours a day."[1]

Soldiers with missing limbs, horrible burns and lacerations were rolled into surgery where doctors and nurses worked beyond the point of exhaustion to clean and repair wounds. Medical breakthroughs — including the use of plasma — saved lives, but sometimes little could be done. Similar scenes unfolded at Canadian general hospitals, which by July were concentrated in the Bayeux area as part of 21st Army Group medical centre.[2]

Inside the wards it was damp and clammy, but a cot was better than a slit trench. The hardest part was getting used to the sound of men tortured by pain, begging for more morphine or another cigarette. Nightmares also left men screaming and thrashing. But what impressed Chisholm was the cleanliness. "I was filthy, rotten dirty, and dead, dogged tired when I arrived, but there were actual sheets on the cot." Chisholm fell asleep within seconds, and when he awoke, he thought he was dreaming. "I was feeling something smooth and cool, and here was this little Scottish nurse. They had pulled off most of my uniform and she is bathing me. God, I looked up and thought I was in heaven."

Young Kurt of the Hitler Youth was not the only wounded enemy soldier in the ward. "I figured there were just as many Germans as there were Allied soldiers," recalled Chisholm.

A very youthful-looking Denis Chisholm, who joined the Regina Rifles straight out of high school.

"Across from the boy was a German sergeant, next to him, an Allied soldier — a Polish lad. The Polish kids really hated the Germans for what they had put their country through. It was hatred like you wouldn't believe. This Polish kid had been hit in the arm and was all bandaged up, but he just wanted to get up and go over and finish off the German sergeant. The orderlies had to separate them, and then move them."

It was mid-summer and much blood had been spilled since June.

* * *

Well before Chisholm suffered his wound in mid-August, the Allies had strengthened their positions in Normandy. By early July, there were more than a million soldiers on the ground, engaged in a battle of attrition. The massive buildup of men, vehicles and supplies did not stop, even after a major English Channel storm on June 19 destroyed or seriously damaged artificial floating harbours. The German high command, meanwhile, was disorganized and frustrated. Hitler remained convinced the main Allied attack would fall in the Pas de Calais. Normandy, he believed, was not the main event, and his stubbornness weighed heavily on the minds of his commanders at the sharp end. In the aftermath of Carpiquet, General Leo Geyr von Schweppenburg, a very experienced officer, knew it was only a matter of time before the Allies took Caen. As the officer responsible for the panzer units in Western Europe, he urged an immediate withdrawal from north of the Orne River. In addition, he favoured the establishment of an armoured reserve to stop any Allied attempt at a breakthrough. Germany's commander-in-chief in Western Europe, General Field Marshal Gerd von Rundstedt, also favoured a strategic withdrawal from Caen, a recommendation that infuriated Hitler, who promptly replaced the two commanders.[3]

Meanwhile, Canadian troops were aiming to break out of their hard-won positions northwest of Caen, against a very formidable enemy.

On July 7, II Canadian Corps, commanded by Lieutenant-General Guy Simonds, became operational, with its headquarters at Amblie, northwest of Caen. It included the newly arrived 2nd Canadian Division, which would be tested again, nearly two years after it was decimated at Dieppe. Up first, though, were the tired, battle-tested soldiers of 3rd Canadian Division, cautiously, but bravely set on defeating a well-known enemy in painfully familiar villages.

While the sun was setting over Normandy that evening, soldiers witnessed something new — and shocking. Those who managed to fall asleep in their narrow slit trenches were jarred awake by the roar of 467 heavy bombers. Heading straight for the medieval city of Caen, the aircraft looked like "a gigantic swarm of bees about to take over the world; passing overhead with a beat of thunder that shook the ground," observed an Allied intelligence officer. The "swarm" included 283 Lancasters, 164 Halifaxes and twenty Mosquito pathfinders. Six thousand bombs fell. In less than an hour, Caen, which had suffered massive Allied bombing on June 6–7, was pummelled by roughly twenty-five hundred tons of explosives.[4] Hundreds died and many more were wounded, most of them civilians.

The enemy, however, was hardly touched. The rectangular area chosen for the bombing on the city's northwest side was nearly five kilometres beyond the Canadian front-line positions and well behind the enemy's main defences. The troops on the ground did not know this; all they saw were the silhouettes of planes as the sky turned orange and red, then filled with towering plumes of dust and ash. To them, it looked like the bombers had done their job, and the infantry's job was going to be easier. "We were dug in and we watched the bombers come in," recalled Jim Parks, the young soldier with the Royal Winnipeg Rifles. "They came over in waves and it was incredible. You could hear the roar. They really weren't that high and the Jerries had pretty good ack-ack. A few of the aircraft got hit, but I never saw any come down, although I saw one bank away with smoke trailing from an engine."

In addition to causing little damage to the enemy's defensive perimeter northwest of Caen, the bombing was poorly timed. It occurred six to eight hours before the infantry from 3rd British, 59th (Staffordshire) and 3rd Canadian Divisions began their attacks for Operation Charnwood, the capture of Caen.

Charnwood included a series of assaults, beginning with British attacks primarily on villages north and northeast of Caen. In the Canadian sector northwest of the city, the Highland battalions of 9th Brigade were awaiting H-Hour. The Stormont,

Dundas and Glengarry Highlanders were to capture Gruchy and the Château de St. Louet, while the Highland Light Infantry faced Buron. The hotly contested villages of Authie and Franqueville were assigned to the North Nova Scotia Highlanders. From there, 7th Brigade's Canadian Scottish Regiment was to pounce on Bitot and Cussy while the Regina Rifles advanced on the Abbaye d'Ardenne. In that medieval stone building, Kurt Meyer, commander of 25th SS Panzer Grenadier Regiment, made his headquarters. Second Canadian Armoured Brigade supported the Canadian infantry attacks, while the larger Anglo-Canadian ground operations were supported by more than 650 field guns of various sizes. Out in the Channel, the navy was ready to lend additional firepower. The final objective for the operation was a line north of the city's core.

Seventeen-year-old Horace Haney, who had left his job at a northwestern Ontario sawmill to enrol in June 1942, also witnessed the powerful bombing of Caen. Loaded down with at least sixty rounds of ammunition, the five-foot-eight lad was exhausted, but carefully biding his time with the Regina Rifles. Since landing on D-Day, he had not had much rest and, like most men, had lost a few kilograms. Now his battalion was only hours away from launching an attack against the heavily fortified Abbaye.[5]

Despite the smoke rising above Caen, 14th Field Regiment's war diary noted that "visibility was fair, but clouds shadowed the moon" at 11 p.m. on July 7, when the artillery began targeting villages behind enemy lines. At 4:20 a.m., the guns opened up again and continued for four hours. Bombardiers Bill Chitty and Bob Muir were with the regiment when it began firing artillery concentrations in support of the British 59th (Staffordshire) Division. The regiment's war diary reported, matter-of-factly, that the British captured their objectives by 6:30 a.m. Chitty and Muir had landed on D-Day in the same self-propelled gun, a Priest dubbed "Easy 4." The first target they destroyed was a

Bill Chitty and Bob Muir arrived in Normandy in Easy-4, a Priest self-pro-pelled, armoured artillery vehicle.

church steeple occupied by an enemy sniper who was firing at soldiers from Le Régiment de la Chaudière. Now north of the flaming city of Caen, Muir and Chitty were too busy to dwell on the circumstances that got them there. Chitty, however, did reflect on it later. "How had I come to be mixed up in this affair? As many of my comrades of the same age and younger, we had all heard plenty about this war from our shores and somehow, one by one, our friends used to enlist and disappear from our towns, villages and farms . . . I believe curiosity, and the possibility of adventure, and the need to be with our friends prompted our determination to join the ranks. I would not deny that, for some, the more noble incentive to serve our country was included in the initiative to become involved."

Chitty arrived overseas in October 1941. While he was set-tling in, his father, Charles, wrote to officials stating his son was underage and needed at home. When Bill was asked if he wanted to return home, his answer was a flat no; he wanted to see the war through. He was sent on courses to learn how to drive tanks and other vehicles until he was deemed old enough to go overseas.[6]

The Canadian infantry attacks began at 7:30 a.m. on July 8, and while the day's objectives were captured, the fighting was chaotic, close and bloody. Herbert Foss, who had enrolled as a teenager, was there when the enemy greeted his battalion, the Highland Light Infantry of Canada, at Buron.[7] After encountering a deep anti-tank ditch, the lads from Ontario's Waterloo County were hit by mortar and machine-gun fire. Throughout the day, the battalion suffered more than 260 casualties. In addition to well-documented cases of courage and individual initiative under fire, there were many brave acts that went unrecorded. Rifleman Horace Haney, the brown-eyed kid from Emo, Ontario, who had once pitched for a local baseball team and enjoyed woodworking and hunting, was among those killed in the vicious fight for the Abbaye. In 1942, when he was asked why he wanted to join the army, Haney's answer was recorded by the interviewer as "because all his friends did."[8]

It is not known if Haney died realizing the Abbaye was in Canadian hands, but the teenager's actions and the bravery of other Canadian and British soldiers shattered the enemy defensive ring around Caen. Moving cautiously into the dusty, rubble-filled streets of a city known for its Romanesque architecture, Allied soldiers were greeted by shocked and dishevelled citizens who emerged from safe havens beneath the destruction. They were glad the Germans were gone, but it was going to take a massive effort to rebuild their beloved city. As the soldiers looked for snipers and booby traps, some witnessed citizens picking through the rubble, searching for belongings. One Canadian soldier saw a woman sweeping the doorstep of a house that no longer existed.[9] Parks recalled how clogged the streets were. "We saw bulldozers trying to make the pathways better, but it was single lane only, and they had

Tanks of the Sherbrooke Fusiliers advance through the war-torn streets of Caen, July 1944.

a tremendous amount of rubble to push out of the way. There were people here and there. It was dusty and hot. The one thing we always worried about was whether something could be booby-trapped." He remembered how tempting it was to enter a house or peer inside a destroyed tank. "Anything like that we kept away from."

Thousands of kilometres away in a muggy apartment in Winnipeg, George and Sarah Haney received the telegram of their son's death. It was dated July 15, but the message read:

*MINISTER OF NATIONAL DEFENCE
DEEPLY REGRETS TO INFORM YOU THAT
H195027 RIFLEMAN HORACE ROY THOMAS
HANEY HAS BEEN OFFICIALLY REPORTED
KILLED IN ACTION NINTH JUNE 1944 STOP*

Members of the Regina Rifles watch for snipers amongst the rubble of Caen, July 1944.

IF ANY FURTHER INFORMATION BECOMES AVAILABLE IT WILL BE FORWARDED AS SOON AS RECEIVED.

The next day, another telegram arrived, correcting what was obviously an error. It stated the official date of death of their son should have read July 9, 1944. "THIS ERROR VERY MUCH REGRETTED."

Nearly a year later, Mrs. Haney received a letter stating that her son's personnel effects, which included a pocket watch, some snapshots and a Bible, would be forwarded to her shortly. In a letter dated October 1, 1945, she wrote to the authorities noting she had not been told where her son was buried.

"So many have [heard] and we have not. I sometimes get anxious to know. As they said as soon as they could they would let us know and it seems so long."

Sarah eventually received a photo of her son's final resting place. It is at Bény-sur-Mer Canadian War Cemetery, not far from Juno Beach.[10]

Gérard Doré prior to heading overseas. He is considered to be the youngest Canadian soldier killed in Normandy.

The day before Haney died, another young soldier was moving towards the battlefield. His name was Gérard Doré and he was just sixteen years old when he stepped off a ship into northern France on July 8, 1944. Five-foot-nine and weighing 140 pounds, Doré told recruiters in Quebec City on April 7, 1943, that he was born on August 29, 1924. His actual birthdate was August 29, 1927. He was only fifteen when he enrolled, making him one of the youngest Canadians to serve in the war.

Doré was from the rural Quebec town of Roberval, roughly two hundred kilometres north of Quebec City on the southwestern shore of Lac Saint Jean. Prior to enrolment, he competed in many of the popular sports young boys enjoyed: hockey, baseball and tennis. In school, his favourite subjects were arithmetic and language, but he also liked to read. After completing Grade 9, he remained in Roberval and worked as a bank clerk, then as an office clerk. His father, Isidore, was a labourer, and his mother, Marie-Anne, a homemaker. Both in their early fifties, they appreciated the extra income their son brought into their crowded little home. The couple raised six girls and four boys. Gérard was the second-oldest boy, nine years younger than his older brother, Maurice, and five years older than his youngest brother, Jean-Joseph. The fourth boy, Rene, was fourteen in 1944, while his sisters, Thérèse, Rita, Hetmance, Hélèn, Irène and Marie, ranged in age from fifteen to twenty-five.

Gérard arrived in France as part of a reinforcement draft, although his parents never expected him to get there so quickly. His service record documents his progression from enrolment to Les Fusiliers Mont-Royal, part of 6th Brigade, 2nd Canadian Division. He began training as a gunner in the Royal Canadian Artillery and took basic training at Lauzon, Quebec. As of October 7, 1943, he was attached to the Canadian Armoured Corps Training Regiment at Camp Borden, Ontario. From there, he was sent to Valcartier on the recommendation he join a French-speaking infantry unit. By the second week of November, the energetic and ambitious young soldier, who was described during the personnel selection process as "eager to go overseas and see action," was working as an orderly room clerk.

On March 20, 1944, Doré was granted embarkation leave of five days. From there, events unfolded quickly. On April 11, he was sent to Debert, Nova Scotia. Fifteen days later, he embarked on a seven-day voyage to England. On June 4, a month before he was shipped to France, Doré was assigned to the historic Montreal battalion. Sadly, his casualty service record features only one short entry after his arrival in France: "S[truck] O[ff] S[trength]. FMR [Les Fusiliers Mont-Royal] deceased 23 Jul. 44, 'killed in action.'"[11]

He was sixteen.

Doré was with D Company when he was killed near Verrières Ridge. He is believed to be the youngest Canadian to die in Normandy. The battle for the ridge occurred after Canadians crossed the Orne into the southeastern suburbs of Caen, where 3rd Canadian Division sustained numerous casualties. The backdrop for those bloody engagements was the heavily damaged industrial area, including the city's mangled steelworks.

Among the new men arriving in Normandy was Corporal Denis Chisholm, who had served as a military policeman at First Canadian Army Headquarters in Britain. During the buildup to the invasion, he applied unsuccessfully to get back to his regiment, the Regina Rifles, in time for D-Day. He was now proud to be back with the Rifles and was slowly getting used to the life of an ordinary foot soldier.

Chisholm joined C Company as a Bren gunner and was fond of the weapon. "The Germans had the MG-42. We called it the widow-maker. It was a high-firing weapon. The old Bren would go tack, tack, tack, tack. The MG-42 sounded like someone pulling or ripping a bedsheet." By then, Chisholm's buddies had taken to calling him "Corporal Pull-Through." At six-foot-three, he was not only tall, but thin, and reminded them of the length of jute cord with a metal weight (usually brass) on one end and a loop on the other, stored behind the butt plate of a .303. It was used to clean the rifle's barrel by dropping the weight through the barrel, putting a piece of flannelette in the loop and then pulling it through the barrel to remove any firing residue. All nicknames stuck in wartime, including his. Chisholm remembered another chap in the Rifles who everyone called "Pelican" because of his large nose.

Although Caen had been liberated, Chisholm was quite aware the area southeast of the Orne was "a dicey place" with numerous perils among the destroyed buildings and mangled steelworks. "Everybody tends to think the worst thing for an infantryman is machine guns or rifles, but the worst is mortars and shelling. You have no idea what it's like. You would come under some of those barrages and they'd be up to an hour you

Seeking cover or finding the low ground was a constant priority for soldiers on the move.

know, just constant, big 88-mm, some of those big shells coming in. Air bursts, they were a bugger; they would explode at just above roof-top level and they were timed to blow up and rain down on you. If you were lucky you would find cover in a slit trench. That's another thing. In Normandy we were digging all the time. It was hard work. The tough part in Normandy was the chalk. There would be about two feet of dirt and then you hit this damn chalk and digging into that wasn't easy. The first thing a soldier asked when he met up with soldiers who were holding a position was not 'How's the enemy?' or 'What's going on up there?' it was 'How's the digging?' You just wanted to get down below ground as quickly as possible. Whenever we were moving we were looking for depressions in the ground, some-place to dive into."

The attacks aimed at Verrières Ridge began on July 20 — three days before Doré was killed — and involved battalions of 2nd Canadian Division's 6th Brigade. Although called a ridge, the geographical feature is more of a slope, rising gradually over a distance of a thousand metres. It gave the enemy an unobstructed view of the countryside, however, especially the waist-high wheat fields south of Caen.

In addition to holding that advantage, the enemy had plenty of armour and was busy reinforcing its positions. Southwest of Caen, the village of St. André-sur-Orne was defended by 272nd Infantry Division. It had been dealt a serious blow since arriving on July 13, but it was still very powerful. Other advantage points and nearby locations were occupied by 2nd SS Panzer Grenadier Battalion, two companies of 1st SS Panzer Division's recon-naissance battalion, two companies of 2nd SS Panzer Battalion, elements of 1st SS Panzer Grenadier Regiment, dozens of tanks and a company of self-propelled guns.[12]

Sixth Brigade began its advance at 3 p.m., supported by strong artillery shelling and Typhoon fighter-bombers. On the right flank, the Queen's Own Cameron Highlanders advanced through wav-ing wheat and reached St. André-sur-Orne with the help of artillery and medium machine guns of the Toronto Scottish. In the centre, the South Saskatchewan Regiment moved quickly and dealt with enemy forward positions at a wireless station and a crossroads. From there, they consolidated their positions on higher ground while awaiting the arrival of anti-tank guns. On the left, Les Fusil-iers Mont-Royal — Gérard Doré's battalion — moved up the long slope towards the village of Verrières and secured two farms, Beauvoir and Troteval. Both were situated along the east-west road connecting Hubert-Folie and St. André-sur-Orne. The plan called for Doré's D Company to capture Verrières village.[13]

Meanwhile, the weather was on the side of the enemy when torrential rain forced the cancellation of artillery observation, armoured fire support and crucial aerial attacks.[14] A powerful German counterattack followed that savaged the forward companies of the Fusiliers and the South Saskatchewans. Around Saint-André-sur-Orne, the Cameron Highlanders were devastated by enemy tanks that also destroyed a number of Sherman tanks. When the Essex Scottish advanced, it too felt the full force of the enemy. The result was a "deep and dangerous salient" between the Highlanders and the Fusiliers, with the latter pinned down and running low of ammunition.

Doré and other members of his unit were exhausted, wet and very hungry. Prior to the attack, they had not had time for breakfast or lunch. And now heavy enemy fire raked them and other Canadian positions along the entire front. Beauvoir Farm was hit especially hard. With B Company of the Fusiliers dug in on the ridge's southern slope and C Company just to the east at Troteval Farm, D Company, under Major Jacques Dextraze (a future Chief of the Defence Staff), was ordered onto Verrières village. The heavy rain interfered with wireless communications, but it was soon learned that D Company was stalled and suffering heavy losses. The death and destruction continued throughout the night and into next day as the Black Watch, supported by tanks from the 1st Hussars and Sherbrooke Fusiliers, fought to prevent further enemy penetration. The Highlanders from Montreal attacked behind a creeping barrage, recaptured the road between Saint-André and Hubert-Folie, and found themselves to the right of the embattled Fusiliers.[15]

In four days, II Canadian Corps lost nearly two thousand men. Third Division suffered 386 casualties with eighty-nine killed, while the butcher's bill for 2nd Division was 1,149, including 254 killed. German losses were also high, but they held the ridge. There are no specifics on how Gérard Doré died,

Casualty Clearing Post, *a watercolour by Alex Colville, depicts box ambulances of 14th Field Ambulance, 3rd Canadian Division, in action.*

but his last moments were spent on the blood- and rain-soaked wheat fields at Beauvoir Farm. Years later, someone cared enough to display their quiet gratitude for the Quebec teenager. During a visit to the small chapel in the village of Verrières, they left behind a photograph of the boy standing proudly in his uniform.

The Canadian Pacific Telegram from the Director of Records reached Roberval on August 2, 1944.

MINISTER OF NATIONAL DEFENCE DEEPLY REGRETS TO INFORM YOU THAT E0584 PRIVATE GERARD DORE HAS BEEN OFFI- CIALLY REPORTED KILLED IN ACTION TWENTYTHIRD JULY 1944 STOP IF ANY FURTHER INFORMATION BECOMES AVAIL- ABLE IT WILL BE FORWARDED AS SOON AS RECEIVED

The devastating news shook the Doré household and sent a shock wave through the quiet community. Isidore and Marie-Anne could not accept that their boy was dead. On August 5, Isidore wrote to the Department of National Defence and his letter was translated into English.

> *We have received yesterday morning a Message informing us that [he] had been killed in action, on July 23, 1944.*
>
> *Well, is there any means of getting further details concerning this matter? We would be very much obliged to you. It is almost unbelievable that this would have happened for again on July 10th, we received a letter from our son, Gérard, and he never mentioned expecting to go to the battle-front. He merely stated he was proud to belong to Les Fusiliers Mont-Royal Regiment.*
>
> *Under what given circumstances has he met death? Accident? Illness or while in action on the battle-field? Was he in Normandy or in Italy and since when? We never heard anything. Was there an Army Chaplain at his side when he died? . . . if this was so . . .*
>
> *Would not a mistake be possible either in the Name or the Regimental Number? We would greatly appreciate information.*

On August 21, the department wrote to Isidore stating his son was "killed through enemy action" and did not die as a result of illness or accident. "It is unfortunate that there is no indication of a mistake having been made in the reporting of this Casualty. You may be absolutely certain that the Overseas Authorities would not forward a report of your son's death without having definite evidence to that effect."

Unaware that this letter was in the mail, Isidore Doré wrote again — on August 25 — asking for details.

> *Could you please . . . tell us the place where he was*
> *killed, if he really was, because I would really like*
> *to be certain of that. It sometimes happens that*
> *there are errors. Secondly, in what way did it hap-*
> *pen? Was it on the battlefield at Normandy, or was*
> *it some kind of accident? Is there any possibility*
> *that we could know the name of his military chap-*
> *lain, and of some of his friends, maybe an address*
> *who could give us information? Did he not write a*
> *last letter? We would like to have back his personal*
> *effects, so that we could then be more certain. Is he*
> *perhaps not only missing? Sometimes that happens.*
> *In any case, please let us know. We still have hope*
> *that he is not dead. Hoping to hear from you as*
> *soon as possible by telegram or otherwise. I remain,*
> *Isidore Doré*

In a letter dated April 12, 1946, Marie-Anne Doré wrote in regards to the war service gratuity she and her husband received. She thanked the authorities for the gratuity, but also stated:

> *When one has a son who has finished his studies*
> *and on whom one counts to help us to live, it is*
> *hard to see him killed at 16 years, and 11 months.*
> *I had already begun to take steps to have him leave*
> *the army, but I could not believe that he would*
> *be sent so quickly to the front, at that age, even*
> *though he was so courageous and he absolutely*

*wanted to go and defend his country because he
enlisted without our knowing, thinking he could
help us that way, but he did not have the chance.
I saw in the paper that you are sending pictures of
the tombs of soldiers who died in France. I would
very much like to have the one of my son, Gérard
Doré. Our best to you, Mme. Marie-Anne Doré*

Since then, visitors to Bretteville-sur-Laize Canadian War
Cemetery have paused to pay their respects in front of the young
volunteer's grave, many moved to tears by the age inscribed on
the headstone. Sadly, Private Doré was not the last sixteen-year-
old to die in the war.

On July 25, during Operation Spring, the Canadians again
ascended the slopes of Verrières Ridge, this time under artificial
moonlight created by bouncing searchlights off clouds. It was
another disaster. The Germans continued to hold an enormous
advantage: excellent observation points, reverse slope positions,
fortified hamlets and plenty of artillery, machine guns and tanks.
The fake moonlight made it easier for them to pick off the attackers. For one battalion, the Black Watch, it was the costliest single
day since the Dieppe Raid. Of the roughly three hundred members of the Black Watch who had begun the advance up the slope
at 9:30 a.m., only sixty made it to the top before they walked into
a trap. Only fifteen lived to tell about it. Overall, Canadian casualties were 1,550 killed and wounded.

While the number of Canadian casualties was reminiscent of
the terrible losses suffered during the First World War, the war
of attrition made it difficult for the enemy to replace significant
troop and *matériel* losses. Meanwhile, west of the Anglo-Canadian advance, American tanks and infantry were heading towards
Brittany, after finally breaking through relatively weak enemy
opposition compared to what the Canadians and British faced.

Mushrooms of flame and oily, black smoke fill the air after Allied bombers attacked enemy lines along Caen-Falaise road.

Hitler, however, made a significant blunder. Instead of ordering his forces to withdraw to the east, he ordered an armoured counteroffensive against the American advance. This gave the Allies the opportunity the trap the enemy in a deadly pocket. For it to work, the Americans had to keep advancing south and southeast while Canadian, British and Polish forces moved south, securing vital east-west roads into and past the town of Falaise. The Anglo-Canadian effort, known as Operation Totalize, was a massive, nighttime attack by armoured columns. For the first time in the history of warfare, armoured personnel carriers were used to carry infantry into battle. These vehicles, quickly fashioned out of M7 Priest self-propelled gun carriers that had been loaned by the Americans, were a Canadian invention. In battle, they provided mobility and protection from small-arms fire.

The air force was also part of the plan.

On the night of August 7, Lancaster bombers unleashed hell on enemy positions. The armoured columns advanced in the darkness, but progress was not as good as expected because of the dust kicked up by the huge number of heavy vehicles and the failure of navigational aids. A second phase was launched the next day and, while American B-17 bombers successfully obliterated enemy positions, many of the aircraft dropped their loads on troops of 3rd Canadian and 1st Polish Armoured Divisions. Jim Parks of the Winnipeg Rifles remembered it well. "They were impact bombs. The moment they hit the ground there was concussion and shrapnel. We had to pass through [where the bombs fell] about an hour or two later and they hadn't cleaned up. Some of the guys were sucked out of their tanks by the concussion. They were hanging out of the turret with blood coming out of their ears . . . The Polish took a beating there; they lost a lot of men and tanks. It was a sad thing to watch them burying their own people, digging trenches for temporary graves."

While stopped in a small forest near the Caen-Falaise road, Parks and the other members of his mortar crew were standing next to their carrier when the area was sprayed with ack-ack fire. "It was over on our right, maybe a couple of hundred yards or so. One landed next to my right leg and pieces of shrapnel punctured my battledress and right shin. It tore it up and it was bleeding. The next one hit the ground between my legs and exploded, and the one after that hit just to the left of my left leg. The same thing happened to the guy on my left. Had the first one been two inches over it would have gone through my shin bone."

With blood dripping off his leg, Parks was loaded onto a jeep and driven to an RAP. "I had my leg propped up on the front fender and as I passed some of the boys I waved to them and told them, 'Hey, I'm going to England!'" At the RAP, Parks removed his boot, and then someone took a knife and sliced through his pant leg to expose his shin. The wound looked ugly with stones and dirt and bits of metal. However, Parks's hope of being evacuated to England began to fade when he was handed some rubbing alcohol and a pair of tweezers and told to finish the job. "So I just sat there taking it out and wiping it clean. I never got my Blighty."

Operation Totalize ended on August 10. The Allied gain was thirteen kilometres, and while the Germans had suffered major losses, they regrouped and managed to slow the effort to close the Falaise Gap. Soon, however, the German Army was in full retreat with the Americans moving quickly eastward towards Argentan and First Canadian Army only a few kilometres from Falaise. Operation Tractable, a daylight attack preceded by another huge bomber assault, involved 3rd Canadian Division, 2nd Armoured Brigade and 4th Canadian Armoured Division.[16] Bad luck entered the picture when a Canadian reconnaissance officer, carrying a copy of the operational plan, was killed by the enemy and the plan was discovered. Responding quickly, the Germans deployed their limited forces and stopped the advance. This was after Canadian and Polish soldiers suffered more serious losses when eight hundred Lancasters and Halifax bombers from the RAF's Bomber Command, which included a large component of RCAF squadrons, dropped their loads on August 14. Most of the bombs were dropped accurately, but many fell short.

It was two days later when Denis Chisholm was wounded, hit in the hand by a piece of red-hot metal, probably from an air burst. "The Germans were trying to get out on this road to the east and our job was to take the road and prevent that. They were on one side and we were on the other. They had a tank dug in there, and also had machine guns, rifles and every damn thing, and there were fields of crops and piles of grain." At least two attempts were made to cross the road until Chisholm's C Company advanced. "The tank began firing at us, but it ran out of ammunition because all of a sudden we heard this roaring and we watched as it backed out. We see this bloody tank and we are thinking he is going to come across the road after us, but he turned and left."

Two French civilians struggle with their belongings through the war-torn city of Falaise.

The shrapnel penetrated Chisholm's right hand and then spun off. "One of the guys took a field dressing from a pocket in my trousers and wrapped it around the wound to stop the bleeding."

Second Canadian Division entered Falaise on August 17. A short time later, Canadian and Polish forces linked up with the Americans. The Falaise Gap was closed, but the Germans — full of fear and desperation — continued to try to escape to the east. East of the Canadians, the bulk of the Polish division was on a wooded hilltop on August 20, engaged in a horrific battle while trying to force the enemy into submission.[17] Another vital point was Saint-Lambert-sur-Dives, where an armoured squadron under Major David Currie of the South Alberta Regiment and an infantry company led by Acting Major Ivan Martin of the Argyll and Sutherland Highlanders of Canada took up positions on August 20.

The main square in Falaise, ripped apart by the path of war.

For a day and a half, the tiny group fought to keep the pocket closed while destroying tanks and killing or capturing scores of enemy soldiers. Martin was killed and Currie, who had joined his hometown militia unit when he was fourteen in 1927 and was a second lieutenant by 1939, earned the Victoria Cross for his valour.[18] For the tens of thousands of Germans caught in the pocket, it was beyond hell. They were strafed by Spitfires and rocketed by Typhoons, and the ground was littered with burning wreckage and mangled bodies. The smell of burning and rotting flesh permeated the nostrils of pilots as they continued their attacks. Of the roughly one hundred thousand men trapped in the gap, it is estimated only twenty thousand to thirty thousand escaped. Between ten thousand and fifteen thousand died and approximately forty thousand to fifty thousand became prisoners. Allied losses in Normandy up to late August were 206,703. First Canadian Army had 18,444 casualties, with

5,021 either killed in action or dead from wounds.[19] Many were still in their teens.

While on the mend at the hospital near Bayeux, Chisholm used his left hand to dole out cigarettes, water and chocolate bars to lads who were a lot worse off. Some men, especially the tankers, had suffered horrific burns. "Those poor devils were all bandaged up — just like a mummy — just an opening for their mouth, eyes and nose. They would want a cigarette and so I would take one to them in a holder, and stick it through the opening and they would puff away. Oh my, I saw some sights."

Young Kurt of the Hitler Youth was also on Chisholm's rounds and his condition was deteriorating. "I learned he was Austrian. He had an awful hole in his back. He'd been hit by shrapnel and was out there for a couple of days. Infection and gangrene got into it, and it smelled like hell when they came in to change the dressing on the wound. He would often look up at me and say, 'Komrade! Komrade! Canadese! Canadese! Cigarette! Cigarette!' So finally I was bumming cigarettes for him. They gave us ten a day. They were Woodbines and . . . a lot of guys claimed they were made out of camel shit."

Three days after he was there — halfway through the night — Chisholm woke to see a couple of orderlies remove Kurt from his cot. "He was gone — dead." It stuck him as strange. He was the enemy, but a kid. At one point in his young life he had been desperately trying to kill Allied soldiers. Yet just before his death, he was only a kid bumming cigarettes. To Chisholm, it made no sense.

The war was never the same for Chisholm after that. He had witnessed a lot of pain and suffering — young men dying on both sides. "I went back and did my job, but you know I looked at them differently. I saw them as human, same as me. That young soldier's death made a big difference on me."

"I FEEL LIKE CRYING MY HEART OUT — HALF WITH JOY, HALF WITH SORROW."

North-West Europe, Falaise to V-E Day
(Map V)

Crouched behind a dike on the southwestern edge of the German village of Bienen, between Emmerich and Rees, east of the Rhine River, Bombardier Bob Muir watched Major David Dickson lead a group of men up the embankment and into a hurricane of red-hot metal. Two platoons from Dickson's D Company of the North Nova Scotia Highlanders had already gone over the top and were being slashed by exploding grenades and machine-gun fire. On the right, Major Lloyd Winhold's C Company was also taking heavy casualties as it attempted to cross the flat, open ground in front of the village, which the Germans had turned into a fortress.

Muir, who was only sixteen when he stood on the back of a flatbed truck in Montreal to encourage other men to enrol, had landed on D-Day in a Priest self-propelled gun. The young soldier was still with the Royal Canadian Artillery's 14th Field Regiment, but was now fulfilling duties as a radio operator. Just before Dickson scrambled up the west side of the dike, he turned calmly to Muir and told him to stay put and await the arrival of the forward observation party's artillery officer.

On the other side of the dike, shrapnel and a steady stream of bullets ripped into buildings like jackhammers. Stone walls, roofs, doors and windows were blown apart or shattered. The enemy's main fire, which was coming from a three-storey house, also targeted the top and east wall of the dike. Although the Germans had been forced back behind the Rhine, they were willing to die defending the Fatherland.

On top of the dike, Dickson paused to urge his men forward. Seconds later, Muir realized the major had been hit. The young radio operator knew he had to act fast.[1]

* * *

After trapping and destroying most of the German Army fighting in Normandy, the Allies moved eastward. By early September, First Canadian Army was busy clearing the Channel ports. Formed overseas in 1942, First Canadian Army was composed of two corps (five divisions and two independent armoured brigades). However, it was broken up in 1943 when I Canadian Corps was sent to Italy. To bolster its strength and satisfy demands at home for a large, identifiable Canadian army, Allied formations were added. When First Canadian Army began clearing the Channel coast on the left flank of the Allied advance, it had more Allied than Canadian soldiers in it.[2] Dieppe was taken on September 1, followed by costly victories at Boulogne, Cap Gris Nez, Calais and Ostend. In October, the objective was to open up the recently liberated port of Antwerp, Belgium, vital for resupplying the Allied advance. To do that, both sides of the Scheldt estuary had to be cleared.

Private John Cremeens of Kenora, Ontario, was among the younger soldiers killed in the fighting for the Channel ports. The seventeen-year-old arrived in France on August 13. Two days later, he was taken on strength of Toronto's Queen's Own Rifles of Canada. Twenty-five days later, on September 9, east of Boulogne, he was killed in action.

Cremeens was only fifteen when he enrolled at Winnipeg in the Non-Permanent Active Militia on April 1, 1942, and was barely sixteen when he joined the Canadian army on December 18 at Vancouver. The eager young lad claimed he was born on October 11, 1924, which made him old enough to join, but someone placed an orange sticker on his file stating he was "underage for overseas service."

The doctor conducting the medical exam noted while Cremeens was five-foot-eight, he weighed only 112 pounds. None of these observations prevented him from enrolling. When he embarked for Britain in November 1943, he was a nineteen-year-old soldier — at least on paper. Like most mothers, Cremeens's mother, Norah Belair, knew how old her son was, but probably felt there was little she could do to stand in the way of an adventuresome teenager. While filling out a form three months after his death, she stated her son was born on October 11, 1927.

After completing Grade 8, Cremeens left school at age thirteen. He could drive a tractor and a truck and was adept at operating heavy equipment for road construction jobs, earning thirty-five dollars a week. Cremeens also worked at a mink farm, as a hunting-and-fishing guide, and raised chickens. When he was not working, he enjoyed going to the movies and attending dances, but also left room for baseball or hockey. His long-term plan was to work for his father's air-conditioning business in Nebraska. During training, Cremeens's experience with heavy equipment singled him out for service with an armoured unit, and while at Borden, Ontario, he qualified as a driver for wheeled and tracked vehicles. A note in his military service file states "he is above average intelligence and learning ability and should be good NCO material."

When he died, he was in the infantry, recently arrived as a much-needed reinforcement in a war that seemed endless.[3]

The battles to clear the Scheldt estuary were among the most physically demanding and violent operations carried out by an already overcommitted First Canadian Army.[4] While the Germans had been pushed out of Antwerp, they controlled the polder country, including the banks of the West Scheldt and the long, exposed causeways connecting the Scheldt estuary islands. It was cold, and the sodden landscape was beyond anything encountered in Normandy. Here, it was mostly reclaimed land — muddy flats interspersed with six-metre-high dikes, deep canals and rivers. Aerial bombing had punched gaping holes in dikes, leading to widespread flooding.

While 2nd Canadian Division focused on clearing the South Beveland peninsula and the flooded island of Walcheren on the north side of the estuary, 3rd Division, supported initially by an infantry brigade from 4th Armoured Division, attacked the southern shore, known as the Breskens Pocket. Two days after 7th Brigade crossed the Leopold Canal from the south on October 6, 9th Brigade launched an amphibious assault on the mud flats between Hoofdplaat and the Braakman inlet and attacked from the east. Originally, these were meant to be simultaneous attacks. However, the amphibious assault had been postponed for forty-eight hours.[5]

Facing the Leopold Canal, Sergeant Denis Chisholm — still known to his buddies as "Corporal Pull-Through" — was not operating a Bren gun. He was with the Regina Rifle Regiment's three-inch mortar platoon when the fighting to cross the twenty-two-metre-wide canal began at 5:30 a.m. It commenced with fountains of liquid fire, spewing like dragon spray from twenty-seven Wasp flamethrowers. Arcing over the canal, the flames lit the sky in a "scarlet glow . . . visible for miles," crashing in molten waves over enemy machine-gun posts. The Germans manning

Darkness is illuminated during a waterborne assault in this watercolour titled A German Flare Goes Up *by Alex Colville.*

those strongpoints had no chance, but other positions, including pillboxes, survived the fiery onslaught.[6]

Seventh Canadian Brigade's Royal Winnipeg Rifles, Regina Rifles and Canadian Scottish Regiment attacked, joined by 8th Brigade's North Shore (New Brunswick) Regiment, under 7th Brigade's command. Over slick terrain, the New Brunswickers hauled collapsible canvas assault boats up and over the exposed canal bank and then ferried the assault troops across the waterway while the Germans poured everything they had at them. After gaining a toehold on the opposite side, the assault companies had very little room to manoeuvre. The bridgehead established by the Reginas, for example, was just 45 metres by 360 metres. Under continuous fire, cold and coated with slime, the men searched for cover. While digging, they discovered they could only go down half a metre before hitting water.

Meanwhile, Chisholm's mortar platoon was firing non-stop. He recalled that in one three-hour period, it laid down more than a thousand mortar bombs on their "immediate front." Canadian artillery and the air force were also busy. As the intensity grew, Chisholm and two other men were ordered to cross the canal to establish better observation to control artillery fire. In front of them was roughly 450 metres of exposed ground. The only cover was the occasional shallow hole or slit trench.

But Chisholm was fast, and he could jump. While growing up in Prince Albert, he represented his school on the track and in high-jump competitions. This time he was wearing a lot more than a T-shirt and gym shorts. In addition to his mud-caked battledress and regular equipment, he carried one hundred rounds of .303 ammunition, grenades and a jerry can full of water. Speed, timing and luck were everything. While preparing to leave, Chisholm and his buddies stared across the open ground towardS the bank over which they would have to scramble. On the other side, they would "run like hell to a pontoon bridge." Their odds of making it to the canal were poor and their chances of getting across the bridge were worse. They would go one at a time, and Chisholm was last in line. "We knew that once we got onto the bridge we would have to just bloody well run. It wasn't too bad getting across at night, but during the day it was under fire — sniper and artillery fire. The two fellas ahead of me went singly and by the time I got to the bridge enemy shellfire had disrupted one of the floats."

Running and breathing as fast as he could, Chisholm reached the damaged bridge and got three-quarters of the way across when he lost his balance and plunged into the cold, murky canal. While the men ahead of him had made it across, Chisholm was sinking in salt water. He was a good swimmer, but was being dragged down by the weight of the equipment he carried. Still, he did not panic. He held his breath and waited for his feet to

A member of the Royal Canadian Engineers works amid the rubble at the east end of the Leopold Canal in the Netherlands, October 1944.

touch bottom. He would then launch himself towards the surface, climb out and run for cover. But the canal was too deep, and he continued to sink. He had instinctively dropped the jerry can, but was hanging on to his .303. He let go of the rifle and rose towards the surface, but began to sink again.

Moments later, a hand grabbed him and hauled his tall frame out of the water and onto a pontoon. While he was catching his breath, a voice told him to get up and get moving. A nearby explosion also convinced him to get across the bridge as quickly as possible. Chisholm dashed to the other side and then threw himself into a shallow slit trench where he noticed another soldier crouched in the corner. "I asked him for a dry cigarette, but he didn't answer. I then realized he was dead."[7]

Chisholm recalled being dug in for about six days. "One company tried to advance further and they got shot up. It was just flat ground and Germans had it all covered. It was bad. It rained all the time — a miserable place. The tragic thing was not being able to go out and move your dead or wounded."

Jim Parks of the Winnipegs recalled seeing some of the dead after they had been moved. "They brought them out at night — across the pontoon bridge — and lined them up on the ground, wrapped in blankets. It was pretty grim and any newcomer or reinforcement going in there would have been shocked to see it." Parks and others spent a lot of time delivering ammunition and other supplies whenever they crossed the canal. He made several trips, hauling mortar shells — three on each side of his tired and wet body. "It really was a miserable place. Everything you crawled into was cold and wet. We wrapped ourselves in our gas capes, which we cinched up around our necks to keep our body heat in."

In seven days of fighting, the battalions of 7th Brigade had 533 casualties, including 111 killed. Chisholm would never forget the bravery he witnessed. Engineers, who are seldom recognized for their efforts, impressed him. "They were just amazing. They would be out there under fire doing many, many things — just doing their job. You had to really admire them."

There is no safe place on a battlefield. Throughout the war, men died horribly — sometimes accidentally — while not engaging the enemy. On October 28, at Bergen-op-Zoom in the Netherlands, seventeen-year-old Dennis Hoare, a trooper with the South Alberta Regiment (SAR), was standing in line in front of the municipal tax building on Steenbergsestraat. The city had been liberated the day before, after the Germans had pulled out, but they were just across the river. Hoare was only sixteen when he enrolled at Kentville, Nova Scotia, and all he wanted to do that day was purchase a few victory bonds at the squadron's office.

The young soldier was with a group of South Albertas. Waiting nearby were members of the Argyll and Sutherland Highlanders of Canada, preparing to advance to the River Zoom as part of a daylight attack. Artillery was being used to "soften up enemy positions" but some of the shells from a Canadian medium regiment were falling short, landing in the city. One of these — a 5.5 inch — struck the deck of a tank belonging to the SAR's C Squadron. The men standing outside the office were sprayed with shrapnel, which ripped through the front of the office building. Captain Alec Scrimger of B Squadron, a number of Argylls, and the forward observation officer from 15th Field Regiment, attached to C Squadron, were killed. Six South Alberta troopers also died, including Hoare, who had only joined the regiment on October 18 after arriving in France on October 4.[8]

At the time of his tragic death, Hoare was more than five months away from celebrating his eighteenth birthday.

Hoare's father, George, 41, was also in the army. His mother, Nellie, 36, was at home in Springhill, Nova Scotia. She was raising three other children — between the ages of seven and sixteen — when the telegram arrived, informing her that her oldest son had been "officially reported killed in action."

When he enrolled, Hoare stated he was born on April 7, 1925, and had quit school while in Grade 10 because he had lost interest and did not like the teacher. He got a job at a newspaper, as a printer's apprentice, and joined the local militia. In his spare time, he studied signalling, played sports and read adventure and animal stories. He joined the army on August 31, 1943, and was described as a "dependable, conscientious young man" with "fairly dynamic physical qualities," an "above average type."

In January 1945, while filling out a form from the Department of National Defence's Estate Branch, Nellie was asked to provide her deceased son's date of birth. She wrote he was born on April 7, 1927.[9]

Near the city of Nijmegen, Bob Muir of 14th Field Regiment had just returned from forty-eight-hours leave in Brussels with his friend Bill Chitty when he learned the young gunner who replaced him at his OP had not reported in. It was November 26 and the soldier was Gunner William Hanley. He was from Montreal and not much older than Muir or Chitty.[10] The 14th's war diary noted that the Regiment had "settled down to a period of static warfare," their first since arrival in the theatre. "Entertainments have been organized and regular 48 hour leaves to Paris, Antwerp, Brussels and Ghent are being granted . . . All personnel have had plenty of opportunity to dig in and make their living quarters as comfortable as possible."[11]

After hopping off the truck from Brussels, Muir was approached by Gunner John Walsh, who wanted to know where Easy Troop's OP was located. Muir immediately thought about the young gunner who had taken his place. The two men jumped into a jeep and roared off towards the OP. They met some stretcher-bearers who — according to Muir — did not want to go to the OP. They offered Muir and Walsh their armlets and helmets with red crosses on them, and this, recalled Muir, angered Walsh, who told them what to do with the equipment.

With adrenalin running high, the two gunners pressed on to the location, which was in ruins. It had been shelled, and the crawl trench joining the slit trench to the OP was filled with debris. Muir and Walsh grabbed a groundsheet and then got on all fours, spending a few anxious moments crawling along the top of the exposed trench. Hanley was found in the bottom of the OP, lying on his stomach with his face in water. "I put my hand under his chin to lift his face out and it was still warm," recalled Muir in an interview years after the war. "I thought that maybe if we had got there a little earlier we might have saved him." When Muir and Walsh rolled the man over onto the groundsheet, only half of him rolled on to it. "So there was no way he had survived that sort of shell. We put him on the groundsheet and the two of us each got a corner . . . and dragged him back up over the hill." Muir and Walsh had seen many casualties since Normandy, but Hanley's death hit them hard. "Unfortunately, this one was very close. He and I were the same age."[12]

The 14th Field Regiment's war diary does not record more than a few details of Hanley's death. It states that it was quiet, clear and cold with a half-moon between 1 and 7 a.m. on November 25. Then, at 7 a.m., Hanley's OP reported "some small arms fire on their right flank." At 4:20 p.m., an officer reported seeing "interesting vapour trails in distant skies — possible V2 [rocket] being launched." Just over an hour later, Hanley's OP reported fire in a church at Zifflich, east of Groesbeek, "probably caused by Typhoon aircraft." The next entry relating to Hanley's OP, made between 9:40 and 9:55 a.m., November 26, notes, "One bomb [dropped] in E Troop area." The day's last entry relating to the OP states, "Between 12:15 and 12:30 p.m. OP 29 shelled. Gnr. Hanley killed and Lieut. J.W. MacKinnon and signaller wounded and evacuated. It is believed shelled [sic] instigated because of movement about OP. CO directs all change overs at OPs to be carried out at dusk forthwith."

The same day Hanley was killed, Private Donald Fowler, who enrolled at the age fourteen in Kingston, Ontario, had to jump for cover while preparing for a church parade. Born in Peterborough, Ontario, Fowler had moved with his family to Kingston when he was five and joined the local militia regiment's bugle band at age eleven. "I went to Connaught Ranges [near Ottawa] for two summers and qualified on the Vickers machine gun and .303 rifle . . . The .303 had quite a kick to it and I felt it on my twelve-year-old shoulder. The trick was to hold it tight, don't let it hang loose and spread your legs wide enough to make sure it doesn't throw you back."

Fowler's father also served, as did a younger brother, Karl, who made it as far as Newfoundland before he was sent home. While in Britain, his father was seriously injured in a motorcycle accident, but before he left Canada, he had some advice for his son. "My mother must have asked him to have a talk 'with your son about the birds and bees.' My father had a couple of expressions that he used. He was getting packed up at Fort Frontenac and he said to me, 'Well, look son, if you are ever out with a woman, make sure you use a rubber. That's all he said, and it was good advice. He didn't have to elaborate because I think he trusted my judgement. I was in Grade 9 at the time."

Fowler arrived overseas with the Stormont, Dundas and Glengarry Highlanders, but was bounced around from unit to unit. His introduction to the horrors of war occurred three months earlier while in Normandy. He was walking between a wire fence and the wall of a building when he noticed a German hand grenade stuck vertically in a pile of dirt, set up as a booby trap. Fowler wisely avoided the potato masher, but curiosity led him to a slit trench — partially covered with logs. The cautious young soldier inched his way forward for a better look inside. "I lost my balance and suddenly found myself seated, with my back against the building, several feet away from the trench filled with the terribly decaying bodies of three members of the 12th SS Panzer Division. The youthful bodies were crawling with maggots and their stench was so powerful it overpowered my senses and thrust me uncontrollably backwards several feet. The memory of that still lingers."

Fowler's narrow escape in mid-November occurred while he was serving with the North Nova Scotia Highlanders. "There were two explosions as we were forming up for the parade. The first one I don't know if it was a bomb or a rocket. I dove under a truck with big tires and got nicked on the forehead. I smashed the back of my head against the truck's differential and blacked out for a few minutes. It hurt like hell when I came to."[13]

Young Donald Fowler learned to ride prior to joining the army at age fourteen in Kingston, Ontario. This photograph shows him in 1939.

Amid the sporadic violence, soldiers welcomed letters from home and early Christmas packages. Sadly, Muir's trusted friend, John Walsh, 32, of Toronto, did not make it to Christmas. He was killed on December 14.[14]

The sacrifices were never forgotten by the Dutch, who remain eternally grateful to men like Muir, Chitty, Fowler and Walsh. Chitty remembered a "lovely day with the local people and all sorts of good food and fellowship." There is a photograph of him, standing smartly in a leather jacket in front of a Dutch home in Nijmegen.[15]

First Canadian Army's operation to clear the Rhineland began on February 8, 1945. Operation Veritable's focus was the heavily defended German homeland between the Maas and Rhine Rivers. It was cold, wet and miserable, and much of the land was flooded. There was also the old Siegfried Line, a series of newly strengthened fortifications in western Germany stretching between the Dutch and Swiss borders.

Donald Fowler is holding a sandbag (second left), while another soldier fills it with dirt. It was the summer of 1944 and they were digging in.

By then, First Canadian Army, which still had other Allied forces under its command, was the largest force ever commanded by a Canadian. However, it had its work cut out for it as it fought across porridge-like terrain to clear such places as the Reichswald Forest, Moyland Wood, Calcar, the Hochwald Forest and Xanten.

Barney McGuigan of the North Shore (New Brunswick) Regiment was only fourteen or fifteen years old when he enrolled on July 8, 1943. He joined the regiment on February 11, but spent just fifteen days on the battlefield before he was killed on February 26 near Udem, thirteen kilometres from the Rhine.

He was sixteen.

McGuigan's story is similar to those of other underage soldiers. He enrolled by giving a false date of birth — May 29, 1925. After his death, while completing a form sent to her by the Estates Branch, his grandmother, Rose McGuigan, stated he was born on May 29, 1929. His parents were Tom and Sadie McGuigan, and the village of Sturgeon, on the east coast of Prince Edward Island, is listed as his place of birth. Rose also noted his mother was deceased. Separate information submitted by his father notes the young soldier was born on May 14, 1928. Other records indicate this as well.

The boy was tall for his age — five-foot-eight — and weighed 133 pounds. Schooling ended after Grade 7. When he was asked about this, he said it was because there was no teacher in the district. He worked as a fisherman and farm labourer, and had no trouble passing basic training. The assessment on his Personal Selection Record states: "Health good. Light, strong build, rugged appearance, plays baseball, likes shooting. Rather limited learning ability . . . and schooling only fair, but this lad would seem likely to absorb training suitably." On November 19, McGuigan — despite his young age — was deemed "suitable for overseas service" and "suitable for reinforcement operation." He shipped out the next day, arriving in Britain nine days later.

In a heartbreaking letter dated March 20, 1945, his grieving father wrote:

> *My son was only 15 when he joined up and was only 16 when he got killed. Its [sic] was strange they wanted to send a Boy 16 years to the firing line and Canada full of A1 Men for years and Still here and [I] did not give my son consent to join. [I would like] the full particulars Re. his death . . .*

A letter from the army, dated April 4, 1945, and addressed to Tom McGuigan, stated:

> *I have to inform that at the time of his enlistment this soldier declared his date of birth to be 29 May 1925, indicating that he reached the age of nineteen years on the 29th of May last. At which age soldiers*

The first heart-wrenching page of
Tom McGuigan's letter enquiring
about the death of his son, Barney,
noting he did not give his consent
for his son to join the army.

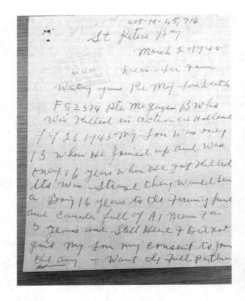

are eligible to serve wherever their services may be
required. Further, there is no record of information
having been received as to his correct date of birth,
prior to your letter under reference. If such information had been received, the services of this soldier
would not have been utilized in combatant duties
before he attained the age of nineteen years.[16]

While young Barney McGuigan fell under enemy fire, other
young men lost their lives or came close to dying on roads torn
up by artillery fire. That same winter, Jim Parks, who enrolled
underage in Winnipeg, nearly died in a motorcycle accident.

"They gave me a helmet that was too big so I stuffed my personal camouflage net inside the helmet to make it fit better. I'm
going along this road at a pretty good clip when I see this shell
hole. Just then a jeep comes around the corner and I had to avoid
him so I swung to the right and hit the shell hole. It threw me
forward in a swan dive, straight up into the air to the right. It was

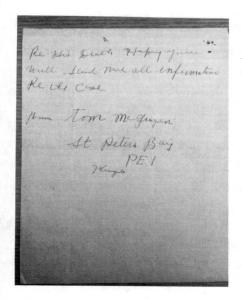

The final words from a distraught father seeking more information on the death of his son.

a good thing I went to the right, not the left. There was mud and trees every 20 feet and I could look between my legs as I was flying through the air and I could see the motorbike following me. I landed on my head and because my helmet was two sizes too big, it was loose on my head. So I went into the mud, ended up with guck all over my face. The bike landed behind me. I remember this English guy running over from the jeep and he said, 'Are you all right corporal?' I shook things off, sat for a while then jumped on the bike. There were a couple of things broken on the bike, and my first thought was I'm gonna get hell for this."

Parks returned the bike and then quietly made his way back to his trench, nursing a sore neck. "I later reported what had happened because they would have put two and two together. They did end up charging me for it."

By March 4, enemy forces were hemmed into a bridgehead in their homeland inside a U-shaped bend on the west bank of the Rhine known as the Wesel Pocket. Desperate and willing to fight to the last man, the Germans held this area while their forces withdrew further eastward across the river. As the Allies tightened their grip on the pocket and established positions along the Rhine, the enemy blew the last bridge over the river on March 10.[17]

The day before the Germans blew that last bridge, a seventeen-year-old Canadian soldier with the Black Watch of Canada was killed in action. His name was Herbert Danielson and he enrolled at age sixteen in Montreal South under his older brother's name, Frank. Sadly, his mother's appeal to have him discharged because of his age did not work. When the letter arrived, it surprised and confused those who had assumed the soldier serving with them was an older private named Frank Danielson, born on March 10, 1923. Even the dreaded telegram sent to his father on March 15, 1945, identified him as Private Frank Danielson, killed in action.

Herbert Danielson, who lived in Montreal, was born on February 22, 1928. His parents, Axle, a veteran of the First World War, and Edith, were married in London, England. The couple had seven children — two daughters and five sons. A third daughter, Kathleen, died in 1930 when she was six months old. Herbert had quit school after Grade 7 and worked as a coal dealer before enrolling on May 13, 1944.

There are four places on his attestation paper, including the Certificate of Medical Examination, where his signature appears as Frank Danielson. Nowhere on the form is he identified as Herbert. His medical sheet, filled out at the time, describes him as a twenty-one-year-old with blue eyes, brown hair, excellent visual acuity and good hearing. Physically, Herbert was exactly what recruiters wanted, and the young lad was anxious to serve. He was five-foot-ten and weighed 157 pounds, with a solid chest measurement of thirty-seven inches. The doctor noted a birthmark on the lad's right thigh and that he had suffered a broken foot ten years earlier.

The shock and disbelief that hit the Danielson home when the dreaded telegram arrived in March 1945 fell squarely on top of another family tragedy. Incredibly, on the same day Herbert was killed, his father was severely injured in a bus accident and died as a result of his injuries on March 23. In a letter following her father's and brother's deaths, Isobelle Danielson wrote to the Department of National Defence.

> *We have had two very hard blows and my mother is in very poor health. My father was a great man . . . I have a brother, William, who is now in Germany. He has been in the army over three years, having been away from Canada two and a half years. Do you think that there would be any possibility of having my brother, William, returned back home? I think it would be the only thing that would comfort her — my mother — in a time like this. She keeps saying that she wished she could only know he was safe and out of danger.*

It took weeks for authorities to sort out the proper identity of Private Herbert Danielson and establish the reason why he was not pulled out of the ranks sooner. This letter, dated February 9, 1945, was from his mother to the Department of National Defence:

> *Dear Sir: I am writing regarding my son who is training in the infantry in England. He says he expects to be leaving soon. As he will not be seventeen until the end of this month I think he is too young to go in action. So if you could do something I would be very glad. He is Pte. Danielson, F. D145261.*
>
> *Yours truly,*
> *Mrs. A. Danielson*

By then, Herbert was well along in the reinforcement stream, having disembarked in North-West Europe on February 10. He was just nineteen days away from joining the Black Watch in Germany.

In a letter dated February 14, the army wrote:

Dear Madam:

This will acknowledge your letter of recent date, requesting that your son . . . be withheld from combatant duties due to his being sixteen years of age. It is not the policy to utilize the services of soldiers who are known to be under the age of nineteen years on combatant duties. They are if under age of seventeen years returned to Canada and if between the age of seventeen and nineteen employed on less onerous and dangerous duties in the United Kingdom until they reach their nineteenth birthday. At the time of his enlistment this soldier declared his date of birth to be 10 March 1923, indicating that he is at present twenty-one years of age. Will you therefore please forward your son's birth certificate to the Secretary, Department of National Defence, Ottawa, in order that his correct date of birth may be definitely established . . .

The birth certificate was sent, but it led to more confusion on the part of the military because it appeared to be for a younger soldier named B. Danielson, not F. Danielson. As the authorities sought clarification, the uncompromising nature of war continued, and Herbert was among those who took his last breath on German soil.

On March 19, Mrs. Danielson wrote again, this time asking authorities to return his birth and baptism certificates:

*Sir. Would you send my son's Birth certificate also
Babtism [sic] paper it was a great shock to me
when I received the cablegram to say he was killed
as he was only a child just seventeen. I do think it
was awful neglect. I am sure you had time to keep
him back in England of which I thought was done
if a mother do not know her son's age who should.
I already have my husband in hospital in a serious
condition as a result of an accident.*

*Yours truly, A Brokenhearted Mother
Mrs. A. Danielson*

P.S. No. D145261. Danielson Herbert, not Frank

A March 28, 1945, memorandum from Canadian Military
Headquarters in London to the Department of National Defence
described the case and concluded,

*. . . all possible steps were taken in an endeavour
to return this soldier to the base. Unfortunately, he
was already in the reinforcement stream going forward at the time advice was received from NDHQ.
These cases of underage soldiers always present difficulties, and it is requested that all possible steps
be taken to prevent underage soldiers being dispatched on reinforcement drafts to the U.K.*[18]

On March 25 — Palm Sunday — the North Nova Scotia
Highlanders were engaged in bitter fighting to destroy the enemy
in the town of Bienen on the east side of the Rhine, north of
Rees. The battalion was part of 9th Canadian Infantry Brigade.
At the time of the attack, however, the brigade was attached to

The letter from a broken-hearted Mrs. Danielson that helped set the record straight in regards to the age of Herbert Danielson and her other children.

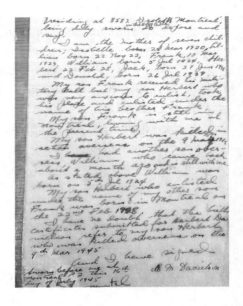

XXX British Corps as part of Operation Plunder, Second British Army's assault crossing of the Rhine. Although history remembers the much larger landing at Wesel — an advance that began with dramatic airborne and commando landings and ended with rapid manoeuvres deep into Germany — the story of XXX Corps' crucial mission has largely been forgotten.

While the mission flanked the main British Second Army attack to the south, it was also aimed at a section of the Rhine — between Rees and Emmerich — where the Germans most expected the Allies to attack. Although backed up behind the Rhine, the enemy was far from beaten and their positions afforded them excellent observation. Their key strongpoints were located in villages, inside stone or brick buildings that rose two or three storeys above the flat, wet landscape littered here and there with bloating carcasses of farm animals. The only cover available southwest of Bienen was a smattering of farm buildings and a dike.

After crossing the Rhine on March 23, 9th Brigade's Highland Light Infantry moved towards the village of Speldrop, on the east

ANSWER FULLY EACH QUESTION ON THIS PAGE
PARTICULARS AS TO IDENTITY

8	Full names of the deceased.	*Enlisted as* *Frank Danielson*
9	Date of his birth.	*Feb 22 nd 1928*
10	Place and date of his marriage.	
11	Place and date of his parents' marriage.	*London Eng.*

PARTICULARS OF DOMICILE

12	Place where deceased was born.	*Ahuntsic Montreal*
13	State, in order, the Province, State and/or County in which he resided before enlistment and the period of time in each.	(a) (b) *Montreal. P.Q.* (c) (d)
14	Nature of employment before enlistment.	*Factory worker*

A government form sent to families of deceased servicemen included a section where next of kin provided the soldier's date of birth. This one was completed by Mrs. Danielson.

flank of the advance. To the west, the Stormont, Dundas and Glengarry Highlanders reached the villages of Wardmannshof, Schultenhof and Grietherbusch by March 25. In the centre, the North Novas established their tactical headquarters in a large windmill southwest of Bienen, at Rosau. Two bloody attempts were made to destroy the enemy in Bienen and it was during the second attack when Bombardier Bob Muir, the young but sturdy radio operator with 14th Canadian Field Regiment, helped save the life of D Company's commander, Major Dave Dickson.

Muir, who had been part of the fighting since D-Day, was with D Company while it prepared to clamber up and over the dike on the southwest side of Bienen. The mission for the fifty men who comprised D Company's No. 16 and No. 17 Platoons was to get into the first few houses opposite the dike. A few minutes later, 18 Platoon, Dickson's headquarters group and the Forward

Observation Officer (FOO) party, of which Muir was part, were
to consolidate the position and plan the attack into the village,
and be ready for the inevitable counterattack.

At 2:30 p.m., the two lead platoons climbed over the dike,
straight into enemy fire. Many men were struck before they got
off the embankment. The men of No. 16 Platoon who managed to escape the hail of bullets dove or crawled into a shallow
depression in the ground on the east side of the dike. One by
one, they were struck by bullets or blown up by grenades lobbed
from trenches metres away. The enemy then began firing Panzer-
faust anti-tank rockets into No. 16 Platoon at point-blank range.
Meanwhile, No. 17 Platoon, which also came under ferocious
fire, had less ground to cover. The men pushed or bombed their
way into houses, attacking the enemy with bayonets, grenades
and small-arms fire. The air was thick with swirling dust and
smoke as they cleared one room after another, killing those too
stubborn to surrender.

On the west side of the dike, Dickson was waiting. While Muir
had arrived, the FOO party's artillery officer had not. The major
understood the importance of having proper artillery support and
was prepared to wait a little longer. Meanwhile, his men on the east
side of the dike were being ripped to shreds in the chaos. Dickson
decided to send No. 18 Platoon over the dike with the idea he
would cross as soon as the FOO arrived. But the enemy was ready.
It slashed the attackers with more machine-gun and mortar fire.
On the right, five men with No. 16 Platoon ran for the dike, but
only a couple made it. When the enemy had mostly finished with
No. 16 Platoon, it directed more fire at the rest of D Company.

All three platoons hadsuffered heavy losses and were barely
hanging on. It had only taken a few minutes, but almost half of
D Company was killed or wounded. Still, the men fought on and
Dickson ordered a party of men that had been left out of battle
to follow him over the dike to reinforce the company's position.

Muir was told to wait for the FOO, and when he arrived, lead him over the dike.

The bullet that struck Dickson penetrated his right side and came out the middle of his back. It sliced through a lung and his liver, took out one of his kidneys and broke several ribs and his diaphragm. Still, he considered himself lucky. "My wife used to send me John Cotton pipe tobacco from England and I never could keep a tobacco pouch. I used to keep the tin of tobacco down inside my battledress blouse."

Before entering his body, the bullet struck the tobacco tin, which may have caused it to deflect past his spinal cord by a few millimetres. "I always felt that perhaps that tin of tobacco saved me from being incapacitated for the rest of my life. Or being dead for the rest of my life, I guess."

While Dickson was lying on the dike, men stopped to help, but he told them to keep going. Then, a mortar blast sent Sergeant Edison Smith of West Point, Prince Edward Island, into the air. The sergeant's body landed on Dickson before rolling off the side of the dike. Thinking he was dying, Dickson reached into his battledress and retrieved a photograph of his wife. The movement caught the attention of Muir, who climbed up and dragged Dickson's large frame off the dike. Muir turned the wounded major over to some other North Novas, who carried him to an ambulance.[19]

While the war in Europe was winding down, First Canadian Army was busy clearing the north of the Netherlands. Many men would become casualties during the final weeks, including Parks, who was nearly vaporized. His nine months in North-West Europe had exposed him to a lot of danger and a lot of noise. The shelling, in particular, had taken a toll on his hearing. "It was all screwed up. My left ear wasn't any good so I depended on my right." Parks did not hear the shell that almost took him out. "We were in a field next to a house, setting up the mortars. I didn't know they were firing until I saw this dust flying around. I got up and there were air bursts so I ran like hell to this house and got my foot on the window sill with my head bent down to get through the opening. That was the last I remember. There was a big white flash, then euphoria."

Parks was blown into the house, and after hitting the floor, he skidded across the room into a closet that held a fold-up bed. "The closet doors were open and I went underneath the bed." The young soldier from Winnipeg eventually got his ears cleaned out, which included the removal of a few stones from his right ear. His battledress jacket took the brunt of it. "It was all torn to pieces with dirt and shrapnel. So that's how close it was. All I remember was that white flash. I was right in the middle of it. It couldn't have been any closer."

The major tasks facing First Canadian Army after the Rhineland campaign were to open the supply routes through Arnhem, in the eastern Netherlands, then move in a north and northeasterly direction towards the North Sea and into Germany. By this time, I Canadian Corps, which had moved from Italy to North-West Europe, had rejoined First Canadian Army. The fighting for Arnhem was costly, but the city on the Nederrijn River was taken in mid-April. By April 17, II Canadian Corps had freed the starving Dutch in the eastern Netherlands from Nazi rule. Their Hunger Winter was over, but more vicious and costly fighting against fanatical Nazis followed into early May, even after Hitler's suicide on April 30.

Parks was in Emden, Germany, when the surrender took place. "We had to still be careful. We were ordered not to fraternize with the enemy. We had to carry our rifle and our gasmask, and we're ordered not talk to anybody. I remember we went into this village and there were two girls there and my buddy and I started to talk to them." The next thing they knew they were spotted by a regimental sergeant major on a motorcycle. "We took off and I ran into a railway yard and in

Donald Anderson's watercolour Dutch Refugees *depicts Canadian soldiers helping refugees in Holland.*

order to avoid him I climbed onto this hospital train [full of Germans]. It had about a dozen cars and was parked on one of the sidings."

Each car was loaded with wounded Germans who suddenly stopped talking when they saw Parks. "I had the sergeant's hooks on and they didn't know if I was a sergeant or what so they all saluted me and stood aside making it easier for me to pass." Through the train's windows, Parks could see the disgruntled sergeant major scanning the cars for him. Luckily, Parks and the other man made their escape.

Chisholm was also in northern Germany, riding on a Bren gun carrier during the advance to the town of Aurich. "We came around this corner and there was a group of Germans on the march without their rifles, but with their bucket helmets on, long coats and jackboots. They were heading one way and we were heading the other. We just stared at them . . . couldn't believe it. Nobody was shooting. Somebody from our side of the road yelled 'Swinehound' in German, but he was quickly told to shut up from one of our guys . . . It just didn't seem possible that it was over . . . that it could stop."

Rifleman R.M. Douglas of the Royal Winnipeg Rifles celebrates with several Dutch women following the liberation of Deventer, Netherlands, April 10, 1945.

Parks felt empty inside on May 5. "I looked around and asked myself, shouldn't I be jumping in the air, yelling, and screaming? Well, I didn't. I was just glad it was over, for sure." Donald Fowler, who had spent the last five years in uniform after enrolling at age fourteen, probably best summed up the emotions he and other men felt when the Germans surrendered that day. In a letter to his mother, he wrote that while the Allies have triumphed, many "men have died . . . good men too . . . names I will never forget. I feel like crying my heart out — half with joy, half with sorrow."

PART IV

DANGEROUS WATERS

"The campaign against the U-boats was won by a precariously narrow margin."

Joseph Schull, *Far Distant Ships: An Official Account of Canadian Naval Operations in World War II*

MAP VI

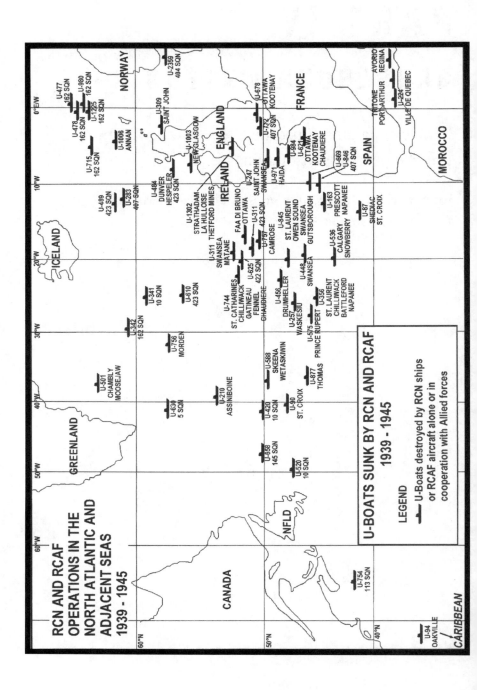

RCN AND RCAF OPERATIONS IN THE NORTH ATLANTIC AND ADJACENT SEAS 1939 - 1945

U-BOATS SUNK BY RCN AND RCAF
1939 - 1945

LEGEND

U-Boats destroyed by RCN ships
or RCAF aircraft alone or in
cooperation with Allied forces

CANADA

NFLD

GREENLAND

ICELAND

NORWAY

ENGLAND

IRELAND

FRANCE

SPAIN

MOROCCO

CARIBBEAN

U-94
OAKVILLE

U-754
113 SQN

U-520
10 SQN

U-658
145 SQN

U-501
CHAMBLY
MOOSEJAW

U-210
ASSINIBOINE

U-630
5 SQN

U-420
10 SQN

U-90
ST. CROIX

U-877
THOMAS

U-588
SKEENA
WETASKIWIN

U-756
MORDEN

U-342
162 SQN

U-341
10 SQN

U-610
423 SQN

U-575
PRINCE RUPERT

U-356
ST. LAURENT
CHILLIWACK
BATTLEFORD
NAPANEE

U-257
WASKESIU

U-456
DRUMHELLER

U-744
ST. CATHARINES
CHILLIWACK
GATINEAU
FENNEL
CHAUDIERE

U-625
422 SQN

U-448
SWANSEA

U-311
SWANSEA
MATANE

U-489
423 SQN

U-283
407 SQN

U-845
OWEN SOUND
SWANSEA

U-757
CAMROSE

U-845
ST. LAURENT
SWANSEA
GUTSBOROUGH

U-536
CALGARY
SNOWBERRY

U-163
PRESCOTT
NAPANEE

U-87
SHEDIAC
ST. CROIX

U-1302
STRATHADAM
LA HULLOISE
THETFORD MINES

U-247
SAINT JOHN

U-311
FAA DI BRUNO
OTTAWA

U-484
DUNVER
HESPELER
423 SQN

U-1003
NEWGLASGOW

U-1006
ANNAN

U-309
SAINT JOHN

U-715
162 SQN

U-478
162 SQN

U-477
162 SQN

U-980
162 SQN

U-1225
162 SQN

U-2359
404 SQN

U-678
OTTAWA
KOOTENAY

U-72
407 SQN

U-984
OTTAWA
KOOTENAY
CHAUDIERE

U-621
KOOTENAY
CHAUDIERE

U-971
HAIDA

U-669
U-846
407 SQN

TRITONE
PORTARTHUR

AVORIO
REGINA

U-224
VILLE DE QUEBEC

MAP VII

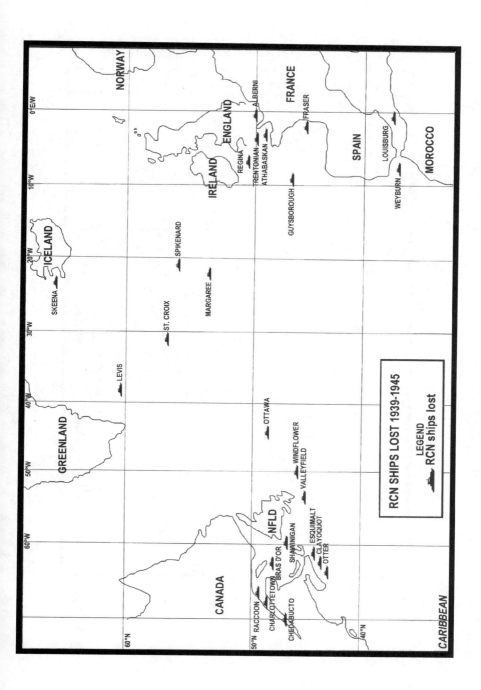

RCN SHIPS LOST 1939-1945

LEGEND
🚢 RCN ships lost

MAP VIII

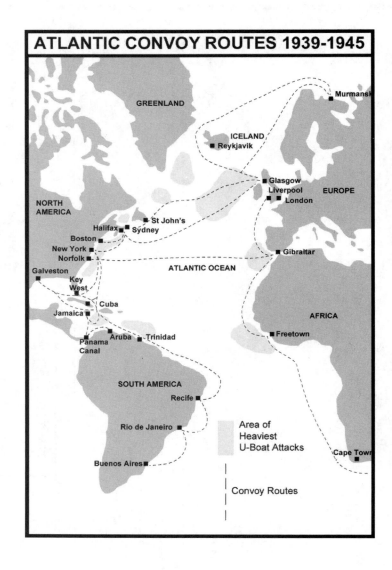

ATLANTIC CONVOY ROUTES 1939-1945

GREENLAND

Murmansk

ICELAND
Reykjavik

Glasgow
Liverpool
London

EUROPE

NORTH
AMERICA

St John's
Halifax Sydney
Boston
New York
Norfolk

Gibraltar

ATLANTIC OCEAN

Galveston
Key
West

Cuba

AFRICA

Jamaica

Aruba Trinidad

Freetown

Panama
Canal

SOUTH AMERICA

Recife

Rio de Janeiro

Area of
Heaviest
U-Boat Attacks

Cape Town

Buenos Aires

Convoy Routes

CHAPTER 10

"ASLEEP IN THE DEEP."
On the Sea, The First Years
(Map VI and Map VII)

The hot, jagged metal caught Ordinary Seaman Kenneth Watson in the arm. It hit him while His Majesty's Canadian Ship *Assiniboine* was engaged in a kill-or-be-killed battle with a surfaced U-boat in the North Atlantic, south of Greenland. Although Watson was the youngest rating on board the one-hundred-metre-long destroyer, he was more than equal to the task. It had been nearly two years since he first dreamed of joining the navy while watching servicemen parade through his hometown of Revelstoke, British Columbia.

Only sixteen years old when he applied for military service and barely seventeen when he was accepted as a Boy (Seaman Class) in 1941, Watson was not big, but he was tough and determined. He had grown up in bear country, along the banks of the Columbia, the largest river in the Pacific Northwest. At Revelstoke, the river's silty, blue waters cut through a valley between the rugged snow-capped Selkirk and Monashee Mountains. The town grew quickly and prospered before hard times blew in with the Depression.

Watson cherished his beloved Pan, a thin, attentive setter. He also had his younger sister, Beryl, and his older brother, Freddy. In one summertime photograph, Kenneth is smiling proudly in his Scout uniform, next to Freddy, who belonged to a local marching band. At the outbreak of war, Watson's parents, Charles and Alice, both in their late forties, had no way of knowing a mountain east of Revelstoke was going to be named after their youngest boy.

After he was knocked down by the flying metal, the five-foot-five Watson got back on his feet — intent on delivering more shells to his gun crew, manning A gun on *Assiniboine*'s forecastle.[1] The young ammunition carrier had no choice but to keep moving during action stations, and he was not the only wounded sailor on board. Nearby, other men pushed themselves to the limit while being slashed by shell fragments or pieces of steel plating, ripped away by *U-210*'s powerful 20 mm flak gun.

It was August 6, 1942, and Watson was prepared to fight to the finish.

* * *

The dramatic duel between *Assiniboine* and *U-210* was one of many battles fought by the often undermanned, overstretched and poorly equipped ships of the RCN during the Battle of the Atlantic. The RCN's role in what was the longest continuous battle of the war was vital to the Allied cause. Canada's navy, which began the war with only six destroyers (a seventh one, *Assiniboine*, was acquired in October 1939), three auxiliary ships, four minesweepers and roughly thirty-five hundred personnel (half full-time professional naval seamen and the rest reservists), achieved much, although it was not always appreciated and was, at times, maligned by the British Admiralty. But without the RCN, especially its little, rust-streaked corvettes hastily built in Canadian shipyards, and other convoy escorts like *Assiniboine*, the delivery of troops and supplies from North America across the Atlantic would have been extremely difficult.

Worse still, the people of the British Isles were in dire straits because, by the spring of 1940, Britain was choked off from North-West Europe by an enemy within easy striking distance across the English Channel. Without the Atlantic lifeline and the delivery of foodstuffs, troops and *matériel*, the British could starve and the Allies would not be able to build up enough forces to invade Europe and crush the Nazis.

By the time *Assiniboine* was facing *U-210*, the RCN had grown considerably. Guaranteeing safety in the North Atlantic, however, was not possible. Early in the war, while the Nazis were seizing France, Canada sent four River-class destroyers overseas to help defend Britain and assist with the evacuation of British and French troops from France. In early 1940, Canada, which had little experience in warship construction, embarked on a massive shipbuilding program to produce sixty-four corvettes and eighteen Bangor-class minesweepers.[2] Many more contracts followed. The first ten corvettes — from a batch of fourteen — were commissioned incomplete as Royal Navy (RN) ships, but crewed by the RCN. When they began their transatlantic crossing in late 1940, they were missing key components and were fitted with fake guns fashioned by their improvising crews.[3] In mid-May 1941, the ten were completed in British shipyards and commissioned as RCN ships.

Measuring roughly sixty metres in length and about ten metres at their widest point, the corvette weighed less than twelve hundred tons fully loaded.[4] These earlier vessels were roughly two-thirds the size of a destroyer with a maximum speed of sixteen knots (roughly thirty kilometres per hour). By comparison, a destroyer's top end was thirty-one knots. However, it was the corvette, which could cover sixty-four hundred kilometres at twelve knots, and those who sailed in them that formed the backbone of Canada's far-ranging convoy escorts.

Finding sailors was another massive undertaking, but the ranks slowly grew with inexperienced boys and men who had never been to sea, fired a gun in anger, swallowed rum or faced a North Atlantic gale. Many of the navy's full-time professionals, which numbered roughly 1,820 officers and ratings at the start of the war, had enrolled years earlier while very young. Officer training had begun in Halifax at the Royal Naval College of Canada (RNCC), which — following the Halifax explosion of 1917 — moved to Kingston, Ontario, then Esquimalt, British Columbia. It closed in 1922 while the navy was busy demobilizing after the First World War.

Some of the more prominent names from the first class of 1911 included Leonard W. Murray, George Clarence Jones and John Moreau Grant. All were between the ages of fourteen and seventeen when they joined the intake of recruits. Murray, who became the only Canadian to command an Allied theatre of operations in either world war, quit high school at age fourteen to attend. Jones went on to serve as chief of the naval staff from 1944 to 1946, while Grant became the first commandant of the Royal Roads Naval College, which opened at Esquimalt in 1940.[5]

Two other teenagers who enrolled in the RNCC and distinguished themselves during the war were Edmond Rollo Mainguy and Harry DeWolf. Mainguy was fourteen when he began his studies in 1915. By 1941, he was in charge of the RCN's destroyers in Halifax and served as chief of the naval staff post-war. DeWolf, born at Bedford, Nova Scotia, entered the RCN at age fifteen at the RNCC in Esquimalt. During the Second World War, his skill, brilliance and boldness, especially in the English Channel, earned him the reputation "Hard-Over-Harry." He was also a post-war chief of the naval staff.

Canada's navy was also served by men who made their hard living at sea — rough and ready fishermen and merchant seamen who joined the Royal Canadian Naval Reserve (RCNR).

Rear Admiral Leonard Murray in 1942, having risen from boy sailor to the Allies' senior naval commander on Canada's east coast.

Nearly 85 per cent of the expanding navy was filled by ordinary sailors, members of the Royal Canadian Naval Volunteer Reserve (RCNVR) — known as the "Wavy Navy" for the wavy stripes its officers wore on their sleeves. A lot of the enthusiastic lads who became ordinary sailors joined straight from high school and had no intention of staying on after peace was won. Officers were drawn from universities, naval reserves and sailing clubs, and, while many of them had been to sea, they were inexperienced when it came to warfare. The RCNVR was the backbone of the navy, and it was the job of the smaller, professional, permanent force, the RCN, to foster, encourage, and train these men for war at sea.

Previous naval experience was not a prerequisite, but those volunteering, especially during the early days, had to be in good health with a Grade 8 education. Throughout the war, volunteers had to be between the ages of eighteen and thirty-two, but as with other branches of the military, birth certificates were rarely produced or asked for.[6] Lads sixteen or seventeen — like Kenneth Watson, who joined the permanent RCN — regularly got in as boy seamen, but most had to wait for promotion to ordinary seamen. The navy's recruitment drives, which began slowly, owing to the government's and the navy's cautious approach towards expansion, created frustration among those eager to join what became the most popular of the armed services.

Those who admitted they were too young were told to scram or obtain permission from home. Others were quietly encouraged to keep their mouth shut and move on to their new life in the navy, which was filled with young men whose average age was just twenty.[7] For many, going to sea promised great adventure, a chance to visit far-off lands, come home, talk about it and impress the girls, most of whom adored the uniform. Suddenly it was easier to get a date. Teenagers also embraced enrolment because it helped them supplant the interdependence of boyhood with the independence of manhood.

Clarence Mitchell's impression was that the navy was more open than the army or air force to accepting seventeen-year-olds. From his southwestern Ontario town of Strathroy, Mitchell hitchhiked to London a day or two after he turned seventeen. "They welcomed me with open arms, but sent me home with a letter that had to be signed by a parent, a merchant, the police chief and a minister from a church. It took some talking to get my mother to sign, but she did." With the signatures in place, Mitchell returned to London's naval reserve division at HMCS *Prevost* where he underwent a quick medical before stepping into a uniform as "a full-fledged member" of the RCNVR.[8]

It took Ralph Frayne of St. Catharines, Ontario, longer to enrol in the navy. He got in at age seventeen following a short stint in the army — when he was only fourteen — and a longer stretch at sea as a second cook in a Norwegian oil tanker, commencing when he was fifteen.

"I've often thought about what prompted me to join the first time. I just figured I didn't have a choice. I wanted to join. My father was an engineer on the railway and he died of gallstones when I was nine. So it was a single-parent family and at fourteen you could leave school to get a job. My mother thought that's what I would do. She didn't know I'd hitchhiked to Hamilton to join the army."

During a layover in Halifax, Frayne got into the navy by lying about his age and place of birth. He told recruiters he was born in Vernon, British Columbia, because he had liked the sound of that name.[9]

Fred Sygrove of Sydney, Nova Scotia, had a more personal reason to enrol, which he did at age seventeen. His father was killed when the SS *Grayburn* — an iron ore carrier that had been making regular hauls between Bell Island, Newfoundland, and the steel mill in Sydney — was torpedoed in the North Atlantic on a convoy run on June 29, 1941. Sygrove's father, a First World War veteran who had been gassed in 1917, was the ship's captain and was on the bridge when the *Grayburn* blew up. Thirty-five of her crew of fifty-three were lost.[10] Sygrove's brother was a cook on the same ship and probably would have died, too, if he had not been hospitalized with appendicitis before the ship sailed. The pain of losing his father prompted Sygrove, who had been born in Britain, to add another year to his age. He got in and joined HMCS *Kentville*, a Bangor-class minesweeper commissioned at Port Arthur (Thunder Bay, Ontario) in October 1942.[11]

Impressed by the uniform and those who had joined, Kenneth Watson had his mind set on the navy's permanent force. He applied to the RCN on June 25, 1940, at Revelstoke. At the time, he weighed 117 pounds and had a chest measurement of thirty-two and a half inches. He did not lie about his date of birth — February 14, 1924 — but was handed a blue consent

*Ralph Frayne was determined to
serve his country during the war and
witnessed plenty of action as a merchant seaman and while serving in
HMCS Haida.*

form for his father or mother to sign. The sixteen-year-old, who
had completed a year of high school, ran home and handed the
slip of paper to his parents. An interesting clause made it clear
who would be responsible for covering any cost should he decide
— for whatever reason — not to join the navy once he arrived at
Esquimalt on Vancouver Island:

> *I agree to refund the Department of National
> Defence the expenses incurred by that Depart-
> ment for my transportation to a Naval Base,
> should I, on arrival at such Base, fail to enrol
> for seven years continuous Naval Service for rea-
> sons which in the opinion of the Department are
> within my own control.*

The form was signed three weeks later — on July 17 — by
his father:

Kenneth Watson's 1940 application to join the Royal Canadian Navy had to be signed by his father because he was under twenty-one years of age.

I hereby certify that my son, Kenneth W. Watson, has my full consent (being himself willing) to enter the Naval Service of Canada for a period of seven years' continuous and general service, from the age of 18, in addition to whatever period may be necessary until he attains the age, agreeably to the King's Regulations. He has not been in a Reformatory, nor has he been sentenced to imprisonment. I declare that he has never had fits. The date of the boy's birth is February 14, 1924.

Sealed in the envelope with the signed form was his birth certificate, a certificate proving he completed two levels of first aid, a statement signed by the vice-principal of his high school that he had finished Grade 9 and a testimonial from an army sergeant.

In a July 26 letter to Watson, the navy returned the references and wrote:

Sir, With reference to your application to join the Royal Canadian Navy, I am directed to advise you that your name has been entered on the list of candidates for consideration in your turn when a vacancy occurs as a Boy (Seaman Class) after you attain the required age of 17 years. When your name is reached, instructions regarding your provisional medical examination will be forwarded to you.

He was advised to keep the department informed of any change of address.

On April 30, 1941 — two months after Watson turned seventeen — the navy told him he was "now under consideration for entry into the Permanent Force of the RCN as a Boy (Seaman Class) for duty at R.C.N. Barracks, Esquimalt, under a Seven Years' Continuous and General Service Engagement to date 2nd June 1941."

Watson was advised it would be necessary to undergo a final medical and educational test.

Provided you are found physically fit and suitable in all other respects, you will be entered in the Permanent Force of the Royal Canadian Navy. If you are not suitable in all respects, the Commanding Officer, R.C.N. Barracks Esquimalt, B.C., will supply you with the following transportation to your home: 1 Steamship ticket — Victoria, B.C., to Vancouver, B.C.; 1 Second Class Railway ticket — Vancouver, B.C., to Revelstoke, B.C.

On a form dated June 4, 1941, there is, under the heading Certificate and Declaration for Boys, the following clause that speaks to the navy's standardized application process:

*This is to certify that we have examined the boy
named on the other side hereof as to his fitness for
the Naval Service of Canada, and we find as follows: He is a well grown, stout, intelligent lad, of
perfectly sound and healthy constitution, and free
from all physical malformation, and we consider
him in all respects fit for His Majesty's Service.
The consent of his parents or guardian has been
obtained in writing, and they are willing and desir-
ous that the boy should be entered for term of seven
years' continuous and general service from the age
of 18, in addition to whatever period may be necessary till he attains that age.*

This last part left the door wide open for just about any lad to join before his eighteenth birthday, so long as a parent or guardian signed off on it.

Young Watson soon said goodbye to his family and his beloved dog, Pan. He began a few weeks of basic training, which taught him how to march, then studied discipline, gunnery, seamanship and signals — scoring average to excellent. By the middle of August 1941, Watson, who could be recognized by the scar on his upper lip, was promoted to ordinary seaman. In early November, he was transferred from the West Coast training establishment, HMCS *Naden*, to the East Coast establishment, HMCS *Stadacona*. On November 26, Watson joined *Assiniboine*, and from a photo — showing him hugging Pan — it appears the teenager got home one last time, in the spring of 1942.[12]

* * *

After the Germans conquered Western Europe in May 1940, enemy submarines roamed from captured French ports, targeting merchant ships coming and going from Britain. Germany's U-boat fleet began to expand at an alarming rate and more submarines ranged further west. In September, U-boats began attacking convoys in groups, known as wolf packs. Between June 1940 and May 1941, total ship losses were 540.[13]

Although still neutral in the war, the United States gave Britain fifty of its old destroyers in exchange for nearly a century of lease access to British bases in Newfoundland and the West Indies.[14] The RCN took possession of seven. Clarence Mitchell's duties on board one of the obsolete American destroyers, renamed HMCS *Annapolis*, included hours on watch high in the crow's nest. He never forgot how the ship rolled from port to starboard and pitched up and down. It made him wondered why he ever joined the navy. With his stomach turning, Mitchell had to be careful not to vomit on the officers below. Instead, he threw up into his cap.[15]

The RCN responded to the rising U-boat threat by contributing to a new escort force based in St. John's, Newfoundland. After local escorts delivered convoys from Nova Scotia, the anti-submarine warships from St. John's escorted them to Iceland. There, they were handed over to RN warships, which took them to Britain. The Newfoundland force refuelled in Iceland, then headed back with a westbound convoy. There remained, however, a serious shortage of escorts.

Additional corvettes from Canadian shipyards along the St. Lawrence and Great Lakes arrived on the East Coast in the spring of 1941, but these vessels and their crews were far from ready. As the U-boat campaign intensified, there was not time to properly train the crews and equip the ships. So, young men and boys went to war against an unseen enemy on an unforgiving sea, knowing they would learn on the job while trying to protect the slowest, most vulnerable convoys without proper equipment. While camaraderie was high, conditions were beyond miserable.

Kenneth Watson with his beloved dog Pan, Revelstoke, British Columbia, 1942.

Gerald Bowen of Ottawa, who joined the navy when he was seventeen and worked as a telegraphist during escort duty, remembered waves fifteen to eighteen metres — the height of a five-storey building. "You'd sort of chug up the side of one of them over the crest and then you'd drop into the trough with a crash and a bang. And the next wave would wash over you." During violent storms, ships in convoy were easily separated from their columns, scattered and hidden among the deep, unforgiving troughs. At such times, the risk of colliding with another ship was huge. "We always feared one of them coming over a crest and falling on top of you."

During one particular vicious storm, Bowen's ship lost all its lifeboats and her crew was smashed against bulkheads and railings, resulting in broken arms, lacerations and bruises. He recalled men on the open bridge or upper deck who lashed themselves to anything solid, out of fear of being swept overboard. Mother Nature's relentless pounding meant the galley was closed, so there was nothing warm to give the men while they kept working through

Besides doing war art, Alex Colville also designed war posters, such as this one from 1941 asking for more ships for the navy to do its job.

storms that turned stomachs and seemed to grind bone and muscle into jelly. "Oh, it was brutal . . . I presume we were scared stiff." Sick, wet, frightened and exhausted, sailors sometimes willed themselves to keep laughing in the face of such danger "because if they ever started to cry, they'd never stop."

Bowen, who was born on October 13, 1925, was thirteen when the war began. He was entering high school, but earning pocket money delivering newspapers in the nation's capital. On Monday, September 4, 1939, Labour Day, he was going door-to-door with a morning edition that carried a banner headline. The SS *Athenia*, an unarmed passenger ship that frequently steamed between Canada and Britain, was sunk by a torpedo from *U-30* in the North Atlantic. One hundred and twenty-eight passengers and crew perished. Bowen recalled customers running out of their houses to grab the paper. He enrolled a few years later, and then — for the first time in his life — boarded a train to Toronto for basic training. Joining the navy changed his life — turned him from boy to man without, he recalled, any teenage years in between.[16]

Torpedoes and bad weather were not the only dangers. Heavy concentrations of ship traffic also posed risks, but were more dangerous when combined with bad weather and threats from below. HMCS *Windflower*, the first Canadian-built corvette to be commissioned, was a victim of all three on December 7, 1941. She was helping to escort SC 58 through dense fog across relatively calm seas when disaster struck at 9:20 a.m. *Windflower*, patrolling on the starboard side, had turned in towards the convoy when the Dutch freighter SS *Zypenberg* emerged from dense fog. The two ships saw each other, but it was too late. The massive merchant vessel struck the corvette on a forty-five-degree angle, slicing off eight metres of her stern. Members of her crew responded by setting the depth charges to safe and drawing down her boiler fires, but it was not enough. Within minutes, cold water rushed over her number-one boiler, which exploded. Alerted by the blast, and presuming it was caused by a U-boat attack, a British corvette dropped depth charges. Those not killed in the collision or when the boiler exploded succumbed in the frigid water, which was barely above 1 degree Celsuis.[17] Among the twenty-three sailors killed was seventeen-year-old Ordinary Seaman Jerome Bright of the RCNVR. He was less than two months past his seventeenth birthday when he enrolled on April 14, 1941.

Bright, who resided in London, Ontario, was not from a large family. There were two boys: Jerome and fourteen-year-old John, both in school. Jerome's father, Denny, was a clergyman, and his mother's name was Violet. They were transplanted Britons, married at Cheltenham, England, in 1918, prior to the end of the First World War. The Reverend Denny Bright was the district secretary for the Western Ontario Bible Society, located downtown, a stone's throw from HMCS *Prevost*, the local naval reserve unit. He worked from what was called the "Bible Room," writing letters and seeing to other Society business. Bright was born on February 28, 1924, and by 1938, he was attending high school at London Central Collegiate Institute.

When he joined the naval reserve, he was nearly five-foot-ten and weighed 123 pounds, prompting the doctor conducting his medical to note the lad was "underweight," but otherwise healthy. On the day he enrolled, his father supported him with a letter of consent. "Sir: This is to say that my son . . . although aged 17 had my full permission to sign on for Active Service with the Royal Canadian Navy and to go wherever his duty may call him."

Bright was also bright. Less than a month after he enrolled, his intelligence was singled out by the instructor of his radio-direction-finding (RDF) course, the commanding officer of *Prevost*, Lieutenant-Commander J.R. Hunter. The CO came to the lad's defence when someone in the personnel section at Naval Service Headquarters in Ottawa noticed that Bright and another young rating from the London Division did not have prior sea cadet training. The May 2 memorandum from the Assistant Naval Secretary to Hunter stated:

> *it is to be ascertained if Ordinary Seamen Jack*
> *Edward Pope and Jerome Denny Bright have had one*
> *year's training as Sea Cadets. If this is so, their entry*
> *as Ordinary Seamen, RCNVR (Temporary) R.D.F. is*
> *approved. If it is found that these ratings have not had*
> *previous training with the Sea Cadets, they are to be*
> *discharged and re-entered as Boy Buglers, observing*
> *that they are under the age of eighteen years.*

The sound of a typewriter rapping out a response was soon heard. Hunter had checked the boys' backgrounds and, while neither had sea cadet training, both had a year in the militia. To the CO, this made sense because both were from inland towns where, he said, sea cadet facilities were not available. Hunter's letter included an assessment from the RDF course instructor who reported Bright and Pope ranked at the top of their class. "In fact, Bright is much superior to anyone in the class . . . the army will take these two if they are released under any condition . . . In view of their abilities, military experience, extreme adaptabilities and proximity to age rates, would it be possible for you to reconsider their case?"

Hunter's credibility was high. People listened. Under his watch, *Prevost* earned the 1941 Commodore Walter Hose Efficiency Trophy, a feat repeated in 1942 and 1943. Three days later, the enrolments were approved.

While Denny and Violet were proud of their son's determination, they — like thousands of other parents — worried and prayed. The telegram informing them of their son's death arrived on December 9 — two days after the tragedy. Also dated that day was a letter from Naval Secretary Captain J.O. Cossette.

> *It is with deep regret that I must confirm the telegram . . . informing you that your son . . . was missing and believed killed . . . The exact circumstances of the unfortunate incident of war must be kept secret for reasons of security. I wish to express the sincere sympathy of the Chief of the Naval Staff, the Officers and men of the Royal Canadian Navy, the high traditions of which your son has helped maintain.*

When a letter from the department regarding application for a war service gratuity arrived, the Reverend stated that neither he nor his wife applied. Nor were they dependent on their son. "My wife and I have the proud distinction of being his parents, and that for us is sufficient. However, our son's expressed wish was in the event of his death, any money he might leave behind should be used for his brother's education." He noted that his youngest son was entering university, planning to serve his country in a "scientific way." The letter concludes with the following: "Both the authorities here and at Halifax offered to recommend O.S. Bright for a shore job, where his capacities for technical matters could both be expanded and made use of. But he insisted in going to sea."

Later, while completing a form for the Estates Branch, the Reverend came across a standardized block of type that asked those filling out the form whether any funeral expenses were incurred. Denny wrote: "None. Asleep in the deep."[18]

The *Windflower* tragedy occurred on the same day that the Japanese attacked Pearl Harbour. With the Americans now fully at war, the Germans sent more U-boats across the Atlantic into Canadian and U.S. coastal waters. In response, the RCN established coastal convoys between Nova Scotia and Newfoundland. The U.S., which was beginning to build large numbers of sub-hunters, did not follow suit, and the U-boats had an easy time sinking lone merchant ships along the eastern seaboard. Ships steaming between Halifax and the U.S. were also hit, so the RCN was tasked with organizing a convoy service between Boston and Nova Scotia. Meanwhile, U-boats continued to wreak havoc on convoys crossing the Atlantic. When subs entered the Caribbean and began picking off tankers, the RCN's escort work was stretched even wider. In the southern waters, U-boats sank up to fifty ships a month.[19] It did not matter where the loaded tankers were when they were hit. "It just stuns you, you know," recalled Gerald Bowen, "dark night and suddenly everything is bright." The RCN escorts fought back, but the added responsibilities left Canada vulnerable and soon U-boats were sinking ships in the Gulf of St. Lawrence.

By the summer of 1942, Germany was launching about twenty U-boats a month, and those operating further out to sea, in what was known as the Black Pit or Mid-Atlantic Air Gap, remained relatively safe from aerial attack. Eastern Air Command of the RCAF contributed greatly to convoy protection, but was short of long-range aircraft to cover the gap.

* * *

When *Assiniboine* encountered *U-210*, she was part of mid-ocean escort group C.1, guarding slow-moving convoy SC 94. The convoy had sailed from Sydney, Nova Scotia, on July 31 with thirty merchant ships, joined by three more out of Newfoundland.[20] Its destination was the historic port of Liverpool, where the River Mersey meets the Irish Sea. In addition to "Bones," as *Assiniboine* was known, the escort group included the Canadian corvettes *Battleford*, *Chilliwack* and *Orillia*, three British warships and one Free French corvette. As SC 94 steamed eastward on August 5, a portion became separated in dense fog and was discovered by *U-593*, which torpedoed and sank the 3,616-ton Dutch cargo ship *Spar*.

Orillia and the British corvette *Nasturtium* gave chase and drove off *U-593* and *U-595*, allowing the convoy to reunite. While Bones was slipping in and out of fog searching for enemy subs, the crew had to remain alert as nearly a dozen U-boats converged on SC 94 with the intention of destroying as many of the merchant vessels as possible. It was hard to see in the silver-grey light that hung between the ocean and drifting fog, but *Assiniboine* used her guns in the hope of destroying *U-595*, which again was threatening the convoy.

Bones did not have to wait long for another chance at a U-boat. Along with HMS *Dianthus*, she chased three subs that had snuck up astern of the merchant ships. While hunting those, *Assiniboine* discovered *U-210*.

Around 8 p.m. the U-boat was on the surface, a short distance from *Assiniboine*'s bow. When the destroyer loomed out of the fog, the sight of her took *U-210* by surprise. At the time, Kapitänleutnant Rudolf Lemcke was below having dinner, and it appears no one on *U-210*'s conning tower noticed the destroyer before it was too late. Lemcke threw his dinner aside when he heard shouts and gunfire. He rushed up into the open conning tower, where he came face to face with Bones. Hoping to gain a steady course to put his U-boat into a dive, Lemcke began issuing orders that sent *U-210* into a series of desperate manoeuvres. *Assiniboine*'s captain, Lieutenant-Commander John Stubbs, did everything he could to prevent the sub from getting away. His goal during the chase was to keep on firing, force the sub to stay on the surface and then ram.

But Lemcke had a lot of firepower. In addition to six torpedo tubes, *U-210* carried an 88 mm deck gun and a 20 mm anti-aircraft gun on the conning tower. *Assiniboine* was better off, with 4.7-inch guns, but for the time being, she was too close to use them.

For nearly forty minutes — at point-blank range — hot metal flew between the two vessels. They were like boxers, battling toe-to-toe in a tight corner. Watson was in the thick of it, hauling ammunition to his gun crew. *Assiniboine*'s .50-calibre machine guns prevented the U-boat's crew from manning the deck gun, but shells from *U-210*'s flak gun pummelled *Assiniboine*'s hull and superstructure. Down below, sailors worked frantically to drive wooden pegs into gaping holes ripped through the hull. Up above, on the starboard side of the wheelhouse, fire broke out when enemy gunfire ignited petrol drums. Thirty-two-year-old Chief Petty Officer Max Bernays, who had joined the RCNVR after he went to sea at an early age with the merchant marine, remained calm while trapped at the helm, surrounded by flames and under intense fire. After ordering two junior sailors to get clear, Bernays executed all the helm orders as the destroyer manoeuvered for position. He dispatched more than

A dramatic photograph of HMCS Assiniboine *ramming* U-210—*whose conning tower is visible on the left — on August 6, 1942.*

130 telegraph orders to the engine room and his bravery earned him the Conspicuous Gallantry Medal.[21]

The outcome was decided when *Assiniboine*'s machine gunners wiped out the crew manning *U-210*'s 20 mm gun. Then a shell from the destroyer's 4.7-inch gun ripped into the conning tower, killing Lemcke and his deck watch. An officer on the U-boat manned the flak gun, but things went from bad to worse. As the U-boat attempted to dive, *Assiniboine* rammed her just aft of the conning tower, but the destroyer's speed was too slow to cause serious damage. The U-boat submerged, but was forced up when water rushed in through the conning tower. *Assiniboine* rammed *U-210* a second time, and then dropped shallow depth charges while a shell from her 4.7-inch gun smashed into the sub's bow. All but six sailors from the sinking U-boat were rescued.

A sailor hangs on as water rushes over Assiniboine's *decks from ramming* U-210.

Many of *Assiniboine*'s men were nursing wounds, but grateful to be alive. The destroyer's only fatality in the dramatic, high-seas battle was lying on the grey, slippery deck. He was Ordinary Seaman Kenneth Watson. The blue-eyed sailor, who was just sixteen when he applied to join the navy, was crossing the open deck to pass another shell to his gun crew when he took a direct hit from a shell that also disabled the gun and wounded three of its crew. The next day, while the ship was steaming towards St. John's, Newfoundland, for much-needed repairs, Bernays and First Lieutenant Ralph Hennessy sewed Watson's broken body into a shroud of canvas. A couple of weights were placed at the teenager's cold feet before his body was solemnly lowered over the side into the deep, buried at sea with full military honours.[22]

An August 11, 1942, letter — sent from the Secretary of the Naval Board to Charles Watson — confirmed the news that had

The painting Burial at Sea *by Harold Beament depicts the solemn committal service aboard a Canadian warship.*

arrived in Revelstoke by telegram. In addition to expressing sympathy to a grieving family, it noted their son was killed in action against the enemy. It also stated it:

> *is for the public interest that the name of the ship in which your son was serving and the fact that she was in action, should not find its way to the enemy until such time as it is desired to publish the fact in an official statement. It is therefore requested that you will treat this information, other than the fact that your son has been killed, as confidential.*

On August 17, Charles wrote to the Naval Service seeking clarification on whether his son died in Canadian territorial or international waters. The stoic father said the information was required for an insurance claim. "This is very sad news to receive, but I suppose we will have to grin and bear it."

Soon another letter arrived, explaining their son was "shot while at his station during an engagement with an enemy submarine." His personal effects included a Bible, mouth organ, book of knots, pocket knife and a darning spool.

Later that year, a parcel containing a Memorial Cross — also known as the Silver Cross — arrived. While taking a closer look, Charles noticed it bore the name of another sailor. He wrapped it up and sent it back to Ottawa with a handwritten note, advising the authorities of the mistake. In early December, the Department of National Defence explained a clerical error was to blame; the Memorial Cross with the right name was on the way. That same month, Watson was posthumously mentioned in dispatches "for courage, resolution and devotion to duty before the enemy."[23] East of Revelstoke, rising more than 2,250 metres, is a mountain that ranks as the 1,828th highest mountain in British Columbia. There are no reports of anyone climbing it, but it is named after the teenager whose remains were sent to the bottom of the sea thousands of kilometres away.[24]

A month later, on September 13, Petty Officer Cliff Power of Mushaboom, Nova Scotia, was in the stoke hole on board HMCS *Ottawa*. The ship, which was completed in 1932, was one of the six destroyers with which Canada entered the war. She was a busy ship. On November 6, 1940, with one of the early graduates of the RNCC in charge, she helped sink an Italian submarine. Unfortunately, Commander Rollo Mainguy died before a post-war assessment — decades later — credited his ship and another one for the sub's demise. For the past fifteen months, *Ottawa* had been operating out of St. John's, part of the Newfoundland Escort Force.[25]

Power, who enrolled in 1939, just after his seventeenth birthday, was one of fourteen children, eleven sisters and three brothers, living in a four-bedroom house along Nova Scotia's Eastern Shore. He was the second oldest. Three of his siblings — two brothers and a sister — died in infancy. Like many families, the Powers raised their own food and so there were daily chores on weekends as well as before and after school. The children grew up respecting the meaning of hard work and the importance of elders. There was time for play, but not as part of any organized sport. In winter it was usually a few kids out on a frozen pond with improvised hockey sticks.

When Power was six, he entered Grade 1 in a one-room schoolhouse offering Grades 1 to 9. He was smart and got through school quickly because all grades were being taught in the same room at the same time by the same teacher. Prior to the outbreak of war, the tall, wiry teenager had his sights on Boston College. He enrolled in November, but was released six months later when his shocked mother, Myrene, caught up to him. His father, Rueben, also hated the idea of any of his boys going to war because he had seen what the First World War had done to his father. Rueben was also familiar with the hardships of a seafaring life, having served many years on the sea both as a fisherman and as the owner of cargo vessel. The weather was one thing, but now there were U-boats. Three months after Myrene intervened, Cliff snuck away and re-enlisted. Exasperated, his parents decided there was nothing they could do.[26]

U-91 sent *Ottawa* to the bottom on September 13. At 11 p.m., the destroyer was screening convoy ON 127 in the mid-Atlantic, roughly nine hundred kilometres east of Newfoundland. Six minutes later, the U-boat fired a torpedo into *Ottawa's* port bow. Although severely damaged, the ship remained afloat. Fifteen minutes later, a second torpedo slammed into the ship's starboard side. The explosion broke her back. She rolled over, broke in two and sank with men trapped inside. Power was among the lucky. "I cheated death

One of the many hazards in the North Atlantic was ice formed by freezing spray, which had the potential to capsize a ship if not kept clear with axes and steam hoses.

that night," he recalled during an interview years after the war. "I was a fortunate man to survive."

After being hit in the stomach by flying steel, Power figured he had no chance, until someone lashed him to a float and threw him overboard. He never learned who that sailor was. In the frigid water, Power and others struggled to hang on amid the swells and debris. Sixty-nine men were saved, but 141 perished, including several RN ratings and a number of merchant mariners rescued earlier by *Ottawa*.[27] Power lost a chunk of his stomach and was hospitalized for twenty-eight days, but he continued to serve, making eight trips across the Atlantic.[28]

By the fall of 1942, more U-boats — with improved technology — could detect long-wave radio emissions from Canadian warships, making it easier to attack while avoiding being killed. The size of the wolf packs also increased, resulting in catastrophic merchant ship losses. In response, the RN assigned its best U-boat–fighting ships to mid-Atlantic support groups. The gaps left in the eastern Atlantic by this decision were filled by three

RCN escort groups moved from the North Atlantic. In Britain, the crews trained under British instructors while their ships were refitted with upgrades, including short-wave radio. However, all three groups were soon escorting convoys between Britain and the Mediterranean. This and the RCN's close escort duty in the North Atlantic were significant contributions at a time when the RN's mid-Atlantic support groups were focused on killing U-boats. Merchant shipping losses dropped dramatically when the enemy headed for safer waters.

But the war at sea was not over. As land slipped away behind the rusty, salt-encrusted ships at the start of another convoy run, sailors, including the youngest of them, tried to steel themselves against familiar enemies: the U-boats, the Atlantic and the weather. Power recalled it was so cold sometimes he thought he was going to die, but the boys who suffered together stuck together, forming lasting bonds.[29] In winter, "ocean spray froze and coated ships with ice," remembered Clarence Mitchell. "It had to be chipped off so our ships would not become unstable and maybe roll over . . . Our clothes would be wet, and we would be soaked to the skin. We would have icicles hanging from our eyebrows, nose and chin."[30]

CHAPTER 11

"I GOT FROSTBITE ALL UP THE LEFT SIDE OF MY FACE. I DIDN'T HAVE TO SHAVE FOR YEARS."

On the Sea, The Final Years

(Map VI and Map VII)

It was dark on the Cabot Strait — approaching 9:30 p.m., HMCS *Shawinigan* was conducting a solo anti-submarine patrol, zig-zagging on a northeastern course towards Port Aux Basques, Newfoundland. Ordinary Seaman Lewis Evans was used to the crowded mess deck, where the air smelled of sweat and damp clothes, and where men ate, slept or relaxed while not on watch. The young Saskatoon rating was among eighty-three other crew members and seven officers in a ship originally designed to accommodate a standard crew of less than fifty.[1] But while privacy did not exist, *Shawinigan* had a good reputation. She had spent the last few years on escort duty, and in 1942, helped rescue survivors of ships sunk by U-boats in the Gulf of St. Lawrence.[2] It was now November 24, 1944, and Evans had been part of the crew since June. He got along with his shipmates and was proud to serve, but had plans to return to the Prairies and work for the railroad after the war.

That changed when an acoustic torpedo, fired from a U-boat

Some of the youthful faces of sailors on board HMCS Shawinigan.

lurking in the icy darkness, struck the corvette in the stern. Evans was among several lads on board who had joined the navy at seventeen. Included in this set were Joseph Breux, Ralph Earp, Arnold Hibbard and Cecil Moss. There was also Petty Officer Howard Parsons — a former newspaper boy from Winnipeg — who first applied to join the RCN at sixteen. Overall, a third of *Shawinigan*'s crew were twenty or younger.[3]

* * *

More than a year before *Shawinigan* was hit, there had been a decisive shift in the war at sea. But while U-boat losses forced the enemy to withdraw from their mid-ocean hunting grounds, the threat remained. More technologically advanced U-boats entered the fray with crews trained in the latest innovations and tactics. These boats headed across the Atlantic, targeting unsuspecting ships with their new weapon that homed in on a ship's propeller.

A corvette's main weapon against
U-boats was depth charges — often
with spectacular results.

Gerald Bowen, who a few years earlier delivered newspapers in an Ottawa neighbourhood, was aware of the acoustic torpedo. On the North Atlantic convoy runs, Bowen was usually crammed into the emergency wireless room in the tiller flats, just above the twin propellers of a frigate. He had to pass through several watertight doors to get down into the room, which featured a steel table bolted to a steel wall. There was a wireless set on the table and, as Bowen stood next to it, he had the usual amount of seawater swirling around his feet. He bravely accepted the fact that if the ship were hit by an acoustic torpedo, he would not know it because his life would end in an instant.

Equipped with a pair of earphones, Bowen was ready to act should the ship's main wireless cabin be knocked out during an attack: "One of the officers on the bridge was to tell me to send a message to the Admiralty, saying we'd been hit. So there I would stand. They'd start dropping depth charges and everything would

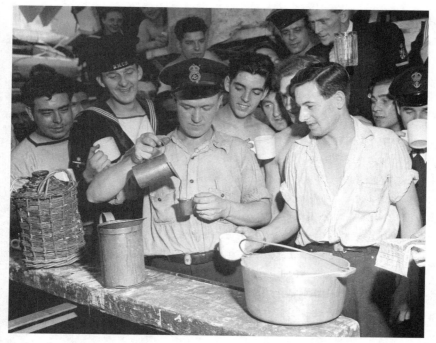

Sailors eagerly await an extra tot of their daily rum ration, or "grog," to celebrate the surrender of Italy in September 1943.

be shaking and shuddering and [I'd] be all alone in my tomb . . ."[4]

Canadian scientists had helped develop a device, known as CAT (Canadian Anti-Acoustic Torpedo) Gear, a noisemaking device that when towed a safe distance astern was meant to draw torpedoes away from a ship's propellers, but ships had to travel at slower speeds to use it. A better answer came in 1943 with the frigate, which was larger and faster than a corvette, and had more endurance.[5] Between late fall and spring, Canadian warships sank or assisted in the sinking of eight U-boats.[6] Air cover also improved with long-range bombers that extended protection over the notorious Black Pit and across the Atlantic. As Allied forces prepared for the Normandy landings, the RCN — with expanded escort groups — rose to the huge challenge of protecting all North

Atlantic convoys. This enabled the RN to concentrate on anti-submarine warfare in the English Channel, where the RCN also made significant contributions and sacrifices.

Able Seaman Ralph Frayne, who joined the navy at seventeen after stints in the army and merchant navy, was in the Channel on board HMCS *Haida*. Prior to joining the 10th Destroyer Flotilla out of Plymouth in January 1944, the destroyer had operated out of Scapa Flow, the RN's main North Sea base. While there, she made two trips to northern Russia, escorting convoys on the infamous Murmansk Run.[7] Sub-zero temperatures, pack ice, enormous seas, and enemy submarines and aircraft kept everyone on alert as the convoys delivered everything from boots to tanks. "It was cold," recalled Frayne, a gunner. "I got frostbite all up the left side of my face. I didn't have to shave for years. I was assigned to B gun. Twin 4.7-inch guns, located on the bow above A gun. There were eight of us in our crew."

Haida was present on December 26, 1943, the day the German Kriegsmarine was dealt an enormous blow by the British Home Fleet. "We were escorting a Murmansk-bound convoy, serving as sucker bait for the *Scharnhorst*, one of Hitler's prized battle cruisers, which had slipped out of Norway," recalled Frayne. Convoy JW 55B was also escorted by the Canadian destroyers *Huron* and *Iroquois*. All three Canadian ships were under strict orders to remain close to the merchant vessels while the trap was set. "We didn't come under attack, but it was colder than blazes. On those runs we had to chip ice off the gun." The Battle of North Cape ended with the enemy battle cruiser on the bottom of the Barents Sea. Of the 1,968 sailors on board, only thirty-six survived.[8]

Frayne recalled stepping off the ship at Kola Bay, a deep, sixty-kilometre-long fjord of the Barents Sea. With a haversack full of medical supplies, he joined five other sailors on a cold trek to a hospital. Getting in was not a problem, but the scene that greeted them on the way out was horrific. "We came out through a different door — a side door and it was bad . . . really bad. The bodies were stacked up and they had no clothes on, just piled up because the ground was frozen and they couldn't dig graves to bury them."

Later, Frayne and other members of the landing party described what they had seen, but their thoughts soon turned to a young shipmate suffering from appendicitis. "He was in severe pain, but wouldn't report it in Russia because he figured they would put him in a Russian hospital. So he suffered until we were a day out of Russia and then reported it. They took his appendix out on the captain's table."[9] Meanwhile, the image of the frozen bodies was hard to shake, even for an adventuresome teenager who had run away from home and toughed it out in a Norwegian freighter before joining the RCN.

Frayne's uninterrupted time in the military would have started sooner if he had not mentioned his enrolment while on leave in St. Catharines, Ontario. When his mother learned her fourteen-year-old son was about to ship out, she instructed her oldest boy to contact the authorities and let them know Ralph was much too young. By then he had been in the army for three months, joining at age fourteen after hitchhiking fifty kilometres to Hamilton. He remembered nobody asked any questions while he was thumbing into the Steel City. "They could care less back then. Kids did what kids did."

At the recruiting centre, Frayne, a big, strapping lad at five-foot-eleven, 175 pounds, was not asked to produce a birth certificate. Instead, he was instructed to state his age. "I lied about it, of course, and nobody questioned it. They were taking everybody and I looked a little older than my years. I didn't have to prove anything because they did not ask. They weren't interested. They just wanted bodies."

Shortly after enrolling, Frayne asked a First World War veteran for advice on how to survive army life. "He thought for a minute and said, 'Ok, eat everything they give you. You never know when you are going to eat again. Sleep every chance you get because you don't know when you will get to sleep again, and look busy. They will leave you alone if you look busy.'"

The keen young greenhorn was all set to head overseas when his older brother showed up and spoke to the authorities. Disappointed, Frayne was handed his discharge papers, at age fourteen. "I told the sergeant who was giving me the papers that I was going to enlist again. He said don't do it here because they will have a record of you. He said go somewhere else."

At fifteen, Frayne and another hopeful teen quietly left home and hitchhiked to Halifax, bent on joining the navy. It took them three days to reach the port city.

"One night while we were out on the road it got quite cold. We didn't have accommodation and it was late fall. The warmest part of the country was the road itself, so we slept on the side of the road — on the warm pavement. I still had my army uniform and it, too, kept me warm. We didn't have much money or food, so we didn't eat a lot. When we got to Halifax we went to the Sally Ann and they looked after us. They were good to us. We got a hot meal and a place to sleep. I then decided to join the Merchant Navy because they were taking guys younger than me."

Frayne's life at sea began when he boarded the *Beth*, a 6,852-ton Norwegian oil tanker that made frequent trips to ports in the Caribbean to take on bunker fuel, which she delivered to North American ports and across the Atlantic.[10]

"We had a telephone pole mounted on the bow so it looked like we had a gun. That was the only 'armament' we had." The ship's crew took a shine to the easy-going Canadian who was a lot younger than he looked. "They wanted to practice their English on me. I loved the Norskies. They were real seamen — a good group of guys — and the tanker was spotlessly clean. We made sure of that by scrubbing it and scrubbing it. It was a good life. I was second cook and pretty good at it. I cooked cod fish, but hated the stuff."

Seasickness did not bother the young cook and there was a lot of comfortable sleeping space — two to a room with bunks, not hammocks.

"On the tanker we could take our clothes off at night if we wanted to sleep. If you were on a straight [non-oil] tanker you slept with your clothes on because if you got torpedoed there was a good chance you would get off. With an oil tanker, there was no chance of that . . . it would just go boom. So we said, 'What's the point of sleeping with our clothes on if it's going to go boom?' We knew it would be game over. There was no stepping back."

Frayne figured he was either too ignorant or too young to be frightened. His first transatlantic crossing in 1941 was in convoy with dozens of ships. There were about thirty crewmembers on board the *Beth*, and Frayne was one of two Canadians. The other Canuck was also fifteen, from an orphanage.

"My job was to prepare breakfast. I would fry up bacon and eggs and it was also my job to clean up — that was the second cook's job as much as anything. There wasn't any down time. When I wasn't in the galley I would be out chipping paint because the ships are inclined to rust quickly. I was low man on the totem pole, so that's what I did. I chipped paint in the morning and painted over it in the afternoon."

It was during a transatlantic crossing when Frayne decided to quit the merchant navy and join the RCN.

"The freighter immediately ahead of us was torpedoed and as we came through we could see men in the water, but we couldn't stop. We had to keep going. That was part of the risk. The corvettes could pick up survivors, but we had no way of knowing if those guys were picked up. After that one I decided, OK, I am going to join up so I can fight back . . . I decided that I wanted to shoot at these bastards."

One day, while up on deck, Frayne witnessed a tanker on *Beth*'s port side turn into a fireball. "She was a bit of a distance, but we could see her burning and go down. It went down very quickly . . . almost like a flash." The *Beth* also lies on the bottom of the Atlantic, southeast of Barbados. She was torpedoed on a moonless night in May 1942, after Frayne — at age sixteen — left the ship in Halifax to join the navy. All but one of her crew of thirty survived.[11]

Following training, Frayne volunteered for a combined operations unit. "They were so-called commandos. They had an army branch and a navy branch. The navy branch was to operate the small ships for landing parties, boardings and night raids." From Halifax, Frayne shipped out to Greenock, Scotland, and spent about four months at HMCS *Niobe*, "an old mental hospital" turned into the navy's manning and accounting depot.[12] From there, he joined HMCS *Arvida*, but left the corvette after it returned to Halifax. "They had too many men and she was crowded. I joined the *Haida* and was there in time for her commissioning, August 1943."

Still mindful of the advice received from the First World War veteran in Hamilton, young Frayne managed to look busy.

"I picked up a clipboard and for the first three weeks I walked up and down the ship like blazes carrying this clipboard, trying to look busy. Finally the chief petty officer caught me and said, 'Frayne, what the hell are you doing?' I said I was looking for a job and he said, 'Well, you got one.'"

A pattern of more constructive work followed.

"I was young and rebellious and if there was trouble I was in it. The chief petty officer and I turned out to be best of friends.

Two ratings wash their laundry at sea, a labour-intensive task known as "dhob-bying" — a term adopted by the British in India.

After the war I said to him, 'My God, you were on my back all the time.' He said, 'You deserved every bit of it' and I asked him why and he said, 'You were the worst underachiever I ever saw.' I took that as a compliment. I was seventeen, going on eighteen."[13]

* * *

Clarence Mitchell, the young sailor from Strathroy, Ontario, whose earlier service had him on board one of the old four-stackers — HMCS *Annapolis* — was drafted to HMS *Puncher*, an aircraft carrier manned largely by Canadians. "Most of the crew were young boys, seventeen- or eighteen-year-olds who had never been to sea. They were like me when I saw the ocean. I put my finger in the water and tasted it — yes — it is salt water." Mitchell made friends with many lads his age — from communities across Canada — "a great bunch of guys who did their duty, often against great odds."

Puncher left Esquimalt in June 1944, bound for Norfolk, Virginia. The training was constant. A lot of Mitchell's time was on the flight deck, learning how to quickly fold up the wings of an aircraft and then get it below to the hangar deck. *Puncher* ferried motor launches from New Orleans to New York, and when she left Norfolk in July for Casablanca, she was hauling forty U.S. aircraft in support of the invasion of southern France, which began in August.[14]

Back at Norfolk, *Puncher* received more aircraft, which were folded up and strapped down millimetres apart. While steaming — via New York — in convoy across the grey Atlantic to the British Isles, Mitchell and others on watch did not have to be reminded about how real the threat was to their cargo. "Even with our escort corvettes, frigates and destroyers on constant patrol, not all of the ships made it to the other side."[15]

* * *

Prior to D-Day, as part of the RN's 10th Destroyer Flotilla, *Haida* attacked and destroyed enemy shipping in the English Channel and Bay of Biscay. For several months, beginning in January 1944, she and other Canadian warships participated in sweeps and patrols, usually at night. By late April, *Haida* had completed nearly twenty night missions.[16] "It was a night time thing," recalled Frayne. "We would come in in the morning because of the German guns in France [and the threat of enemy aircraft at first light]. Most of us would get some sleep during the day and then we'd be back out at night." In all, Frayne's ship participated in the sinking

The oil painting Canadian Tribal Destroyers in Action, *by serving naval officer Tony Law, depicts one of several intense night actions in the English Channel fought by HMCS Haida and her sister ships.*

of several enemy warships, including destroyers, a minesweeper and a submarine. On April 26, she and her sister ships, *Huron* and *Athabaskan*, helped sink the German torpedo boat *T-29*. Three days later, *Athabaskan* was sunk with the loss of 128, including her captain, Lieutenant-Commander John Stubbs, who had been in command of *Assiniboine* when she sank *U-210* in 1942.

"The *Athabaskan* took a torpedo fairly early," recalled Frayne, who was helping to man *Haida*'s B gun when *Athabaskan* was hit at 4:15 a.m. In the early morning darkness, *Haida* remained next to her sister ship long enough to lay a smoke screen. She then pursued two enemy vessels fleeing towards the French coast. As she put more distance between herself and *Athabaskan*, an explosion lit the sky. *Athabaskan* sank at 4:42 a.m. *Haida*, skippered by Commander Harry DeWolf, who had joined the RCN years before at age fifteen, scored hits on both enemy vessels before they veered in different directions. One of them — *T-27* — was hit repeatedly by *Haida*'s guns, and amid the explosions, elected to run herself ashore, where she was pummelled again by the Canadian destroyer. "The shell we fired was a 4.7-inch high explosive. We loaded them and loaded them and by the time we were finished we were dead tired," recalled Frayne. "I didn't have any trouble with my back, but my ears took a constant pounding."

Since there was always something to bet on, Frayne and other members of his gun crew played a little game if they were not too exhausted after a shoot. "When we were off duty we would go below. We couldn't hear anything at all until suddenly your ears popped. We would put a penny on the table to see whose ears — whose deafness — lasted the longest and the last one whose ears popped got the pennies."

There was no time or desire to do that when *Haida* returned to the scene of *Athabaskan*'s destruction. Floating amid the oil and debris were dozens of men, supported by life vests equipped with locator lights. Scramble nets and ropes were thrown over the side and boats were lowered, including *Haida*'s port motor cutter. Altogether, forty-four men were rescued. With daylight approaching, *Haida* could not stay long. She was also drifting towards an enemy minefield. All available hands worked to save as many men as possible as the gunners, including Frayne, remained alert at their stations. DeWolf, meanwhile, waited patiently, adding precious minutes to the rescue bid. Eighty-six other seamen were taken prisoner after the Canadians left and German warships arrived.[17]

In the early morning darkness of June 6, 1944, Frayne was staring into the sky over the Channel. He saw hundreds of planes, heading south in small groups towards the Normandy coast. It was an amazing sight for the young sailor. "It looked like they had a guide plane that led a group of five or six other planes. Only the guide planes had a light on and the sky was filled with these lights." The attack on Hitler's Fortress Europe had begun and the RCN was there, protecting the massive invasion fleet. More than ninety-four hundred Canadian naval personnel and 110 RCN ships participated in the assault phase, including sixteen mine-sweepers that cleared the approach lanes to the beaches. Harry Payne was an anti-aircraft gunner on board HMCS *Mulgrave*, part of the 31st Minesweeping Flotilla.[18] "I just sat there, looking out for enemy planes. If they came in, I shot them." The Canadian minesweepers were busy well before, during and after the historic invasion. Payne, who was under eighteen when he joined the navy in Toronto, recalled the grim task of recovering bodies in the water. "You pick them up, take off their identification, anything in their pockets, put it in a bag and throw them back in again. We had no choice because there was no room for them on the ship, all those people. That was the worst of my time in the navy."[19]

Peter Germaniuk, who joined the navy in April 1942 at seventeen, was serving as a gun loader on a motor torpedo boat, part of the Canadian 29th Motor Torpedo Boat (MTB) Flotilla. While pounding over the waves and through the spray off France in a twenty-two-metre-long MTB, Germaniuk was usually hunkered down or lying next to a torpedo, ready for action. During the Normandy landings, he was in MTB 463, deemed unsalvageable after striking a mine on July 8. Incredibly, the boat had struck several small mines without serious damage before the last one took its toll. Germaniuk, three other crew members and an officer were wounded and later transported — on another Canadian MTB — to a Polish destroyer. "I had a knife in my slot, in my back pocket, you might say, and it bent into a 90 degree. After that I spent 32 days in hospital in England . . ."[20] Seven months later, on the afternoon of February 14, 1945, a fiery explosion killed dozens of sailors, twenty-six of them Canadian, and destroyed five of the 29th Flotilla's MTBs

*Peter Germaniuk in his sailor's uni-
form, 1943. At the time he was likely
serving in HMCS* Cape Breton.

tied up at Ostend, Belgium, including MTB 459, in which Germaniuk had served.[21]

Before getting into "the good stuff" and "lots of action" with the MTBs, Germaniuk served in a variety of ships, including the minesweeper HMCS *Caraquet*, which took about seven weeks to travel from Esquimalt to Halifax. He also served in the frigates *Cape Breton* and *Charlottetown* before making it overseas. Life on board an MTB was an exciting change of pace until he was wounded and later drafted to another frigate.

While D-Day marked the beginning of the end of the war in Europe, it did not eliminate the U-boat threat. Equipped in early 1944 with a new breathing apparatus called a schnorkel, U-boats could remain underwater for weeks on end. They could lie in wait — undetected — near harbours or along coastal shipping routes. Stoker Alec Lovell, who enrolled at age sixteen under his older brother's name, Lorne, was on board HMCS *Regina* on the night of August 8. The corvette had stopped off the Cornish coast to assist a damaged merchant vessel. Twelve minutes before 11 p.m., *Regina* was torpedoed by *U-667* and sank within seconds. Thirty men died, including Lovell, who was from Brantford Township in southwestern Ontario.[22]

Lovell, who had completed Grade 8 and was employed as a welder for Massey-Harris-Verity, enrolled on July 27, 1943. He could proudly point to his service — at age fifteen — with the 2nd (Reserve) Battalion of the Dufferin and Haldimand Rifles of Canada. On December 15, 1943, at the tender age of seventeen, he joined the *Regina*, which had sunk an Italian submarine while on convoy duty in the Mediterranean.[23]

Regina's convoy duty on the North Atlantic in the winter of 1944 was followed by a series of exhausting patrols in the Channel prior to D-Day. After the invasion, she, like other ships, remained busy escorting convoys hauling munitions and supplies to the Allied forces in France. It was hard, dangerous work, and the number of wrecks littering the bottom of the Channel and Bay of Biscay made it difficult to locate enemy submarines.

Within a few days of *Regina*'s sinking, families of the missing received a naval telegram. The Lovells got theirs on August 11, less than a month before their son would have turned eighteen. In block letters, the cable stated their son, identified as Lorne Lovell, was missing at sea. The matter of Lovell's identity was clarified in 1945. "I did not know he had joined in his brother's name until we got word of his brother's death which was 30 days [earlier]," stated his grieving mother, Annie, in a letter to naval authorities. "I always called him Bud & when he gave me his address it was Bud Lovell. Hope this is clear."

Although Private Lorne Lovell was older than Alec, he was only a month past his sixteenth birthday when he enrolled in the army on June 21, 1940. Lorne, who was trained as a meat cutter, but worked as a brick setter for Brantford Brick and Tile, was born on May 6, 1924. Two days after landing on Juno Beach with the Highland Light Infantry, Lorne was struck in the face by a mortar fragment. The bloody injury to his nose did not end his time in France, but his parents received a telegram stating he was wounded in action. A month later, on July 8, while his younger brother Alec was on board *Regina*, Lorne was part of the attack to capture and clear the heavily defended village of Buron. The enemy was rooted out and destroyed, but the blood flowed into the next day (Chapter 8). Lorne was hit again and died July 9.

A report by the Department of Veterans Affairs, dated April 19, 1945, stated Alec enrolled using his older brother's identity, without his parents' knowledge to "obviate need of parents' consent . . ." The steps he took to enrol reflect how anxious he was to serve. The report also sheds light on what many families faced while struggling to make ends meet and mourning the loss of loved ones. It noted his father, Alec, was forty-five and in poor health after losing two sons. Annie, who was forty in 1945, had worked nights at Slingsby Textiles in order to be home during the day to care for her youngest children, including an infant. She was earning about fourteen dollars a week at a produce company. Her two oldest children — still at home — were working and paying room and board. It was noted the Lovells contributed to the construction of their "tidy and comfortable" home, which had an estimated value of seven hundred dollars with a three-hundred-dollar debt for lumber. "The mother seems healthy and employable, but tired. She does not complain, displays great fortitude, but is anxious about the debt on the home."[24]

* * *

When HMCS *Shawinigan* steamed out of Sydney on the night of November 24, 1944, she was accompanied by the U.S. coast guard cutter *Sassafras*. The two ships escorted the ferry SS *Burgeo* on her regular trip across the strait to Port aux Basques. While the

MEN of VALOR
They fight for you

Two-man boarding party from the Canadian corvette 'Oakville' subdues crew of German sub in Caribbean

Lads looking for excitement at sea may have been pulled into the recruiting centres by this poster by Hubert Rogers, depicting HMCS Oakville's *dramatic sinking of* U-94 *in 1942.*

U.S. ship departed after the crossing, *Shawinigan* remained in the area, watching for U-boats. The plan was to rendezvous with the Newfoundland ferry in the morning, for her return trip to Sydney. *Shawinigan's* captain, Lieutenant W.J. Jones, did not know *U-1228* was lying in wait. The U-boat had sailed from Bergen, Norway, on October 12 and her mission was to sink ships in Canadian waters. She was heading to the Gulf of St. Lawrence when her captain decided to linger in the Cabot Strait — the same deep body of water where the Newfoundland ferry SS *Caribou* was sunk in October 1942 by a U-boat. The loss of *Caribou's* 136 passengers and crew, many of them women and children, was still fresh.

Shawinigan's youngest sailors were sleeping, relaxing or going about their duties. Ordinary Seaman Lewis Evans was from a relatively small family. His father, William, was fifty-eight and his mother, Mable, forty-nine. He had two brothers and a sister, all of whom were older. His parents were married in 1914 and he was born on February 9, 1926. He had attended school, but was stacking bags of flour in the warehouse at Robin Hood Mills when he decided to visit the Saskatoon naval division, HMCS *Unicorn*, and join the RCNVR. At five-foot-eight, 138 pounds, Evans was solid at seventeen. Nine months later, he was with *Shawinigan*.[25]

Joseph Breux, Ralph Earp, Arnold Hibbard and Cecil Moss followed similar paths. All of them volunteered at age seventeen for the RCNVR. Able Seaman Breux was born in Chambly, Quebec, about twenty-five kilometres southeast of Montreal. He was from a French-Canadian family that moved to Montreal. Breux entered his teen years without his father, Yvon, who died in 1938. His mother, Anna, carried on, raising two sons and three daughters. Breux had finished Grade 8 and was working for Noorduyn Aviation as an assistant on a drop hammer, a large, heavy tool used during metal forging. He enjoyed his six months at Noorduyn and had plans to return after the war. At five-foot-eight, 125 pounds, Breux was no heavyweight, but he was a hard worker, and when he applied to the navy on June 15, 1943, he could point to a year's service with a local reserve unit.[26]

That same summer, Able Seaman Earp was working as a clerk in the accounting department of the City Hydro Company in Winnipeg. He was the oldest of three children raised by William and Lillian Earp, who were in their thirties when he applied to the navy on August 16, 1943. His training began shortly after at the local naval reserve unit. During his medical examination, the doctor noted the brown-haired, brown-eyed rating was five-foot-eight-and-a-half and weighed 136 pounds. He also recorded the scar where his appendix had been removed. Earp grew up in a modest home, a few blocks from the Red River. He attended Lord Roberts and Earl Grey schools before entering Kelvin high school, where he completed Grade 10. From Winnipeg, Earp's

Young Ralph Earp, along with the entire crew of HMCS Shawinigan, *died when his ship was torpedoed in the Cabot Strait.*

path led him through the training establishments at *Cornwallis* and *Stadacona*, and on May 5, he began a two-month stint in the Bangor-class minesweeper *Gananoque*, part of the Sydney Escort Force. He was drafted to *Shawinigan* on June 11.[27]

Ordinary Seaman Hibbard grew up in Grand-Mère, Quebec, along the St-Maurice River, northeast of the town of Shawinigan, his ship's namesake. He was a confident, solid lad at six-foot-one, 198 pounds when he enrolled in November 1942. His favourite courses at Laurentian high school were history, physics and electricity. He was a fast learner and his abilities carried over into summer employment as an assistant to a superintendent in an aluminum plant, where he supervised and recorded the work of other employees. The navy judged him to be "mentally alert and physically energetic — nerves seem to be steady." He was also described as a "clean-looking person of good appearance," interested in "group activities," owing to his experience as a scout leader. He loved rugby and swimming, and "evidently plays a good game of golf." When he shared his hopes of becoming a dentist after the war, "foresight and ambition" were added to his assessment.[28]

The household where Ordinary Seaman Moss spent his younger years was crowded, but less so during the war when three of his older brothers, Harry, Thomas and Angus, also left home to join the military. Cecil, the youngest of eight children, had completed Grade 11 and was working as a busboy at the Palliser, the Canadian Pacific Railway's flagship hotel in Calgary. It was an honour to work at the luxury hotel, which attracted the rich and famous. During the 1930s, the big-band sound of the Jerry Fuller Orchestra filled the ornate ballroom and was broadcast live on national radio.[29] The Palliser was the highest building in the city when Moss stepped away, after six months of clearing tables, to enrol in the navy. By then, his mother, Emma, was in her early fifties and his father, John, was over sixty. On the East Coast, Moss, who was five-foot-eight, 140 pounds, continued his training and joined *Shawinigan* on June 12, 1944.[30]

Howard Parsons of Winnipeg was willing to devote at least seven years of his young life to the RCN when he applied in November 1940 at age sixteen. The former newspaper delivery boy set his sights on becoming a telegrapher on board a warship. The navy's response, dated November 28, was not good, but it did suggest a course of action.

> *Sir, With reference to your application dated 19 November, I am directed to inform you that you are below the educational standard at present required for entry in the Telegraphist Branch of the Royal Canadian Navy, viz. completion of 2 years' high school. If you are desirous of having your application considered for entry as a Boy*

*(Seaman Class) you should advise Naval Service
Headquarters, Ottawa, to that effect and forward
a Certificate of Birth or Declaration sworn to
before a Notary Public as to date of birth, together
with two character references, one of which must
confirm your answer to Question 21, 'Have you
ever been convicted of a criminal offence?'*

After mulling it over, Parsons requested his application for
entry into the RCN as a telegrapher be changed to an application
for entry as boy seaman. He enclosed his birth certificate and
two references, including a character reference and a statement
proving he did not have a criminal record. When nothing was
heard by the end of April, Parsons wrote again. Finally, in a letter
dated June 18, he learned he was "under consideration for entry
into the Permanent Force of the Royal Canadian Navy as a Boy
(Seaman Class)." He was instructed to report to the Winnipeg
Division, RCNVR, on July 15, 1941, "not before and not after"
and submit to a medical exam and educational test.

In late November, while training at Esquimalt, Parsons fell out
of a truck and landed on his right arm. The pain was excruciating,
but the arm was not broken. When he left hospital on December
5, he was wearing a sling and assigned to light duties. Parsons was
soon promoted to ordinary seaman and his progression continued after arriving at East Coast training establishments. Between
April and May 1944 he was instructing at the anti-submarine
training centre and counted that towards advancement. On May
13 — two days after he joined *Shawinigan* — Parsons was promoted to petty officer.[31]

It is impossible to record exactly what happened to *Shawinigan* during her final moments on November 24, 1944. All of
these young sailors and everyone else on board perished, killed
instantly by the horrific explosion or dying in the icy water as the

ship sank. Some managed to get into their life vests, but the water was too cold. *Shawinigan* was all alone when *U-1228* fired a single T-5 GNAT torpedo from a range of about twenty-seven hundred metres at around 9:30 p.m. The torpedo struck the corvette in the stern, causing her to sink quickly. It is also believed *Shawinigan*'s depth charges exploded as she sank, adding to the destruction. When the SS *Burgeo* departed Port aux Basques for Sydney the next morning, the corvette was not in sight. Her master elected to continue on alone to Cape Breton while maintaining radio silence. When the ferry arrived in Sydney without her escort, the naval officer there ordered an air and sea search, but bad weather put a stop to much of that. An empty Carley float was found on November 26, and five bodies, identified as members of *Shawinigan*, were recovered from the frigid sea.

A board of inquiry was held, but specific details of the sinking only emerged when the U-boat commander was interrogated in May 1945. He stated the ship sank quickly, followed by two underwater explosions, and he saw no survivors in the water. The master of *Burgeo* was severely criticized by the Department of National Defence for not radioing the fact that his escort had failed to show up as planned, and for continuing his solo trip across the strait. He responded by stating that visibility was poor at the rendezvous point and he could not find sufficient cause to break radio silence.[32]

The family of any sailor lost at sea usually received a telegram within days. Most of them were a few lines stating the name of the sailor, his service number and whether he was missing or dead. Specific details on where and how a ship was sunk — even if they were known to naval authorities — were not released until the navy deemed it safe. Other sons and husbands were still fighting and the navy did not want to divulge anything that could compromise them or the operations they were involved in. As the old saying went: "Loose lips sink ships."

Young Lewis Evans had plans to work for the railroad after the war.

Evans's mother received her telegram on November 29. All it stated was her son was "missing at sea." It did not explain where he went missing nor did it mention the ship in which he was serving. On December 7, she received a letter from the secretary of the Naval Board, stating her boy was on board *Shawinigan*, lost while on operational duty at sea: "It is regretted that slight hope is held for your son's survival."

The letter also noted five bodies were recovered, and her son's body was not one of them. The Breux, Earp, Hibbard, Moss and Parsons families got the same sad news. It was not until February, when the Evanses received final word on their son's fate, that the secretary of the Naval Board wrote, "In view of the length of time which has elapsed since your son . . . was reported missing from HMCS *Shawinigan*, and as no news has since been received to the contrary, the Canadian Naval Authorities have now presumed his death to have occurred on the 24th of November, 1944." It concluded with an expression of sympathy on behalf of the defence minister, the chief of the naval staff and officers and men of the Royal Canadian Navy, "the high traditions of which your son has helped maintain."[33]

Two years later, on November 30, 1946, Breux's mother, Anna, was carrying on as a single parent, bereaved of her husband and her son. Suddenly, her hopes were raised by a photograph in a local newspaper. The young man looked just like her boy Joseph, could the navy investigate? Sidestepping the newspaper's editorial department, the Naval Secretary learned the photo was taken at a hospital in California. Through an exchange of correspondence between the navy and the hospital's chief social worker, it was determined the man in question was not Breux. Anna's bid for closure touched the chief social worker, who wrote back, expressing deep sympathy for the family's loss.[34]

Breux, Earp, Evans, Hibbard, Moss and Parsons were among the youngest of the 2,024 Canadian sailors killed in the war, most of them in the North Atlantic. Such loss of life was a grim sacrifice, but not without tremendous achievement. Thanks to all of them and the merchant mariners, the vital convoys crossed the Atlantic, the troops landed in Italy and Normandy and supplies reached northern Russia.[35]

"ONE LAD WAS ONLY TWELVE YEARS OLD — SO I WASN'T ALWAYS THE YOUNGEST ONE."

The Boys of Canada's Merchant Navy

(Map VIII)

Gordon Hovey was thirteen years old when he climbed into the cab of a potato truck and headed down a snow-covered road towards Saint John, New Brunswick. He was in the driver's seat, but unlike shorter kids, Hovey, who was over six feet, had no trouble seeing over the steering wheel. It was December 1942 and his goal was to join the war effort — one way or another — and he was not about to let his age stop him.[1]

* * *

Roy Spry and Joseph Kenny were fifteen when they decided to leave home amid the latest news and rumours from overseas. Spry, whose father was serving at a Canadian army depot in southern England, was pining for adventure when he hit the road in 1944. He was living at his grandmother's place at Leskard, Ontario, a farming community northeast of Bowmanville, where he and his older brother, Earl, created a swimming hole by damming a creek in a farmer's field. For them, it was all about making their own fun between chores and other obligations. In the long, blistering heat of summer, the makeshift pool drew youngsters from neighbouring farms, including a young girl who made quite an impression on Spry before he embarked on a wartime journey that took him into danger on the high seas.[2]

Kenny's wartime adventure began in the fall of 1939, shortly after the outbreak of war. He was in school, studying a map of the world, when he realized Germany was a tiny country compared to Canada. People were scared, but based on the map, it seemed to make sense that little Germany could be defeated quickly. Hoping to follow an older brother into the army, Kenny left the family farm at Sainte Rose, in northeastern New Brunswick, and headed south to Newcastle on the Miramichi. The recruiters there promptly told him to go home — he was too young. Instead of heeding the advice, Kenny turned to the RCAF. That looked promising until someone in Fredericton discovered his true age. From the provincial capital, he headed to Halifax, where he zeroed in on the first merchant ship he saw.[3]

* * *

Hovey, Kenny, Spry and Ralph Frayne (Chapters 10 and 11) were among hundreds of adolescents, some as young as twelve, who joined Canada's Merchant Navy during the war. And like many of the young lads who enrolled in the regular navy, their brief backgrounds hardly prepared them for a life in the merchant marine among old salts whose weathered, dark faces were in sharp contrast to their own. There were boys still too young to need a razor blade and others who — until they boarded a ship — had never tasted alcohol or indulged in adult stories involving female anatomy. They found adventure at sea, but the experience was far less romantic than what most had envisioned before

Roy Spry enjoying his early adolescent years at Leskard, Ontario, 1943.

leaving home. While some took to the sea easily, others never got used to the food, the harsh weather and the threat of U-boats. It was often an uncomfortable, nerve-racking existence, especially for those on board a ship loaded with munitions or aviation fuel. But for those who stuck it out and survived, the Merchant Navy experience was, on the whole, no less transformative than what was encountered by adolescents who joined the regular navy, the air force or the army.

It was their call to arms.

Altogether, some twelve thousand Canadian and Newfoundland sailors of various ages joined the Merchant Navy during the war, and regardless of whether they were crossing the Atlantic to deliver cargo to Britain or steaming to some other far-off port, they were up against incredible odds. And although it took decades for the federal government to grant them veteran's status with the attendant benefits, the wartime service of Allied merchant mariners earned high praise, especially their achievements during the war's longest continuous battle. "The Battle of the Atlantic was not won by any Navy or Air Force," said Canadian Rear-Admiral Leonard W. Murray, who during the war was commander-in-chief, Canadian Northwest Atlantic. "It was won by the courage, fortitude and determination of the British and Allied Merchant Navy."[4]

Merchant navy ships made more than twenty-five thousand voyages between North America and Britain during the Battle of the Atlantic. By war's end, approximately 170 million tons of supplies were delivered to Britain and to Allied forces in North-West Europe. Of this amount, 41.4 million tons were loaded on 7,357 ships that sailed from Canadian ports, primarily Halifax and Sydney. This massive life-saving contribution, together with the Merchant Navy's other wartime responsibilities around the globe, came at a cost. During the war, 1,629 men, women and boys from Canada and Newfoundland died while serving in the Merchant Navy, where the casualty rate was higher than that suffered by the individual branches of Canada's armed forces.[5] The true number, however, is higher — and unknown — because Canadians and Newfoundlanders also served on Allied and neutral ships, where there was a serious lack of standardized record-keeping.

* * *

It helped that Gordon Hovey was comfortable behind the wheel of the potato truck. Indeed, driving a large truck or a tractor was second nature for boys who grew up on farms, and besides, in many jurisdictions across Canada, it was legal during the war for adolescents to do so. Hovey's parents, William and Cedelia, appreciated how their son and another lad had volunteered to deliver spuds from their farm near Florenceville to Saint John, a distance of more than two hundred kilome-

Detail from a poster by Hubert Rogers shows sailors of the Merchant Navy in action on the dangerous Murmansk Run to northern Russia.

tres. What they did not know was how long their youngest boy would be away.

Like many large, rural families, the Hoveys survived on their ingenuity and fortitude during the Depression. They also owed their existence to the United Empire Loyalists who settled along the Saint John River during the late 1700s. Disease and farm accidents reduced the size of many families, and the Hoveys were not spared. Two infants died of illness and another child, in his early teens, succumbed after eating poison berries. Young Gordon, whose birthdate was January 4, 1929, was all brawn and capable of hard work. "He was six-foot-three and had a physical presence. And I know that people tend to overestimate people who are big," explained his daughter Marilyn Gillich. "A thirteen-year-old who looks the size of a grown man is going to get treated differently than a thirteen-year-old who hasn't had a growth spurt. One gets treated as a child and the other gets treated as a young man. The fact that he was a big person opened a few doors that made it easier for him to do the things he wanted to do."

Hovey also had an open mind. He did not want to follow what was considered the "normal path to adulthood." He was a free-spirit, somewhat of a risk-taker, but sensible — fuelled by a restless desire to travel the world and sample whatever it offered.[6]

Hovey's Second World War adventure began when he arrived in Saint John and joined a merchant ship. It was December 27, 1942, and he was not yet fourteen, but was immediately hired on as a "Peggy," working primarily as a cabin boy. There was plenty to learn, but he worked at it. "They were a pretty rough crowd, but they had your back all the time. You had to have that . . . One lad was only twelve years old — so I wasn't always the youngest. He, too, was Canadian — a fireman [a stoker]. Firemen hated sailors and sailors hated firemen. It was a rivalry, but it wasn't really a serious rivalry — kind of like opposing hockey teams."

For Hovey, work entailed delivering food from the ship's galley to the men in the mess. It was hazardous, especially during rough seas when the ship slammed into waves that sent walls of foaming water hurtling across the deck. During such times, it was a combination of luck and experience that helped a Peggy move from the galley to the mess, a trip that usually began from a position of relative safety, such as on the leeward side of the ship's bridge housing. To avoid being bowled over or swept away by a wave, these young sailors had to time their trips carefully, like a circus performer. Once on their way, they faced the challenge of maintaining speed and balance while carrying swinging buckets of soup or other food across the slippery deck as the ship rolled

Gordon Hovey had no trouble joining the Merchant Navy at age thirteen. He was tall and looked older than his years.

or pitched. Sometimes the food would have to be unceremoniously scooped up off the deck and placed back into the container. The trick, as the old saying goes, was to "keep one hand for yourself and one for the ship."

Hovey spent a lot of time delivering food, in all kinds of weather. When asked years later what type of food was in the buckets, he just smiled and said, "Shit. I was a farm boy. Food was food." Hovey served in three ships, including the *Riverdale Park* and *Lorne Park*. "These were big ships hauling big loads. They were 10,000 tons." Between 1942 and 1946, he made more than half a dozen trips across the North Atlantic and into the Caribbean, on ships hauling a variety of cargo, from artillery shells to whiskey. It was all part of the fight to win the war. "The main thing for me was my keenness to get in there and kick the ass of the Germans."[7]

* * *

For young Roy Spry, who was born on June 22, 1928, the road to Halifax went through Cobourg, on Lake Ontario, where he was hired on as a "pot-walloper." His dishwashing duties were on board the *Ontario No. 2*, one of two twin-funnelled coal/ passenger ferries operating between the southern Ontario town and the Genesee River dock, near Rochester, New York. By then, Spry, who stood about five-foot-six, was anxious to move on with his life and possibly get overseas to reconnect with his father, Ernest, who had owned a hardware store in Toronto. When the business was sold, Roy, along with his brother and mother, moved in with their grandmother in Leskard. He was thirteen when his father was posted overseas. "I missed him of course and was bound I was going to get over and see him. Looking back, that desire to see him got me through some wild and woolly days at sea and ashore."

While applying to the Ontario Car Ferry Company, the blue-eyed, blond-headed boy could point to his schooling — a period that clearly did not hold his interest — and his time in the army cadets, something he did enjoy. He had no idea what lay ahead, but working in the big ferry's galley was a start. He washed dirty pots, pans and fine china plates, polished silver until the skin fell off his fingers, and performed other duties on board the gleaming white *Ontario No. 2*, which kept a tight schedule across the vast and sometimes angry lake.

In addition to providing an international passenger service, the inbound ferries hauled railcars full of Pennsylvania coal used to power locomotives. The experience helped Spry prepare for his time in the Merchant Navy, which began after he quit Cobourg and hitchhiked with a chum to Montreal. He worked in construction, earning enough cash for train fare to Halifax. Years later, his widow, Betty Spry, the young girl whom met him at the swimming hole behind her grandfather's farm in Leskard, recalled that he was a quiet, easy-going boy who did

Roy Spry at Leskard, Ontario, before taking a job with the Ontario Car Ferry Company and then heading east to join the Merchant Navy.

not see wartime service as dangerous. "You were invincible at that age," she said. "He was on a mission and it was not hard to get into the Merchant Navy."[8]

* * *

Joseph Kenny's mother was worried about her young son, but she knew there was nothing she could do. His mind was made up. All that was left for her to do was to pray for his safety and hope he would do his best. In Halifax, Kenny made his way to the busy harbour, keen to find whatever work he could on one of the giant grey cargo ships that loomed sharply above the water. When asked to state the type of work he was interested in, he uttered two words: "A job." Kenny was soon introduced to the captain of a foreign vessel, who right away wanted to know how old he was and what kind of experience he had. Sixteen was his answer, but in addition to working on the farm, he had been employed as a "cookie," hauling pails of water at a lumber camp. After looking him up and down, the captain told him there are no farms on the ocean, but help was needed in the galley. That is where Kenny began his seafaring, peeling potatoes next to the main cook, a highly respected old-timer with clubbed feet and enough patience to teach the young lad.[9]

* * *

In September 1939, well before Hovey, Kenny and Spry made their moves, Canada's deep-sea merchant fleet was quite small, just thirty-eight ships. Two weeks before the war began, these vessels were confiscated by the federal government and placed under the control of the RCN. The size of the wartime fleet grew when 133 vessels from the Great Lakes fleet were called up and assigned to ocean-convoy duties. Canada also embarked on a massive shipbuilding program that by war's end produced 403 cargo ships. Most went to the U.S. and Britain, but many sailed under the Canadian flag. In 1942, the Park Steamship Company Limited, a Crown corporation, assumed ownership of the Canadian vessels, commissioning shipping firms to operate them on its behalf. Before the war ended, it had taken over 127 10,000-ton Park-class ships, forty-three 4,700-ton Gray-class freighters, and six 3,600-ton tankers — all built in Canada.

Finding sailors to crew them was not easy. There were approximately 1,450 merchant sailors prior to the outbreak of war, but most had joined the RCN. Others had signed on with the air force and the army. Sailors were found among the shipping companies that operated on inland and coastal waterways, but a lot more bodies were needed, and they were found among those who were medically unfit or too old for the regular forces, including retired naval officers in their sixties and seventies.[10] And, of course, there were boys, like Hovey, Kenny and Spry. Not every young teen made it through, but many did. Hovey just walked to the end of a pier in Saint John, where he met a man who was not a stickler for detail. Indeed, "becoming old enough" or "being young and healthy enough" were outweighed by the need to keep the ships moving with the right number of crew. Hovey was quickly assigned to a ship and left harbour almost immediately to join a convoy. "At the start there were a lot of ships that got torpedoed. They would sink one and all the sailors would likely get off because there were rafts and boats. The corvettes and destroyers would pick them up and they would be dumped into another [merchant] ship that was also running with half a crew." Hovey remembered that once a ship was loaded and had enough men, it was not unusual for it to sail right away.[11]

Another young lad who had no trouble joining the Merchant Navy was Ken Luttrell of North Bay, Ontario. He left school at fourteen and worked as a welder in a steel plant, assembling defensive guard shields for Bren gun carriers. Luttrell belonged to the sea cadets, and while working in the factory, he followed the news from overseas, yearning "to get into action." But instead of waiting until he was old enough to join the navy, he left home and joined the merchant navy, banking on the idea that the navy would take him after six months in the merchant navy. This "turned out to be untrue because they still said I was too young. And so I did my time on a merchant ship . . . a year on the SS *Hastings*."[12]

When Roy Spry got to Halifax, he took his place in line at the Canadian Seamen's Union office. "The union rep was sitting at a desk with his back to the door. He never saw me, just asked my name and rank and made out a pass to the docks. I said I was a trimmer, but didn't know what that was. When we got on board the ship [*Mayfair Park*] they called me into the officer's mess room, where they were signing on the crew. The captain blew his stack, and asked if my mother knew where I was. The union rep slowly turned purple." When the captain told him he was too young to work below, the chief mate jumped in and said they needed a fireman's Peggy. Spry said he would do it, even though he had no idea what a Peggy was.[13]

A trimmer helped the fireman look after the fires that heated the massive boilers, which produced steam to power the ship's engine and other machinery. But a trimmer's shift also included hours in the dark, dusty bunkers, shovelling coal into the chutes that fed the boiler room. George Evans, who toiled as a trimmer and fireman on board the Dutch ship SS *Pieter de Hoogh*, later wrote about his youthful experiences at sea. "The tools of a trimmer's trade were a coal shovel, wheelbarrow, sledge hammer (to break up knobs of coal) and a steel plate used for shoveling coal in the main bunker. For a teenage boy of 16 years of age, this was very strenuous work." Evans, who was born in St. John's, Newfoundland, was only fifteen when he began working as a mess boy in the SS *Einvik*, a Norwegian ship that was sunk in September 1941. After piling into lifeboats, Evans and the rest of the crew endured several miserable days at sea before reaching Iceland.[14]

* * *

Although inexperienced boys and men joined ships without delay, many other lads benefited from courses at the St. Margaret's Sea Training School in Hubbards, Nova Scotia, and in Ontario at the Prescott Marine Engineering Instruction School.[15] Time in the classroom was well spent, but nothing matched the excitement of going to sea.

Drawing on experience from the First World War, the British Admiralty ordered cargo ships to sail in convoy, escorted by warships. The first convoy — HX 1 — left Halifax on September 16, 1939.[16] With so many steamships pressed into service, it was

Atlantic Convoy, *a watercolour by Leonard Brooks, depicts a ship of 5th Escort Group escorting a convoy.*

necessary to separate them into slow and fast convoys. A fast or regular convoy could cross the Atlantic in ten to twelve days. A convoy of slower, less reliable ships could take sixteen days or longer. Ships joined convoys from a variety of ports along the eastern seaboard. In Halifax, the ships departed Bedford Basin and followed each other through the harbour out to an assembly point, where they were arranged in columns that formed a large grid or box. An average convoy could be composed of well over a hundred vessels, plus escorts, covering a huge expanse of ocean. With roughly a thousand metres separating the columns and approximately six hundred metres between ships in a column, the captains and crews remained vigilant, especially when fog set in or seas ran high.

Edward Bain from central Ontario emerged from the St. Margaret's school in 1943 at age sixteen. He was suitably impressed when his ship, the ten-thousand-ton *Westmount Park*, joined an eastbound convoy in mid-October. "As far as the eye could see there were ships . . . This great sight lasted only for that day; on the fifteenth, off the Grand Banks of Newfoundland, we ran into a very heavy fog and lost the convoy."

Bain's ship then ran into a hurricane that lasted five days. No one, he recalled, could approach the port side, and early one morning, two lifeboats were lost when they were torn from their davits. The force ripped the thirteen-millimetre steel deck plating "as if it were a piece of paper." The *Westmount Park* arrived safely at Liverpool where Bain saw — for the first time — destruction caused by Germany's bombing campaign.[17] Bad weather was particularly worrisome when ships were empty, heading west. "It was real bad coming back because you had no load in the ship," recalled Hovey. "The boat was light, riding high. I have seen that sucker go right up over to forty-four — forty-five degrees. All you could do was grab a post or something and hang on like hell. But even grabbing the post you would have been flying around in the air. You could get slapped by a few tons of water — slapped around pretty severely." Asked years later whether he ever thought he was going to die, Hovey smiled while recalling his youthful bravado: "Impossible. I was on it [the ship]. Nothing was going to happen to it." He did acknowledge, however, "one hell of a lot of damn good luck" came into play.[18]

Joseph Kenny remembered getting up at 4 a.m. — on a regular basis — to chop ice before heading to the galley to prepare breakfast. "We would have a storm, a snowstorm and the rain and that would build up on the ship. And that was just as bad as a torpedo. Just as bad. You'd have to chop [because] the cable and the winch and everything got full of ice. So you have to cut [it] up . . . [to] take the weight off."[19]

These were serious hazards, but being caught in the cross-hairs of a U-boat was terrifying. During the first three years of the war, the German U-boat fleet increased from about thirty to three-hundred. They also began to hunt smarter — in wolf packs

(Chapters 10 and 11). During June 1941, U-boats sank 454,000 tonnes of shipping. In the first half of 1942, nearly four hundred Allied ships were sunk with only seven U-boats destroyed.[20] The bulk and speed of a merchant ship meant it could not outmanoeuvre a surface raider, U-boat or aircraft. Instead, the merchantmen depended on escorts for defence. However, merchant ships were "stiffened" and authorized to carry defensive weapons and equipment — everything from small arms to deck guns to torpedo nets.[21] Ken Luttrell recalled gun drill on the SS *Hastings*. While lining up the axis of the gun barrel in the direction of the target, he had to take into account the downward and upward movement of the ship. Fish barrels were tied together and dropped over the side. Target practice commenced when the barrels were roughly two hundred to four hundred metres away. "The only thing that is humorous about this is that our ship travelled so slow that when you went to fire the gun you had to undo all the lightbulbs on the stern or in any area around where the vibration of a gun going off would be. And that's to save the lightbulbs from blowing out. But also, I swear to God, the ship would almost stop as the gun fired because of the recoil. But it was rather interesting, and at that young age it was quite an experience."[22]

Lighter moments and maintaining a sense of humour relieved boredom and stress, but nothing quelled the fear of U-boats. Sixteen-year-old Victor Pageau and his seventeen-year-old brother, Romeo, knew they were in dangerous waters on November 23, 1941, but may not have suspected they were going to die in the minutes before their ship sank in the Caribbean. The cause of the demise of the SS *Proteus* is unknown, but sabotage is suspected. The Pageau brothers were from Bagotville, Quebec, the sons of Odina and Marie Pageau.[23] Similar circumstances surround the SS *Nereus*, which sank with sixty-one people, including Pantry Boy Alan Garrett and Able Seaman Paul Starkey, both sixteen

Defensively Equipped Merchant Ships (DEMS) gunners pass ammunition for a Bofors 40-mm anti-aircraft gun, May 5, 1941.

from Montreal. Also killed were Steward William Couture of Quebec City and Pantry Boy Douglas Whitelaw of Hamilton, both seventeen.

Experienced seamen, if not fatalistic, were realistic about their chances of surviving in colder waters, especially the North Atlantic or off Norway or northern Russia on the infamous Murmansk Run (Chapter 11). The men and boys on the cargo ships slept with their clothes on, but the lads on the tankers, Frayne included, slept in the raw because they knew there would be no time to abandon ship if a torpedo struck. Joseph Kenny was lucky when the cargo ship he was in got torpedoed by a U-boat that crept inside the convoy. Knocked down by the blast, he still had time to get off the ship after regaining consciousness. Bruised and cold, he spent seventy-two hours alone in a raft,

Smoke billows from a damaged Park-class merchant ship (similar to an American Liberty ship) as she limps into Halifax for repairs.

praying for his survival and another chance to see his mother. "That's the part that kind of hurt . . . I didn't know if I could make it or not . . ."[24] Ordinary Seaman Gerard Martell of Halifax and Saloon Mess Man Charles Tooker of Hamilton were not so lucky. The two seventeen-year-olds were on board the SS *Victolite* when she was attacked by *U-564* northwest of Bermuda, February 10, 1942. The 153-metre-long oil tanker with a crew of forty-seven was sailing in ballast from Halifax, bound for Las Piedras, Uruguay, where she was to take on light diesel. She was hit by a torpedo amidships around 9:30 p.m., and while she managed to send an emergency radio signal, she exploded and sank after being raked by gunfire. There were no survivors. Her demise occurred close to where her sister ship, the SS *Montrolite*, was destroyed six days earlier.[25]

Roméo Gaudet of Verdun, Quebec, and Harry Kaminsky of Montreal, both seventeen, were firemen in the engine room of

Roy Spry's gunnery certificate obtained at the DEMS Training Centre in Saint John, New Brunswick.

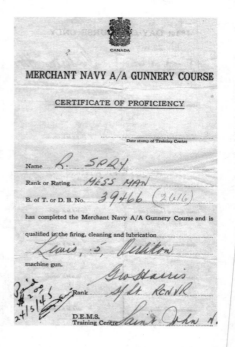

the SS *Donald Stewart* around 1:30 a.m., September 3, 1942, when a torpedo from *U-517* slammed into the ship, just forward of their work station. The *Donald Stewart* was in convoy in the Strait of Belle Isle, steaming towards Goose Bay, Labrador, with a load of high-octane aviation fuel and cement. The fuel was needed for aircraft providing North Atlantic convoy protection while the cement was earmarked for runway construction. She was just northwest of present-day Gros Morne National Park when the torpedo found her and sent her to the bottom in seven minutes. Most of her crew managed to escape and get away from the flames on the water. Three perished in the inferno, including Gaudet and Kaminsky.[26]

The destruction of merchant ships and RCN vessels continued well into the final days of the war, with serious losses, including many young teenagers. On Christmas Eve, Roy Spry was leaving the crew's quarters aft on the *Mayfair Park* when a torpedo

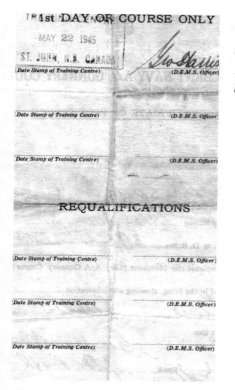

1st DAY OF COURSE ONLY

MAY 22 1945

ST. JOHN, N.S. CANADA
(Date Stamp of Training Centre)

(D.E.M.S. Officer)

(Date Stamp of Training Centre)

(D.E.M.S. Officer)

(Date Stamp of Training Centre)

(D.E.M.S. Officer)

REQUALIFICATIONS

(Date Stamp of Training Centre)

(D.E.M.S. Officer)

(Date Stamp of Training Centre)

(D.E.M.S. Officer)

(Date Stamp of Training Centre)

(D.E.M.S. Officer)

The second half of Roy Spry's gunnery training certificate, dated late May 1945. Hostilities in Europe had ended, but the war was not over.

from *U-806* slammed into the minesweeper HMCS *Clayoquot* off Sambo Light, near the entrance to Halifax Harbour. The *Mayfair* was in convoy, heading south, when Spry noticed her off the port side. The warship was steaming by when the acoustic torpedo found its mark, mangling more than eleven metres of her stern. Eight sailors, including four officers, perished, but for a while, it looked like more had died. "We watched her go down, seeing only one life raft of survivors," recalled Spry. Amid the terrible excitement, the gun layer on the merchant ship instructed Spry and two others to join him on the after gun deck. Roughly ten minutes after *Clayoquot* was hit, the stealthy U-boat fired a torpedo, which exploded near the minesweeper *Transcona*. The immediate hunt for *U-806* involved several ships and aircraft,

Roy Spry (second from top) poses with some shipmates aboard an unknown merchant vessel.

but the elusive sub slipped away. Spry recalled the convoy was ordered back to Halifax, where he spent his first Christmas away from home, but glad to be alive.[27]

Months later, Spry finally got overseas in the *Tweedsmuir Park,* arriving at the port of Avonmouth, where he was reunited with his father. It happened on the morning after the seventeen-year-old had been out celebrating the end of the war. "I was awakened by shipmates who told me my dad was at the gate. He had met them on the train, but couldn't get into the dock area without a pass. I wasted no time getting to the gates. It was wonderful seeing him again after all that time. He never mentioned my hungover appearance or even my tattoos, but he must have got a shock remembering me as the scrawny thirteen year old he'd last seen."[28]

* * *

In the Atlantic, the Caribbean, the Mediterranean, on frozen runs to northern Russian, off Normandy, in the Pacific and Far

East, Canadian and Newfoundland merchant mariners served and sacrificed. Many were very young, and remained that way, lost to the deep. Others grew older and either hung on to memories or tried hard to forget them. "It was an honour to be with those men," recalled Hovey. "It was one of the greatest experiences I ever had, and I probably didn't start to get really smart until I was about twenty-five or so, which was still more than ten years away when I joined."[29]

PART V
DANGEROUS SKIES

"The strategic bomber offensive was, by 1941, the only way to strike directly at Germany."

Brereton Greenhous, Stephen J. Harris, William C. Johnston & William G.P. Rawling, *The Crucible of War, 1939-1945: The Official History of the Royal Canadian Air Force, Volume III*

MAP IX

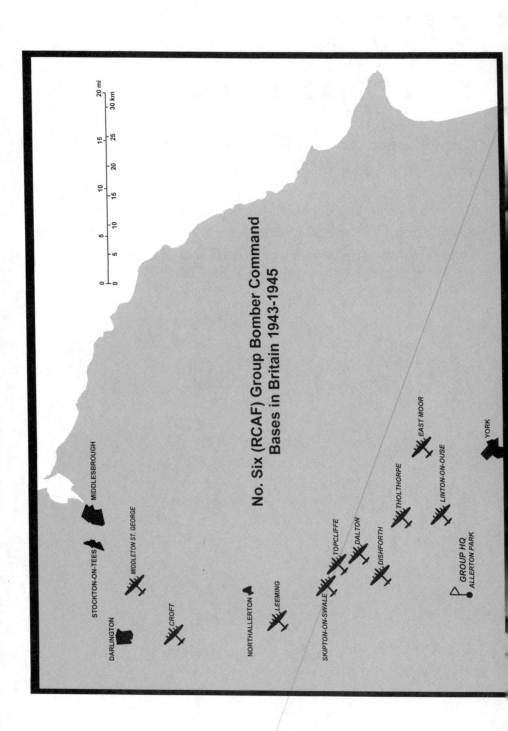

No. Six (RCAF) Group Bomber Command
Bases in Britain 1943-1945

MAP X

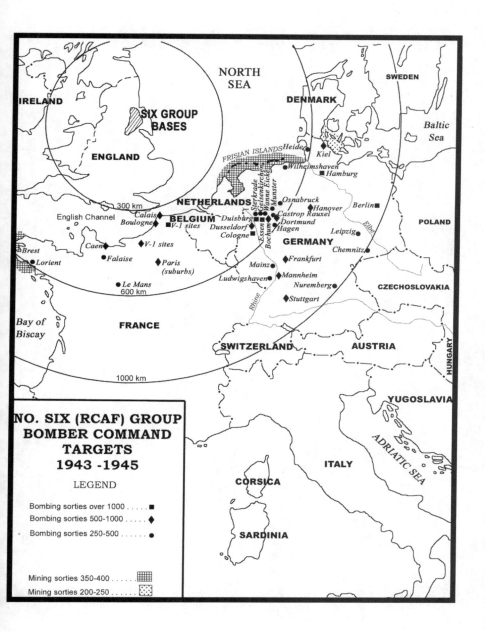

NORTH SEA

SWEDEN

IRELAND

SIX GROUP BASES

DENMARK

Baltic Sea

ENGLAND

FRISIAN ISLANDS Heide

Kiel

Wilhelmshaven

Hamburg

300 km

NETHERLANDS

Osnabruck

Hanover

Berlin

POLAND

English Channel

Calais
Boulogne

BELGIUM

Sterkrade
Gelsenkirchen
Hanne Eickel
Munster

Duisburg

Castrop Rauxel

V-1 sites

Dusseldorf

Dortmund

Brest

Caen

V-1 sites

Cologne

Essen
Bochum

Hagen

Leipzig

Lorient

Falaise

Paris
(suburbs)

GERMANY

Chemnitz

Mainz

Frankfurt

Le Mans
600 km

Ludwigshaven

Mannheim

Nuremberg

CZECHOSLOVAKIA

FRANCE

Rhine

Stuttgart

Bay of
Biscay

SWITZERLAND

AUSTRIA

HUNGARY

1000 km

YUGOSLAVIA

ADRIATIC SEA

ITALY

CORSICA

NO. SIX (RCAF) GROUP BOMBER COMMAND TARGETS 1943 -1945

LEGEND

Bombing sorties over 1000 . . . . . ■

Bombing sorties 500-1000 . . . . . ◆

Bombing sorties 250-500 . . . . . . ●

Mining sorties 350-400 . . . . . ▦

Mining sorties 200-250 . . . . . . ▨

SARDINIA

CHAPTER 13

"AS I REMEMBER HIM, HE WOULD HAVE FOUND ANOTHER WAY."

No. 6 (RCAF) Group Bomber Command in Britain

(Map IX)

At 10:35 on the night of May 27, 1944, Wellington bomber DF641 of 30 Operational Training Unit (OTU) took off from its home station at Hixon airfield in England, about eighty kilometres southeast of Liverpool. It was in the company of eight other aircraft for a "bull's-eye" detail — a training flight intended to simulate as closely as possible an operational night flying mission. DF641, with seven crew members on board — five of them Canadian — was last heard from about half an hour after departure. Then, thirty-five minutes into the next day, the bomber's dinghy, which was housed in a hatch behind a starboard engine, broke free from its housing. The dinghy was blown back by the slipstream and may have snagged the elevator and/or the rudder, which could have caused a violent pitch up or down. Despite the unique geodetic structure of the "Wimpy" (as the Wellington was affectionately known by those who flew it) and its ability to absorb tremendous amounts of damage, this sudden direction change probably caused the aircraft to break up without any warning.[1]

The geodetic structure of a Wellington bomber is clearly visible as a crew member prepares to use its flare chute.

All crew members were killed, including air gunner Sergeant J.R. Pollon of the RCAF.

Pollon was seventeen years old.

Joseph Pollon was born on June 13, 1926, in the tiny hamlet of Clanwilliam, Manitoba, between today's Riding Mountain National Park and the city of Brandon. After finishing Grade 9, Pollon helped on a farm for a while and, for the three months prior to his enrolment in March 1943, worked at a smelter in Trail, British Columbia. When the five-foot-ten, 153-pound Pollon joined the RCAF, he claimed a birthdate of June 13, 1924, making him two years older than his actual age of sixteen. He also stated he smoked at least two packs of cigarettes a week, but seldom drank alcohol.

Training claimed the lives of many young airmen, including that of air gunner Sergeant Joseph Pollon.

Notations on his file by recruiting personnel describe him as "Physically fit. Quiet retiring type. Should improve with training. Low average aircrew material . . . Motivation satisfactory," while his course report for wireless operator (air gunner) and air gunner notes he was "very intelligent, works well, shy and quiet." Pollon received a nice Christmas present in 1943: he was promoted to flight sergeant on Christmas Eve, the day his formal course training ended. He embarked from Halifax to sail to Britain on May 3, 1944, and arrived at his new home nine days later.[2]

In an effort to provide some degree of comfort to Pollon's family after his death, a letter to his mother, Lillian, from the station commander at Hixon dated June 9, 1944, noted, "I am assured by the Station Medical Officer, and am myself satisfied, that death was instantaneous, and that your son would not have suffered at all." He also noted, "Your son was an excellent air gunner who, during his stay at this unit, proved himself an excellent member of aircrew. He will be mourned by all who knew him."

Pollon's service file closes with two letters. The first is from an obviously distraught Lillian Pollon inquiring about her son's personal effects, after she received a parcel supposed to contain her son's belongings. "I don't consider them his personal effects," she wrote in mid-March 1945, "and I am still waiting for them. I know he had a good watch, ring, wallet and fountain pen besides a few other things. We did receive a carton containing a sweater, 4 pairs of socks and a money belt, some underwear, clothes brushes and razor and also a picture frame with two snaps in it and one dress shirt."

In response, the RCAF director of estates explained a month later — in a letter that may have satisfied the authorities but would have provided cold comfort at best to the grieving mother — that several articles belonging to her son were not located at his unit in Britain. "It is suggested," he wrote, "possibly your son was wearing his watch and ring and carrying his fountain pen and wallet with him on his last flight."

* * *

When the Second World War began, the RCAF had one bomber squadron. It had been formed at Halifax only on September 5, 1939, four days after Hitler's invasion of Poland and five days before Canada declared war on Germany. No. 10 Squadron was equipped with obsolete, two-man, open-cockpit Westland Wapiti biplanes, which could carry a 260-kilogram bomb load 850 kilometres.[3]

By the time the war ended, the RCAF had expanded to fifteen bomber squadrons overseas, all but one allocated to No. 6 (RCAF) Group in Bomber Command.[4] The No. 6 Group bomber squadrons flew out of ten operational airfields and

Nissen huts and ablution buildings at the Skipton-on-Swale airfield, a typical bomber station, which was home to Lloyd Hyde's 424 Squadron.

one training aerodrome in northern England, ten in a crescent-shaped swath through the Vale of York in North Yorkshire and one in the southern part of County Durham. Group Headquarters was at Allerton Hall (known to airmen as "Castle Dismal"),[5] a rambling, seventy-five-room mansion near Knaresborough.

Securing Allerton Hall had not been without its difficulties. According to Air Vice-Marshal George Brookes, the officer selected to command No. 6 Group, "the resentful owner — 'the worst pessimist I have ever met . . . no patriotism & full of himself & his troubles' raised so many questions and complaints about the inevitable alterations (and where he was to live in the meantime)" that it was not completely ready when the group became operational on New Year's Day 1943.[6]

Three of the earlier-formed squadrons initially flew two-engine Handley Page Hampdens. But at one time or another, most of the

Aircrew pose next to a Wellington bomber at an OTU in Britain.

squadrons were equipped with two-engine Vickers Wellingtons (eleven squadrons), before moving on to the "heavies": various marks of four-engine Handley Page Halifaxes (thirteen squadrons), followed by Avro Lancasters (also thirteen squadrons). The Lancaster could carry an 8,165-kilogram bomb load four thousand kilometres.[7]

Bomber Command carried out a strategic bombing campaign against occupied Europe and the German heartland, quickly resorting to night bombing when daytime raids rapidly led to unacceptable losses. While losses were less with night-time bombing, bomber crews initially had great difficulty in navigating to their intended targets in the dark.[8]

When a member of a bomber crew arrived in Britain from training in Canada, he did not immediately serve on operations. Before that happened — and after he staged through No. 3 Primary Reception Centre (PRC) — he was usually posted to an OTU. There, each new intake group was paraded in a hangar and told to form themselves into five-man crews: pilot, navigator, wireless operator, bomb aimer and air gunner. At an OTU, where crews flew mainly two-engine Whitleys or Wellingtons, they acquired all-important team skills and completed a lot of flying. Occasionally, an "easy" operation might be undertaken, such sowing mines over water or dropping leaflets.

Once a crew successfully completed training at an OTU, it was normally posted intact to an operational flying squadron. If, however, it were destined for a "heavy" squadron flying four-engine bombers (which by late 1942 was most of them), further training followed at a Heavy Conversion Unit (HCU), where a flight engineer and a second air gunner joined the crew. At the HCU, crews converted to four-engine bombers through a short course and were then sent to a flying squadron. Those destined for Lancasters also completed a very short course at a Lancaster finishing school.

Aircrews in Commonwealth squadrons were normally of several nationalities. In fact, there were more Canadians serving in the Royal Air force (RAF) than there were in the RCAF. Conversely, no RCAF squadron overseas was composed entirely of Canadians. Most of them had a number of Britons, Australians, New Zealanders, South Africans and other Commonwealth nationalities, as well as a few Americans, Poles, French or others.[9]

Losses throughout Bomber Command were high. Of the 14,541 RCAF dead from all causes throughout the war, the overwhelming majority were in Bomber Command: some 8,240 killed on operations and another 1,740 from non-operational causes.[10]

* * *

Notification of the death of a member of an aircrew during the Second World War arrived in several ways. First; a telegram:

RCAF MESSAGE CYPHER

TO: MR IL DOWDING 162 JOHN STREET
SARNIA ONTARIO

FROM: RCAF CASUALTIES OFFICER (REPORT
DELIVERY)
DATE: OCT 20
DEEPLY REGRET TO ADVISE THAT YOUR
SON PILOT OFFICER JOHN FREDERICK
DOWDING J FOUR SIX NOUGHT FOUR
ONE WAS KILLED ON ACTIVE SERVICE
OVERSEAS OCTOBER SEVENTEENTH STOP
PLEASE ACCEPT MY PROFOUND SYMPATHY
STOP LETTER FOLLOWS[11]

Then, a second telegram:

RCAF MESSAGE

TO: MR. I.L. DOWDING 162 JOHN STREET
SARNIA, ONT.

FROM: RCAF CASUALTIES OFFICER
DATE: OCT. 22
YOU WILL WISH TO KNOW THAT FUNERAL
YOUR SON PILOT OFFICER JOHN FRED-
ERICK DOWDING TAKES PLACE 7:30 P.M
OCTOBER TWENTY THIRD AT HARROGATE
REGIONAL CEMETERY HARROGATE YORK-
SHIRE ENGLAND STOP LETTER FOLLOWS

Next, a letter:

27 Oct. 1944

Dear Mr. Dowding,
I find it my unfortunate task to confirm the
telegram which you will have received informing
you that your son was killed whilst flying on active
service on the 17th October, 1944.
As air gunner of his aircraft, he took off in the
evening of Tuesday, 17th October to carry out a cross-
country detail. Contact was maintained with the
aircraft until 21.22 hours, which was the last contact
made. Information was received later that the aircraft
had crashed at approximately 21.30 hours, a few
miles inland west of Seaham Harbour, near Durham.
It may be of some consolation to you to know that
death must have been instantaneous. The cause of the
accident has not yet been established.
Your son's Flight Commander spoke very highly
of him and his loss is a great blow to his fellow
members of this unit. Your son's fellow officers, the
N.C.O.s of his station and I wish to convey to you
our sympathy in your bereavement.
I have delayed writing to you in order to give
you the details of your son's funeral which took place
on Monday the 23rd October at R.A.F. Regional
Cemetery, Harrogate, the service being conducted by
the Revd. McLean of the Royal Canadian Air Force.
Full service honours were accorded and officers from
this station attended the funeral as representatives
of the unit. Wreaths were sent from the officers,
N.C.Os. and myself.
You will wish to know that all war graves are
taken care of by the Imperial War Graves Commission

*who will erect a temporary wooden cross pending the
provision of a permanent memorial by them.*

*Your son's effects have been gathered together
and sent to the Royal Air Force Central Depository,
from where they will be forwarded to the Administrator of Estates, Ottawa, who will be writing to you
in this regard in due course.*

*The names of all who lose their lives or are
wounded or reported missing whilst serving in the
RCAF will appear in the official casualty lists published from time to time in the press. Publication of
the date, place and station of a casualty and, particularly, any reference to the unit concerned, might
give valuable information to the enemy and for this
reason only the name, rank and service number are
included in the official lists. Relatives are particularly requested to ensure that any notices published
privately do not disclose the date, place and circumstances of the casualty or the unit.*

*Please do not hesitate to ask for any assistance
that I or my staff may be able to give you to relieve
your sorrow in any way.*

*[signed] R. G. G. Cole, Group Captain
Commanding R.A.F. Station Kinloss*

Then, a second letter:

*Ottawa, Canada
24th October, 1944
Mr. I.L. Dowding
162 John St., Sarnia,
Ontario*

Dear Mr. Dowding:

It is with deep regret that I must confirm our recent telegram informing you that your son, Pilot Officer John Frederick Dowding, was killed on Active Service.

Advice has been received from the Royal Canadian Air Force Casualties Officer, Overseas, that your son lost his life during flying operations at 9:25 P.M. on October 17th, 1944, at Slingby Hill Farm, East Murton, Durham County, England. The aircraft of which he was a member of the crew, fell to the ground. His funeral took place at 7:30 P.M. on October 23rd, at the Harrogate Regional Cemetery, Harrogate, Yorkshire, England.

You may be assured that any further information received will be communicated to you immediately.

I realize that this news has been a great shock to you, and I offer you my deepest sympathy. May the same spirit which prompted your son to offer his life give you courage.

Yours sincerely,

[signed] J.A. Sully, Air Vice-Marshal
Air Member for Personnel

Finally, a third letter:

Oct. 30, 1944
Mr. I.L. Dowding,
162 John Street,
Sarnia, Ontario

Dear Mr. Dowding:

I have learned with deep regret of the death of your son, Pilot Officer John Frederick Dowding, on Active Service Overseas on October 17th and I wish to offer you and the members of your family my sincere and heartfelt sympathy.

It is most lamentable that a promising career should be thus terminated and I would like you to know that his loss is greatly deplored by all those with whom your son was serving.
Yours sincerely,

[signed] J.A. Sully, Air Vice-Marshal
Acting Chief of the Air Staff

[The above line is crossed out in red with the letters CAS (Chief of the Air Staff) added next to it.]

Such telegrams and letters were the pieces of correspondence every serviceman's parents dreaded receiving during the war. In the case of Ivan and Rhea Dowding of Sarnia, Ontario, it confirmed the death of their son, Pilot Officer John Frederick Dowding. The air gunner was only seventeen when he was killed.

Mementoes of their son's funeral were also sent to Dowding's parents:

RAF Kinloss
Forres, Morayshire
31 October 1944

Dear Mr. Dowding.

I am enclosing a set of photographs taken at the funeral of your son at the R.A.F. Regional Cemetery, Harrogate on the 23rd of October, 1944.

Three crewmen are laid to rest after their Wellington bomber crashed.

Although these may prove to be a painful reminder of your sad loss, I feel sure you would wish to have them.

May I once more express my deepest sympathy in your bereavement.

Yours Sincerely,

R. G. G. Cole, Group Captain
Commanding R.A.F. Station Kinloss

When he enrolled, Dowding signed a will as a requirement of his service. Like most single males, he left all his estate to his mother in the event of his death. After notification of his death, the mundane routine of administrative action to handle his estate eventually followed:

Estates Branch
Ottawa,
April 20, 1945

Dear Mrs. Dowding:
    Your son's personal belongings which could
be located at his unit Overseas immediately after
he lost his life have reached this Branch, and will
be forwarded to you within the next few days in
a carton and a Gladstone bag by prepaid express.
We trust that they will reach you in good order,
and would ask you to complete the enclosed receipt
form and return it to this Branch after the carton
and Gladstone bag have reached you.
    The key to the Gladstone bag is enclosed herewith.
Yours faithfully,

Director of Estates

The teenager's worldly effects arrived shortly afterwards in the Gladstone bag and cardboard box. Among the non-issue items were a Kaschi lighter, fancy tie, brushes in a case, thirteen letters, Kodak box camera, pocket wallet with snaps, gold signet ring and a brooch. There was also a cheque book with twenty-three unused cheques, cash amounting to three pounds, four shillings and a certificate for a one-hundred-dollar Victory Loan Bond.

* * *

John Frederick Dowding bluffed his way into the RCAF because he wanted to follow his older brother, Harry, who was a squadron leader and a Spitfire ace with seven victories while serving with

403 (Wolf) and 442 (Caribou) Fighter Squadrons overseas.[12] As a courtesy, the British Air Ministry had informed Harry of his younger brother's death two days after it occurred.

Dowding was born on October 26, 1926, in Sarnia, Ontario, a town on Lake Huron where the Canadian petroleum industry began in the mid-nineteenth century, and which grew substantially during the war. At school, he swam and played rugby, hockey and basketball, and also served three years in cadets, rising to the rank of cadet lieutenant. He left part way through Grade 11 in February, 1943, and worked briefly in a couple of jobs: two months at the Imperial Oil Limited laboratory, followed by two months as a welder's helper at a construction company.

Dowding applied to join the RCAF at No. 9 Recruiting Centre in London, Ontario, on August 3, 1943, and immediately underwent a series of assessments and interviews. On an aircrew information sheet — one of the first forms he completed — Dowding put an "X" beside "19 or less" in the age column. Strictly speaking, it was an honest enough answer, although the "or less" was obviously not intended to include anyone below 18, the minimum age to enrol. Dowding was only sixteen. His claim of a birthdate in October 1925 was a year earlier than his actual one and was supported by a letter from parents, which not only gave him permission to join, but also claimed the same earlier 1925 birthdate. His size reflected his true age: at the time he weighed 148 pounds and was five-foot-seven.

During his recruiting interview, when he was asked "the length of time he [had] been considering joining one of the armed forces," the interviewer wrote: "Made up mind about 8 months ago to enlist." He also noted Dowding found "Aircrew more exciting. Action at higher pitch." When he asked Dowding about the factor or factors that brought him to apply to the air force, the interviewer noted: "Two of his friends are being enlisted. Three have been chums and want to go together." The interviewer also remarked that Dowding was "prepared to do his best to make success of any training for which he is selected."

The blue-eyed, fair-complexioned youth was accepted into the RCAF on August 4, 1943. The interviewing officer's assessment noted, "neat appearing . . . Average material . . . Alert, energetic young applicant . . . likely looking . . ." A later fitness assessment sheet notes a score of 86 out of 100. Dowding scored high in "staying power" and was "capable of prolonged and strenuous activity. He also "puts all he's got into the workouts, energetic approach to all sports, attends sports parade with enthusiasm on all occasions."

On enrolment, Dowding immediately began initial training at a series of air force stations in Edmonton, Regina and Saskatoon. Although he commenced the aircrew course for pilots and observers at No. 4 Initial Training School at the end of January 1944, his heart was not in it as he had always wanted to be an air gunner. He got his wish. The school's commanding officer removed Dowding from training in mid-March and re-mustered him to air gunner, with the comment "very keen and interested in being an Air Gunner — Confident — Good Type — Conscientious."

Dowding's final training in Canada was at No. 3 Bombing and Gunnery School in Macdonald, Manitoba, a few kilometres northwest of Portage la Prairie, where the bombing and gunnery ranges were over nearby Lake Manitoba. He qualified as a wireless operator (air gunner) and an air gunner in June 1944. In Macdonald, aerial gunnery was conducted on Bolingbrokes — obsolete aircraft used only for training purposes. Dowding learned to fire Browning .303 machine guns on the ground before advancing to firing them in the air. Sometimes the training did not go according to plan, especially if students took matters into their own hands. On one gunnery course at Macdonald, a nameless gunner "narrowly missed hitting a group of terrified fishermen in a lake below when he opened fire at a flock of ducks."[13]

On completion of the course, Dowding was promoted sergeant. His course report noted he was an "above average student; clean-cut; enthusiastic; dependable; proficient at his trade." He was then offered a commission as a pilot officer, which he accepted "for the duration of the present war and for the period of demobilization thereafter." He also indicated he understood "His Majesty may exercise the right at any time to dispense with the services of an Officer on probation." After a short period of leave, Dowding embarked for overseas at Halifax on July 11, 1944, and arrived in Britain a week later. In Britain, he was posted to No. 19 OTU in Scotland for final training prior to undertaking bombing missions over Germany.

But John Dowding never got to go on an operation.

Armstrong Whitworth Whitley V twin-engine bomber AD685 took off from RAF Station Kinloss near Forres in Morayshire, Scotland at 7:06 p.m. on October 17, 1944, on a five-hour solo cross-country flight, piloted by Flying Officer Ken Reed. Flying Officer Walt Wall was the navigator, Sergeant Ernie Leivers the radio operator, and Sergeant Leslie Olmstead the bomb aimer. Pilot Officers Alex Sunstrum and John Dowding, both air gunners, made up the rest of the crew. All were members of the RCAF except for Leivers, who was in the RAF.

It was the fourth cross-country night flight for this crew. AD685 was described in the subsequent "Report on Flying Accident or Forced Landing Not Attributable to Enemy Action" as "one of our best machines." The same report described Flying Officer Reed as "of average ability" and someone who "should have been capable of dealing with any normal [sic] emergency," while another report noted he had "no outstanding fault" and was an "above average Captain of Aircraft."

Shortly after 9 p.m. — halfway into the flight — the Whitley was flying south at 3,658 metres in clear weather and with visibility of twenty-two and a half kilometres, as reported by another

A Whitley bomber makes a cross-country flight over the British countryside.

bomber on a similar training flight in the area. The last known contact with AD685 was at 9:22; eighteen minutes later, it broke up in the air prior to crashing inland about five kilometres from the North Sea at Slingby Hill Farm, near East Merton, County Durham. Wreckage was dispersed over a wide area.

The exact reason for the crash was never ascertained, although "control lost in cloud" was listed on accident documents. "Fairly frequent flashes of lightning" were later reported by the other Whitley bomber in the area, and the Durham Royal Observer Corps reported a "violent localized electrical storm moving through the area from the west" at 9:30. This storm could have led to the bomber breaking up in the air.

The crash killed all six aircrew instantly, the result of terrible injuries. The medical officer's report on Dowding noted "Multiple Injuries . . . Head completely pulped; multiple abrasions with extensive tissue loss, fracture right humerus, fractured ribs both sides, complete fracture right tibia and fibula."

It was a horrendous end for an enthusiastic youth who wanted to serve his country.

The epitaph on Dowding's headstone in the Commonwealth War Graves Commission cemetery in Harrogate was chosen by his family and reflects the young airman's aspirations: "He challenged those who would destroy the innocent and the way of life he loved so well."[14]

* * *

On Monday, April 30, 1945, Sergeant Ron Cranston was a tail gunner in a three-aircraft formation of Lancaster bombers from the RCAF's 428 (Ghost) Squadron. The formation was on a routine cross-country training flight over the countryside of northern England. The crew had taken off at 10:59 that morning from their base at Middleton St. George in County Durham, just north of the Yorkshire border. Cranston had a clear view of one of the other aircraft in the flight some nine hundred metres below his fifty-five-hundred-metre altitude. For some time now, Lancaster KB879 had been behaving erratically, flying with a slip-sliding motion. Cranston advised his pilot, Flying Officer Dave Archer.[15]

Aboard KB879 were seven crew members. Pilot Flight Lieutenant Billie Campbell, twenty-three, hailed from Hamilton, assisted by flight engineer Flight Sergeant Walter Ward, twenty, a Scot and the lone RAF member on board, who was also a qualified pilot. The navigator was Sergeant John Kay, twenty-six, of Calgary, while the bomb aimer was Flight Sergeant Stuart Berryman, just turned twenty-three. Warrant Officer Second Class Tom Lawley was the wireless operator. Like the pilot, Berryman and Lawley were also from Hamilton. The remainder of the crew

Lancaster bombers of 428 Squadron line up prior to takeoff from their base at Middleton St. George.

were two air gunners and the youngest aboard: Flight Sergeant Lester Tweedy, nineteen, of Loughheed, Alberta, and Flight Sergeant Teddy Wright of Winnipeg, only sixteen. All were single except for Kay, a former Mountie, whose wife, Ann, and three-year-old son, Johnny, lived in Brooks, Alberta.[16]

Lawley, the radio operator, had already been in contact with RAF Station Hixon — which was now within sight — to confirm their arrival in the area. Despite being on a routine flight, both air gunners — Tweedy and Wright — remained on the lookout for German intruder fighters; although the chances at this late stage of the war were extremely slim.

About twenty to twenty-five minutes later — just before noon — Cranston noticed KB879 "going down in a spiral dive with white vapour trails or smoke coming from the starboard engine.

It appeared that nothing was done to counteract the dive. No parachutes appeared to open and no part of the aircraft seemed to fall off."

But according to the RAF investigation into the accident, the bomber in fact broke up in the air, likely the result of stress and pressure caused on the airframe by the dive. The wing tips flew off first, followed by parts of the fuselage. The separated metal pieces of the aircraft then tumbled down, hit the ground and caught fire.

Debris fell over a wide area.

The fuselage and wings landed in a farmer's field near the A51 highway, while the tail section rolled across the road and hit a farm building. One of the bomber's big wheels bounced along the ground and ended up in another farm. All seven crew members were killed, the result of "multiple injuries." Wright was the first fatality to be identified, found in a sitting position some distance from the crash site.[17]

The RAF investigation also discovered the oxygen supply cock was partially closed. This could have led to some — or even all — crew members to pass out from oxygen deprivation and to the bomber's "erratic" flight. Another finding noted the autopilot was faulty, something that had occurred on a previous flight. It, too, could have contributed to the accident.

At sixteen years of age, Teddy Wright may have well been the youngest aircrew member killed on flying duty during the Second World War — from any country.

* * *

When Edward James Wright enrolled in the air force at No. 6 RCAF recruiting station on November 18, 1943, he was a fifteen-year-old, five-foot-six, 129-pound, fair-haired teenager.

How such a slight youth was able to get past the recruiter remains a mystery.

Teddy Wright managed to join the
air force at fifteen and was killed
when he was only sixteen.

Wright was ten years old and living in Halifax when the war began in September 1939, where he attended Grade 5 at Sir Charles Tupper School in the port city's west end. His father, James, was a superintendent in the Royal Canadian Mounted Police and had only been recently posted there from Campbellton, New Brunswick. Wright had fought in the First World War as a pilot in the RAF. The rest of the family consisted of mother, Alfreda, older sister, Ada, and younger twins, Patsy and Richard.

A few months later, his father was posted again, this time to Charlottetown, where Wright quit school after completion of Grade 8. Always a bit of a free-spirited dreamer, Wright was already focused on a loftier goal. He returned to Halifax and worked as a cook for three months for the Canadian National Railway and at the Knights of Columbus canteen. Then he joined his family in Winnipeg, where his father had been sent in May 1943 prior to his retirement three years later.

Wright had set his sights on joining the RCAF for some time, and even threatened to run away unless his parents gave him permission to apply for the air force. His father agreed, believing his son would be rejected.[18] To everyone's surprise, Wright was accepted. He had entered November 7, 1925, on his application — making him the minimum eligible age to join at eighteen. It was the right day, but three years earlier than his actual birth year of 1928. Perhaps the two months he claimed he had served in the militia and an earlier attempt to join the Merchant Navy had also helped persuade the recruiter to enrol him.

But undoubtedly, it was the National Registration Certificate Wright produced showing his age as eighteen that cinched the deal. The certificate had been introduced by the government in 1940 and all Canadians sixteen years of age and older were legally required to carry it at all times. The penalty for non-compliance was twenty dollars.[19] Yet, despite the certificate, many underage youths were able to slip through the recruiting system and enrol.

Six months later, on July 27, 1945, after basic training at No. 3 Manning Depot in Edmonton, academic upgrading at Montreal's McGill University and air gunnery school, Wright found himself in Britain. Before he sailed overseas, he spent some of his embarkation leave in Winnipeg with his family. Years later, his sister, Patsy, who was nine years old at the time, remembered the farewells at the train station. She recalled being excited about the bagged lunch her mother had made for him for the journey and waving a last goodbye. Although she was only six years his junior, Patsy regarded her older brother as a grown man and her hero; a handsome knight in his air force blue armour.

She also recalled she always wished his application had been rejected, but added, "as I remember him, he would have found another way."[20]

Wright's initial posting in Britain was to 26 OTU in Buckinghamshire, where he flew in Wellington bombers. During this period, he also made several operational flights over Nazi Europe in diversionary raids, and on one occasion (according to a letter home), flew the bomber while the pilot "took a break."

Wright's last letter home was dated April 25, 1945. In it, he noted he was flying with 428 Squadron. He also had some good news: "Well, Mom, I've been a flight sergeant for a few months and never knew it. I just found out today." After speculating that the squadron was going to the east, he added a request. "I wonder if you could send me a Sheaffer's pen and pencil set. I lost a fellow's pen and want to get him another." In closing, he asked his mother to "write soon."[21]

Less than a week later, the sixteen-year-old Winnipeg teenager was dead. He had served in 428 Squadron for eight days.

* * *

At two o'clock on the afternoon of May 4, 1945, at the regional cemetery in Blacon, near Chester in northwest England, a full military funeral took place for six of the seven crew members of Lancaster KB879. The body of the seventh member, Flight Sergeant Walter Ward, had been returned to his native Scotland for private burial.

Immediately after the war, Wright's parents and the twins moved to England and settled in Brighton on the Channel coast. Wright's father, James, visited his son's gravesite at Blacon and spoke to many of the locals in Sandon who had witnessed the crash. When his mother, Alfreda, died in Florida in 1974, her purse contained the last letter he had written home from England.

More than half a century after the flying accident, on August 28, 1999, a memorial was unveiled at the crash site of KB879, attended by members of the Wright, Campbell and Ward families. In Manitoba, the home province of Campbell and Wright, two northern lakes have been named after them. Campbell Lake is west of Waskaiowaka Lake, while Edward Wright Lake is northeast of Windy Lake.[22]

* * *

Lloyd Bernard Hyde joined the RCAF for a very simple reason.[23] "Girls. That was a big reason to join the air force." Everybody wanted to be a pilot because of the glamour associated with it, including Hyde. But the young Ottawa lad was not to get his wish, although he did join the RCAF.

Hyde was born in Ottawa South on July 15, 1925, into a typical middle-class family of the time, when the father worked and the mother looked after the house and raised the family. At a young age, he worked at a local drugstore for ten cents an hour: forty cents for the six-to-ten evening shift. He was a delivery boy, running packs of cigarettes and cokes by bicycle to the "highfalutin people" who lived along The Driveway, an upscale area of the city.

One day he walked into Hyde's Meat Market on Bank Street and asked if the store was hiring for Saturdays. It was not, but someone said they would take his name and give him a call if something came up. Although there was no family connection with the store, his name must have carried some weight as he started to work that Saturday. He got a dollar a day for delivering groceries and scrubbing the butcher block long after the store was closed. His next job was at Loblaw's as a "Saturday Boy," stocking shelves and parcelling up groceries for $1.90 a day.

Hyde was fourteen and in Grade 7 when war was declared. In common with his chums, he thought the war would end before he had a chance to join. Three years later — still underage at seventeen, but five-foot-ten and weighing 175 pounds — he enrolled in the air force. He trained as a tail gunner at No. 9 Bombing and Gunnery School at Mont Joli, Quebec, on Fairey Battles. There,

Sunshine and glamour add light to this RCAF recruiting poster designed by Joseph Hallam.

air gunners were taken up three at a time and crammed into the small, single-engine airplanes to practice and test their shooting skills. They shot at towed targets using four .303 machine guns that fired simultaneously using a central joystick.

Six months later, Hyde was overseas.

Before he went, he asked the father of his girlfriend, Alice, to bless their engagement. "Certainly not!" was the reply from her outspoken father. "You get knocked off, she gets knocked up, and we will have to look after the kid."

Despite the abrupt parental response, Alice and Hyde carried on a long-distance relationship. Hyde noting that "one thing we did sounds kind of silly." The five-hour time difference between Britain and Ottawa meant when Hyde took off on a mission — normally at 11 p.m. — it was six o'clock her time. They agreed to "stare up at the same moon and send a message of love to each other" at the same time each night.

Ground crew prepare to install oxygen cylinders in a Halifax bomber.

He remembered the crossing on the Cunard liner *Mauritania* with less than fond memories: "We got served kidney stew and hard tack three times a day. I don't know what was in it, but it was terrible." Each dining table had twelve airmen seated at it and they took turns getting a bucket of stew for the group. Soon, Hyde got to the point where he could not go anywhere near the stew; the smell was enough to make him sick. And, coupled with rough seas, he did become sick.

His saving grace was an old Dutch sailor who told Hyde he had been vomiting straight bile because he had nothing in his stomach. The seaman told him to eat hardtack to help dissolve the bile. It worked — and Hyde was not seasick again.

In Britain, Hyde flew in his first bombers — Whitleys and Wellingtons. On a training mission one night, Hyde told the pilot via the intercom he was getting cold, so the pilot told him

412 TOO YOUNG TO DIE

to come up to the cabin, where there was heat. He never made it. Halfway up the fuselage, other crew members found him passed out from a lack of oxygen. They carried him forward and put him alongside the wireless operator, who every once in a while would take off his oxygen mask to let Hyde have a whiff.

Each crew member had his own oxygen bottle, and Hyde's had run out. "The trouble is you don't know that you are not getting oxygen," Hyde recalled years later. After time on two-engine bombers, Hyde moved to four-engine ones: Halifaxes.

Bomber aircrew like Hyde who survived the rigorous training regime in Britain went on to the next phase of their wartime careers: bombing targets in Nazi-occupied Europe. In the face of anti-aircraft fire and Luftwaffe night fighters over the Continent, the losses in personnel and aircraft were several times those that occurred during training. Statistically, only twenty-two airmen out of a hundred survived a tour of operations without being killed, wounded, taken prisoner or shot down and evading capture.[24]

CHAPTER 14

"I WENT AWAY AS A BOY AND CAME BACK AS A MAN."

Bombing Germany and Occupied Europe

(Map X)

Halifax II DT575 of the RAF's No. 76 Squadron took off from its base at Linton-on-Ouse in North Yorkshire at 8:49 p.m. on April 16, 1943. The aircraft was part of a 327-bomber raid against the large Skoda arms factory at Pilsen in occupied Czechoslovakia. Although 249 aircraft claimed to have hit the target between 1:30 and 2:10 a.m. early the next morning, in fact the bombing was centred on the small village of Dôbrany, eleven kilometres southwest of Pilsen, where "several factory-like buildings" — actually an insane asylum — and a German barracks were mistaken for the Skoda works, as confirmed by daylight reconnaissance.[1] Yet, in keeping with the upbeat tempo of war reporting to the public, several newspapers put a positive spin on the mission, with one of them noting "the good bombing must have done enormous damage."[2]

After dropping their bombs along with the other aircraft on what the crew thought was the Skoda factory, DT575 turned back for the return flight to Britain. The twin-engine bomber never made it.

The oil painting Bombs Away
*by Paul Goranson depicts a
bomb-aimer as he releases his
bomb load over enemy territory.*

At four o'clock the next morning, high in the air between the northeastern French villages of Pierrepont and Marle, a German night fighter suddenly attacked DT575 before the crew had time to return fire. The bomber exploded in a brilliant geranium-coloured fireball that lit up the dark predawn sky, plummeted earthwards and burst into flames on impact.

French gendarmes quickly arrived on the scene and found the bodies of seven airmen near or among the debris. The five in the wreckage were "terribly burnt," but the other two were intact. Although they had bailed out, they were killed on impact as the aircraft was too low for a safe parachute drop. German soldiers showed up shortly afterwards and took charge of the crash area. Just before the enemy soldiers showed up, a local baker, M. Baton, arrived and had time to see the name "Brown" on a bag before the soldiers told him to leave.

The next day, all seven bodies were buried by the Germans in adjoining graves in the communal cemetery at Liesse-Notre-

Dame, a village next to Pierrepont. The seven-man crew of DT575 were all sergeants except for the bomb aimer, who was a flight sergeant. Five were British: pilot and aircraft captain Brian Wedderburn, flight engineer John Strachan, navigator Brodie Clinging, wireless operator/air gunner Frank Fidgeon and tail gunner Steve Brown, while two were Canadians: bomb aimer Frank Ross and mid-upper gunner Leonard Jonasson. One of the bodies that was not burnt and so could be identified was Jonasson's, a member of the RCAF who was serving in the RAF. Len Jonasson was killed three months to the day after his seventeenth birthday, making him possibly the youngest airman in Bomber Command killed in action during the war.[3]

Jonasson's mother had been advised by a letter dated April 18 from the commanding officer of 76 Squadron that her son was missing, but the letter stated "unfortunately, we have no indication at all of what could have happened." He went on to note that "according to statistics of past losses, more men who are reported missing are prisoners-of-war than otherwise, and at the very worst his chances of being safe are at least fifty-fifty."

Similar telegrams and letters followed from air force authorities until she received an RCAF casualty notification dated September 21, 1943, stating her son's previous status of "Missing Believed Killed" was now "Presumed Dead" for all official purposes.

Jonasson was born in Winnipeg on January 17, 1926, the son of Otto and Asrun, of Icelandic heritage. His father, a dairyman, died in late 1939, leaving Asrun to raise Len, who was then thirteen, an older brother, Victor, and younger sister, Olive. Jonasson attended high school — where he joined cadets — and left after completion of Grade 10 in 1940. He worked as an errand boy at the Winnipeg General Hospital before moving to Pilot Mound, a small farming community southwest of Portage la Prairie and close to the United States border, where he lived with an uncle.[4] In late June 1942, when he was sixteen,

*Leonard Jonasson was shot
down over France when he was
seventeen, making him possibly
the youngest Bomber Com-
mand airman killed in action.*

he joined the Manitoba Mounted Rifles, a militia unit, where he
served in A Squadron.

A month later, Jonasson showed up at the RCAF's No. 6
Recruiting Centre in Winnipeg and applied to join the air force.
The medical officer's assessment notes, "Athletic build. May be
excitable." At the time, Jonasson was five-foot-eight and weighed
135 and 3/4 pounds and claimed to play hockey and rugby, as
well as being a swimmer. He also stated he drank alcohol occasionally and smoked ten to fifteen cigarettes a day.

An assessment from the interviewing officer added, "Alert.
Intelligent . . . Appears to be a good type . . ." and mentions Jonasson "has had some shooting with the reg't." Although he was
deemed suitable for wireless operator (air gunner), the interviewing officer recommended Jonasson for air gunner as he wanted
to serve in that capacity with a friend. Under suitability for commission, the same officer wrote "a little immature at present."

Lockheed Hudsons warm up at No. 9 Bombing and Gunnery School in Mont Joli, Quebec, the same school where Lloyd Hyde trained.

Years after the war, Jonasson's girlfriend, Joyce Landerkin, admitted she didn't know why he had enrolled, noting only "he probably wanted to fly — he was quite adventuresome." She recalled him as quiet, serious, intelligent, a lot of fun, a gifted conversationalist and "dreamy."[5]

Jonasson was taken on strength of the RCAF on August 5, 1942, as an aircraftsman second class. Air gunnery training followed at No. 3 Bombing and Gunnery School at Macdonald, Manitoba (the same school where John Dowding would train in 1944), from the end of September to mid-December, where the young airman fired Browning .303 machine guns on the ground and in the air from a variety of aircraft turrets. Although Jonasson passed the course, he finished only forty-sixth out of sixty-nine students.

His assessment by his instructors was not good. On his course report, the school's chief instructor commented, "Below average student, does not try very hard — is liable to sleep in class or divert his attention — poor discipline. Basic qualities poor; mental process slow; needs watching; not responsible." Jonasson was deemed "not at all suitable" for further training as a gunnery instructor, nor was he recommended for commissioning. Such assessments were not unheard of as an influx of young men — most without any form of military experience — flooded training centres, where pre-war-vintage staff were more used to dealing with older, more mature trainees. Often, such a training assessment was an inaccurate predictor of an airman's performance at his squadron, where most of them rose to the challenge and bravely did their duty. In Jonasson's case, he succeeded and qualified as an air gunner and was promoted sergeant when the course ended.

After a short Christmas leave, Jonasson embarked for overseas and arrived in Britain on January 12, five days before his seventeenth birthday. There, he was first posted to No. 3 PRC, "a kind of a stockpile of [RCAF] air crew awaiting posting to A[dvanced] F[lying] U[nits] and a clearing house for airmen waiting for maybe three or four weeks for a posting to squadrons."[6] The PRC was headquartered at Somerset House in Bournemouth, a city on the English Channel coast about 130 kilometres south-west of London. Even for Canadian airmen, the RAF controlled the movement of personnel throughout the training chain, from Bournemouth to operational squadrons for most of the war.[7]

RCAF Pilot Officer Murray Peden had arrived at No. 3 PRC two months before Jonasson and remembered Bournemouth as "a lovely city in which to be introduced to the war-time way of life in England." Before the war, "it had been a restful south-coast haven, catering not so much to the younger, racy set, as to the middle-aged and older citizenry," who went to Bournemouth for "its mild climate, beautiful beaches and headlands, its stately gardens and lush parks, and the handsome pavilion in which brass band and orchestra concerts, tea dances, and a variety of other pleasant affairs were presented." The city's "vast numbers of palatial hotels" had since "fallen on evil days," having been taken over by the Air Ministry and filled with transient Canadian airmen, "most of whom must have struck their hosts as over-active thyroid cases compared with the sedate clientele" of pre-war days.[8]

The official purpose of a PRC was to orient aircrew as they arrived, organize refresher training and arrange postings in conjunction with the Air Ministry. In reality, its main role was to keep aircrew gainfully employed until they could be sent for further training. Among the practical happenings at PRCs were additional medical examinations, briefings on responsibilities and duties, lectures from experienced aircrew and the issue of battledress and flying gear. Officials tried to keep the time airmen spent at PRCs to a minimum, as morale could deteriorate by idleness when there was a war being fought.

Robert Collins, another Canadian airman, remembered his time at No. 3 PRC with mixed emotions:

> We detrained at Bournemouth on the south coast, to be billeted in hotels of faded elegance. They had no staffs or services — just damp, chilly, barren rooms with beds, communal toilets, and crumbling plaster — but were infinitely more romantic than Mont Joli's comfortable puke-green barracks [RCAF Station Mont Joli, where Lloyd Hyde trained as an air gunner]. I dreamed of a day when I might return as a wealthy correspondent to a hotel like this, with morning tea served on a silver tray.[9]

RCAF and RAF aircrew parade at No. 3 Personnel Reception Centre in Bournemouth prior to inspection by King George VI.

After six weeks at No. 3 PRC, even though he was already a qualified air gunner, Jonasson moved in February to No. 7 Air Gunnery School (AGS) for refresher and confirmation training. The AGS was located at RAF Stormy Down near the village of Pyle, between Cardiff and Swansea in South Wales. It used a mixture of Avro Ansons, Boulton Paul Defiants and Westland Lysanders to teach air gunnery, using local beaches on the nearby coast and the Bristol Channel for target practice. "Stormy," as it was known to those who served there, came by its name honestly. Its three grass runways suffered from strong crosswinds, which, when coupled with poor drainage, made the airfield marginal at best.

Russell Margerison, an eighteen-year-old RAF Lancaster gunner, recalled the kind of moments air gunners went through

Patrick Cowley-Brown's oil painting Air to Ground *shows an aircraft firing its machine guns against a ground target during a practice run.*

when he qualified at Stormy Down in July 1943, undoubtedly similar to what Jonasson had experienced a few months earlier. On a hot day, "dressed in fur-collared outer flying suit and fur-lined flying boots . . . a sticky mixture of glycol antifreeze, petrol and warm air replaced the clean air I had been breathing. The temperature in the plane would have wilted tomato plants." Once in the air, the pilot headed for the Bristol Channel, where each of the three new gunners aboard would fire two hundred rounds at a towed target drogue.

> *At a height of 5,000 ft, with the Anson rising and sinking at irregular intervals, the instructor called the first gunner to the mid-upper turret. He quickly rattled off his rounds and in the process filled the*

*fuselage with cordite fumes which, mixed with the
other smells, produced a nauseating stench, doing
nothing to help my stomach, my sweating or my
headache.*

Now, it was Margerison's turn and "after struggling to lever
myself into the turret I found myself sitting in the smallest
smoke-filled sauna ever seen. My head was stuck up in the
Perspex dome like a light bulb in an upturned goldfish bowl.
Sweat dripped from my nose." When the instructor ordered
the young gunner to fire, Margerison discovered the combined
motion of his seat and the plane, coupled with the stench and
the heat, turned him green.

*I squeezed the triggers of the guns to get the whole
performance over as quickly as possible. The turret vibrated, the deafening noise drowned out
the drone of the engines. Cordite fumes invaded
my nostrils until I could hardly breathe. It was a
bedraggled, disillusioned airman who eventually
half fell out of the turret to be violently sick.*

Margerison qualified as an air gunner and became the mid-
upper gunner of a seven-man Lancaster crew — four of whom
coincidentally were Canadian — in the RAF's 625 Squadron
and went on to survive "one of the most dangerous jobs in the
Second World War."[10]

With the successful completion of his refresher training at No.
7 AGS, Jonasson next moved to No. 1652 HCU at RAF Marston
Moor in mid-March 1943. Although it was in North Yorkshire,
Marston Moor was not one of the stations used by the RCAF's
No. 6 Group. The purpose of HCUs (originally known as Con-
version Units — CUs) was to qualify crews trained on medium

Night Target, Germany, *by Miller Brittain, an artist who initially served as a bomb-aimer and flew thirty-four missions, depicts the spectacle of a night-time raid.*

(two-engine) bombers to operate heavy (four-engine) bombers prior to posting to an Operational Training Unit to gain experience before a final posting to an operational squadron.

Although training at Heavy Conversion Units normally took several weeks, on March 25, after only eleven days at No. 1652 HCU, Jonasson was posted to 76 Squadron RAF in No. 4 Group, which had been stationed at Linton-on-Ouse since September 1942. In mid-June, Linton became home to two RCAF bomber squadrons — pushing 76 Squadron to another Yorkshire base. In addition to a considerably shortened time at an HCU, Jonasson bypassed additional familiarization training at an OTU.

Jonasson arrived at 76 Squadron in the early days of the Battle of the Ruhr, which began on March 5 and ended July 12. It was one of Bomber Command's three great bomber offensives of 1943, along with the Battle of Hamburg and the Battle of Berlin. Night after night, bomber crews flew to some of the most heavily defended areas of Germany to attack their assigned targets, some of which were not even located in the heavily industrialized Ruhr Valley. Altogether, bomber crews carried out forty-three major attacks during this battle — and lost almost a thousand aircraft missing over Germany or crashed in Britain.

"Coned" by searchlights, flying through a wall of flak, attacked by German night fighters and risking collision with nearby bombers — even having "friendly" bombs drop on them from above — the courageous airmen pressed on to their targets, avoiding the overwhelming urge to turn aside before reaching their designated aiming-point. Such missions were the equivalent of a giant crap shoot in the sky. Sometimes Bomber Command would have a catastrophic night and lose scores of aircraft, while any particular squadron would return home unscathed. On the other hand, on some occasions, a squadron would lose far more than the average: as many as four, five or six bombers. In 76 Squadron's case, it lost a steady one, and sometimes two, aircraft on each mission.[11]

It was on one of these missions — less than three weeks after he joined 76 Squadron and only seventeen years old — that Len Jonasson was killed on his third and last trip over occupied Europe, flying as the mid-upper gunner in a Halifax bomber. His three operational flights had spanned just one week. Jonasson was not alone. The rate of missing aircraft for this raid was eleven per cent, the highest in the Battle of the Ruhr. In 76 Squadron alone, three crews failed to return. "Being that the raid was carried out in perfect moonlight," the squadron record book noted, "heavy losses were to be expected."[12]

In July 1946, Asrun Jonasson received a letter from the RCAF records officer containing her son's air gunner wings and a certificate "in recognition of the gallant services rendered by your son." The letter went on:

> *I realize there is little which may be said or done*
> *to lessen your sorrow, but it is my hope that these*

*"Wings," indicative of operations against the
enemy, will be a treasured memento of a young
life offered on the altar of freedom in defence of his
Home and Country.*

Mrs. Jonasson also received her son's war service gratuity of $98.71 and was awarded a pension of twenty-five dollars a month in respect of the death of her son.

* * *

Sixteen-year-old Manitoban Eric Fedi followed much the same route and timings as Len Jonasson before arriving at an operational squadron in Britain: a brief stint in the militia (but with a signals unit as opposed to mounted rifles), enrolment in Winnipeg (on July 13, 1942 at age sixteen), air gunner training at No. 3 Bombing and Gunnery School in Macdonald, promotion to sergeant at the end of the course, deployment to Britain, reception at No. 3 PRC in Bournemouth, additional gunnery training at No. 7 AGS at Stormy Down, conversion training at No. 1652 HCU at Marston Moor and a posting to an RAF flying squadron. Jonasson and Fedi sailed overseas together and the dates of their movements in Britain coincide exactly, with one exception: while Jonasson went to 76 Squadron at Marsden Moor, Fedi ended up in 77 Squadron at Elvington — one day after Jonasson.[13]

And Flight Sergeant Eric Fedi — who turned seventeen on March 3, 1943 — lived eighteen weeks longer on operations than Sergeant Len Jonasson did.

Fedi was born on March 3, 1926, in Winnipeg. He left high school during Grade 9 when he was fifteen and worked at the Ashburn Service Station as a mechanic from 1940 until he joined the RCAF two years later. His workplace was near the house of his parents — car salesman Bill and his wife Fran — on Ashburn

Street. His older brother, Ken, was serving overseas in the Canadian Provost Corps at the time, while sisters Betty, Loraine, June and Gloria were still at home. Fedi's father had served overseas during the First World War and in the Veterans' Guard during the Second.

Fedi played hockey and baseball, built model planes and smoked occasionally, but did not drink. He hoped one day to become an electrical engineer. When he enrolled, the sixteen-year-old was in good health, but his size reflected his age: five-foot-six and 123 pounds. Fedi had made up his mind to be an air gunner — and he got his wish. His air force interview report

Flight Sergeant Eric Fedi died at age seventeen when his bomber was lost during a raid over Germany.

noted "average appearance — alert. Neat, clean — should make a satisfactory Air Gunner," although it also stated he was not suitable for a commission.

Fedi's air gunner training did not quite live up to the expectations of his intake interview. Although he qualified as an air gunner, his course report noted "below average — slow to learn and lacks willingness and effort — very quiet and retiring," ending somewhat paradoxically with the remark "good practical man." Two months after arriving at 77 Squadron in Britain, Fedi had a run-in with an officer on May 28, when he failed to carry out an order to proceed to a range. He was charged, found guilty and given a reprimand.

When Halifax DT793 of 77 Squadron took off from its base at Elvington, just southeast of the ancient city of York on the

Paul Goranson's oil painting Marshalling the Hallies *depicts Halifax bombers of 419 Squadron at Middleton St. George being readied for a night-time raid against Wuppertal, Germany.*

night of September 6, 1943, for a bombing raid over Munich, Fedi had been serving in the unit for five and a half months. The Halifax was flown by Pilot Officer Reg Munns, and his crew were all sergeants: flight engineer Bill Smirk, navigator Bill Smith, air bomber Cliff Tomlinson, wireless operator Dick Wilson and two air gunners: Doug Webb and Eric Fedi. The young Manitoban was the lone member of the RCAF in the crew, the rest were RAF.

Fedi's Halifax was officially listed as "failed to return," one of the many aircraft losses suffered by 77 Squadron during its time at Elvington. From October 1942 to May 1944, the squadron suffered 529 aircrew killed, missing or taken prisoner (out of a total of eleven hundred for the entire war), as well as the loss of 72 Halifaxes (out of a total of 112). Like Fedi, another ninety-six of the total killed were members of the RCAF. No trace was ever found of DT793 and its crew; or at least, they were never identified as such. One other 77 Squadron Halifax was lost that night, along with all seven of its crew.

During the two-month period of August and September 1943, 77 Squadron carried out 284 sorties on eighteen raids. Including Fedi's aircraft, it lost 21 Halifaxes, while among aircrew it suffered 119 killed or "missing believed dead" and thirty-two taken prisoners of war. Remarkably, three aircrew who were shot down or crashed managed to evade capture and return to Britain. With these gruesome statistics — which amounted to almost the equivalent of squadron strength in both aircraft and aircrew — the probability of completing a tour of operations of thirty missions declined to one in ten.[14]

Before he flew on operations, Fedi left a letter at his air base addressed to "the Padre or those looking after my luggage." Its mundane approach to the chance of his capture or death is perhaps an indication of how most young men regarded these possibilities:

> *In case I come down in enemy territory, I would like my suitcase, wallet, and all the personal clothing etc to be sent to my brother whose address is H.16627 L./Cpl. Ken Fedi. The key in my wallet opens my blue kit bag, there are cigarettes in it, and a few sweaters, please send them also and give him the letter also. Also my razor blades and soap, & brown shaving box to him. The blades and stuff are in a little white bag in my kit bag. I thank yow [sic].*

After his death, the seventeen-year-old Fedi was promoted in arrears to flight sergeant, effective June 4, 1943. It took until June 1952 before the RCAF told Fran Fedi officially that it had been determined her son had no known grave. Because of this, the letter noted that his name "will appear" eventually on a memorial to be erected at Runnymede in Britain.

In October the next year, the Air Forces Memorial or Runnymede Memorial was unveiled by the Queen. It is on a hill overlooking the River Thames, just six and a half kilometres downstream from Windsor Castle. The memorial commemorates Commonwealth airmen and airwomen, as well as those from occupied countries in continental Europe, who flew with the RAF and were lost during operations from bases in Britain and North-West Europe and who have no known grave.

On Panel 181, Flight Sergeant Eric Fedi's name is listed, along with an incredible 20,455 of his fellow aircrew on the impressive memorial.[15] In a field below the memorial is the spot where English noblemen forced King John to affix his seal to the Magna Carta on June 15, 1215. Eric Fedi and his comrades died continuing the fight for freedom that began with John's barons in that pleasant sunlit meadow so many centuries ago.

* * *

Lloyd Hyde flew his first operational missions in the spring of 1944, when he was eighteen.[16]

He had joined 424 (Tiger) Squadron at Skipton-on-Swale, Yorkshire. Formed at nearby Topcliffe on October 15, 1942, it was the RCAF's twenty-third squadron established overseas and its sixth bomber squadron. The unit was also known as the City of Hamilton Squadron because the Lake Ontario city sponsored the squadron, sending sports equipment such as baseballs, mitts and bats, among other items. The squadron adopted a tiger's head on its badge in honour of Hamilton's rugby team — the Tiger Cats (later the name of the city's football team). Unlike the majority of bombers, Hyde's Halifax did not have any "nose art" — colourful drawings that often depicted cartoon characters or impossibly curvaceous women. "The funny thing," Hyde remembered, "was our bomb aimer made money painting

This 424 Squadron Halifax displays typical nose art, although Lloyd Hyde's bomber had none.

because he was an artist. But we never put one on ours. I don't know why."

Life in the tail gunner's turret was cold and lonely. The rear turret was the only unheated crew position in the aircraft and the one farthest away from the rest of the crew. An attempt at providing heat — an electric flying suit — proved less than successful:

"They were no good for the simple reason there was no compass [control] on them to adjust the heat. They were either on or off . . . it was 30, 35 below back there. After a while when the electric suit was on you started to sweat in the armpits and in the crotch and you would get a shock. So we didn't use them."

Most of Hyde's operational flying was done at night. If an enemy aircraft — even a suspected one — were spotted by the tail gunner, he took over and shouted instructions to the pilot over the intercom, "Port Go!" or "Starboard Go!" as the situation demanded. The pilot would then start a wild corkscrew dive to the left or right in an attempt to escape the German fighter. Enemy flak was another constant worry as the bombers approached hostile territory. Hyde recalled how important it was for pilots to react accordingly when the first puff of black smoke — caused by exploding flak — appeared. "When you saw [that] you didn't have to worry because the smoke comes after the shell. You would be dead if you were in that area before you saw the smoke." He noted when it came to anti-aircraft fire, the Germans were very methodical, firing a shell on one side, one on the other and then one up the middle. "That is the way they opened up . . . If the first burst came up on the right, you'd think the best thing to do was to turn away from it, but we knew it was better to turn into it."

During the D-Day landings in June, the eighteen-year-old Hyde had his "worst fright":

"We came in low over the beach. Unbelievable numbers of ships and men. I could see men running and falling. Then we started our bomb run and then there was the impact of hits on the airplane. I was convinced we couldn't survive that many hits and I was sure we were going down. It turned out we were so low we were feeling the blast from our own bombs."[17]

That was not the only time Hyde's bomber was hit. On one occasion after returning from a mission, the crew noticed a hole in front of his position and another one through the door behind him. "When we looked at it we came to the conclusion that there wasn't enough room for me between the two holes, but still I didn't get hit." An observer from Group Headquarters offered the suggestion that Hyde must have "sucked in his gut awful fast."

Over London one night on the way to another raid, suddenly "everything quit . . . and we started going down." Somebody

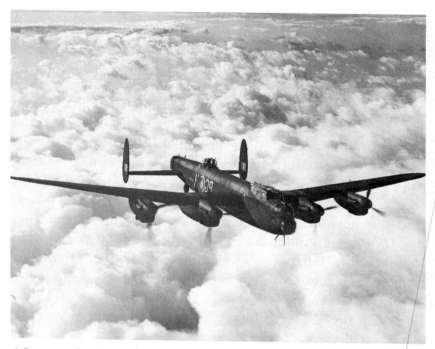

A Lancaster bomber from Lloyd Hyde's 424 Squadron flies over Britain.

said they should bail out, but with five and a half tons of bombs aboard and the aircraft's location over the city, that option was quickly ruled out. Somehow, the pilot succeeded in restarting two of the bomber's engines and made for the English Channel to jettison the bombs, although they were still losing height.

That posed another problem, as a convoy of British ships was making its way up the Channel — with clearance to shoot down anything in the air. The aircraft's bomb bay doors were already open before they reached the Channel so the crew could jettison anything of weight and the bombs followed once they were over the water. Miraculously, they were not fired upon by any of the ships.

With the bombs away, the pilot circled around to land at an emergency airfield on the south coast that was used for returning aircraft, about "a mile and a half long and half a mile wide." The only lighting was two troughs full of oil on either side of the runway. "They would light that — and woof," the airfield was lit up. Thanks to the fact Hyde had a good pilot — an ordained priest who gave up the priesthood to enrol in the RCAF — the bomber landed safely.

On another occasion, the landing gear came down, but it collapsed when the bomber touched down. "We came in on our belly . . . the smoke . . . was streaming out behind us and we were out of that plane and running before it even stopped moving." Hyde and his fellow crew members threw themselves to the ground and waited for an explosion, but nothing happened. Gradually, they looked back and, although the bomber was smoking, it did not explode.

The crew were given instructions to return to their home airfield by train, but left their parachutes aboard to be brought back when the bomber was repaired and flown home. Unfortunately, someone stole the parachutes and they were charged for them. At the time, parachutes were made of silk and could be sold for "good money" to make wedding gowns. Hyde remained philosophical about the incident: "We were negligent."

Hyde's most moving memory, one that made him cry whenever he thought about it, occurred on return from a mission. The bomber's instruments had been knocked out, the aircraft was above the clouds and there was no way of knowing where they were. Then, the bomb aimer went up into the hatch and took star shots with a sextant, which he passed to the navigator. Finally, the navigator said to the pilot, "OK, you can let down, we should be just over the coast of England." Hyde remained skeptical: "We didn't know whether we were coming down over the ocean. When we broke through the clouds, there were the cliffs of Dover . . . that's the one song that gets me today: the White Cliffs of Dover."

Once Hyde completed thirty-three operational missions (raised from an original thirty) in late 1944, he was entitled to return home to Canada. Even though he had volunteered for a second tour, he was part of a group that was told they would be home for Christmas. Then, "some silly bugger got small pox or something and we were quarantined in Liverpool over Christmas."

He returned to Canada via New York City, a voyage made all the more pleasurable for the nineteen-year-old by the presence of thirteen hundred American servicewomen. The fact that "the food was good" was an added bonus. The troops were given "cartons and cartons" of cigarettes, so many so that Hyde recalled he was "pulling stuff out of my kitbag and jamming it full of cigarettes."

It was an emotional homecoming:

"One thing I will never forget was coming into New York Harbour. It was dense fog and all of a sudden the lights broke — the sunlight broke [through]. And there was the Statue of Liberty [sobs] . . . I still do this whenever I think of that morning. Anyway there was one tremendous cheer. You wouldn't think that after all this time I would react this way [referring to his breaking up]. We got off the boat and I've never seen the statue again and I've travelled the world pretty well."

After disembarkation, the Canadians were taken to Montreal, where Hyde received thirty days leave. He returned to Ottawa and lived at home. His brother, who was eight years older and in the army, welcomed him the first morning with a less-than-heartwarming greeting: "I will be damned if I have to salute you."

That was when Hyde concluded "I went away as a boy and came back as a man."

Like so many other Canadians who served in the air force, Lloyd Hyde played his part in his squadron's history. By war's end, in exactly three years of existence, 424 Squadron had flown 3,257 sorties (a sortie is one flight by one aircraft) and dropped

8,776 tons of bombs. On operations and training, it lost a total of 327 aircrew (282 killed — 236 of whom were originally reported as missing but never found — fifteen injured, fourteen prisoners of war) and fifty-six aircraft.[18]

"I WASN'T SLEEPING OR EATING WELL SO THEY PUT ME IN WHAT THEY CALLED THE BOMB-HAPPY WARD."

Post-war, Back Home

Readjusting to civilian life is not easy for any battle-tested soldier. Many of Canada's youngest Second World War soldiers, sailors and airmen had dropped out of school or had given up a job to join. They left behind family and friends, skipped abruptly past their adolescence and entered a war that, if it did not kill them, it changed them. Most moved on with their lives and accomplished much.

* * *

Quebec City native Ken Cambon went on after his experience as a prisoner of war of the Japanese to a distinguished medical career. He enrolled at McGill University as an undergraduate and was accepted into its medical school in 1947, where he met his wife, Eileen. They graduated together as doctors in 1951 and settled in Vancouver after working in British Guiana and Texas — along the way completing additional medical training in Britain. In

In retirement Dr. Ken Cambon was an avid winemaker and tennis player, who had a love of good company and stimulating debates.

Vancouver, the husband and wife doctor team established practices in their respective fields. Additionally, Cambon taught in the ear, nose and throat department of the University of British Columbia's medical school, where he was named clinical professor emeritus of surgery in 1988.

Cambon initially swore he would never return to Japan, not even to attend medical conferences. Then his daughter went to Asia and visited Niigata — where he had spent time in Camp 5-B — only to be told by municipal authorities that there had never been a prisoner of war camp there. After writing to the mayor and receiving an apologetic reply, Cambon travelled to Niigata, where he was welcomed and honoured as the first returning member of Camp 5-B. His attitude towards the Japanese softened; he noted before his visit: "I had come filled with doubts, fears, and prepared for catastrophe," but afterwards he "left with renewed hope and warmth." He died in 2007 after a seven-year struggle with dementia and other medical problems. He left a valuable record of his war-time experiences in *Guest of Hirohito*.[1]

* * *

When pre-war militiaman George MacDonell returned home from Japanese captivity, he realized his whole life, since he was seventeen, had been spent in the army. With only a Grade 10 commercial certificate — and a great deal of trepidation — he decided to return to school. "On that day in March," he later wrote, "this soldier's story ended." The Veterans' Educational Rehabilitation Programme had been designed by the government to assist qualified service personnel whose education had been disrupted by the war to complete their schooling. It was a tough go for MacDonell, who had to cram three years of high school academic courses into thirteen months. He passed, achieved his senior matriculation with honours and entered the University of Toronto's University College in the fall of 1947. He met his future wife, Margaret — an MA graduate and a university lecturer in sociology — at a college dance and graduated two years later with a BA.

The next fall, he married Margaret and returned to university to commence his MA studies. When one of his professors passed a paper on labour relations MacDonell had written to a friend — who just happened to be the president of Canadian General Electric — MacDonell was asked to see him. That interview resulted in a job offer and the opportunity to still complete his MA. The company president had arranged for MacDonell to work for him in the mornings and at the university in the afternoons, starting at an unheard-of fifty dollars a week. MacDonell

Hong Kong survivor George Mac-Donell in 2012.

was ecstatic. He stayed with Canadian General Electric for the next twenty years before moving on to a series of executive positions in other companies for another twelve years.

In 1982, he joined the government of Ontario for a short-term contract that resulted in an appointment as deputy minister in the Department of Industry, Trade and Technology. Finally, in 1990, MacDonell retired. After several years in retirement, he penned *One Soldier's Story 1939-1945: From the Fall of Hong Kong to the Defeat of Japan*, an account of his time in the army and his successful transition back to civvy street.[2]

* * *

On the transfer of I Canadian Corps from Italy to North-West Europe, Reginald Roy moved to Belgium with his unit and finished the war in Holland. After the war, the high school dropout resumed his education and earned a BA and an MA. He worked

During his career as a university professor, Reg Roy also wrote several books of military history.

as an archivist for both federal and provincial agencies and spent three years in Ottawa helping to write the official history of the Canadian army in the Second World War. In 1958, he became a member of the University of Victoria's history department and obtained a PhD in 1965, remaining with the university for thirty years.

Roy became one of Canada's leading chroniclers of military history, and in the late 1960s, he initiated teaching courses in military history at the University of Victoria. He authored twelve books, from his best known, *For Most Conspicuous Bravery: A Biography of Major-General R. Pearkes, VC., through Two World Wars* (1977) through to his most important, *1944: The Canadians in Normandy* (1984) to his last, *D-Day! The Canadians and the Normandy Landings, June 1944* (2001). He also wrote well-received regimental histories of the British Columbia Dragoons, the Seaforth Highlanders of Canada and the Canadian Scottish

Regiment (Princess Mary's). As well, Roy pioneered recording veterans' oral histories, a project that ensured veterans' memories — recorded in their own words — would long outlive them and be available to younger generations. In "Reg Roy Remembers" he chronicled his own war-time experiences in a series of articles for the Cape Breton Highlanders regimental newsletter. "Boy" Roy died at Saanich on Vancouver Island, January 22, 2013. He was ninety.[3]

* * *

Denis Chisholm was twenty-one when the war ended. He had served for five years and nearly died dashing across a slippery pontoon bridge over the Leopold Canal. The war was still with him when he returned to Prince Albert, Saskatchewan, in 1945. "I had a bit of a bad time when I came home. I thought the world was crazy, not me. Things weren't the same. I could not get over how everything was so organized . . . how people did certain things at certain times. When I was overseas the adrenalin was going all the time and there was no such thing as certainty."

Going to the Legion helped. "I'd go down there and have a few beers with the guys. At the time I didn't know what I was going to do with my life, but it was a place where I could go and talk. Folks wanted me to go back to school, but I couldn't see myself in Grade 11, sitting in a classroom." Chisholm idolized his father, a First World War veteran gassed on the Somme. Now he too was wounded, but in a different way.

"About two weeks after I got home — before I got my discharge — I woke up and was nothing but big blisters. There were hives all over my body. My eyes were closing and my scalp felt like it was on fire. Dad took me to the hospital and I was there twelve or fourteen days. It turned out to be nerves.

"I wasn't sleeping or eating well so they put me in what they called the 'bomb-happy ward' in Regina. It was an army hut in the west end of the city. There were quite a few guys in there, and oh my God, some of them were in really bad shape — some couldn't hold a cigarette. I spent two weeks or more there, and as soon as I could sleep and eat I was out."

Chisholm applied to the Royal Canadian Mounted Police, and headed south to Regina for training. "We were all ex-servicemen, except for one guy. I think the only reason we got through was because the OC [Officer Commanding] had a son — his only son — killed in the air force. So the veterans couldn't do much wrong in his eyes. He stuck with us that guy — I admired him."

Chisholm later joined the Regina city police, where he reached the rank of deputy chief before retiring in 1980. As a Legionnaire, he attended numerous events and often spoke to schoolchildren about the importance of remembrance. He was ninety when he died in January 2015, surrounded by family spanning four generations, including Edith, his wife of sixty-seven years.[4]

* * *

Donald Fowler was only nineteen when it ended. He had served in Britain, France, Belgium and the Netherlands, even though he did not reach the qualifying age for overseas service until the final months of the war. His teenage years were in uniform, facing an enemy that had to be defeated.

Discharged from the army in October 1945, Fowler returned to Kingston and re-entered high school. A few months later, he headed to Brockville, where he earned his Grade 12 and 13 at a school for returning veterans. "I've always been curious as hell and very inquisitive," he recalled. "Back then I was well aware of

Donald Fowler met his future wife, Eva, on a bridge in Gananoque, Ontario, in 1940. It was a love that lasted well past the war.

my lack of education, and well aware of my need to do something about that."

After returning to Kingston, Fowler joined the Canadian Officers' Training Corps at Queen's University. His practical but ambitious nature — coupled with his affection for a girl whom he had met prior to going overseas — led him back to Brockville, where he eventually landed a good job with a large telecommunications firm. He married his sweetheart, Eva, in 1949, and fathered a son, and he continues to lead an active social life in Brockville. His younger brother, Karl, who also joined as a boy soldier during the war, earned the Military Medal while serving with the Royal Canadian Regiment in the Korean War. Karl died in October 1988 at age sixty.[5]

* * *

Bill Chitty and Bob Muir, considered to be the youngest members of 14th Field Regiment, also survived. When Chitty arrived home in August 1945, he came up with the "crazy idea" to "make a go of the family farm" at Midgic, New Brunswick. "It didn't work out for a lot of reasons so I started looking for work in the area." He found it in the woods — cutting logs — and in foundries, making cooking stoves. The young man saved his money, bought a truck and hauled gravel to highway construction sites. He kept listening for new employment opportunities, but never would have guessed that his next job — as a temporary guard at Dorchester prison — would bring him face-to-face with Kurt Meyer, formerly of the 12th SS — the nemesis of the Canadian troops who fought in Normandy. The former SS general had been tried for the cold-blooded murders of Canadian troops and a court-martial in December 1945 found him guilty. He was sentenced to death, but the punishment was commuted to life imprisonment. He served five years at Dorchester, before he was transferred to a prison in Germany, in the British zone of occupation. By 1954, Meyer was a free man.[6]

Chitty's part-time work schedule at Dorchester depended on the rise and fall of the inmate population. At one point, Meyer asked him if he could try on his penitentiary hat. It is not known what Chitty thought of the request, but he let the prisoner wear it, according to his widow, Margaret.[7]

Chitty had met Margaret outside a drugstore in Sackville, while his career was trending upwards. He was transferred to Collins Bay Penitentiary in Kingston and when he returned east, it was to marry Margaret at Pugwash, Nova Scotia. The two spent their honeymoon driving back to Ontario. In 1972, Chitty was appointed warden at Joyceville Penitentiary. Five years later, the Correctional Services of Canada promoted

Post-war Bill Chitty in his federal prison guard uniform.

him to regional director, not bad for a boy who grew up on a farm without running water and who answered to the name "Git Wood." Chitty retired in 1979, but continued working as a member of the Ontario Parole Board. He died on February 16, 2008.[8]

* * *

Bob Muir joined the regular force in December 1948. He enrolled as a private in Princess Patricia's Canadian Light Infantry and qualified as a parachutist and glider pilot. He went to Korea in October 1951 as a sergeant and returned to Canada the following year. In 1953, he attended the officer candidate school at the Royal Military College and earned his commission in 1954, the same year he married a teacher named Grayce, whom he met in Kingston.

Muir's military service took him to Germany from 1955 to 1957 and to the Gaza Strip in 1964. He was a captain when he retired in 1969.

A very pleasant surprise occurred in 1998, following the ice storm that devastated Eastern Ontario and Western Quebec.[9] The Muirs were at home in Jasper, Ontario, when the phone rang. It was David Dickson, the former major of the North Nova Scotia Highlanders whose wounded body Muir pulled off the dike at Bienen, Germany, in March 1945. "From that day, until that phone call, Bob wondered whether Dave had made it through the war," explained Grayce. "It was a major revelation for him. All I heard him say on the phone was, 'Really, it's the major!'" The two old soldiers were reunited in June 1998 when Muir and Grayce attended a D-Day dinner organized by the North Novas in Fredericton. By then, Muir had suffered three heart attacks.

Muir died of cancer on January 7, 1999. He was seventy-four.[10] Dickson died on June18, 2014. He was ninety-four.

After the war, Dickson enrolled at the University of New Brunswick law school and went on to study overseas. He returned to Fredericton, where he practised law until he was appointed as a judge to the Supreme Court of New Brunswick in 1964. Justice Dickson retired in 1994.[11] Five years later he drove through a snowstorm to attend Muir's funeral.[12]

* * *

Jim Parks, who also landed on D-Day and fought through North-West Europe, returned home to Winnipeg in September 1945. His slightly older brother, Jack, was already home. "Two days after I got home my mother was in the hospital. She died two months later . . . It was good to see her, but it was sad because she didn't have long to go. I went to see her every second night. My

Jim Parks meets Prince Charles during commemorations outside the Juno Beach Centre in Normandy.

half-brother, Greg, never did get home in time — he was seven days too late."

In his free time, Parks joined a small group of veterans who made regular trips to a local veterans' hospital.

"Some of the guys weren't allowed out so we would sneak in a change of clothes. They would put them on and we would sneak them out. One guy from the Fort Garry Horse had a wound in his forehead — a serious gash, but was always smiling. I think it was because of his wound. There was another guy named Black who had a shoulder wound and he'd lost an eye. We were looking for some cash to buy a bottle of booze and some beer. So we went into a jeweler's shop and asked if there were any pawn shops nearby. We were told there weren't. He asked us what we had to pawn and I showed him my wristwatch. This guy Black piped up and said, 'Hey, how about my glass eye?' The jeweler started to laugh and gave us twenty dollars."

"Different people managed to carry on and some of them did reasonably well," recalled Parks, who got married and raised a family.

"One guy I knew in the navy became a doctor — another one a veterinarian. One guy — a lad who had been poking around for landmines over there — had blown off parts of both arms. When he drank beer he had to put both elbows together to pick up the glass and tilt it towards his mouth. We used to go to wrestling matches with him and he would always get a bit corned. He'd climb into the ring and go after the villain. They would have to carrying him out and put him in a taxi. He later committed suicide."

Parks suffered hearing loss and his feet were damaged by all the marching he did, but he remains grateful for what he has.[13]

* * *

Ralph Frayne finished high school after returning home to St. Catharines, Ontario. He held no regrets about his time in the Merchant Navy and RCN, but his nerves were shot. "I was a mess. I couldn't lift a cup of coffee up to my lips with one hand. I had ulcers and they had to take out three quarters of my stomach . . . It was just nerves and stress." He graduated from law school and practised for more than sixty years in his hometown, insisting the nicest thing about him was his wife, Alice. He died on May 15, 2015, in his ninety-first year.[14]

* * *

Back home in Ottawa and living with his parents after his time as a bomber tail gunner during the war, Lloyd Hyde was pushed by his father to get a job. Streetcars, where his father worked, the police or the post office were his father's choices. Hyde dutifully went to the local police station and applied to join the force. During the interview, he was asked how old he was, and when he replied he was twenty, he was asked when he would turn twenty-one. When Hyde told him July, the interviewer noted he had to be twenty-one to carry a gun. Hyde burst out laughing. "I have been carrying four machine guns for quite a while," he chuckled.

In any case, his heart was not set on becoming a policeman. He went to the local high school, where the sheet-metal teacher — a veteran of the First World War — got him talking to the students about the war. The teacher was so impressed with his talk that he wrote a letter of recommendation to the president of the local Legion branch. Hyde had quite a talk with the president, who told him to go to the Canadian Bank Note Company.

Hyde got a job there and married his sweetheart, Alice. He stayed with the company for forty-one years, and in retirement, spent time sailing his five-and-a-half metre sailboat on the Ottawa River.[15]

* * *

Merchant Navy veterans Gordon Hovey and Roy Spry also survived the war. Hovey enrolled in the air force and then joined a private company that did a lot of work for the military. "He was a vehicle systems engineer. The winterization of equipment became a real specialty for him," explained his daughter Marilyn Gillich. "He spent a lot of time up in Churchill, Manitoba, taking armed forces vehicles up there to make sure they could function in that climate."[16] Hovey died at the Perley Rideau Veterans' Centre in Ottawa on May 15, 2015, less than a month after he was interviewed for this book.[17]

Roy Spry remained in the Canadian Merchant Navy and travelled all over the world. The arrival of Hal Banks and the Canadian government's selling of the Canadian fleet in spite of promises for peacetime jobs ended his sailings days.[18] He and Betty — the girl he met before leaving Leskard, Ontario, in 1944 — met again when he returned home and were later married. In 1979, Spry met up with a group of former merchant seamen, which soon grew into the Canadian Merchant Navy Veterans Association. Spry was a charter member and served as its president from 1987 to 1989. He died on February 12, 1995.[19]

ACKNOWLEDGEMENTS

The credit for this book goes beyond its authors.

While it represents three years of research and writing, *Too Young to Die* draws its strength from many people and organizations. At the top of the list are Canada's youngest Second World War veterans, among them Denis Chisholm, William Chitty, Donald Fowler, Ralph Frayne, Gordon Hovey, Lloyd Hyde, Bob Muir, Jim Parks, Jack Shepherd and Roy Spry. We are most grateful for the time these gentlemen or their families took to patiently listen to and answer our questions. The veterans we talked to shared their memories freely, knowing at times their words would take them into moments they would sooner forget.

Sadly, some of the veterans we interviewed have since died, and are deeply missed by families and friends and by those with whom they served. While their lives are irreplaceable, it is sincerely hoped this book will — in some way — serve to keep alive part of what they experienced in a war the Allies had to win.

Written personal accounts of the experiences of several veterans — both published and unpublished — formed another invaluable part of our research. Among these are Kenneth Cambon's *Guest of Hirohito*; Bill Chitty's *On The Road To Midgic*; Robert Collins's *The Long and the Short and the Tall: An Ordinary Airman's War*; George S. MacDonell's *One Soldier's Story 1939-1945: From the Fall of Hong Kong to the Defeat of Japan*; Russell Margerison's *Boys at War*; Murray Peden's *A Thousand Shall Fall*; and Reginald Roy's *Reg Roy Remembers* (serialized in The Cape Breton Highlanders Association and Regimental Newsletter).

Their wives, sons, daughters, sisters, brothers, nephews, nieces and acquaintances also grasped the importance of this book and patiently took time to speak or write to us. Among them:

Rosemary Boutilier and Robert Power, for sharing memories of Clifford Power; Margaret Brown and Erin Mucha for information and photographs relating to Denis Chisholm; Hanna Burnett for photographs and details about her uncle Jimmie Burnett; Margaret Chitty and her daughter Karen Wand for sharing memories of Bill Chitty; Jeff Foss, Jason Robinson and Paul Robinson for talking to us about Herbert Foss; Marilyn Gillich for sharing her memories and for arranging a timely interview with her father, the late Gordon Hovey; Franklyn Roy for photographs of her father, Reg Roy, and Ian Macintyre for sharing details of Reg Roy's diary and letters; Grayce Muir and her daughter Andrea Breen for reminiscing and sharing photographs and other keepsakes left behind by Bob Muir; Larry Rose and Sue Beard for photographs of George MacDonell; Betty Spry for photographs and memories of her husband, Roy Spry. In addition to trusting us with family treasurers, these relatives helped us "see" aspects of the soldiers, sailors and airmen about whom we were writing. Their crucial assistance and role as guardians of family history reinforces the belief that there are generations of Canadian families who actively cherish and want to accurately share the wartime stories passed down to them.

Discovering the stories of Canada's youngest soldiers, sailors and airmen also required widespread research at organizations ranging from small local libraries and military museums to national institutions. Many people who work at these organizations assisted in bringing this largely unknown Canadian story to light. They ranged from professional historians, archivists, curators and librarians to volunteers. Additionally, Don LaPointe deserves special thanks for drawing the ten very informative maps used in the book, as does independent British Second World War aircraft accident researcher Duncan Robinson for providing us with a detailed perspective on aircraft crashes.

At the Canadian Agency of the Commonwealth War Graves Commission, Johanne Neville prepared lists of Canadian servicemen under the age of eighteen buried in the commission's cemeteries around the world. This compilation was an excellent starting point for this book and for *Old Enough to Fight: Canada's Boy Soldiers in the First World War*, published in 2013, and now available in soft cover. At Library and Archives Canada, we reviewed dozens of service files and are grateful for the assistance provided by its courteous and knowledgeable staff.

We are also deeply indebted to Veterans Affairs Canada for its Virtual War Memorial and Heroes Remembered websites, and other online resources; to the Historica-Dominion's Memory Project website — in particular Alex Herd — for a valuable and popular online collection of first-hand accounts from veterans spanning all categories of military service. Collectively, these websites lend voice to history.

For writing the thoughtful and in-depth Foreword to this book, we thank one of Canada's former top soldiers and ambassadors to the United States, General John de Chastelain. Encouragement, inspiration and support came from Geraldine Chase, Guillaume Charest, Tim Cook, Bruce Ferguson, Donald E. Graves, Mary-Kate Laphen, Ken MacLeod, Patricia Remmer, D-Day veteran Okill Stuart, Gary Weir, Jim Williams, Glenn Wright, and overseas from Diana Beaupre and Adrian Watkinson.

We are also very grateful to publisher Jim Lorimer, who immediately grasped the subject's historical significance and then signed contracts with us for two books. His steady support for this project and for Canadian book publishing in general is deeply appreciated. At Lorimer's Toronto and Halifax offices, Robin Studniberg, Nicole Habib, Dana Hopkins, Emma Renda, Laura Cook, Tyler Cleroux and Meredith Bangay were first-rate throughout the editing and production process. In addition to being very professional, they are excellent people to work with.

TOO YOUNG TO DIE

Additionally, copy editor and reader Laurie Miller's thorough edit and succinct and thoughtful comments and observations were most useful to the writing process.

Finally, it goes without saying (but we will) that our wives, Miriam and Alice, and our families and closest friends, have been outstanding in their encouragement and support of this project. We could not have done it without them.

ENDNOTES

INTRODUCTION

1   Ralph Frayne interview, February 2, 2013.
2   Wartime Minister of Transport J.E. Michaud, cited by Robert G. Halford, *The Unknown Navy: Canada's World War II Merchant Navy* (St. Catharines, ON: Vanwell Publishing Limited, 1995) p. VIII.
3   Jonathan F. Vance, *Maple Leaf Empire: Canada, Britain, and Two World Wars* (Don Mills, ON: Oxford University Press, Huron University College, 2012), p. 149.
4   Donald E. Graves, *South Albertas: A Canadian Regiment at War* (Toronto: Robin Brass Studio, South Alberta Regiment Veterans Association, 1998), pp. 29–30.
5   Vance, p. 149.
6   Denis Chisholm interview, February 15, 2013.
7   Colonel C.P. Stacey, *Six Years of War: The Army in Canada, Britain and the Pacific* Vol. I of the *Official History of the Canadian Army in the Second World War* (Ottawa: Queen's Printer, 1957), pp. 182–183.
8   Robert Power and Rosemary Boutilier interviews, October 15, 19, 2015.
9   Tim Cook, *The Necessary War, Vol. 1: Canadians Fighting The Second World War 1939–1943* (Toronto: Penguin Canada Books Inc., 2014), p. 35.
10 Lori A. Mayne, *Journal Pioneer* (Summerside, PE), November 1, 2008.
11 Historica Canada, www.thememoryproject.com/stories/1167:gerald-bowen.
12 Unless otherwise noted, all information about Jim Parks comes from interviews conducted May 11–13, 2015.
13 Donald D. Tansley, *Growing Up and Going to War: 1925–1945* (Waterloo, ON: The Laurier Centre for Military Strategic and Disarmament Studies, Wilfrid Laurier University, 2005), p. 4.
14 Cynthia Comacchio, "To Hold on High the Torch of Liberty," *Canada and the Second World War: Essays in Honour of Terry Copp* (Waterloo, Ontario: Wilfrid Laurier University Press, 2012), p.36.
15 Jack Shepherd interview, 2013.
16 Donald Fowler interviews, April 15, 2009.
17 Vance, p. 150.
18 Ibid., 173.
19 LAC, RG24, Vol. 27790, John Huggins; LAC, RG24, Vol. 25732, Evan Desjardins.
20 www.railways.incanada.net.
21 Vance, p. 177.
22 LAC, RG24, Vol. 25519, John Callahan; LAC, RG24, Vol. 25854, Ian Ferguson; LAC, RG24, Vol. 27111, Thomas Steed; LAC, RG24, Vol. 25473, Hubert Blanchard.
23 Chisholm interview.

CHAPTER 1

1   www.veterans.gc.ca/eng/video-gallery/video/9806.
2   Ibid.
3   Brereton Greenhous, *"C" Force to Hong Kong: A Canadian Catastrophe 1941-1945* (Toronto: Dundurn, 1997) pp. 15–18, 25, 27, 29.
4   George S. MacDonell, *One Soldier's Story 1939-1945: From the Fall of Hong Kong to the Defeat of Japan* (Toronto: Dundurn, 2002), p. 49.
5   Ibid., p. 21.
6   Ibid., p. 23.
7   Ibid., p. 31.
8   Ibid., pp. 33-37, 41-43, 47, 49.
9   www.veterans.gc.ca/eng/video-gallery/video/6407.
10 Details from Sandra Martin, "Kenneth Cambon, Soldier, PoW and Doctor 1923-2007," *The Globe and Mail*, March 17, 2007.
11 www.hkvca.ca/historical/accounts/stebbe.htm.
12 www.veterans.gc.ca/eng/video-gallery/video/9802.
13 www.veterans.gc.ca/eng/video-gallery/video/9803.
14 Kenneth Cambon, *Guest of Hirohito* (PW Press: Vancouver, 1990), p. 2.
15 www.veterans.gc.ca/eng/video-gallery/video/9805.
16 www.veterans.gc.ca/eng/video-gallery/video/9506.
17 www.veterans.gc.ca/eng/video-gallery/video/6408.
18 Stacey, pp. 448-449.
19 Cambon, p. 5.
20 www.veterans.gc.ca/eng/video-gallery/video/5304.
21 Cambon, pp. 5-6.
22 MacDonell, p. 51.
23 www.veterans.gc.ca/eng/video-gallery/video/5304
24 Brigadier G.D. Johnson, "The Battle of Hong Kong," *After the Battle*, No. 46, 1984, p.3.
25 Stacey, pp. 459-460.
26 Carl Vincent, *No Reason Why: The Canadian Hong Kong Tragedy — an examination* (Stittsville, ON.: Canada's Wings, 1981), pp. 109-110.
27 Cambon, p. 6.
28 www.veterans.gc.ca/eng/video-gallery/video/5305.
29 www.hkvca.ca/historical/accounts/stebbe.htm.
30 www.veterans.gc.ca/eng/video-gallery/video/9636.
31 Stacey, p. 481.
32 www.veterans.gc.ca/eng/video-gallery/video/6409.
33 MacDonell, pp. 73-74.
34 Stacey, p. 490.
35 www.hkvca.ca/historical/accounts/stebbe.htm.
36 Cambon, pp. 18-22.
37 Ibid., pp. 23-24.
38 MacDonell, pp. 76-78.
39 Ibid., pp. 78-80.
40 Ibid., pp. 80-81.

41   www.veterans.gc.ca/eng/video=gallery/video/6409.
42   Cambon, p. 24.
43   Ibid., p. 26.
44   MacDonell, pp. 81-82.
45   Ibid., pp. 81-83.
46   Ibid., pp. 83-85.
47   Vincent, pp. 1, 197.
48   MacDonell, p. 85.
49   Cambon, p. 30.
50   Ibid., p. 31.
51   www.hkvca.ca/historical/accounts/stebbe.htm.
52   Stacey, pp. 488-489.

CHAPTER 2

1   G.C. Marston, unpublished diary, quoted in MacDonell, pp. 99-101.
2   www.veterans.gc.ca/eng/video-gallery/video/6410.
3   Tony Banham, *Not the Slightest Chance: The Defence of Hong Kong, 1941* (Vancouver: UBC Press, 2003), pp. 105-106; Greenhous, p. 73.
4   Ibid., p. 129.
5   Ibid., p. 203.
6   J.H. Marsman, *I Escaped from Hong Kong* (New York: Reynal & Hitchcock, 1942) pp. 80-83.
7   Banham, p. 250.
8   Nathan M. Greenfield, *The Damned: The Canadians at the Battle of Hong Kong and the POW Experience, 1941-45* (Toronto: HarperCollins, 2010), pp. 214-215.
9   Greenhous, pp. 115-116.
10   Greenfield, pp. 215-217.
11   Greenhous, pp. 73-74.
12   John Masters, *The Road Past Mandalay* (New York: Harper, 1961), pp. 162-163.
13   Vincent, p. 210.
14   Ibid., pp 210-211.
15   www.veterans.gc.ca/eng/video-gallery/video/5307.
16   Cambon, p.34.
17   MacDonell, p. 96.
18   Vincent, pp. 210-211.
19   www.veterans.gc.ca/eng/video-gallery/video/9637.
20   Cambon, p. 32.
21   www.hkvca.ca/historical/accounts/stebbe.htm.
22   www.veterans.gc.ca/eng/video-gallery/video/6411.
23   Vincent, p. 211; MacDonell, pp. 96-97.
24   Cambon, p. 35.
25   www.veterans.gc.ca/eng/video-gallery/video/9639.
26   Lance Ross, unpublished diary, quoted in MacDonell, pp. 97-98.
27   Ibid., pp. 98-99.
28   G.C. Marston, unpublished diary, quoted in MacDonell, pp. 99-101.
29   www.veterans.gc.ca/eng/video-gallery/video/6411.

30 www.veterans.gc.ca/eng/video-gallery/video/5308.
31 MacDonell, p. 102.
32 Greenfield, pp. 242, 271-272; Greenhous, pp. 121-122.
33 www.veterans.gc.ca/eng/video-gallery/video/5308; www.veterans.gc.ca/eng/video-gallery/video/6412 .
34 www.veterans.gc.ca/eng/video-gallery/video/6412.
35 MacDonell, p. 104.
36 www.hkvca.ca/historical/accounts/stebbe.htm.
37 Greenhous p 126-127; Greenfield p 268-269.
38 MacDonell, p. 105.
39 Vincent, pp. 211-212.
40 MacDonell, pp. 102-103.
41 Cambon, pp. 41-42.
42 Greenhous, pp. 129-130.
43 www.veterans.gc.ca/eng/video-gallery/video/9779.
44 MacDonell, pp. 105-106.
45 www.hkvca.ca/historical/accounts/stebbe.htm.
46 Cambon, p. 51.
47 Ibid., pp. 55, 57-59.
48 www.hkvca.ca/submissions/vpearson.htm; www.hkvca.ca/submissions/vpearson1.htm; www.hkvca.ca/lastpost/obits/blisscole.htm.
49 www.hkvca.ca/historical/accounts/johnjames.htm; Marcine Hefner James, "The Ladies' Side of the Story," *The Spirit of the Torch*, Vol. V, No. 2 (9), December 2005, pp. 10-12.
50 Greenhous, p. 148.
51 MacDonell, p. 90.
52 Cambon, p. 117.

CHAPTER 3

1   Stacey, p. 381.
2   Mark Zuehlke, *Tragedy at Dieppe: Operation Jubilee, August 19, 1942* (Vancouver: Douglas & McIntyre, 2012), p. 309-314.
3   John Boileau, "Battle Honours of the Canadian Forces, Part 32: Second World War — Dieppe," *Legion Magazine*: Vol. 88, No. 2, March/April 2013, p. 58; Brigadier General Denis Whitaker and Shelagh Whitaker, *Dieppe: Tragedy to Triumph*, (Toronto & Montreal: McGraw-Hill Ryerson, 1992), p. 256.
4   www.2ndww.blogspot.ca/2012/08/i-want-to-be-at-peace-with-god.html.
5   Zuehlke, p. 272.
6   Major D.J. Goodspeed, *Battle Royal: A History of the Royal Regiment of Canada, 1862-1962* (Toronto: The Royal Regiment of Canada Association, 1962), pp. 394-396, 398.
7   Unless otherwise noted, all information about Burnett is taken from LAC, RG24, Vo l. 25285, James Burnett.
8   Boileau, p. 58.
9   Goodspeed, pp. 365-368, 376-386.
10 Stacey, pp. 334-336.

11 Goodspeed, pp. 386-387.
12 Boileau, p. 58.
13 Unless otherwise noted, all information about Boulanger is taken from LAC, RG24, Vol. 25498, Robert Boulanger.
14 www.2ndww.blogspot.ca/2012/08/i-want-to-be-at-peace-with-god.html. Original letter in French; translation from website.
15 Ibid. Original letter in French; translation by Patricia Remmer and John Boileau.
16 Zuehlke, p. 361.
17 www.2ndww.blogspot.ca/2012/08/i-want-to-be-at-peace-with-god.html.
18 Roland Paillé, "Dieppe se souvient du Grand-mérois Robert Boulanger," *le Nouvelliste* (Trois-Rivières, QC), February 14, 2014.
19 Hanna Burnett, "The Uncle I Never Knew: A journey to Dieppe to discover Jimmie Burnett," *Canadian Military History.* Vol. 21, Issue 4, 2015, p. 79.
20 Hanna Burnett interview, July 22, 2015. Jimmie Burnett is Ms. Burnett's great-great uncle.
21 Burnett, p. 80.
22 *Ajax* was one of three Royal Navy cruisers that had engaged and forced the powerful German pocket battleship *Admiral Graf Spee* to seek refuge in the River Platte near the Uraguayan capital of Montevideo in December 1939. Cornered, and with no chance of escape, the German captain scuttled his ship.
23 Charles Kipp, *Because We Are Canadians: A Battlefield Memoir* (Vancouver: Douglas & McIntyre, 2002), p. 18.
24 Burnett, p. 80; Burnett interview.
25 Burnett, pp. 80-81.
26 Ibid., pp. 82-84.
27 Burnett interview.
28 Burnett, p. 83.
29 Of the 907 total, 807 were killed during the raid, 28 died of wounds and 72 died while in captivity.
30 Boileau, p. 59.

CHAPTER 4

1 James A. Wood, *We Move only Forward: Canada, the United States and the First Special Service Force 1942-1944* (St. Catharines, ON: Vanwell, 2006), pp. 90-91.
2 Alex Morrison and Ted Slaney, *The Breed of Manly Men: The History of the Cape Breton Highlanders* (Sydney, NS: The Cape Breton Highlanders Association and Peacekeeping Education Associates, 2002), pp. 1-2, 6.
3 Reginald Roy, "Reg Roy Remembers" The Cape Breton Highlanders Association and Regimental Newsletter, January-April 2009, pp. 4-6. The term "short-arm inspection" is a military euphemism for the routine medical inspection of soldiers' penises ("short arms") for signs of sexually transmitted diseases and other medical problems.
4 Andrew Clark, *A Keen Soldier: The Execution of Second World War Private Harold Joseph Pringle* (Toronto: Alfred A. Knopf, 2002), pp. 18, 22-23, 25, 28, 32-34, 37-38, 43.
5 LAC, RG 24, Vol. 26845, Harold Joseph Pringle. There is some discrepancy

about the date Pringle arrived in Italy. Based on interviews with unit personnel, Clark believes it was December 1943, but Pringle's file clearly states March 1944. Where other discrepancies exist between Pringle's LAC file and Clark's book, his file has been used as the authority. Canadian army personnel records are unusually accurate.

6   Morrison and Slaney, pp. 28-30.

7   Ibid., p. 34.

8   Excerpted from the diary of RH Roy, courtesy of Ian Macintyre, Honorary Colonel of the Cape Breton Highlanders.

9   Morrison and Slaney, pp. 35-36, 40.

10   Ibid., pp. 40-41.

11   Ibid., p. 99.

12   Unless otherwise noted, all information about Grant is taken from LAC, RG24, Vol. 25997, Freeman Hector Grant.

13   Thomas H. Raddall, *West Novas: A History of the West Nova Scotia Regiment* (Liverpool, NS: s.n., 1986), pp. 84-153.

14   John Boileau, "Battle Honours of the Canadian Forces, Part 46: Second World War—The Moro," *Legion Magazine*: Vol. 90, No. 5, September/October 2015, pp. 38-39.

15   John Boileau, "Battle Honours of the Canadian Forces, Part 47: Second World War—Prelude to Ortona," *Legion Magazine*: Vol. 90, No. 6, November/December 2015, pp. 56-57.

16   Raddall, pp. 159-165.

17   Unless otherwise noted, all information about Innanen is taken from LAC, RG24, Vol. 30830, Victor Innanen.

18   Wood, pp. 30, 35, 37-38, 45, 56-57.

19   Ibid., pp. 64-68, 70.

20   Ibid., pp. 71, 80-92.

CHAPTER 5

1   Clark, A Keen Soldier, pp. 273, 277, 286-287. As noted in Chapter 4, endnote 5, where discrepancies exist between Pringle's LAC file and Clark's book, his file has been used as the final authority.

2   www.canadiansoldiers.com/regiments/cavalry/2nd10thdragoons.htm.

3   Unless otherwise noted, all information about Anderson is taken from LAC, RG24, Vol. 25327, John Edward Anderson.

4   Stacey, p. 175.

5   Stafford Johnson, *The Fighting Perths: The Story of the First Century in the Life of a Canadian County Regiment* (Perth Regiment Veterans' Association: Stratford, ON, 1964), online version at www.perthregiment.org/index3.html, n.p., chapters 8-12.

6   Unless otherwise noted, all information about Rose is taken from LAC, RG24, Vol. 26933, Alexander McEachern Rose.

7   Robert Tooley, *The Carleton and York Regiment in the Second World War* (Fredericton: New Ireland Press, 1989), pp. 201-206.

8   Morrison and Slaney, p. 99.

9   Roy diary.

10　Morrison and Slaney, p. 270.

11　Roy diary.

12　Morrison and Slaney, p. 274.

13　Morrison and Slaney, p. 277-279.

14　Morrison and Slaney, p. 286-288.

15　Morrison and Slaney, p. 290.

16　Reginald Roy obituary in *The Globe and Mail,* February 25, 2013.

17　Roy diary.

18　Clark, pp. 62-63.

19　Ibid., pp. 63-65.

20　Ibid., pp. 67, 69, 70-72, 78, 80.

21　Ibid., pp. 81, 83, 85-87.

22　Ibid., pp. 91, 104.

23　Ibid., pp. 105, 114-116.

24　Ibid., pp. 123-124, 126-127.

25　Ibid., pp. 130-134.

26　Ibid., pp. 143-149.

27　Ibid., pp. 157, 162-163, 165.

28　Ibid., pp. 166-184.

29　Ibid., pp. 193, 214, 221, 246.

30　Ibid., pp. 215, 229-230, 265-266, 273-274.

31　Ibid., pp. 284-286.

32　Ibid., pp. 176-177.

CHAPTER 6

1　Unless otherwise noted, all information about Jim Parks comes from interviews conducted May 11-13, 2015.

2　Mark Milner, *Stopping The Panzers: The Untold Story of D-Day* (Lawrence, Kansas: University of Kansas, 2014), pp. 66, 93.

3　Col. C.P. Stacey, *The Victory Campaign: The Operations in North-West Europe, 1944-1945, Vol. 3* (Ottawa: Queen's Printer, 1960), p. 76; Mark Zuehlke, *Juno Beach: Canada's D-Day Victory: June 6, 1944* (Maderia Park, British Columbia: Douglas and McIntyre, 2004), p. 103.

4　J.L. Granatstein and Desmond Morton, *Bloody Victory: Canadians and the D-Day Campaign 1944* (Toronto: Lester & Orpen Dennys Publishers, 1984), p. 23.

5　Milner, pp. 63, 81.

6　Margaret Chitty interview, February 9, 2013; Bill Chitty, unpublished memoir *On The Road To Midgic,* p. 86.

7　Granatstein and Morton, p. 22.

8　Chitty, p. 86.

9　Ibid., p. 87.

10　Bill Tindall, Historica Canada, The Memory Project, www.thememoryproject. com/stories/2756:bill-tindall.

11　Milner, p. 112.

12　Jean E. Portugal, *We Were There: The Army: A Record for Canada, Vol. 2*

(Shelburne, ON: The Royal Canadian Institute Heritage Society, 1998) p. 635.

13 William Heron, Historica Canada, The Memory Project, www.
    thememoryproject.com/stories/297:william-hallet-bill-heron; www.obitsforlife.
    com, November 2012.

14 Grayce Muir interview, July 31, 2012.

15 Chitty, pp. 5, 7.

16 Ibid., p. 9.

17 Ibid., pp. 22, 24.

18 Ibid., p. 52.

19 Ibid., pp. 66, 83, *84*.

20 Ibid., p. 87.

21 Dianne Pinder-Moss, Smiths Falls Record News, June 1, 1994.

22 Email correspondence between Grayce Muir, David Muir and Babs Webber,
    January 26, 2015, April 22, 2012.

23 Bob Muir with Sam Malkin, June 1994, courtesy Andrea Breen.

24 Pinder-Moss, *Smiths Falls Record News*, June 1, 1994.

25 Gerry Macdonald, Historica Canada, The Memory Project, www.
    thememoryproject.com/stories/1566:gerry-edward-mac-macdonald; Jane Taber,
    Globe and Mail, November 11, 2012.

26 LAC, RG 24, Vol. 26048, Horace Haney.

27 Granatstein and Morton, p. 60.

28 Zuehlke, p. 333.

CHAPTER 7

1   Portugal, Vol. 6, pp. 2936-2937.

2   Howard Margolian, *Conduct Unbecoming: The Story of the Murder of Canadian
    Prisoners of War in Normandy* (Toronto: University of Toronto Press, 1998), p.
    6.

3   Ibid., pp. 9, 10,15.

4   Milner, p.162.

5   Granatstein and Morton, p. 63.

6   Portugal, Vol. 6, p. 3000.

7   Historica Canada, www.thememoryproject.com/stories/865:sheldon-dennis-
    nattrass. From here on: Nattress, The Memory Project.

8   Milner, p. 199.

9   Nattrass, The Memory Project.

10 Ibid., p. 110.

11 Mark Zuehlke, *Holding Juno: Canada's Heroic Defence of the D-Day Beaches:
    June 7-12, 1944* (Vancouver: Douglas & McIntyre, 2005), p. 79-80.

12 Portugal, Vol. 4, p. 1725.

13 Zuehlke, p. 85.

14 Portugal, Vol. 4, p. 1725.

15 Milner, p. 189.

16 Portugal, Vol. 3, p. 1164.

17 Historica Canada, www.thememoryproject.com/stories/1339:herbert-foss; Jeff
    Foss, Paul Robinson, Jason Robinson interviews, July 17 and 20, 2015.

18   Milner, p. 236; Margolian, p. 77.
19   Milner, p. 247.
20   Portugal, Vol. 6, p. 3044.
21   Portugal, Vol. 6, p. 2937.
22   Portugal, Vol. 6, p. 2938.
23   Milner, p. 254.
24   Granatstein and Morton, p. 70; *Normandy 1944: Canada Remembers* (Veterans Affairs Canada), p. 34.
25   Historica Canada, www.thememoryproject.com/stories/1555:william-leland-berrow.
26   Terry Copp, *A Canadian's Guide to the Battlefields of Normandy* (Waterloo, ON: Laurier Centre for Military Strategic and Disarmament Studies, Wilfrid Laurier University, 1994), p. 83.
27   Granatstein and Morton, p. 112.

CHAPTER 8

1   Unless otherwise noted, all information about Denis Chisholm comes from interviews conducted February 15, 2013, and May 11-13, 2015.
2   www.junobeach.org/canada-in-wwii/articles/the-army-medical-organization.
3   www.britannica.com.
4   Granatstein and Morton, p. 112.
5   LAC, RG 24, Vol. 26048, Horace Haney.
6   Unpublished, undated memoir by Bill Chitty; interviews with Margaret Chitty and his daughter Karen Wand, 2013, 2015.
7   Historica Canada, www.thememoryproject.com/stories/1339:herbert-foss.
8   LAC, RG 24, Vol. 26048, Haney.
9   Granatstein and Morton, p. 113.
10   LAC, RG 24, Vol. 26048, Haney.
11   LAC, RG 24, Vol. 26359, Gérard Doré.
12   Mark Zuehlke, *Breakout From Juno: First Canadian Army and the Normandy Campaign, July 4-August 21, 1944* (Vancouver: Douglas & McIntyre Publishers Inc., 2011), p. 152.
13   Ibid., p. 159.
14   Copp, p. 100.
15   Copp, p. 100; Zuehlke, p. 175.
16   Zuehlke, p. 344.
17   Granatstein and Morton, p. 179.
18   Graves, p. 24.
19   Zuehlke, pp. 413-414.

CHAPTER 9

1   Lee A. Windsor, "Too Close for the Guns! 9 Canadian Infantry Brigade in the Battle for the Rhine Bridgehead," *Canadian Military History Journal*, Winter/Spring 2003. Waterloo, ON: Wilfrid Laurier University; Grayce Muir interviews, 2013, Andrea Breen interview, 2014.
2   www.thecanadianencyclopedia.ca/en/article/first-canadian-army/.

3   LAC, RG 24, Vol. 25666, John Cremeens.
4   Gordon Brown and Terry Copp, *Look To Your Front . . . Regina Rifles: A Regiment At War: 1944-45* (Waterloo, ON: Laurier Centre for Military Strategic and Disarmament Studies, Wilfrid Laurier University, 2001), pp. 135-136.
5   John Marteinson, *We Stand On Guard: An Illustrated History of the Canadian Army* (Montreal: Ovale Publications, 1992), pp. 307-308.
6   Reginald H. Roy, *Ready for the Fray: History of the Canadian Scottish Regiment* (Calgary: Bunker To Bunker Publishing, 2002), pp. 334-335.
7   Brown and Copp, pp. 146-147.
8   Graves, pp. 231-232; LAC, RG 24, Vol. 26119, Dennis Hoare.
9   LAC, RG 24, Vol. 26119, Dennis Hoare.
10   www.veterans.gc.ca/eng/remembrance/memorials/canadian-virtual-war-memorial.
11   War Diary, 14th Field Regiment, RCA.
12   Grayce Muir and Andrea Breen interviews.
13   Unless otherwise noted, all information about Donald Fowler comes from interviews conducted in 2009.
14   www.veterans.gc.ca/eng/remembrance/memorials/canadian-virtual-war-memorial.
15   Chitty memoir, p. 93.
16   LAC, RG 24, Vol. 26467, Barney McGuigan.
17   Angus Brown and Richard Gimblett, *In the Footsteps of First Canadian Army: Northwest Europe 1942-1945* (Ottawa: Canadian War Museum, Magic Light Publishing, 2009), p. 117.
18   LAC, RG 24, Vol. 25698, Herbert Danielson.
19   Historica Canada, www.thememoryproject.com/stories/1228:david-masterton-dave-dickson; Grayce Muir interview; Lee A. Windsor, Canadian Military History Journal, Winter/Spring 2003, pp. 5-27.

CHAPTER 10

1   Tim Cook, *The Necessary War: Vol. 1, Canadians Fighting The Second World War 1939-1943* (Toronto: Penguin Canada Books Inc. 2014), p. 290.
2   Ken Macpherson and John Burgess, *The Ships of Canada's Naval Forces 1910-1981* (Don Mills, ON: Collins Publishers, 1981), p. 29.
3   Mac Johnston, *Corvettes Canada: Convoy Veterans of WW II Tell Their True Stories* (Whitby, ON: McGraw-Hill Ryerson, 1994), p. 7.
4   Granatstein and Morton, *p. 66.*
5   Joel Zemel, svpproductions.com/rncchistory.pdf.
6   Cook, p. 101.
7   William Pugsley, *Saints, Devils and Ordinary Seamen: Life On The Royal Canadian Navy's Lower Deck* (Toronto: Collins, 1945), p. 19.
8   Clarence Mitchell, *From Boys To Men*, www.veterans.gc.ca/eng/remembrance/those-who-served/diaries-letters-stories/second-world-war/cmitchell. From here on: Mitchell.
9   Ralph Frayne interview, February 3, 2013.
10   Britain Ship Losses 1941, Military Records Online, www.world-war.co.uk/

warloss_172brit.php3.
11 www.thememoryproject.com/stories/1940:fred-sygrove.
12 LAC RG112, Vol.30783, Kenneth Watson; www.veterans.gc.ca/eng/
    remembrance/memorials/canadian-virtual-war-memorial/detail/2641152.
13 Roger Sarty, *The Battle of the Atlantic: The Royal Canadian Navy's Greatest
    Campaign 1939-1945* (Ottawa: CEF Books, 2001) p. 12.
14 Granatstein and Morton, p. 67.
15 Mitchell.
16 www.thememoryproject.com/stories/1167:gerald-bowen.
17 Fraser McKee and Robert Darlington, *The Canadian Naval Chronicle 1939-1945*
    (St. Catharines, ON: Vanwell Publishing, 1998), p. 41.
18 LAC RG24, Vol. 29028, Jerome Bright.
19 Sarty, p. 22.
20 www.warsailors.com/convoys/sc94.html.
21 Marc Milner, "Fire And Fog: *Assiniboine* Rams *U-210*," *Legion Magazine*, Vol.
    89, No. 4, July/August 2014; McKee and Darlington, pp. 56-59; Joseph Schull,
    *Far Distant Ships: An Official Account of Canadian Naval Operations in World
    War II* (Toronto: Stoddart Publishing Co. Ltd., 1950) p. 136.
22 Milner, *Legion Magazine*.
23 LAC RG112Vol. 30783, Kenneth Watson. Watson was one of fourteen on board
    mentioned in dispatches.
24 www.peakery.com/mount-kenneth-canada.
25 McKee and Darlington, p. 71.
26 Robert Power and Rosemary Boutilier interviews, October 15, 19, 2015.
27 Ibid., p. 73.
28 Scott Haskins, *Laughing In The Face Of Danger* (Edmonton: TMH Marketing
    Inc., 2006), pp. 223-224; Robert Power interview, October 8, 2015.
29 Power interview.
30 Mitchell.

CHAPTER 11

1   Granatstein and Morton, p. 66.
2   McKee and Darlington, pp. 193-195.
3   www.uboat.net/allies/merchants/crews/ships3379.html.
4   Veterans Affairs Canada, Heroes Remembered, www.veterans.gc.ca/eng/
    video/8634.
5   Macpherson and Burgess, p. 44.
6   Sarty, p. 34.
7   Macpherson and Burgess, p. 42.
8   www.bbc.co.uk/history/worldwars/wwtwo/scharnhosrt_01.shtml.
9   Frayne interview.
10 www.uboat.net/allies/merchants/1672.html.
11 www.warsailors.com/singleship/berth.html.
12 Commander Tony German, *The Sea Is At Our Gates: The History of the
    Canadian Navy* (Toronto: McClelland & Stewart Inc., 1990), p. 178.
13 Frayne interview.

14   Macpherson and Burgess, p. 34.
15   Mitchell.
16   German, p. 161.
17   McKee and Darlington, p. 142.
18   Macpherson and Burgess, p. 129.
19   www.thememoryproject.com/stories/1282:harry-payne.
20   www.thememoryproject.com/stories/385:peter-gery-germaniuk.
21   German, p. 167; Macpherson and Burgess, p. 142.
22   McKee and Darlington, p. 169.
23   Macpherson and Burgess, p. 94.
24   LAC RG 24, Vol. 29091, Alec Lovell; LAC RG24, Vol. 29091, Lorne Lovell.
25   LAC RG 24, Vol. 29054, Lewis Evans.
26   LAC RG 24, Vol. 29027, Joseph Breux.
27   LAC RG 24, Vol. 29052, Ralph Earp.
28   LAC RG 24, Vol. 29072, Arnold Hibbard.
29   www.theroadtriphound.com/2012/11/05/castle-by-the-tracks-the-palliser-hotel.
30   LAC RG 24, Vol. 29111, Cecil Moss.
31   LAC R112, Vol. 30774, Howard Parsons.
32   McKee and Darlington, p. 194.
33   LAC RG 24, Vol. 29054, Lewis Evans.
34   LAC RG 24, Vol. 29027, Joseph Breux.
35   During the Battle of the Atlantic, RCN escorts and RCAF aircraft ensured the
     safe passage of more than 25,000 merchant ships that delivered approximately
     165 million tons of cargo to Britain and the Allied cause in Europe. During that
     time, the tiny Canadian navy grew to become one of the largest navies in the
     world.

CHAPTER 12

1   Gordon Hovey interview, April 30, 2015.
2   Betty Spry interview, November 14, 2015; files from Betty Spry, including
     accounts from Roy Spry.
3   Joseph Kenny, VAC Heroes Remembered, www.veterans.gc.ca/eng/video-
     gallery/video/7570.
4   Admiral Leonard W. Murray interview, CBC, 1967.
5   Speech by Hon. Stephane Dion during unveiling of Historic Sites and
     Monuments plaque, Halifax, September 11, 2005; www.veterans.gc.ca/historical-
     sheets/merchant.
6   Hovey interview; Marilyn Gillich interview, April 30, 2015; obituary for Claude
     Hovey, www.inmemoriam.ca.
7   Hovey interview.
8   Spry interview.
9   Kenny.
10   John Boileau, "Canada's Merchant Navy: The Men That Saved The World,"
     Legion Magazine, Vol. 85, No. 4, July-August 2010, pp. 21-22.
11   Hovey interview.
12   www.thememoryproject.com/stories/229:ken-raymond-fritz-curly-luttrell. From

here on: Luttrell.

13 Spry interview and notes from her.

14 George Evans, "Life As A Merchant Marine," *The Red Duster*, Spring 2009, pp. 4-5.

15 Robert G. Halford, *The Unknown Navy: Canada's World War II Merchant Navy* (St. Catharines, ON: Vanwell Publishing Limited, 1995), p. 69.

16 Joseph Schull, *Far Distant Ships: An Official Account of Canadian Naval Operations in World War II* (Toronto: Stoddart Publishing Co. Limited, 1950), p. 17. In 1939, sixty-three per cent of Canada's export trade and thirty-nine per cent of its import trade moved by sea. Schull, p. 10.

17 Ibid., pp. 174, 196.

18 Hovey interview.

19 Kenny.

20 www.veterans.gc.ca/historical-sheets/merchant.

21 These were known as Defensively Equipped Merchant Ships or DEMS.

22 Luttrell.

23 www.veterans.gc.ca/eng/remembrance/memorials/canadian-virtual-war-memorial/detail/2640435. For Victor Pageau, same website, but detail 2640436. From here on: CVWM, followed by detail number.

24 Kenny.

25 McKee and Darlington, p. 232; CVWM, detail 2640170, detail 2641062.

26 McKee and Darlington, p. 237; CVWM, detail 2558219, detail 2558580.

27 Halford, p. 186; accounts from Roy Spry.

28 Spry.

29 Hovey interview.

CHAPTER 13

1 Accident details provided by Duncan Robinson, independent British Second World War aircraft accident researcher.

2 Unless otherwise noted, all information about Pollon is taken from LAC, RG24, Vol. 28439, Joseph Raymond Pollon.

3 Brereton Greenhous, Stephen J. Harris, William C. Johnson, and William G.P. Rawling, *The Crucible of War, 1939-1945: The Official History of the Royal Canadian Air Force Vol. III* (Toronto: University of Toronto Press, 1994), p. 523.

4 No. 405, the first bomber squadron formed, was transferred to No. 8 (Pathfinder Force) Group RAF in April 1943, shortly after the new group had been established in January.

5 David Brown, *Aerodromes in North Yorkshire and Wartime Memories* (Stockton-on-Tees, England: self-published, 1996), pp. 2, 5-7, 12.

6 Greenhous et al., p. 635. Allerton Hall's owner was William Marmaduke Stourton, 25th Baron Mowbray, 26th Baron Segreve, 22nd Baron Stourton. After No. 6 Group took over the hall, he lived in Allerton House on the estate.

7 Aircraft details from Chaz Bowyer, *The Encyclopedia of British Military Aircraft* (London: Arms and Armour Press, 1982).

8 Greenhous et al., p. 523.

9 Rob Davis, "Royal Air Force (RAF) Bomber Command 1939-1945," www.

elsham.pwp.blueyonder.co.uk/raf_bc/

10   Larry Milberry (ed.), *Sixty Years: The RCAF and CF Air Command 1924-1984* (Toronto: CANAV Books, 1984), p. 159.

11   Unless otherwise noted, all information about Dowding is taken from LAC, RG24, Vol. 27407, John Frederick Dowding.

12   www.acesofww2/Canada/aces//dowding.htm.

13   Dan McCaffery, *Battlefields in the Air: Canadians in the Allied Bomber Command* (Toronto; James Lorimer, 1995), p. 69.

14   Dan McCaffery, "Historian honours Sarnia gunner's bravery," *The Observer* (Sarnia), July 14, 2009.

15   Unless otherwise noted, all information about Wright is taken from LAC, RG24, Vol. 28987, Edward James Wright.

16   Williston, Floyd, "Too young to fly, old enough to die," *Winnipeg Free Press*, May 1, 2005.

17   Ibid.

18   Ibid.

19   Ibid.

20   Ibid.

21   Ibid.

22   Ibid.

23   All information about Lloyd Bernard Hyde comes from an interview conducted in January 2013.

24   Davis, Ibid.

CHAPTER 14

1   Greenhous et al., p. 667; *Bomber Command Report on Night Operations No. 312*, 16/17th April, 1943.

2   For example, see "Fierce Blows by Allied Raiders," *The Advertiser* (Adelaide, Australia), April 19, 1943.

3   Unless otherwise noted, all information about Jonasson is taken from LAC, RG24, Vol. 27861, Leonard Norman Jonasson.

4   www.lh-inc.ca/index.php/icelandic-paper/home-page-archives/42-2010/92, "One airman who didn't return."

5   Ibid.

6   Brown, p. 16.

7   Greenhous et al., p. 7.

8   Murray Peden, *A Thousand Shall Fall* (Toronto: Stoddart Publishing, 1988), p. 110.

9   Robert Collins, *The Long and the Short and the Tall: An Ordinary Airman's War* (Saskatoon: Western Producer Prairie Books, 1986), p. 80.

10   Excerpt from Russell Margerison, *Boys at War* (London: Northway Publications, 2006), in the *Mail Online*, May 10, 2009.

11   Max Hastings, *Bomber Command* (New York: Dial Press, 1979), pp. 221-222.

12   Ibid., p. 223.

13   Unless otherwise noted, all information about Fedi is taken from LAC, RG24, Vol. 27490, Eric Fedi.

14   Mike Varley, "A Concise History of 77 Squadron RAF," http://homepage.
     ntlworld.com/r_m_g.varley/77%20Squadron%20Association.html.
15   www.cwgc.org/find-a-cemetery/cemetery/109600/RUNNYMEDE%20
     MEMORIAL.
16   Unless otherwise noted, all information about Lloyd Bernard Hyde comes from
     an interview conducted in January 2013.
17   Dave Brown, *Ottawa Citizen*, July 30, 2012.
18   S. Kostenuk and J. Griffin, *RCAF Squadron Histories and Aircraft: 1924-1968*
     (Toronto: National Museum of Man, National Museums of Canada, 1977), p.
     119.

EPILOGUE

1   Kenneth Bambon obituary, *The Globe and Mail*, March 3, 2007; "Kenneth
     Cambon, Soldier, PoW and Doctor 1923-2007, The Globe and Mail, March 17,
     2007.
2   MacDonell, pp. 161-197.
3   Reginald Roy obituary.
4   Chisholm interview.
5   Fowler interviews.
6   Margolian, p. 182.
7   Margaret Chitty interview.
8   Ibid.
9   www.canadianencyclopedia.ca/en/article/ice-storm-1998.
10   Grayce Muir interviews.
11   David Dickson obituary, www.mcadamsfh.com/obituaries/89250.
12   Grayce Muir interviews.
13   Parks interview.
14   Frayne interview.
15   Hyde interview; Dave Brown, *Ottawa Citizen*, July 30, 2012.
16   Gordon Hovey and Marilyn Gillich interviews.
17   Gordon Hovey obituary, *Ottawa Citizen*, May 23, 2015.
18   The Canadian government, supported by the Canadian shipping industry,
     brought in Hal Banks from the United States to lead the brutal suppression of
     the Canadian Seamen's Union "whose leadership, though not its rank and file,
     was Red-tinged." Halford, p. *x*.
19   Correspondence with Betty Spry, November 16, 2015.

BIBLIOGRAPHY

BOOKS

Banham, Tony. *Not the Slightest Chance: The Defence of Hong Kong, 1941.* Vancouver: University of British Columbia Press, 2003.

Black, Dan and John Boileau. *Old Enough To Fight: Canada's Boy Soldiers in the First World War.* Toronto: James Lorimer and Company Limited, 2013.

Bowyer, Chaz. *The Encyclopedia of British Military Aircraft.* London: Arms and Armour Press, 1982.

Brown, Angus and Richard Gimblett. *In The Footsteps of First Canadian Army, Northwest Europe 1942-1945.* Ottawa: Canadian War Museum, Magic Light Publishing, 2009.

Brown, David. *Aerodromes in North Yorkshire and Wartime Memories.* Stockton-on-Tees, England: Self-published, 1996.

Brown, Gordon and Terry Copp. *Look To Your Front...Regina Rifles A Regiment At War: 1944-45.* Waterloo, ON: Laurier Centre for Military Strategic and Disarmament Studies, Wilfrid Laurier University, 2001.

Cambon, Kenneth, M.D. *Guest of Hirohito.* Vancouver: PW Press, 1990.

Clark, Andrew. *A Keen Soldier: The Execution of Second World War Private Harold Joseph Pringle.* Toronto: Alfred A. Knopf, 2002.

Collins, Robert. *You Had To Be There: An Intimate Portrait of the Generation that Survived the Depression, Won the War, and Re-Invented Canada.* Toronto: McClelland and Stewart, 1997.

----------. *The Long and the Short and the Tall: An Ordinary Airman's War.* Saskatoon: Western Producer Prairie Books, 1986.

Cook, Tim. *The Necessary War: Volume One, Canadians Fighting The Second World War 1939-1943.* Toronto: Penguin Canada Books, 2014.

Copp, Terry. *A Canadian's Guide to the Battlefields of Normandy.* Waterloo, ON: Laurier Centre for Military Strategic and Disarmament Studies, Wilfrid Laurier University, 1994.

German, Tony. *The Sea Is At Our Gates: The History of the Canadian Navy.* Toronto: McClelland and Stewart, 1990.

Goodspeed, Major D.J. *Battle Royal: A History of the Royal Canadian Regiment of Canada, 1862-1962.* Toronto: The Royal Regiment of Canada Association, 1962.

Granatstein, J.L. and Desmond Morton. *A Nation Forged In Fire: Canadians and the Second World War 1939-1945.* Toronto: Lester and Orpen Dennys Publishers Limited, 1989.

----------. *Bloody Victory: Canadians and the D-Day Campaign 1944.* Toronto: Lester and Orpen Dennys Publishers Limited, 1984.

Graves, Donald E. *South Albertas: A Canadian Regiment at War.* Toronto: Robin Brass Studio, South Alberta Regiment Veterans Association, 1998.

Greenfield, Nathan M. *The Damned: The Canadians at the Battle of Hong Kong and the POW Experience, 1941-45.* Toronto: HarperCollins, 2010.

Greenhous, Brereton. *"C" Force to Hong Kong: A Canadian Catastrophe, 1941-1945*

(Canadian War Museum Historical Publication No. 30). Toronto: Dundurn, 1997.

----------, Stephen J. Harris, William C. Johnson and William G.P. Rawling. *The Crucible of War, 1939-1945: The Official History of the Royal Canadian Air Force Vol. III.* Toronto: University of Toronto Press, 1994.

Halford, Robert G. *The Unknown Navy: Canada's World War II Merchant Navy.* St. Catharines, ON: Vanwell Publishing Limited, 1995.

Haskins, Scott. *Laughing In The Face Of Danger: World War True, Real People, Real Heroes, Real Funny.* Edmonton: TMH Marketing, 2006.

Hastings, Max. *Bomber Command.* New York: Dial Press, 1979.

Johnston, Mac. *Corvettes Canada: Convoy Veterans of WW II Tell Their True Stories.* Whitby, ON: McGraw-Hill Ryerson, 1994.

Kipp, Charles. *Because We Are Canadians: A Battlefield Memoir.* Vancouver: Douglas and McIntyre, 2002.

Kostenuk, S. and J. Griffin. *RCAF Squadron Histories and Aircraft: 1924-1968.* Toronto: National Museum of Man, National Museums of Canada, 1977.

MacDonell, George S. *One Soldier's Story 1939-1945: From the Fall of Hong Kong to the Defeat of Japan.* Toronto: Dundurn, 2002.

Macpherson, Ken and John Burgess. *The Ships of Canada's Naval Forces 1910-1981.* Don Mills, ON: Collins Publishers, 1981.

Margolian, Howard. *Conduct Unbecoming: The Story of the Murder of Canadian Prisoners of War in Normandy.* Toronto: University of Toronto Press, 1998.

Marsman, J.H. *I Escaped from Hong Kong.* New York: Reynal and Hitchcock, 1942.

Masters, John. *The Road Past Mandalay.* New York: Harper, 1961.

Marteinson, John. *We Stand On Guard: An Illustrative History of the Canadian Army.* Montreal: Ovale Publications, 1992.

McCaffery, Dan. *Battlefields in the Air: Canadians in the Allied Bomber Command.* Toronto: James Lorimer and Company Limited, Publishers, 1995.

McKee, Fraser and Robert Darlington. *The Canadian Naval Chronicle, 1939-1945.* St. Catharines, ON: Vanwell Publishing Limited, 1998.

Milberry, Larry (ed). *Sixty Years: The RCAF and CF Air Command 1924-1984.* Toronto: CANAV Books, 1984.

Milner, Marc. *Stopping The Panzers: The Untold Story of D-Day.* Lawrence, Kansas: University Press of Kansas, 2014.

Morrison, Alex and Ted Slaney. *The Breed of Manly Men: The History of the Cape Breton Highlanders.* Sydney, NS: The Cape Breton Highlanders Association and Peacekeeping Education Associates, 2002.

Nicholson, Lt.-Col. G.W.L. *Official History of the Canadian Army in the Second World War, Vol. II: The Canadians In Italy 1943-1945.* Ottawa: Minister of National Defence, Queen's Printer, 1957.

Peden, Murray. *A Thousand Shall Fall.* Toronto: Stoddart Publishing, 1988.

Portugal, Jean E. *We Were There: The Army: A Record for Canada, Vol. 2.* Shelburne, ON: The Royal Canadian Institute Heritage Society, 1998.

----------.Vol. 3.

----------.Vol. 4.

----------.Vol. 6.

Pugsley, William. *Saints, Devils and Ordinary Seamen: Life on the Royal Canadian Navy's Lower Deck.* Toronto: Collins, 1945.

Raddall, Thomas H. *West Novas: A History of the West Nova Scotia Regiment.* Liverpool, NS: s.n., 1986.

Roy, Reginald. *Ready for the Fray: History of the Canadian Scottish Regiment.* Calgary: Bunker To Bunker Publishing, 2002.

Sarty, Roger. *The Battle of the Atlantic: The Royal Canadian Navy's Greatest Campaign 1939-1945.* Ottawa: CEF Books, 2001.

Schull, Joseph. *Far Distant Ships: An Official Account of Canadian Naval Operations in World War II.* Toronto: Stoddart Publishing Company Limited, 1950.

Stacey, Colonel C.P. *Six Years of War: The Army in Canada, Britain and the Pacific,* Vol. 1. *The Official History of the Canadian Army in the Second World War.* Ottawa: Queen's Printer, 1957.

----------. *The Victory Campaign: The Operations in North-West Europe, 1944-1945,* Vol. 3. *The Official History of the Canadian Army in the Second World War.* Ottawa: Queen's Printer, 1960.

Tansley, Donald D. *Growing Up and Going to War: 1925-1945.* Waterloo, ON: The Laurier Centre for Military Strategic and Disarmament Studies, Wilfrid Laurier University, 2005.

Tooley, Robert. *The Carleton and York Regiment in the Second World War.* Fredericton: New Ireland Press, 1989.

Vance, Jonathan F. *Maple Leaf Empire: Canada, Britain, and Two World Wars.* Don Mills, ON: Oxford University Press, Huron University College, 2012.

Vincent, Carl. *No Reason Why: The Canadian Hong Kong Tragedy—an examination.* Stittsville, ON: Canada's Wings, 1981.

Whitaker, Brigadier General Denis and Shelagh Whitaker. *Dieppe: Tragedy to Triumph.* Toronto and Montreal: McGraw-Hill Ryerson, 1992.

Wood, Herbert Fairlie and John Swettenham. *Silent Witnesses.* Toronto: A.M. Hakkert Limited, Canadian War Museum Historical Publications, Department of Veterans Affairs, 1974.

Wood, James A. *We Move only Forward: Canada, the United States and the First Special Service Force 1942-1944.* St. Catharines, ON: Vanwell, 2006.

Zuehlke, Mark. *Breakout From Juno: First Canadian Army and the Normandy Campaign, July 4-August 21, 1944.* Vancouver: Douglas and McIntyre, 2011.

----------. *Holding Juno: Canada's Heroic Defence of the D-Day Beaches: June 7-12, 1944.* Vancouver: Douglas and McIntyre, 2005.

----------. *Juno Beach: Canada's D-Day Victory: June 6, 1944.* Maderia Park, BC: Douglas and McIntyre, 2004.

----------. *On To Victory: The Canadian Liberation of the Netherlands, March 23-May 5, 1945.* Vancouver: Douglas and McIntyre, 2010.

----------. *Tragedy at Dieppe: Operation Jubilee, August 19, 1942.* Vancouver: Douglas and McIntyre, 2012.

GOVERNMENT PUBLICATIONS

Granatstein, J.L. *Normandy 1944: Canada Remembers.* Veterans Affairs Canada, 1994.

MAGAZINE, NEWSPAPER, JOURNAL ARTICLES, ESSAYS

Boileau, John. "Canada's Merchant Navy: The Men That Saved The World," *Legion Magazine*: Vol. 85, No. 4, July/August 2010.

------------------. "Battle Honours of the Canadian Forces, Part 46: Second World War—The Moro," *Legion Magazine*: Vol. 90, No. 5, September/October 2015.

------------------. "Battle Honours of the Canadian Forces, Part 47: Second World War—Prelude to Ortona," *Legion Magazine*: Vol. 90, No. 6, November/December 2015.

Brown, Dave. "Old enough for war, but not to be an officer: War vet Lloyd Hyde was turned away by Ottawa police force." *Ottawa Citizen,* July 30, 2012.

Burnett, Hanna. "The Uncle I Never Knew: A Journey to Dieppe to discover Jimmie Burnett," *Canadian Military History: Vol. 21, Issue 4,* 2015.

Calder, Mark. "Glad to have served, glad to have survived: Gananoque's Bill Chitty remembers the D-Day landing," *The Brockville Recorder and Times,* June 5, 2004.

Comacchio, Cynthia. "To Hold on High the Torch of Liberty: Canadian Youth and the Second World War." Found in *Canada and the Second World War: Essays In Honour of Terry Copp.* Geoffrey Hayes, Mike Bechthold, Matt Symes (ed). Waterloo, ON: Wilfrid Laurier University Press, 2012.

Evans, George. "Life As A Merchant Marine," *The Red Duster,* Spring 2009.

James, Marcine Hefner. "The Ladies' Side of the Story," *The Spirit of the Torch* Vol. V, No. 2 (9), December 2005, pp. 10-12.

Johnson, Brigadier G.D. "The Battle of Hong Kong," *After the Battle,* No. 46, 1984.

Margerison, Russell. Excerpt from *Boys at War,* London: Northway Publications, 2006, in the Mail Online, May 10, 2009.

Martin, Sandra. "Kenneth Cambon, Soldier, PoW and Doctor 1923-2007," *The Globe and Mail,* March 17, 2007.

Mayne, Lori A. "Union Corner man mourns brother lost to military tragedy," *Journal Pioneer* (Summerside, PE), November 1, 2008.

McCaffery, Dan. "Historian honours Sarnia gunner's bravery," *The Observer* (Sarnia, ON), July 14, 2009.

Milner, Marc. "Fire And Fog: Assiniboine Rams U-210," *Legion Magazine,* July/August 2014.

Paillé, Roland. "Dieppe se souvient du Grand-mérois Robert Boulanger," *Le Nouvelliste* (Trois-Rivières, QC), February 14, 2014.

Pinder-Moss, Dianne. "D-Day: June 6, 1944," *Smiths Falls Record News,* June 1, 1994.

Roy, Reginald. "Reg Roy Remembers" *The Cape Breton Highlanders Association and Regimental Newsletter,* January-April 2009.

Windsor, Lee A. "Too Close for the Guns! 9 Canadian Infantry Brigade in the Battle for the Rhine Bridgehead," *Canadian Military History Journal, Winter/Spring 2003.*Waterloo, ON: Wilfrid Laurier University.

WEBSITES

Britain Ship Losses 1941, Military Records Online. www.world-war.co.uk/warloss_172brit.php3.

British Broadcasting Corporation. www.bbc.co.uk/history/worldwars/wwtwo.
Canadian Soldiers. www.canadiansoldiers.com/regiments/cavalry/2nd10thdragoons.
    htm.
Commonwealth War Graves Commission. www.cwgc.org.
Historica Canada, The Memory Project. www.thememoryproject.com.
Hong Kong Canadian Veterans' Association. www.hkcva.ca/historical/accounts.
Mike Varley, "A Concise History of 77 Squadron RAF," www.homepage.ntlworld.
    com/r_m_g.varely/concise%20history%20of%2077520sqd.
Rob Davis, "Royal Air Force (RAF) Bomber Command 1939-1945," www.elsham.
    pwp.blueyonder.co.uk/raf_bc/.
Perth Regiment. Stafford Johnson, *The Fighting Perths: The Story of the First
    Century in the Life of a Canadian County Regiment,* Perth Regiment Veterans'
    Association: Stratford, ON., 1964. Online version at www.perthregiment.org/
    index3.html.
Veterans Affairs Canada, *Canadian Virtual War Memorial.* www.veterans.gc.ca/eng/
    remembrance/memorials/Canadian-virtual-war-memorial.
----------, *Heroes Remembered.* www.veterans.gc.ca/eng./collections/hrp.

UNPUBLISHED MATERIALS

Bill Chitty, On The Road To Midgic, unpublished memoir.
G.C. Marston, Lance Ross, Reginald Roy: unpublished diaries.
War Diary, 14th Field Regiment.

INTERVIEWS AND CORRESPONDENCE

Dan Black interviews: Betty Spry, November 14, 2015; Denis Chisholm, February
    15, 2013; Donald Fowler, 2009-2015; Gordon Hovey with daughter Marilyn
    Gillich, April 30, 2015; Grayce Muir, July 31, 2012, December 19, 2015, and
    correspondence between Grayce Muir, David Muir, Babs Webber, April 22,
    2012 and January 26, 2015; Jack Shepherd, September 17, 2013; Jeff Foss, Jason
    Robinson, Paul Robinson, July 17, 20, 2015; Jim Parks, May 11-13, 2015; Lloyd
    Hyde, January 15, 2013; Margaret Chitty, February 9, 2013; Ralph Frayne,
    February 2, 2013; Robert Power, Rosemary Boutilier, October 8, 15, 19, 2015;
    Karen Wand, July and August 2015.
John Boileau interview: Hanna Burnett, July 22, 2015.
Sam Malkin interview with Bob Muir, courtesy Andrea Breen and Grayce Muir,
    June 1994.

IMAGE CREDITS

FRONT COVER
TOP RIGHT: Muir: Grayce Muir.
BOTTOM LEFT: Frayne: Ralph Frayne.
BOTTOM RIGHT: Chisholm: Margaret Brown.

BACK COVER
TOP LEFT: A Canadian sapper: LAC PA-131415.
TOP RIGHT: MacDonnell: The Memory Project.
BOTTOM LEFT: Shepherd: Jack Shepherd.
BOTTOM MIDDLE: Youthful sailors: www.forposterityssake.ca, J.T. Williams
Collection, courtesy Jim Williams.
BOTTOM RIGHT: German POWs: LAC PA-114486.

INTRODUCTION
Recruits Wanted (41): Orville Fisher, 1941, watercolour, CWM 12584.
Spry (44): Betty Spry.
Civilian encouragement (46): McGill WP2.R3.F1.
Parks (47): Jim Parks.
Shepherd (48): Jack Shepherd.
Fowler (50): Donald Fowler.
Dispatch Rider (52): Donald Anderson, 1944, watercolour, CWM 10768.

CHAPTER 1
Royal Rifles (61): M. Gagnon, 1941, CWM 19750317-052.
MacDonnell (63): Seargant Major George McDonnell, Susan Beard. *A Dog Named Gander.* (2014.)
Camp Valcartier (65): LAC PA-116794.
Winnipeg Grenadiers (68): LAC PA-116790.
Military equipment (70): LAC PA-116789.
HMT Awatea (71): LAC PA-116288
Kowloon disembark (72): LAC PA-037419.
Crown Colony (74): LAC PA—155527.
Lye Mun Battery (82): LAC PA-114877.

CHAPTER 2
North Point POW Camp (86): LAC PA-116796.
MacWhirter identification card (91): The Memory Project.
Stebbe (92): The Memory Project.
Cambon (93): Ken Cambon, *Guest of Hirohito.* (Vancouver: PW Press, 1990.)
MacDonnell (96): The Memory Project.
MacWhirter and friends (98): The Memory Project.
Winnipeg Grenadiers marker (100): LAC PA-136277.

Ohashi POW camp (104): The Memory Project.
HMCS *Prince Robert* (108): LAC PA-116788.
Canadian POWs (109): LAC PA-193015.

CHAPTER 3

Assault craft (112): LAC PA-183770.
The Dieppe Raid (113): Charles Comfort, 1946, oil painting, CWM 12276.
Bodies on Dieppe beaches (115): LAC C-014160.
Evacuation exercise (116): LAC PA-113242.
Boulanger (119): www.lapresse.ca/le-nouvelliste/opinions/201211/06/01-4590869-la-
    derniere-lettere-du-soldat-boulanger-a-ses-parents-de-grand-mere.php.
Les Fusiliers Mont-Royal (120): LAC PA-177146.
Mopping Up After the Battle (125): Martin Lunstroth, 1942, watercolour on paper,
    CWM 14422.
Burnett family (127): Hanna Burnett.
Burnett death announcement (133): Hanna Burnett.
King George VI letter (134): Hanna Burnett.

CHAPTER 4

Roy identification (140): Franklyn Roy.
Cape Breton Highlanders (141): Franklyn Roy.
Pringle (142): Andrew Clark, *A Keen Soldier.* (Toronto: Vintage Canada, 2004).
Cape Breton Highlanders' platoon (144): Franklyn Roy.
Moro River (149): LAC PA-114486.
Ortona Front (151): LAC PA-167912.
Inannen (152): www.specialforcesroh.com.
Mule pack (156): LAC PA-171189.
Soldiers prepare a meal (158): LAC PA-128973.
Wounded First Special Service Force (160): LAC PA-128985.

CHAPTER 5

Rain-soaked road (168): LAC PA-173549.
Soldiers eat a meal (168): LAC PA-129778.
Buried alive (170): LAC PA-152748.
Battlefield grave (173): LAC PA-129784.
Damaged Pay Book (176): LAC RG24 Vol. 26933.
Captured Nazi flag (180): Franklyn Roy.
Reinforcements Moving up in the Ortona Salient (182): Lawren P. Harris, 1946, oil
    painting, CWM 12712.
Campobasso (183): Charles Comfort, 1945, oil painting, CWM 12244.
The Hitler Line (184): Charles Comfort, 1944, oil painting, CWM 12296.
Execution novel (191): John Boileau.

CHAPTER 6

Training exercise (199): LAC PA-135889.
Parks brother (201): Jim Parks.

Chitty with friend (203): Margaret Chitty.
Vessels prepare to disembark (204): LAC PA-137130.
D-Day — The Assault (208): Orville Fisher, 1945, oil painting, CWM 12469.
Chitty (211): Margaret Chitty.
Chitty on the farm (213): Margaret Chitty.
Muir (215): Grayce Muir.
1944 poster (220): McGill WP2.M1.F1.

CHAPTER 7

Cameron Highlanders of Ottawa (226): LAC PA-162455.
German 12th SS Division (229): LAC PA-131397.
Wounded on Juno Beach (231): LAC PA-132384.
Dispatch rider takes cover (237): LAC PA-140855.
Emerging from dugout (240): LAC PA-131415.
Rifleman keeps watch (245): LAC PA-167297.
Machine-gunners (247): LAC PA-138358.
Battle for Carpiquet Airfield (248): Orville Fisher, 1946, oil painting, CWM 12421.

CHAPTER 8

Chisholm (251): Margaret Brown.
Chitty and Muir (255): Margaret Chitty.
Sherbrooke Fusiliers (257): LAC PA-162667.
Regina Rifles (258): LAC PA-131404.
Doré (259): Canadian Virtual War Memorial, Veterans Affairs Canada.
Seeking cover (262): LAC PA-140849.
Casualty Clearing Post (265): Alex Colville, 1945, watercolour, CWM 12133.
Allied bombers attack (269): LAC e010858649.
French civilians (272): LAC PA-132820.
Falaise (273): PA-116503.

CHAPTER 9

A German Flare Goes Up (279): Alex Colville, 1944, watercolour, CWM 10189.
Engineer working (281): LAC PA-131259.
Fowler (287): Donald Fowler.
Fowler and soldier (288): Donald Fowler.
McGuigan letter first page (290): LAC RG24 Vol. 26467.
McGuigan letter final page (291): LAC RG24 Vol. 26467.
Danielson letter (296): LAC RG24 Vol. 25698.
Danielson government form (297): LAC RG24 Vol. 25698.
Dutch Refugees (301): Donald Anderson, 1945, watercolour, CWM 10773.
Douglas (302): LAC PA-140683.

CHAPTER 10

Murray (311): Naval Museum of Halifax LW/CF NF-895.
Frayne (314): Ralph Frayne.
Watson's application (315): LAC RG112 Vol. 30783.

Watson with dog (319): The Canadian Virtual War Memorial, Veterans Affairs Canada.
Navy poster (320): Toronto Public Library.
HMCS *Assiniboine* (327): Naval Museum of Halifax.
Water on deck (328): Naval Museum of Halifax.
Burial at Sea (329): Harold Beament, 1943, oil on canvas, CWM 10005.
Ice hazard (332): Naval Museum of Halifax.

CHAPTER 11

HMCS *Shawinigan* (335): www.forposterityssake.ca, J.T. Williams Collection, courtesy Jim Williams.
Depth charges (336): Naval Museum of Halifax.
Daily grog (337): LAC PA-142439.
Laundry duty (343): LAC PA-204338.
Canadian Tribal Destroyers in Action (345): Tony Law, 1946, oil painting, CWM 10248.
Germaniuk (348): Peter Germaniuk, The Memory Project.
HMCS *Oakville* poster (351): McGill WP2.V3.F1.
Earp (353): www.forposteri tyssake.ca.
Evans (357): www.forposteri tyssake.ca

CHAPTER 12

Spry (361): Betty Spry.
Merchant Navy poster (363): LAC C-103326.
Hovey (365): Marilyn Gillich.
Spry at Leksard (367): Betty Spry.
Atlantic Convoy (371): Leonard Brooks, date unknown, watercolour, CWM 10078.
Ammunition (374): LAC PA-105353.
Damaged merchant ship (375): Public Archives of Nova Scotia.
Spry gunnery certificate first half (376): Betty Spry.
Spry gunnery certificate second half (377): Betty Spry.
Spry with shipmates (378): Betty Spry.

CHAPTER 13

Wellington bomber (386): DND PL-4661.
Pollon (387): LAC RG24 Vol. 28439.
Bomber stations (389): DND PL-45597.
Aircrew with Wellington bomber (390): DND PL-7998.
Three crewmen buried (397): DND PMR-93293.
Whitley bomber (402): DND PL-3099.
Lancaster bombers (404): DND PL-44319.
Wright (406): LAC RG24 Vol. 28987.
RCAF recruiting poster (410): McGill WP2.R13.F3.
Oxygen cylinders (412): DND PL-22425.

CHAPTER 14

Bombs Away (414): Paul Goranson, 1947, oil painting, CWM 11327.

Jonasson (416): LAC RG24 Vol. 27861.

Gunnery school (417): DND PL-11799.

Aircrew parade (420): DND PL-4753.

Air to Ground (421): Patrick Cowley-Brown, 1945, oil painting, CWM 11078.

Night Target, Germany (423): Miller Brittain, 1946, oil painting, CWM 10889.

Fedi (426): LAC RG24 Vol. 27490.

Marshalling the Hallies (427): Paul Goranson, 1947, oil painting, CWM 11402.

Nose art (430): DND PL-29628.

Lancaster bomber (432): DND PL-44203.

EPILOGUE

Cambon retired (437): Ken Cambon, *Guest of Hirohito*. (Vancouver: PW Press, 1990.)

MacDonell (439): Larry Rose.

Roy author (440): Franklyn Roy.

Fowler and wife (443): Donald Fowler.

Chitty post-war (445): Margaret Chitty.

Parks and Prince Charles (447): Jim Parks.

INDEX